# Hegel's Critique
# of Modernity

# Hegel's Critique of Modernity

## Reconciling Individual Freedom and the Community

Timothy C. Luther

LEXINGTON BOOKS

A division of
ROWMAN & LITTLEFIELD PUBLISHERS, INC.
Lanham • Boulder • New York • Toronto • Plymouth, UK

LEXINGTON BOOKS

A division of Rowman & Littlefield Publishers, Inc.
A wholly owned subsidiary of The Rowman & Littlefield Publishing Group, Inc.
4501 Forbes Boulevard, Suite 200
Lanham, MD 20706

Estover Road
Plymouth PL6 7PY
United Kingdom

Copyright © 2009 by Lexington Books
First paperback edition 2010

*All rights reserved.* No part of this publication may be reproduced,
stored in a retrieval system, or transmitted in any form or by any
means, electronic, mechanical, photocopying, recording, or otherwise,
without the prior permission of the publisher.

British Library Cataloguing in Publication Information Available

**Library of Congress Cataloging-in-Publication Data**

The hardback edition of this book was previously catalogued by the Library of Congress
as follows:

Luther, Timothy C., 1954– Hegel's critique of modernity : reconciling individual
freedom and the community / Timothy C. Luther.
     p. cm.
   Includes bibliographical references and index.
1. Hegel, Georg Wilhelm Friedrich, 1770–1831—Political and social views. 2.
Liberty—Philosophy. I. Title.
   JC233.H433L87 2009
   323.44—dc22

                                                                2009007664

ISBN: 978-0-7391-2979-1 (cloth : alk. paper)
ISBN: 978-0-7391-2980-7 (pbk. : alk. paper)
ISBN: 978-0-7391-2981-4 (electronic)

Printed in the United States of America

∞ ™ The paper used in this publication meets the minimum requirements of American
National Standard for Information Sciences—Permanence of Paper for Printed Library
Materials, ANSI/NISO Z39.48–1992.

To my wife: Melissa

# Contents

# Acknowledgements

I would to thank California Baptist University for granting me a sabbatical to research and write this book, awarding me a research grant, and generously supporting travels to many professional conferences to present various versions of the ideas developed more fully in this book and to receive valuable feedback from the panel discussions. I would also like to thank Claremont Graduate University for the opportunity to be a visiting scholar while working on Hegel and for my colleagues there for the many fruitful discussions and seminars that they provided. Professors Patrick Horn, Anselm Min, and the late D. Z. Phillips warrant special mention.

Many people helped me along the way with helpful comments and suggestions. There is no doubt that their suggestions have improved this manuscript; the deficiencies that remain are my responsibility alone. Friends, family, and colleagues patiently listened to my ideas and offered their criticisms. A few deserve special mention: Melissa Conway and Joyce Luther read parts of the book, Nick Peterson read the entire manuscript, and Mack Brandon read it twice. I am also grateful for the comments and suggestions of the readers commissioned by staff at the Lexington Books Division of Rowman & Littlefield Publishers. These "masked" reviewers greatly contributed to the organization and substance of the book; it is a better work for their criticisms. It is important to acknowledge that my thought on Hegel benefited greatly from the many Hegelian scholars sited in this book. I truly owe them all a debt of gratitude.

Finally, I would like to thank the staff at Lexington Books. The editors, Joseph Parry, Jana Wilson, Paula Smith-Vanderslice, and Melissa Wilks, were helpful professionally and personally. I greatly appreciate their diligence in navigating me through the process. A writer could not ask for more from the editors and staff.

# Chapter One

# Introduction

It was the best of times, it was the worst of times, it was the age of wisdom, it was the age of foolishness, it was the epoch of belief, it was the epoch of incredulity, it was the season of Light, it was the season of Darkness, it was the spring of hope, it was the winter of despair, we were all going to Heaven, we were all going direct the other way—in short, the period was so far like the present period.[1]

—Charles Dickens, *A Tale of Two Cities*

Georg Wilhelm Friedrich Hegel is one of the greatest philosophers in the Western tradition. For some, he is a Romantic critic of the Enlightenment and a source of antirationalism, and, for others, he is an opponent of Romanticism and a defender of modern reason. Similarly, for some, Hegel is a theological philosopher trying to uphold Christian orthodoxy, while others see him as a radical seeking to undermine religious faith. Moreover, his comprehensiveness and ability to bring diverse, even contradictory elements of reality together into a unified system is unparalleled. For Hegel, the history of philosophy is an organic process in which previous philosophies converge toward the goal of universal enlightenment.[2] Thus, he not only explores the foundations of thought and culture but also claims to have discovered a pattern of progression in the evolution of philosophical thought itself toward an ever-increasing, more unified comprehension of the natural world and human reality. My interest in this pattern is that while much of modern political philosophy before Hegel was preoccupied with the legitimacy of authority, he introduces a dimension of change and historicity to political thought and makes important contributions to reconciling individual freedom within the community and economics with politics.

1

While Hegel does not suggest that poverty originates in modern society, he thinks that modern society exacerbates the problem. Unlike traditional methods of production, the modern economy pulls individuals away from the family. Self-sufficient individualism and unmitigated pursuit of private interests spawns an atomistic principle that frequently abandons individuals to contingency. Each person is supposed to fend for herself. While the market brings employment opportunities and labor together, it has a downside. Today's neoliberal ideology insists that the market can solve every problem. This has led to the acceptance of privatization, marketization, and the outsourcing of public tasks to the private sector. Well-trained workers often find their skills redundant in the modern economy, and through no fault of their own, they become unemployed when their skills are no longer needed. Increasing economic efficiency and production creates surplus production and replaces workers with machines. The modern economy frequently renders workers superfluous and wreaks havoc on their personal lives, especially with the outsourcing of so many jobs to take advantage of cheap foreign labor. Moreover, by failing to earn a livelihood, the victims of poverty are deprived of the opportunity to exercise their autonomy as a rightful member of the community.

In the *Philosophy of Right*, Hegel recognizes that poverty is not only absolute, but can be relative as well. The poor are poor not only in that they have been deprived of the possibility of acquiring property; this deprivation also leads to others, such as nonrecognition and marginalization. The denial of recognition and the exclusion from civil society while living in its midst can constitute a spiritual death. The poor are pushed to the margins of society and become invisible. Deprived of resources and recognition, they are without determinate being or status in civil society. The recognition of universal freedom disappears, or turns out to be freedom for a few, and the general recognition [*Anerkanntsein*] is thereby undermined.[3] This greatly resembles the situation for most of the homeless in contemporary United States. Most Americans move through their daily lives with little to no contact with the homeless and the desperately poor. In fact, we barely see them. This deprivation, according to Hegel, threatens the possibility of membership and inclusion in civil society. Life itself has needs, and property resources are among the most basic way of meeting life's needs; to be deprived of the resources to meet these needs is to be deprived of one's ultimate right to life itself.[4] Since recognition, for Hegel, is a condition of having rights, the poor do not really have any rights in civil society in a meaningful fashion.

Hegel's conception of ethical life [*Sittlichkeit*] requires that civil society and the state be balanced. At times, government intervention is required to address some of the harsh side-effects of life in civil society. Hegel does not advocate complete laissez-faire. Hegel points out these problems and suggests the method for redistributing wealth that avoids them, while ensuring the greatest fairness and respect for the exercise of economic freedom:

> redistribution not through transfers of goods and services, but through monetary taxation and reimbursement. . . . [R]eliance on taxation allows the equitably determined transfer to be mediated through the choice of all parties concerned. By virtue of taxation, the economically privileged, be they individual or private or public enterprises, are allowed to fulfill their economic duty to the disadvantaged without relinquishing their freedom to decide what commodities to exchange and what services to render in obtaining the money they must pay. Similarly, monetary reimbursements leave the disadvantaged with the full prerogative to decide how to translate the abstract form of wealth they have received into particular goods and earning opportunities.[5]

Even though the separation between government and economy is a key dimension of Hegel's modern state, the state has specific powers and responsibilities in the economic realm. Hegel would not likely be pleased with the political direction taken by the United States over the last couple of decades. A significant "danger is posed by the autonomization of globalized networks and markets that simultaneously contribute to the fragmentation of public consciousness."[6] Democratic government is being stripped of its ability to regulate the economy responsibly and to protect the public. This tendency not only harms responsive citizenship, Hegel would find the number of people living below the poverty line unacceptable.[7]

The recent wave of globalization is exacerbating the gulf between individualism and community, and excessive privatization is threatening the public realms and commons. Hegel recognizes that self-interest exists and is important; however, that is not to say that self-interest is all that exists or that it should be given free rein. For him, while self-interest must be given room to work, it also needs to be limited at times and channeled for the public good, which is the job of public law. Benjamin Barber observes that today freedom is indistinguishable from selfishness and is corrupted from within by apathy, alienation, anomie; equality is reduced to market exchangeability and divorced from its necessary familial and social contexts; happiness is measured by material gratification to the detriment of spirit.[8] He further notes that there is something profoundly schizophrenic about liberal democracy. Failing to acknowledge any middle ground, it often trades in contrasts, in polarities, in radical dichotomies and rigid dualisms: terror or anarchy, force or freedom, hate or love. Bertrand Russell warns us that the two dangers facing every community are anarchy and despotism.[9] Consequently, we need to rediscover

Hegel's conception of *Sittlichkeit* and the reconciliation of individualism and community, liberty and morality, that it offers.

## THE PURPOSE OF THE BOOK

One of the great difficulties confronting a reader of Hegel is an impenetrable style and a notoriously technical vocabulary. He makes his readers work very hard, and his writings are open to diverse appropriation. In the *Philosophy of Right*, for instance, he asserts that "what is rational is actual and what is actual is rational."[10] Or, he claims that the *Rechtsstaat* [Modern State, based on Rule of Law] is the concrete unity of the particularity and universality in Idea.[11] Such technical conceptions appear on virtually every page of Hegel's writings. Consequently, the aim of this book is primarily expository. I utilize his esoteric terminology as necessary, but I will present the major tenets of his political philosophy in more accessible language. That said, this book is also my interpretation of Hegel's political thought and I hope that it will be of interest to professional philosophers. In order to bring Hegel to life, I have critically reconstructed his ideas for a contemporary context. In other words, Hegel's critical and dialectical approach needs not only to be applied to Hegel himself, but must also be continued up to the contemporary era, including today's economic globalization. His work addresses the important philosophical disputes of his day; however, the dialectical character of his thought means that with many conflicts Hegel does not try to resolve them. Rather, by taking up one side or the other, he demonstrates that the dichotomy underlying the dispute is false. Hence, his dialectical method establishes the possibility of integrating elements from both positions.

I will show how Hegel's philosophy is an important break from the Cartesian and Kantian heritage that he inherits. Specifically, he develops the Kantian/Cartesian "I" into a "we," that is, the focus on individuality into a focus on community. For Descartes and Kant, the individual subject is the source of knowledge; however, for Hegel, knowledge is a collective achievement. This represents a crucial shift from the first person singular to first person plural standpoint, and it has much in common with the paradigm shift from the philosophy of consciousness to the philosophy of intersubjectivity in the late twentieth century. The implications of this shift are still being explored today. Human knowledge is no longer dependent upon the precarious ability of the individual human subject to synthesize his or her own experience.

> Hegel's dialectic of self-consciousness passes over the relation of solitary reflection in favor of the complementary relationship between individuals who

know each other. The experience of self-consciousness is no longer considered the original one. Rather, for Hegel it results from the experience of interaction, in which I learn to see myself through the eyes of other subjects. The consciousness of myself is the derivation of the intersection [*Verschränkung*] of perspectives. Self-consciousness is formed on the basis of mutual recognition.[12]

This responsibility is now collective, or to use technical vernacular, it is the realm of intersubjectivity. The *Philosophy of Right* is Hegel's last published book and is his attempt to describe the harmonious political system in which the conflict between the individual and the community are reconciled into a higher synthesis. However, I will argue that this political system cannot be understood adequately without a full appreciation of his conceptions of philosophy, history, self-consciousness, and the dialectic.

Thus, even though there are some excellent commentaries on particular aspects of Hegel's thought and some superb general introductions to his work, there is warrant for a more systematic examination of his political thought.[13] While these works are philosophically interesting and furnish important contributions in elucidating Hegel's place in the Western philosophical tradition, they each leave out something of importance. It is my contention that appreciating Hegel requires a discussion of his technical use of some key concepts: *Geist*, self-consciousness, freedom, the dialectic, and reconciliation [*Versöhnung*]. These concepts are intricately connected in Hegel's work and are combined to form his philosophical method. This means placing each concept in the wider context of Hegel's entire corpus. His *Phenomenology of Spirit*, *Science of Logic*, *Philosophy of History*, and *Philosophy of Right* all fit together as a single approach to human understanding and need to be discussed as a single system.

To a large part, today's failure to reconcile individual liberty with community interest is due to our inability—or unwillingness—to treat the economy as an ethical concern. A careful examination of globalization and the recent economic meltdown demonstrates the need for a reconstruction that makes place for an ethical economy. In brief, economic theory must be purged of the natural and monological conceptions that condemn economics to ethical neutrality.[14] It is my contention that Hegel is one of the first thinkers to establish a framework for a more ethical and balanced approach to modern economics. With his notion of *Sittlichkeit*, he sees economy as a crucial part of the realm of ethics. Thus, Hegel conceives of the economy as a place of social freedom, one that is often undermined by natural and monological factors. Although his efforts are fragmentary, they provide an important starting point for addressing a just economy. Even though Hegel appreciates classical economists' success in describing the lawful motion of a given economy, he rejects their framework of a strictly social rather than political economy:

This reflects his understanding that just economic relations can neither be natural, monological, nor political, but must belong within a civil society whose
structures of freedom are not committed to the same ends as civil government,
nor derivative of the state of nature construct of social contract theory. In contrast to the political economists, Hegel argues that if economic relations are to
be matters of justice falling within a civil society, then both they and that society
must consist entirely in nonnatural, intersubjective structures of freedom, distinct from the other conventional modes of freedom comprising just property,
moral, household, and political relations.[15]

For Hegel, the economic freedom that would constitute a just economy cannot be founded on liberty alone. By repudiating a narrow interpretation of
liberty, Hegel paves the way for a systematic investigation of what a properly
constituted economy ought to look like.

The American economy is undergoing rapid changes these days. Everywhere around us is evidence that economic and technological changes are
transforming the international landscape. Like many changes, there are both
positive and negative aspects. One of the changes is the "size" of the world.
While not actually shrinking, the world is getting more interconnected—even
interdependent, and the number of countries whose economic activities are
closely entangled with our own has increased greatly. Economies and people
around the world are more closely linked that ever before. Information circles
the globe in an instant. Business is conducted largely without regard to international borders. Capital markets are integrated worldwide. For example,
while the computer was once an "all-American" product, today it is likely to
come from Korea, Taiwan, or Singapore. Decisions made in London or New
York are felt in Tokyo and Jakarta. While only a few decades ago, most businesses operated within national economies and oversea markets, today the
world's major corporations are truly global.

This process is part of what is called globalization. If it continues as it
has the last three decades, it will deeply affect American economic life to an
even-greater extent than it already has. The impact will likely have mixed
results: Korean computer monitors cost less for consumers, but with the
result of fewer jobs in Seattle and more in Seoul. Financial instability in
one seemingly remote country can threaten economies around the world.
Growing economic interdependence is changing the political landscape of
the world too. Countries rise and fall depending on their ability to operate
within a rapidly evolving world economy. Fueled by trade and investment,
China is rising to global prominence. The Soviet Union fell in part because it
could not compete with the dynamic growth of Western capitalism. By pursuing market-friendly trade and investment strategies, many countries in the
developing world have experienced rapid economic growth. However, they

have also felt the insecurity and dislocations of currency crises and market fluctuations.[16] Hegel reminds us that economies are supposed to be embedded in a moral context. He comprehends that since market societies are an antagonistic interrelationship of compulsions, political communities must have substantial power in the face of this type of society. Nonetheless, the Hegelian state is less a utilitarian and calculating enterprise than a political power that re-establishes the absolute morality of an Aristotelian order aiming at the good life.[17]

Another change is income distribution. To put it bluntly, the stream of incomes going to the richest families in America have been growing rapidly, while the stream going to the less affluent has been shrinking.[18] In other words, the rich have been getting richer, and the middle class and the poor have been getting poorer in a relative sense. A third tendency concerns the use of technology. While technological innovation has always been a part of capitalism, the new technologies differ from previous ones in eliminating certain kinds of work. For example, the ATM and computer have put many banktellers out of work. Pressures of economic competition would seem to dictate rapid deployment of robots and artificial intelligence in industrial production and service industries—the specter of rising world unemployment may spawn opposing reactions.[19] Political struggles have erupted all over the world as a response to globalization and the threat it poses to sovereignty, cultural tradition, environmental protection, and workers rights.[20] The interconnectedness of societies is creating new sorts of changes. Environmental pollution is increasingly spreading beyond national borders. To be sure, globalization is not simply the unfolding of an iron law of economics; politics and governmental decisions are at the heart of the process.

Modernization has involved the destruction of traditional meaning and the creation of marginal people.[21] As Hegel notes, healthy societies depend upon healthy, empowered communities that build caring relationships among people. Hegel's *Sittlichkeit* recognizes that such societies must be built through the integration of family, civil society, and government. In the name of science, economics reduces all values to market values, as revealed in market price. Today neoliberalism—the new global ideology—is closely tied to the global expansion of markets. Market principles are portrayed as pervading even the most intimate dimensions of our social existence. Although marketization is portrayed as an objective process, the implication is that its effects are nonetheless beneficial, which is a normative judgment.[22] It offers a guide for action, since markets are seen as reflecting a natural and superior way of ordering the world. The implication is that good citizens should demand that their governments facilitate globalization as understood in market terms. Neoliberalism offers a simplification of complex social reality, and

Hegel's discussion provides a much better foundation for social analysis and prescription.

In the last two decades, proponents of the nineteenth-century market utopia have found in the concept of globalization a new guiding metaphor for the neoliberal message. The central tenants of neoliberalism include the primacy of economic growth; the importance of free trade to stimulate growth; the unrestricted free market; individual choice; the reduction of government regulation and the public domain; and the advocacy of an evolutionary model of social development anchored in the Western experience and applicable to the entire world.[23] Neoliberalism is rooted in the liberal ideals of British philosophers, such as Adam Smith, David Ricardo, and Herbert Spencer. The market system is seen as a self-regulating mechanism tending toward equilibrium of supply and demand, thus securing the most efficient allocation of resources. Any constraint on free competition is said to interfere with the natural efficiency of the market. The principle of laissez-faire was complemented with free trade and the elimination of tariffs. It was David Ricardo's "theory of comparative advantage" that became the gospel of modern free traders. Ricardo argued that free trade was a win-win situation for all trading partners, because it allowed each country to specialize in the production of those commodities for which it had a comparative advantage.

Making a case for free-market policies of the past, neoliberals draw on the neoclassical laissez-faire economic theories of Friedrich Hayek and Milton Friedman. By the 1980s, Ronald Reagan and Margaret Thatcher advanced neoliberal polices in their nations respectively. Since then, the neoliberal project has been expanded into a full-blown global ideology. Neoliberal globalists seek to cultivate in the popular mind the uncritical association of globalization with what they claim to be the universal benefits of market liberalization: Rising global living standards, economic efficiency, individual freedom, and unprecedented technological progress.[24] Some see neoliberal globalists as "market fundamentalists" who believe in the creation of a single, global market in goods, services, and capital.[25] Neoliberals believe that all peoples and states are equally subject to the logic of globalization. Societies have no choice but to adapt to this world-shaping force. Globalization is driven by the irresistible forces of the market. Neoliberals reject Keynesian principles and advocate reducing the welfare state, the downsizing of government, and the deregulation of the economy. They envision a shift from a community-dominated to a market-dominated world. Neoliberals follow Hayek's theory that the free market represents a state of liberty, because it is a state in which each can use his knowledge for his own purpose.[26] Globalization is about the triumph of markets over politics. Privatization, free trade, and unfettered capital movement are portrayed as the best and most natural way for realizing individual liberty and material progress. The driving idea behind globalization is that the more you let market forces rule with free trade, the more efficient your economy will become.[27]

After World War II, American officials systematically tried to open markets and integrate regions economically. They determined that the American interest necessitated the expansion and integration of the world economy. This goal was the inspiration for the conference on post-war economic cooperation held at Bretton Woods, New Hampshire in July of 1944. American politicians wanted to make sure that after helping Great Britain and Western Europe rebuild, American business would not be shut out of their markets. This agreement was particularly important because it established the basis for a global trade system. Along with an agreement on a new monetary order, this paved the way for broader economic agreements. The Bretton Woods agreements allowed political leaders to envisage a post-war economic order in which multiple and otherwise competing objectives could be combined.[28] The Bretton Woods agreements served as a basis on which to build broader coalitions around a relatively open and managed global order. With the advent of the Bretton Woods institutions, such as GATT, IMF, and WTO, we have made a concerted effort to disconnect the economy from other social and political organizations, which runs against the grain of Hegel's thought.

As I write this introduction, the American economy appears to be caught in a severe meltdown within a global economic crisis. The stock market has been in a free fall, the housing and lending industries have collapsed, automakers are going bankrupt, unemployment is on the rise, and since national and state governments cannot pay their bills, essential public services are being cut. In fact, the recently elected president, Barack Obama, faces problems that have not been confronted by an incoming administration since the election of Franklin Roosevelt. It is time to reconsider the primacy of neoliberal tenets and to balance short term economic goals with other social values and needs. Although Hegel supports an economic system based on free enterprise, he recognizes that it is merely a subsystem of a larger socio-political system. In fact, while the economy is essential in meeting many vital human needs and interests, it needs to be monitored and managed by a rational political system. Moreover, the economy also should be viewed as a subsystem of the larger, but finite and nongrowing, ecosystem. Consequently, it becomes desirable, and even necessary, to begin to take steps to identify the optimal scale for both the human population and its economy.[29] Our society must also learn to live in peace with the planet and its biosphere. To project forward on the basis of current trends is to foresee a planet denuded of most of its species through global warming, whose natural resources and water have been spoilt or worn out, whose storms are too violent and whose sun is too warm.[30]

Hegel's conception of civil society [*bürgerliche Gesellschaft*] establishes the framework within which ethical claims of a purely economic kind can be realistically raised without eliminating the distinct ethical norms of other coexisting spheres, such as justice and a healthier environment. Hegel recognizes that the economy is a subsystem that is nestled into a more encompassing social context, that is, a *Sittlichkeit*. His thought can help us get beyond the monological discourse of neolilberalism.

## HEGEL'S PHILOSOPHICAL IMPORTANCE

The importance and applicability of Hegel's work to contemporary thought lies in the fact that his philosophy can shed some light on many contemporary problems. More specifically, he has contributed to the formation of philosophical concepts that are indispensable for tackling some modern dilemmas. For instance, Hegel's conception of freedom enables us to reconcile many of the differences that divide liberalism and communitarianism. While liberalism tends to overemphasizes the individual and devalue the community, communitarianism tends to do the reverse. Even though some communitarians try to use Hegel as a foundation for their arguments, he does not fit communitarianism very well.[31] In fact, one of his central aims is to integrate liberalism's concern for the political rights and interests of individuals within the framework of a moral community. The advancement of *Geist* [Absolute Spirit] and the actualization of freedom mean that while the classical notions of community and modern individualism are both partially right, they are also part wrong—that is, they are each extreme in one direction or the other. His *Philosophy of Right* tries to reconcile the individual and community in a way that creates the proper mix of liberty and authority. As noted above, this reconciliation also has applications for today's economic problems. While economic individualism—laissez-faire principles—neglect economic duty, economic collectivism neglects individual economic rights. Hegel's *Sittlichkeit* balances the two economic values as well. To be sure, individuals do play an important part, but only within the context of their communities.

Hegel's goal was to comprehend all reality philosophically. In order to probe the nature of reality, he investigates the whole spectrum of human life—art, religion, philosophy, history, morality, politics, and science. Philosophy is able to support the rigorous self-scrutiny of thought, and is thus uniquely able to render concepts in a conceptually adequate fashion. Since philosophy provides a cognitive framework for discerning the pattern of development in all spheres of human activity, Hegel thinks that it can be designated as the truest source of understanding of the world.[32] Philosophy is not merely historical in a chronological sense, rather it is historically constituted in a profound sense. Each philosophy has its own time, place, and context, and since it is temporally and culturally situated, it cannot be understood properly if removed from its context. Nevertheless, for Hegel, all past philosophical projects collectively make up the whole of philosophy.[33] Simply put, the task of the philosopher is to observe the "dialectic of consciousness," and Hegel assures us that a system—the organized totality of all the stages of consciousness—emerges from this dialectic.[34]

Since philosophy and culture are the self-awareness of their age, all aspects of a given culture form a single whole and follow their own organic laws of development. Hegel asserts that the order in which philosophies follow one another chronologically is a logical order.[35] He has a difficult and precise idea of this purpose—the self-consciousness of freedom. Based on this idea, he sees a systematic unity and organization to all of history, which consists in the stages of development in self-awareness of freedom.[36] Moreover, the final "true" philosophy is a comprehensive system that preserves the truths and cancels the errors of all past philosophers:

> [E]very philosophy has been and still is necessary. Thus none have passed away, but all are affirmatively contained as elements in a whole. But we must distinguish between the particular principle, and the realization of this principle throughout the whole compass of the world. The principles are retained, the most recent philosophy being the result of all preceding, and hence no philosophy has ever been refuted. What has been refuted is not the principle of this philosophy but merely the fact that this principle should be considered final and absolute in character.[37]

Thus, for Hegel, the history of philosophy is an organic whole, the essence of which is expressed in his system. His philosophical method is thus drawing together and fulfilling all of those who went before him: "In philosophy the latest birth of time is the result of all the systems that have preceded it, and must include their principles; and so, if, on other grounds, it deserves the title of philosophy, will be the fullest, most comprehensive, and most adequate system of all."[38] The logical consequence of Hegel's theory is that his own philosophy is the culmination of the history of philosophy and completes its progression.

From Kierkegaard to Karl Popper, many thinkers accuse Hegel of being an idealist whose system is not based on existing reality (which is ironic since Hegel is also accused of providing a justification of the status quo).[39] On the contrary, he does not leave experience behind and remains faithful to the world. He neither doubts nor denies the existence of the physical world. To be sure, he is an idealist in the technical sense that he regards the activity of the mind as formative in obtaining knowledge:

The special conditions which call for the existence of philosophy may thus be described. The mind or spirit, when it is sentient or perceptive, finds its object in something sensuous; when it imagines, in a picture or image; when it wills, in an aim or end. But in contrast to, or it may be only in distinction from, these forms of its existence and of its objects, the mind has also to gratify the cravings of its highest and most inward life. That innermost self is thought. Thus the mind renders thought its object.[40]

Hegel does not mean that thought simply invents a world. Instead, he should be understood as asserting that a rational reflection is responsible for refining and clarifying how the nature of things is to be understood. Meaningful experience is constructed by thought, and cognitive life is saturated with sensory input and continually engaged in testing its constructions with experience.[41] It follows that Hegel is not an abstract thinker whose concerns are entirely removed from ordinary life: To the contrary, he is a concrete thinker who is interested in gathering up ordinary experiences in order to make sense of them in a unified way.

The concept of *Geist* occupies a central place in Hegel's philosophy. *Geist* is a real, concrete, objective force that remains unified, yet is particularized as spirits of specific nations and embodied in human beings. "The History of the world is none other that the process of consciousness of Freedom. . . ."[42] Consequently, Hegel identifies the specific forms of freedom associated with each particular historical era. While each era displays an important aspect of freedom, freedom is still incomplete. For example, with ancient Greece, freedom is bound up with a deep subjective attachment to the *polis*. Thus, Greek citizens are so attached to their *polis* that social membership is the major part of individual identity.[43]

The concept of the individual as the basic unit of identity was born in ancient Rome, with its emphasis on the abstract freedom of the individual.[44] In Rome, all citizens are legally recognized as possessing personal and property rights. However, this conception of freedom is inadequate:

But the fact that man is in and for himself free, in his essence and as man, free born, was known neither by Plato, Aristotle, Cicero, nor the Roman legislators, even though it is this conception alone which forms the source of law. In Christianity the individual, personal mind for the first time becomes of real, infinite and absolute value. . . . It was in the Christian religion that the doctrine was advanced that all men are equal before God. . . . These principles make freedom independent of any such things as birth, standing or culture.[45]

With the idea that individuals are equal before God, the early modern world adds an important dimension to freedom. Individuality is further developed with Kant's morally autonomous subject that is bound only by principles immanent to its own reason.[46] Hegel's goal is nothing less than the reconciliation of individual freedom and community in modern Sittlichkeit.[47] From very early on, there has been a tension between the individual and social nature of man. Since the values of individuality and social membership are not mutually exclusive, Hegel hopes to reconcile them.

One of Hegel's goals is to discover social structures that will allow individuals to escape the alienation and sense of drift that characterize contemporary life, a method of reconciling his contemporaries to the modern world by overcoming the things that split the self from the social world.[48] Hegel's *Rechtsstaat* is a place where this alienation is overcome and people are at home in the social world. Alienation is not only a concern of Hegel's day but is also a problem in today's world.[49] A sense of estrangement and homelessness is all too common in contemporary life, even for those who enjoy more personal freedom and material abundance than ever thought possible. While Hegel is speaking directly to and about his contemporaries, their social world bears much in common with ours. Consequently, his attempt to reconcile philosophical and social contradictions can elucidate our own condition. While the modern world reflects important contributions to the development of *Geist*, with the advent of modern liberalism it leads to *excessive* individualism. Hegel refers to this as atomism, since it fragments social life, and individuals feel disconnected and adrift from meaningful social life. The major goal of Hegel's political philosophy is the reconciliation of the individual with his or her political community in a way that overcomes the alienation of modern life. To be sure, it is essential that this reconciliation not result in the excessive collectivism found in much of classical political philosophy, in which individuals are merely part of an organic whole with no free individual will (such as the citizens of Plato's *Republic*). Hegel's *Rechtsstaat* represents the integration and transcendence [*Aufhbung*] of the merits of antiquity and modernity.

## A PREVIEW OF THE CHAPTERS

This book consists of nine more chapters that are intended to elucidate the context, development, components, and political consequences of Hegel's philosophical system. Chapter 2 provides a brief introduction to Hegel's thought and establishes the philosophical background needed to appreciate his philosophy. Hegel is not merely an uncritical advocate of modernity, but instead develops a framework for the continued critique of modernity. The chapter also contains an overview of his dialectic method and its relationship to *Geist*. Chapter 3 follows with the specifics of Hegel's philosophy of history and movement and development of freedom within specific historical civi-lizations and political cultures. The chapter studies the relationship between *Geist* and actual human beings. Since *Geist* needs to be concrete, it must manifest itself in the actual world. For Hegel, human beings are vessels for *Geist* and play an intrinsic role in *Geist*'s development and the actualization of freedom. The chapter also covers the origin and advancement of freedom in historically existing societies in order to trace the development of freedom and witness how *Geist* overcomes and reconciles contradictions. The dialec-tic of history includes sections on the development of freedom from ancient Greek and Roman civilizations through medieval Christianity, the Reforma-tion, and the Renaissance to the Enlightenment and Hegel's world.

Chapter 4 analyzes Hegel's conception of *Sittlichkeit*, or ethical life. This is an essential aspect of his attempt to reconcile the individual and community. The chapter is broken into four sections: The first examines Hegel's discus-sion of Greek *Sittlichkeit*, and the next two provide an overview of Kant's metaphysics of morals and Hegel's critique of Kant. The chapter concludes with Hegel's modern *Sittlichkeit*, which plays a key role in the development of his political philosophy. Chapter 5 deals with Hegel's conception of fam-ily and *bürgerliche Gesellschaft*, or civil society, since these are the first two parts of modern *Sittlichkeit*. The first section contains a discussion of place of the family in modern ethical life. Drawing from English economists, such as Adam Smith and David Ricardo, Hegel notes that civil society is the nec-essary realm of individuality. The next section examines Hegel's conception of *bürgerliche Gesellschaft*, including the system of needs, the administra-tion of justice, police and community welfare, and corporations. For Hegel, civil society is the realm of free enterprise, and therefore political economy promotes an essential realm of freedom and individuality, such as personal property and mutual recognition. Hegel's *Sittlichkeit* balances economic duty with economic right, that is, individual wants with public needs. The chapter concludes with a section on Hegel's conception of the particular and subjec-tive freedom.

Democracy should be conceived as the right of the people to oversee col-lectively their common good. Today democracy is under assault by privatiza-tion and neoliberalism. Chapter 6 describes Hegel's conception of *Rechtsstaat*, which promises to reconcile individual autonomy and social solidarity. The state, the third part of modern *Sittlichkeit*, is the true home of the universal and works against the fragmenting impact of the particular, represented in civil soci-ety. Hegel's political institutions are reconstructed. To this end, the chapter is or-ganized into five sections. The first section examines Hegel's criticisms of social contract theory, and the second discusses his attempt to reconcile individualism and community. The third section describes the specific institutions of Hegel's modern state, constitutional monarchy, the universal estate, and the legislative assembly. Hegel's views on the separation of church and state and religious toleration are addressed in the fourth section. The chapter concludes with Hegel's critique of liberalism, which he views as excessive individualism.

The final four chapters draw conclusions regarding Hegel's philosophy. Chapter 7 looks at Hegel's immediate impact upon philosophy. It consists of three sections: The first section assesses Hegel's conception of philosophical reconciliation [*Versöhnung*] and defends it against nineteenth-century criticisms. The following sections examine reactions to Hegel by the left Hegelian movement, Ludwig Feuerbach, and Karl Marx. Chapter 8 discusses existentialism as a response to Hegelianism, specifically addressing Kierkegaard's and Nietzsche's criticisms. Chapters 9 and 10 advance the argument that Hegel's thought is of particular importance today. It is not an accident that many philosophers now see Hegel as the chief antidote and alternative to many problematic positions, such as Cartesian subjectivism, naïve realism, extreme liberalism and mental-physical dualism, or reductivist materialism.[50] Chapter 9 contends that Hegel's political philosophy is not caught up in the philosophy of subjectivity but rather that it moves into the realm of intersubjectivity, thus reconciling the gulf between liberalism and communitarianism. To this end, it is organized into four sections that explore the philosophical relationship between Hegel and contemporary schools of thought—critical theory and negative dialectics, postmetaphysical intersubjectivity, poststructuralism and deconstruction, and phenomenology and philosophical hermeneutics. Chapter 10 argues that Hegel's philosophy can help us to understand better the basic problems of modern political life. To this end, the first section of the chapter assesses the relationship between Hegel's philosophy and economic justice, and includes subsections on political economy and alienation and issues in contemporary globalization. The other section of the chapter looks to Hegel for remedies for modern dilemmas. In particular, his philosophy is very useful as an antidote for excessive individualism, and his conception of *Sittlichkeit* provides firm basis for the reconciliation of individual rights within the social framework of a community and the reestablishment of economics as a subsection of the socio-politico system at large.

## NOTES

1. Charles Dickens, *A Tale of Two Cities* (New York: Signet Classic, 1980), 13.

2. Georg W. F. Hegel, *Lectures on the History of Philosophy, Volume 1: Greek Philosophy to Plato*, trans. E. S. Haldane (Lincoln: University of Nebraska Press, 1995), 1.

3. Robert R. Williams, *Hegel's Ethics of Recognition* (Berkeley: University of California Press, 1997), 247. To be sure, the external state is supposed to provide opportunities to all in principle, but the disappearance of the possibility of property and the opportunity to work from the situation of the poor means that their freedom no longer can have any determinate existence in the world.

4. Williams, *Hegel's Ethics of Recognition*, 244.

5. Richard Dien Winfield, *The Just Economy* (New York: Routledge, 1988), 221.

6. Jürgen Habermas, *The Inclusion of the Other: Studies in Political Theory*, ed. Ciaran Cronin and Pablo De Greiff (Cambridge: MIT Press, 1998), 158. If these systemic pressures are not met by politically capably institutions, there will be a resurgence of the crippling fatalism of "old empires" in the midst of highly modern economies.

7. Mark R. Rank, *One Nation, Underprivileged: Why American Poverty Affects Us All* (New York: Oxford University Press, 2005), 25. Currently, there are 34.6 million Americans, about 12% of the population, who live below the poverty line. Furthermore, another 26.3 million live precariously close to the poverty line.

8. Benjamin Barber, *Strong Democracy: Participatory Politics for a New Age* (Berkeley: University of California Press, 2003), 24.

9. Bertrand Russell, *Roads to Freedom* (London: Allen and Unwin, 1966), 73.

10. Georg W. F. Hegel, *Philosophy of Right*, trans. T. M. Knox (Oxford: Oxford University Press, 1967), 10.

11. Hegel, *Philosophy of Right*, 155–156.

12. Jürgen Habermas, *Theory and Practice*, trans. J. Viertel (Boston: Beacon Press, 1973), 144–145.

13. For example, Frederick Neuhouser, *Foundations of Hegel's Social Theory: Actualizing Freedom* (Cambridge: Harvard University Press, 2000), focuses on freedom, Michael O. Hardimon, *Hegel's Social Philosophy: The Project of Reconciliation* (New York: Cambridge University Press, 1994), concentrates on reconciliation, and Allen W. Wood, *Hegel's Ethical Thought* (New York: Cambridge University Press, 1990), examines Hegel's conception of ethical culture.

14. Winfield, *The Just Economy*, 87.

15. Winfield, *Just Economy*, 88.

16. Joseph Grieco and G. John Ikenberry, *State Power and World Markets: The International Political Economy* (New York: W. W. Norton, 2003), 2.

17. Habermas, *Theory and Practice*, 191.

18. Robert Heilbroner and Lester Thurow, *Economics Explained* (New York: Touchstone, 1998), 7.

19. Willis Harmon, *Global Mind Change: The Promise of the Last Years of the Twentieth Century* (Indianapolis: Knowledge Systems, 1988), 150.

20. Grieco and Ikenberry, *State Power and World Markets*, 2.

21. Harmon, *Global Mind Change*, 151.

22. Manfred Steger, *Globalism: The New Market Ideology* (Lanham, Md.: Rowman & Littlefield, 2002), 6.

23. Steger, *Globalism*, 9.

24. Steger, *Globalism*, 12.

25. George Soros, *The Crisis of Global Capitalism: Open Society Endangered* (New York: Public Affairs, 1998).

26. Friedrich Hayek, *Laws, Legislation, and Liberty, Volume 1* (London: Routledge & Kegan Paul, 1979), 55.

27. Thomas Friedman, *The Lexus and the Olive Tree* (New York: Farrar, Strauss & Giroux, 1999), 9.

28. Grieco and Ikenberry, *State Power and World Markets*, 138.

29. Herman Daly and Kenneth Townsend, "Introduction," in *Valuing the Earth: Economics, Ecology, Ethics*, eds. Herman Daly and Kenneth Townsend (Cambridge: MIT Press, 1993), 8.

30. Teresa Brennan, *Globalization and Its Terrors: Daily Life in the West* (London: Routledge, 2003), 31.

31. I realize that there are contemporary thinkers who see themselves as liberals or communitarians and do not fall prey to either excessive individualism or collectivism. For instance, Amitai Etzioni, *The Golden Rule: Community and Morality in a Democratic Society* (New York: Basic Books, 1996), offers a version of communitarianism that is very Hegelian in blending aspects of tradition and modernity; excessive liberty is curbed by an ethical context. "[I]t is not only possible but highly necessary *to combine some universal principles with particularistic ones to form a full communitarian normative account*" (248). Moreover, in *The Moral Dimension: Toward a New Economics* (New York: The Free Press, 1988), 8–9, Etzioni, like Hegel, recognizes that both individual and community are completely essential to social theory, that is, the individual and community make each other and require each other. Etzioni applies his findings to both political theory and economics, since they are both intrinsic aspects of ethics.

32. Georg W. F. Hegel, *Logic*, trans. William Wallace (Oxford: Clarendon Press, 1975), 8.

33. Hegel, *Logic*, 20.

34. Georg W. F. Hegel, *Science of Logic*, trans. A. V. Miller (Amherst, Mass.: Humanity Books, 1969), 28.

35. Hegel, *Logic*, 19.

36. Georg W. F. Hegel, *Reason in History: A General Introduction to the Philosophy of History*, trans. Robert S. Hartman (Indianapolis: Bobbs-Merrill, 1953), 15.

37. Georg W. F. Hegel, *Lectures on the History of Philosophy: Greek Philosophy to Plato, Volume 1*, trans. E. S. Haldane (Lincoln: University of Nebraska Press, 1995), 37.

38. Hegel, *Logic*, 19.

39. For a classic statement of the argument that Hegel's work defends the status quo, see Rudolf Haym, *Hegel und siene Zeit* (Berlin: Rodolf Gaertner, 1857). For a more recent statement of this position, see Ernst Tugendhat, *Self-Consciousness and Self-Determination*, trans. P. Stern (Cambridge: MIT Press, 1986), 315–320.

40. Hegel, *Logic*, 15.

41. Hegel, *Logic*, 18.

42. Georg W. F. Hegel, *The Philosophy of History*, trans. J. Sibree (Buffalo, N.Y.: Prometheus Books, 1991), 19.

43. Hegel, *The Philosophy of History*, 253.

44. Hegel, *The Philosophy of History*, 278–279.

45. Hegel, *Lectures on the History of Philosophy, Volume 1*, 49.

46. Hegel, *Lectures on the History of Philosophy: Medieval and Modern Philosophy, Volume 3*, trans. E. S. Haldane and Frances H. Simson (Lincoln: University of Nebraska Press, 1995), 459.

47. Hegel, *Philosophy of Right*, 105.

48. Hardimon, *Hegel's Social Philosophy*, 2.

49. For example, in the United States voting turnout has continued to decline and public opinion surveys indicate that more and more Americans perceive that government responds to the rich few, or big business. People are alienated from government and cynical. See Timothy C. Luther, *Congress, Interest Groups, and Democracy: Private Money v. Public Interest* (Boston: Houghton Mifflin, 2002), for a discussion of how the increasing amount of money in American elections undermines legitimacy and fosters alienation.

50. Frederick Beiser, *Hegel* (New York: Routledge, 2005), 3.

## Chapter Two

# Georg Wilhelm Friedrich Hegel:
# His Philosophy and Context

Hollier says the same thing, in a different way. He says that people don't by any means all live in what we call the present; the psychic structure of modern man lurches and yaws over a span of at least ten thousand years. . . . He's deep in the Middle Ages because they really are middle—between the far past, and the post-Renaissance thinking of today. So he can stand in the middle and look both ways.[1]

—Robertson Davies, *The Rebel Angels*

Few thinkers in the history of philosophy are as controversial as Hegel, and reading him is a trying and difficult experience. Challenging traditional philosophy, he argues that the development of human capacities within a given social stage leads to changes in human nature and human objectives. Humanity feels constrained by the inherited social forms and overthrows them to make way for new liberating ones. Philosophers alternatively dismiss Hegel as a charlatan and obscurantist and praise him as one of the great minds of philosophy, but rarely regard him with detachment or indifference. He has also been depicted as an apologist for the Prussian state and a prophet of statism.[2] As a result of such extremes, Hegel has for decades been either completely neglected or studied closely. Whether one loves or despises Hegel, his enormous historical significance should not be ignored.

Most subsequent forms of philosophy have either been influenced by Hegel or have reacted against him. This is as true of Marxism and existentialism as it is of critical theory, phenomenology, hermeneutics, and much of analytic philosophy. In addition to his historical importance, Hegel's work merits close attention by virtue of his claim that it is his system alone that provides a viable middle path between every philosophical synthesis. He asserts that it preserves the strengths and cancels the weaknesses of realism and idealism, dualism and materialism, relativism and absolutism, skepticism and dogmatism, nominalism and Platonism, pluralism and monism, radicalism and conservativism.³ In his day, philosophical reflection seemed to be stranded between positivistic obtuseness and transcendental abstraction. His system reacts against the rational tradition with its antiquated doctrines and methods, specifically the metaphysics of Descartes, Leibniz, and Wolff, which had been discredited by Kant's critique of knowledge. For this reason, many see Hegel as the last great systematic thinker in Western philosophy, a thinker seeking to render all facets of reality accessible to philosophical understanding and to integrate them into an intelligible whole.⁴ Hegel held from the beginning of his career that the purpose of his work is to aid philosophy in its quest for the rational knowledge of *Geist* [Spirit, or the Absolute].

A striking feature characteristic of Hegel's thought is that he historicizes philosophy, explaining its purpose, principles, and problems in historical terms. His historicism amounts to nothing less than a revolution in the history of philosophy. It implies that true philosophy is possible only if it is historical, only if the philosopher is aware of the origins, context, and development of his doctrines.⁵ Consequently, Hegel throws the Cartesian revolution that founds modern philosophy into question. With this historical dimension, it is no longer possible to create a system of philosophy free of presupposition merely by abstracting from the past and relying on one's individual reason. He asserts that metaphysics is possible only if its central concepts are explicable in historical terms.⁶ Hegel accepts Kant's critical teaching that metaphysics is not possible as speculation about a realm of transcendent entities but is possible only if metaphysics does not transcend the limits of possible experience. The central concepts of metaphysics therefore must be explained in empirical terms. Doing so, however, means defining these concepts in historical terms, since experience consists not only in present sense perceptions but also in the totality of all forms of human experience, past, present, and future.⁷

Hegel's response to this challenge is the famous dialectic that he begins to develop in 1800 with the *Fragment of a System*.⁸ His early work searches for a logic that would demonstrate the viewpoint of absolute knowledge by beginning with the concepts of understanding. This logic demonstrates how the concepts of the understanding necessarily contradict themselves, and how their contradictions can be resolved only by seeing them as parts of a wider whole.⁹ Hegel modifies his approach in 1807 with the *Phenomenology of Spirit*, which deals not with concepts of understanding but with standpoints of consciousness. Here, Hegel demonstrates how the attempt by ordinary consciousness to know reality in itself ends in contradiction, and how this contradiction can be resolved only through rising to a more inclusive standpoint.¹⁰ More specifically, the dialectic proceeds through three stages: First, a finite concept, true only of a limited part of reality, exceeds its limits in attempting to know all reality by claiming to be an adequate concept that explains reality completely. Second, this claim encounters an inherent conflict between its claims of independence and the fact that it is de facto dependent upon its own negation of its existence. Third, the only way to resolve the conflict is to reinterpret the claim to independence so that it applies to both concepts. The same stages are repeated, and the dialectic continues until a standard of knowledge is found that conforms to the experience of consciousness. What Hegel attempts to provide in the *Phenomenology of Spirit* is nothing less than a transcendental deduction of absolute knowledge.[11]

Today, many postmodern theorists claim to be antifoundationalist. Although most previous philosophies do in fact rest upon foundations of some sort, Hegel pursues systematic philosophy with the recognition of the need to overcome foundations; that is, his task is to provide a critique of foundational thought without making foundational claims:

> The first thinker to have raised the possibility of such nonmetaphysical, nonphenomenological systematic philosophy is Hegel. In his *Phenomenology of Spirit*, he has attempted to demonstrate how phenomenology does in fact complete itself with the self-elimination of knowing as it appears, thereby providing the starting point for a presuppositionless systematic philosophy.[12]

As discussed in a later section of this chapter, his phenomenology requires overcoming the oppositions in consciousness. He works out a dialectical logic with no primitive terms or principles.[13] As illustrated in Chapter 9, Hegel's system not only is antifoundational, it also escapes the relativism of many postmodern theories. In fact, his discussion of ethical life is normative.

Besides furnishing a brief overview to Hegel's thought, this chapter provides the philosophical background necessary to appreciate Hegel's unique perspective. His philosophical attempt to overcome the fragmentation and contradictions between the individual and society can only be appreciated fully within the context of the Western tradition. Like modern libertarians, Hegel celebrates the separation of civil society and the state as a great achievement of modernity. However, even though he approves of the liberation of self-interest from oppressive collectivization, Hegel is highly critical of those commercial societies where everything is judged in terms of exchange, like modern globalization and its mantra of free trade. As indicated above, the metaphysical subjectivism of Descartes, Locke, and Kant completely lacks a historical dimension. They are unable to explain how the subject emerged or give a historical account of it. There is no transcendental subject capable of standing outside society or outside experience.[14] For Hegel, human beings must be comprehended historically and in relationship with other subjects;

that is, intersubjectively. Thus, the subject is transformed through an ongoing interplay, or dialectic, of forces.[15] This means that human beings are defined by more than raw economic self-interest alone. Moreover, Hegel recognizes that absolutist conceptions of individual rights can lead to anarchism. While the anarchist disposition of liberalism has stood as a sentinel against tyranny, it also stands as a stubborn obstacle to community forums and justice.[16]

Hegel is not an alienated critic of modernity. On one hand, he approves of the general direction of Western culture and society, and supports what he saw as the key developments of modernity. On the other hand, modern philosophy and life are understood in terms of oppositions, such as the individual versus the community, man versus nature. This chapter is organized into four sections. The first section provides an overview of Hegel's history of philosophy. Understanding previous philosophy is crucial because it not only influenced Hegel's intellectual growth but is also part of the development of *Geist*. Hegel recognizes that each philosopher has important truths to offer, but he also demonstrates that each contains only partial or incomplete truth. According to Hegel, we can only appreciate his philosophy by understanding the past. The second section of the chapter places Hegel's philosophy in its historical and intellectual context. This includes Hegel's appreciation of his philosophical place in the Western tradition. The third section examines Hegel's dialectic method, illustrating the power of contradiction and reconciliation to synthesize and gain a higher level of understanding. The chapter concludes with a brief discussion of Hegel's critique of modernity.

## HEGEL'S HISTORY OF PHILOSOPHY

The history of philosophy is of great importance to Hegel. Philosophy has an internal history, which consists of the genesis, development, and transformation of its very subject matter.[17] In essence, it is impossible to separate philosophy from the history of philosophy. In the introduction to his 1820 Berlin lectures on the history of philosophy, he says: "I would only remark this, that what has been said reveals that the study of the history of Philosophy is the study of Philosophy itself, for, indeed, it can be nothing else."[18] Since the history of philosophy is the necessary development of the true system of philosophy, Hegel holds that philosophy is learned through its history. History not only teaches us how to philosophize, but the history of philosophy is also crucial because it is the means for knowing the truth. That is, truth emerges as a consequence of historical development. It is through its history that we see what philosophy is; therefore, the history of philosophy is the philosophy of philosophy. This Hegelian notion of philosophy means that "reason itself must constantly recognize that it is not rational enough, that it is rational only to the extent that it *becomes* more rational, that being rational is a process which no philosophy exhausts."[19] Thus, Hegel is not interested in merely interpreting Plato, Augustine, Locke, or Kant; rather he wants to show what has been going on through the process of which these thinkers constitute an integral part.

The final system is developed at the end of the history of philosophy, and Hegel does not hesitate to suggest near the end of the lectures that his system is the result of all the labors of *Geist* in the past 2,500 years.[20] Since Hegel argues that the history of philosophy is the exposition of the true system of philosophy, and since he maintains that his own philosophy is the next logical step, he regards the history of philosophy as an introduction to and justification for his own philosophical system. Being the culmination and reconciliation of all past philosophy, Hegel thinks that his philosophy preserves the truths and cancels the errors of all past philosophy. Furthermore, the process of thought is the process of becoming free: Self-determination is freedom. For Hegel, philosophy proper commences in the West, since it is in the West that the freedom of self-consciousness begins.[21] In particular, the progress of *Geist* and actualization of freedom move from the realm of classical political philosophy to that of modern political theory. For Hegel, "thought is an ongoing process whose past is integral to its present, and whose present can be what it is only because its past has been what it has been, whose present is knowable only if its past is also known."[22]

## The Development of Western Philosophy

The Western intellectual tradition is a confluence of two traditions that arose in the ancient world—the Judeo-Christian and the Greco-Roman. The great achievement of the Greeks lay in the development of rational thought. With the Greeks, the human mind discovered its capacities for thinking, and thus philosophizing. Subsequently, they conceived of a new way of viewing nature and human society that became the basis of Western scientific and philosophic traditions. They conceived of nature and society as following general rules that could be discovered through the use of reason. Their achievement made theoretical thinking and the systematization of knowledge possible.

Socrates (469–399 BC) argues that human beings should regulate their conduct according to universal standards that are arrived at through, and are upheld according to, rational reflection—in short, reason is the only guide to rational action. By examining all behavior critically, Socrates wants to remove ethics from the realm of authority, tradition, and dogma. Reason alone should determine questions of good and evil. Hegel says: "Athenians before Socrates were objectively, and not subjectively, moral, for they acted rationally in their relations without knowing that they were particularly excellent."[23] Socrates further advances philosophy through his questioning attitude. The Socratic Method consists in applying critical inquiry and reasoning to those who profess knowledge, and in this way determining whether stated truth stands up to critical thinking. In other words, philosophy must begin with a puzzle in order to bring about reflection; everything must be doubted, and all suppositions given up to reach truth.[24] Plato (429–347 BC) uses Socrates' teaching to create a comprehensive system of philosophy that embraces both the natural and social world, and he is the first to write systematically about political matters. To that extent at least, he stands at the head of the Western philosophical tradition, being the first to produce a body of writing that touches metaphysics, epistemology, science, religion, and ethics.[25] Building on the insights of Socrates, Plato insists on the existence of a higher world of reality that is independent of the world of things that people experience—the realm of Forms, or ideas [*eidos*], which are absolute, eternal, universal truths or standards.[26] Empirical things only exist through their participation in the Forms. Hegel notes that Plato's philosophy is the science of the implicitly universal, as contrasted with the particular.[27]

For Plato, human beings are to use reason to study and arrange human life according to these universally valid standards. Moreover, these absolutes, or Forms, are not discoverable through experience, but rather through pure reason unhindered by the senses.[28] Forms are the most difficult thing for human beings to comprehend fully. In fact, very few will ever come close. Thus, to remedy the problems within the human condition, Plato asserts the necessity of uniting philosophy with government.[29] Since Plato sees true knowledge as being beyond the reach of average human beings, he unveils his plan for the "philosopher-king" in the *Republic*. These philosopher-kings alone would approach human problems with reason and wisdom, derived from knowledge of the eternal Forms.[30] A just society must be governed by reason and have unity and order. Plato's political philosophy conveys a lack of concern for individuals, who are essentially sacrificed to the unity of the whole. In fact, justice is each individual performing the work that he was born to do without reflection—a caste system of sorts. According to Hegel, Plato's thought leaves no room for subjective freedom.[31]

Aristotle (384–322 BC) was a research scientist and much of his time was devoted to observation.[32] He possessed an inductive habit of mind that made him accumulate and catalogue all available information on a variety of subjects. Aristotle examines things that exist by nature in order to discover their principles, causes, and elements.[33] The circumstances that render a fact necessary are referred to as its causes. He basically rejects Plato's theory of Forms.

Both form and matter are necessary for reality to exist. While universals exist, they must be combined with physically existing matter. He would not accept Plato's claim that what is real is an eternal, unchanging idea. Since the world is real, any explanation of change, growth, and decay could be discovered only by studying actual instances themselves. Aristotle sees the state as natural and argues that political life can be rationally understood and intelligently directed. Like many in his day, he does not approve of democracy, but instead advocates blending aristocracy and democracy into the best practical state.[34] Since democracy's principle of equality is blended with aristocracy's elitism, there is room for some popular participation. Hegel asserts that Aristotle subordinates the individual and his rights to the state, since the whole is greater than its parts.[35] Aristotle's politics intends to protect the common good by balancing the contending classes within society. Since virtue is living in accordance to the universal law of nature, Hegel says that individuals merely find their place in the natural order.[36]

In general, Hegel associates modernism with the movement in philosophy running from Francis Bacon (1561–1626) and Descartes (1596–1650) through the Enlightenment toward the twentieth century. Greatly influenced by science, the modern way of thinking is distinguished from ancient and medieval conceptions. Specifically, it arose out of the Renaissance, the Protestant Reformation, and the scientific revolution. From the beginning, modernism can be characterized by its challenge to traditionalism. Bacon takes experience as the true and only source of knowledge. In the *Organon*, he tries to establish a new method of learning, one that is founded on the observation of the external nature of man in his desires and rational qualities.[37] The rise of the scientific method and the faith in human reason creates an atmosphere that questions established customs, belief systems, and authority. Reason becomes artificial calculation that strives to control the world of necessity by understanding and then by exploiting its laws. For Hegel, early modernism advocates overturning whatever cannot satisfy its new criterion of rational justification.

Modernism characterizes a form of logocentric metaphysics that seeks to realize philosophy's traditional goal of achieving a basic, fundamental knowledge of "what is" by turning inward, into the knowing subject, where it tries to discover grounds that will allow for certainty in knowledge of the outside world. Modern rationality requires reflection, and it arises when "the subject" stands back from lived experience in order to determine abstract principles that explain and structure experience. In brief, modernism is grounded in the assumption that the order of the universe is natural, accessible to reason and observation, and describable in impersonal, materialistic, mechanical, and mathematical terms. Descartes' critical stance toward tradition and his discovery of conceptual certainty in the *cogito* of the subject embody much of the modern paradigm. Self-conscious reflection thus becomes the essence of thinking and a new reference point for the objectification of nature, and now serves as the foundation of knowledge. Descartes can rightly be seen as the father of modern philosophy, since he proclaims the mind's inviolable autonomy and its ability to comprehend truth. Because Descartes holds that philosophy must begin from thought alone, Hegel says that he makes the abolition of all determinations the first condition of philosophy.[38] Descartes attempts to overcome skepticism and establish a new foundation for human reason and action, an "Archimedean point" from which to organize and master the world.

With Descartes, there is a turn to human beings as the ultimate reference point for philosophy. The emphasis upon individualism is explicit in his writings. Descartes establishes his secure standpoint beyond worldly influences. More specifically, he uses skepticism to destroy the idea that human experiences connect people to a wider world. Methodical doubt is employed to raise the possibility that all human experiences are delusions of dreams that say nothing about the world.[39] Nonetheless, this opens up the way to positive developments—the establishment of a standpoint beyond doubt. First, if the premise that all experience might be deceptive is accepted, what remains beyond doubt is an "I" that is required in order to have these experiences, to sustain them, however deceptive they may be.[40] Second, from the standpoint of the Cartesian subject, it is possible to reinterpret experiences subjectively, as sensory perceptions, or sense impressions. Experiences have become forms of thinking, and are subordinated to the self: "I am something real and really existing, but what thing am I? I have already given the answer: a thing which thinks."[41] Hence, individualism is wedded to rationalism: knowledge comes from individual thinking subjects.

In this manner, Descartes establishes his secure standpoint beyond worldly influences. With *cogito ergo sum*, he plays the role of a god and places himself—and all thinking individuals—at the center of a world in which he—as an isolated individual—is both discoverer and creator. According to Hegel: "Nothing is true which does not possess an inward evidence in consciousness, or which reason does not recognize so clearly and conclusively that any doubt regarding it is absolutely impossible."[42] Hence, Cartesian certainty is knowledge that is self-relating. The thinking self is the first step in the construction of a firm and permanent structure in the sciences. Once assured of the certainty of one's own existence, the Cartesian subject can proceed to the construction of a system of knowledge by moving from the inside outwards. With the Cartesian subject, which is egocentric or a first-person standpoint, perceptions can only ever be interpreted as sense-impressions. Everything is encountered subjectively by individuals. So thought is caught up in a solipsistic circle. Thus, totalizing thought and its solipsistic self-enclosure are at the heart of modern philosophy.[43] Nothing in experience can shake the self's faith in itself. With this Cartesian move, a gulf has opened up between the self and the world. Moreover, with Descartes, the natural world is seen to be purely mechanical:

> Extension and motion are the fundamental conceptions of mechanical physics; they represent the truth of the corporeal world. It is thus that ideality comes before the mind of Descartes, and he is far elevated above the reality of the sensuous qualities. . . . He thus remains at the point of view of mechanism pure and simple. Give me matter (extension) and motion and I will build worlds for you, is what Descartes virtually says.[44]

Subsequent philosophical developments continue to be caught in the subjectivist trap. John Locke (1632–1704) takes up the struggle to escape the circle of the self and regain access to the world. He does this by rejecting internal reflection and its innate ideas, and turns to the world of concrete experience.[45] In reaction to Descartes, Hegel says that the human mind, for Locke, is a *tabula rasa*, which means that it is an empty vessel that is filled with what we call experience.[46] Consciousness obtains all its conceptions and notions from experience. Locke and his fellow empiricists do not get very far, however, since they retain too much of the Cartesian baggage. The problem is that concrete experience continues to be interpreted subjectively because empiricists keep Descartes' notion of sense-experience. So, instead of the world, empiricists find only a series of isolated subjective sense-impressions.

For Hegel, Immanuel Kant (1724–1804) sees empiricists as being trapped in the subjectivist interpretation of experience and attempts to go beyond the limitations of the empiricist picture in order to re-establish the possibility of knowing the world.[47] Nonetheless, Kant questions neither the subjective interpretation of experience nor the modern subject. Instead, he reasserts the idea of the foundational subject. With Kant, the subject itself is now used to overcome the limitations of the subjectivist picture. With the transcendental subject, the self actively organizes its sense impressions, which Kant calls empirical intuitions, in accordance with the universal, *a priori* categories of the understanding.[48] Even though knowledge is no longer confined to immediate sense-impressions, the problem of solipsism remains in the form of the self-enclosure of Kant's transcendental idealism. The self is still the sovereign, God-like creator and source of the world and the basis of moral law. Although Kant's thought may have regained access to the world, the world is entirely subordinate to the organizing self. Experience is still interpreted from the standpoint of the subject—that is, it is shaped and ordered in accordance with the subject's categories of understanding.[49] For Kant, human beings only have access to the phenomenal world, the world of appearances. The subject is still prior to and independent from its objects.

## The Modern Conflict Between the Individual and Community

With Thomas Hobbes (1588–1679), the Baconian ideal of knowledge as power begins to pervade the liberal conception of natural man. Since individual selves are all that exist in nature, the natural gulf is artificially bridged through the social contract. Liberal democracy is derived from Hobbes' and Locke's metaphysics of the subject. Hobbes begins his political inquiries from the state of nature, a pre-political situation where isolated individuals exist. He starts his analysis on a Cartesian base, and deduces natural rights from this individualistic starting point. All human beings have rights simply by virtue of their "humanness." In their natural state, human beings possess the right to everything. Since people are highly selfish, they only leave the state of nature when they find it to their personal advantage.[50] For Hobbes, both society and its institutions are artificial human constructs. Moreover, institutions are designed to serve the selfish interests of individuals. The bond that holds the state together and gives the state its power is derived from individual self-interest.[51] According to Hegel, the common good is replaced by individual self-interest as the criteria for the legitimacy of authority. Due to the risks in the state of nature, Hobbes draws the conclusion that mankind must leave the natural condition and go forth into the newly created—and improved—political world.[52]

Following Hobbes' Cartesian lead, John Locke (1632–1704) uses a state-of-nature argument to make his case. Autonomous individuals precede society and possess natural rights. Although there are differences, Locke too believes that people leave the state of nature and form society purely out of self-interest.[53] Lockean liberalism is clearly a response to threats towards individuals and their liberty by absolutist government. Thus, from the very beginning, liberalism attempts to deal with the war between liberty and government authority, even democratic government. Since liberty is defined as the absence of government, government is seen as jeopardizing individual liberty. The epistemological presumptions of early liberalism are Cartesian, and the solipsism of Cartesian epistemology serves to reinforce the excessive individualism of Lockean liberalism.[54] Excessively individualistic conceptions of liberty tend to empty the concept of citizenship of any meaningful content. The difficulty is that a disproportionate emphasis upon individuals and their rights threatens the idea of a community. In order for a society to be a community, it must be constitutive of the shared understandings of the participants and embodied in their institutional arrangements. Since the modern subject is installed as sovereign and is freed from the dictates of nature and the sanction of social roles, it is the author of the only moral meanings there are.[55] So conceived, liberal democracy and natural rights tend to be anti-democratic. Properly conceived, the democratic citizen is neither completely the individual nor the collective.[56]

Jean-Jacques Rousseau (1712–1778) challenges the mathematical-logical spirit that had converted nature into a mere mechanism. He draws a sharp distinction between civilized and natural human beings. Against the proponents of the Enlightenment, he charges that society distorts and perverts human nature.[57] Against Hobbes, Rousseau asserts that the unpleasant characteristics of human beings derive not from nature but from society.[58] Not content with satisfying natural need, civilized people are envious and greedy, obsessively pursuing luxury and sinking into debauchery. In fact, Rousseau rejects the contention that individuals could have begun to conceive thoughts without language, any more than they could have formed a society without it. In the absence of both society and language, the establishment of a right to property, such as Locke describes it, would have been impossible. Furthermore, Rousseau dismisses Hobbes' claim that individuals are innately brutish and violent. Since human beings are free agents and capable of choice, Rousseau thinks that they have a unique capacity to change their nature. The perfectibility of natural man did not ensure their moral advancement, since the real advancement of humanity depends upon the actual choices made in the adoption of social and political institutions. According to Rousseau, human beings have in fact misapplied their freedom and brought about their own corruption. Freedom does not mean arbitrariness but the overcoming and elimination of all arbitrariness. The essential qualities of human nature could be uncovered only if envisioned apart from the contemporary features of human conduct.

Rousseau's political theory seeks to facilitate the achievement of moral goodness. Like Hobbes and Locke, he believes that people are free and independent. Although he rejects Hobbes' version of the social contract, he agrees that society rests on convention and is the product of deliberate contrivance.[59] Human beings unite together and form an association: "Find a form of association which will defend and protect with the whole of its joint strength, the person and property of each associate, and under which each of them, uniting himself to all, will obey himself alone, and remain as free as before."[60] Rousseau's social contract replaces the scientific justification of society with an ethical one.[61] While Hobbes and Locke advocate natural rights, Rousseau asserts that rights are born of the social order and repudiates the idea of natural rights that people carry over from the state of nature.[62] Rights are conventional, or political, and are possessed by members of a community. In effect, Rousseau seems to be reacting against the excessive individualism

and atomism of the English contract theorists. It is not a question of eman-
cipating and liberating the individual in the sense of releasing him from the
community; rather, it is a question of finding the kind of community that will
protect every individual with the whole concerted power of the political organization.[63] For Rousseau, freedom depends upon the state for its continued
existence. As illustrated in the next chapter, Rousseau's political philosophy
contributes greatly to Hegel's critique of modernity.

The "general will," or interest of the community, is the cornerstone of
Rousseau's political philosophy, and nothing may legitimately be done
against it. The excessive individualism of English contract theory leads to a
mere aggregation, not a community. The general will is intended to reconcile
interest and authority, and autonomy and solidarity. In society, one's civil
liberty is regulated by the general will. The general will is binding, and by
forcing individuals to obey it, they are merely forced to be free.[64] Although
most people will freely follow, Rousseau argues that force must be available
against destructive individuals who refuse to abide by the conditions of social
solidarity. Forcing one to be free means binding individuals to accept political decisions reached collectively after public deliberation. Every act of the
general will is an act of self-legislation by society as a whole, and it is binding because everyone has already agreed to be bound by it. The general will
makes people into free citizens because it protects them from the fate of being subjected to the will of others. For Rousseau, true freedom is only found
through obedience to the general will: "Political membership is a precondition of civil freedom, which Rousseau takes to be the ability of individuals to
act unconstrained by the particular wills of others within a sphere of activity
deemed by society to be external to the vital interests of the community as
a whole."[65] While some hold that Rousseau's general will is abstract at best
and totalitarian at worst, Hegel sees the general will as offering a necessary
starting point for criticisms of modern liberalism.


## HEGEL'S PHILOSOPHY IN CONTEXT

Hegel sees the history of philosophy as a long dialogue regarding truth. For
him, there is no question either of simply rejecting preceding philosophical
views or beginning again anew. Instead, his goal is to construct a new system, a new philosophy, which will include all that is positive, that is, every
conceptual advance from his predecessors. No philosopher ever begins from
scratch, since all thought depends upon the philosophical tradition to which
it responds. An understanding of Kant requires a familiarity with Leibniz
and Hume and so on. Paul Redding argues that Hegel's achievement is his

ability to continue the unfinished revolutionary modernization of ancient philosophical thought initiated by Kant: "Putting hermeneutic ideas together with Kant's Copernican philosophy, transcendental idealism, he was able to extend Kant's project of a modern postmetaphysical philosophy, a philosophy that stands in relation to the dogmatic metaphysics of its antecedents in a way analogous to that in which the modern scientific Copernican cosmology stood to its ancient geocentric precursor."[66] Responding to the conflicting tendencies within the Enlightenment, Romanticism, and Kantian philosophy, Hegel tries to establish a complete metaphysical system by synthesizing them. Hegelian philosophy completes the projects of its great predecessors, Kant, Fichte, and Schelling, and answers Hume's argument that the locus of concreteness is in the immediacy of reality's presence to sensation.[67]

The Enlightenment culminates the movement toward modernity initiated by the Renaissance. Galileo pioneers in experimental physics and advances the modern idea that knowledge should be derived from direct observation.[68] His scientific method stresses that temporary hypotheses should be tested, and the traditional explanations of natural behavior should be verified empirically. By penetrating beyond the superficial appearance of things, new knowledge can be discovered through the scientific method. The invention of new scientific instruments advances the exactness of observation. The drift of this new scientific method helps pave the way for a radically new conception of man and of nature; it also leads to a mechanistic conception of nature and knowledge. Francis Bacon attacks scholastic thinkers for engaging in an arid verbalism and constructing elaborate systems that have little to do with the empirical world. He describes those "idols," or false notions, that hamper human understanding.[69] In order to penetrate into the inner recesses of nature, Bacon asserts that a new, more certain method is necessary. He advocates the inductive way to truth, which leads to the colonization of philosophy by the scientific method. Isaac Newton uncovers universal laws that explain the physical phenomena of the empirical world.

The Romantic reaction to the Enlightenment in Germany arises with the diffuse movement known as *Sturm und Drang*. In part, Romanticism is a direct response to what is perceived as the Enlightenment's tendency to glorify the objectification of nature. Modern science threatens the unity of human life, and isolates individuals from society and cuts them off from nature. Romanticism is a protest against the Enlightenment's view of man as both subject and object of an objectifying scientific analysis. Specifically, Romanticism is a reaction to the view that nature and society are only a means of fulfilling the desires and drives of the human ego. German thought in this period also reflects a nostalgia for premodern ideas and classical studies, particularly those of ancient Greece. The Greeks are seen as achieving a unity with self and communion with nature. Modern man, for the Romantics, is at war with himself. Thus the fundamental challenge is to legitimate the ideal of unity in face of the growing divisions within modern life. The modern state tends toward domination and control, and the atomistic trends of civil society are perceived in Germany toward the end of the eighteenth century. While the Enlightenment stresses reason and its secular status, Romanticism focuses on religion and passion.

Ancient Greece is supposed to have achieved the most perfect unity between nature and the highest human expressive form.[70] The Greeks represent the paradigm of perfection for many Germans of the late eighteenth century. For example, Friedrich Schiller's *On the Aesthetic Education of Man* traces cleavages which man has suffered in the evolution from ancient Greeks to modern society. Modern man has divided human faculties that were united in classical times.[71] Specifically, Schiller illustrates the contrast between the harmony of the ancient world and the fragmentation of modern life. With modernity, people have become specialized so that instead of expressing the whole, each is only a fragment of humanity. The specialization of functions makes for increased efficiency, but Schiller says that it replaces an organic system with "an ingenious clockwork in which out of the piecing together of innumerable but lifeless parts, a mechanical kind of collective life ensued."[72] Through the division of labor, human faculties become enervated and narrow, until people are only a caricature of what they once were. For Schiller, this transformation happens when the primordial natural harmony is destroyed by the growth of speculative intellect.[73]

The Romantics reject utilitarianism because it sees human beings as passive consumers of pleasure and neglects the active development of human powers. Schiller holds out the possibility of a new civilization where the current antagonism between sensuousness and reason will be overcome. This requires a society that produces not for needs or utility but rather according to the laws of beauty. He alludes to a higher unity based on exposure to art.[74] For Schiller, beauty is to be the unifying principle for collective life. Since beauty is crucial to freedom and morality, the beautiful work of art contributes something important to the formation and education of humanity. The Romantics seek a deeper bond of unity between human beings, one where people's highest concerns are shared and woven into the community rather than remaining the preserve of individuals. Thus, Romantics shift the conception of freedom away from the idea of rational self-determination toward the ideas of authenticity and feeling. As an expressive being, man has to recover communion with nature, which has been broken by the analytic stance of objectifying science. Even though Hegel is attracted to many aspects of Romanticism, he never fully embraces the movement. In true Hegelian fashion, he tries to reconcile the philosophical contradictions between Romanticism and the Enlightenment.

Hegel thinks that the union of the two is the key to an adequate account of the realization of freedom in the modern world. In his eyes, Romanticism partially completes the development of subjective idealism and the modern world in that it both renders the contradictions of that world fully apparent and creates the "social space" in which the possibility of a resolution of those contradictions finally appears (even though Romanticism itself does not offer that resolution on its own).[75] In spite of his criticisms of Romanticism, "Hegel's absolute idealism, his organic conception of nature, his critique of liberalism, his communitarian ideals, his vitalized Spinozism, his concept of dialectic, his attempt to synthesize communitarianism and liberalism—all these ideas are sometimes seen as uniquely Hegelian; but they were part of the common romantic legacy."[76] On the one hand, he sees Romanticism as the completion of a certain line of historical development; on the other hand, he thinks that it is deeply flawed, and often conveys his distain for its more extravagant expressions. Nevertheless, Hegel values Romanticism's account of freedom in terms of existing, concrete subjectivity.[77] The Romantics shift the conception of freedom away from the idea of rational, self-determination toward something with authenticity and feeling. Romanticism further helps to restore the idea of a community as the true seat of freedom.

Hegel's philosophy is significantly influenced by and draws upon the work of his immediate predecessors, especially Immanuel Kant. Not only is Kant the dominant figure in German philosophy, his writings set the philosophic agenda.[78] Thus, any ambitious philosopher wishing to assert his or her own identity must intellectually react to Kant's authority. Since Kant dominated the philosophical debate when Hegel began to write, he sees Kant as his most important interlocutor in contemporary discussion. In attempting to revindicate a radically free subjectivity, Kant's critical philosophy takes a new direction and defines the subject by transcendental argument. Kant's world of experience is distinguished from ultimate reality, and it takes its shape partly from the subject's mind. Since the beginning, philosophy has always been concerned with the theory of knowledge, and it is central to Kant's critical philosophy. Furthermore, it is the primary thread linking the views of Kant, the post-Kantians, and Hegel.[79]

Chronologically and conceptually, Kant's theory belongs to the Enlightenment. "Kant was defending the clarity of reason at a time when the general sympathy of the German intellectuals was turning increasingly toward mysticism and anti-intellectualism."[80] In fact, Kant sees the Enlightenment as the emergence of human beings from a self-imposed tutelage. With his *Ideal for a Universal History with a Cosmopolitan Purpose*, Kant's teleological doctrine of nature presupposes that mankind's natural dispositions are destined, in time, to develop in accordance with a purpose.[81] Just as Kepler discovered the natural laws of the planets, Kant claims to have discovered the natural laws of history. Moreover, Kant demonstrates that human development is found in history, and his philosophy of history is guided by a philosophical idea that understands historical change as the development of natural predispositions of the human race as a living species.[82] As Chapter 3 will make clear, Hegel's philosophy of history is foreshadowed in Kant's conception of universal history as the rational development of the human species. Kant's assertion that the history of the human race as a whole can be regarded as the realization of a hidden plan of nature seems to anticipate Hegel's notion of the cunning of reason.[83] One might even say that Kant's notion of Providence is a proto-type for Hegel's *Geist*. Furthermore, both thinkers recognize that reason does not transform the world overnight, but rather the advance of reason is extremely slow.

Since Kant's Providence sees to the development of the rational capacities of the human species, reason also manifests itself in human life as freedom. He further views freedom as the keystone of the whole architecture of the system of pure and speculative reason.[84] For Kant, moral law and freedom reciprocally imply each other. If people are not free, they are not able to make moral decisions. Human beings are subject to the laws of reason alone.[85] Progress can only be expected in the establishment of laws that are in accord with practical reason. In true Enlightenment fashion, Kant frees people from the domination of theological absolutism and the bonds of teleological natural law. Thus, reason is the history of freedom, and freedom takes a distinctly political form for Kant as it does with Hegel: The history of the human race can be regarded as the realization of a hidden plan of nature to bring about a perfect political constitution.[86] Political institutions, for Kant and Hegel, are regulated by laws that are based on reason, and they are intended to protect freedom. Both also assert that the principle of right [*Recht*] derives solely from the exercise of rational faculties that are historically conditioned.

In Kant's day, philosophy is divided by controversies among rationalists, skeptics, and empiricists. He neither sidesteps the issue nor joins the parties to the controversy, but instead adopts a previously undiscovered way to liberate metaphysics from its muddled situation.[87] Kant argues that the only way to defeat skepticism and explain the reliability of knowledge is by positing that the human mind structures sense experience in accordance with certain innate categories. His critique is not a condemnation of reason, but rather is a determination of its source, extent, and limits. He rejects both rationalism and empiricism as completed epistemological theory. Although he admits that knowledge begins with experience, it does not follow that knowledge originates solely in experience. The human mind contains its own inherent logic and is equipped with categories of understanding that give form and content to sense-data. This initiates the philosophical movement known as German Idealism, which includes Fichte, Schelling, and Hegel.[88] According to German Idealism's theory of knowledge, there is someone who experiences and there is that which is experienced, that is, there is a subject and an object. The distinctive feature of German Idealism is the claim that the subject is never passive but always active with respect to what it experiences.

Kant compares his philosophy to the work of Copernicus, who inverts the traditional claim regarding the relation between the earth and the universe. Kant's critical philosophy depends upon a revolutionary new concept, called the Copernican Revolution, which similarly inverts the relation between subject and object, between the perceiver and the perceived.[89] For Kant, the mind is active with respect to and influences what the subject perceives. His transcendental philosophy tries to determine the conditions of knowledge from a perspective prior to and thus isolated from all experience. Kant's epistemology therefore attempts to go beyond the limits of experience. Nevertheless, Kant has an important empirical dimension, since he refuses any knowledge of what is not either given or related to experience. Without a doubt, all knowledge begins with perception and sense-experience.[90] Put differently, transcendental simply refers to that which precedes experience and renders it possible. Mental concepts must be combined with sense-date for experience to be intelligible. Human consciousness of the world requires a combination of two very different types of representations [*Vorstellung*]. Passively received sense-representations of objects are combined with discursive representations, or concepts. Hegel asserts that the main point of Kantian philosophy is that reason is thought of as self-consciousness.[91] Kant's critical philosophy asserts that behind "all our experience of the world is an ineluctable fact of human spontaneity, of our actively taking up our experience and rendering it into the shape it has for us. Neither nature nor God could do that for us; we must do it for ourselves."[92]

Johann Gottlieb Fichte's theory is the first step toward the creation of post-Kantian German Idealism. When they were young, Schelling and Hegel — who were then committed to Kantian theory in general — regarded Fichte (1762–1814) as the true successor of Kant, that is, the one who provided the correct interpretation of the critical philosophy.[93] Fichte furnishes an important contribution to the reconstruction of critical philosophy in systematic form. Ever since Descartes, the discussion of the concept of a system turns on the concept of an undeniable foundation. Simply put, there is no science without system, and no system without foundation. In the debate regarding the reconstruction of critical philosophy, Fichte takes a bold and decisive step. In fact, he is convinced of his ability to finish the philosophical revolution initiated by Kant.[94] Although he agrees with Kant that it is impossible to surpass critical philosophy, Fichte claims that critical philosophy has still not been successfully formulated. Since objects are the objects of human experience, he rejects Kant's idea of objects "in themselves" beyond experience. Hegel notes: "Fichte created a great sensation of his time; his philosophy is the Kantian philosophy in its completion, and, as we must specifically notice, it is set forth in a more logical way."[95] For Fichte, the problem of self-authorization is the problem that must be solved in order to complete Kant's system.

Like Kant's *The Critique of Pure Reason*, Fichte's *The Science of Knowledge* provides an epistemological theory. Fichte shares Kant's view that philosophy must be science and that science requires a system. To this end, philosophy consists in the search for a first and absolute principle of human knowledge. Such a principle is unlimited and undemonstratable when it is a question of a true first principle:

> Our task is to discover the primordial, absolutely unconditioned first principle of all human knowledge. This can be neither *proved* nor *defended*, if it is to be an absolutely primary principle. It is intended to express that Act which does not and cannot appear among the empirical states of our consciousness, but rather lies at the basis of all consciousness and alone makes it possible.[96]

Fichte accepts the Cartesian view that philosophical science and knowledge are only possible in the form of a system, but he refuses the idea of an indubitable foundation and thus rejects Descartes' contribution to the theory of knowledge. In its place, he substitutes a concept of system in which there is a first principle, but where there is no foundation.[97] Thus, Fichte advances the idea of an unfounded system—that is, a foundationless theory of knowledge. He believes that the only possible account of justification has to see the mind as capable of grasping certain necessary a priori features of reality through an act of what he calls "intellectual intuition:"

> This intuiting of himself that is required of the philosopher in performing the act whereby the self arises for him, I refer to as *intellectual intuition*. It is the immediate consciousness that I act, and what I enact: it is that whereby I know something because I do it. We cannot prove from concepts that this power of intellectual intuition exists, nor evolve from them what it may be. Everyone must discover it immediately in himself.[98]

That is, we apprehend a necessary truth that can serve to justify some other claim. In most of his writings, Fichte stressed the same point: since the first principle of all science can only be given by an intellectual intuition, no further justification should be sought for it.

With respect to the initial principle intended to subtend the scientific system, there are only three possibilities: foundationalism, which rests on a first principle known to be true and from which the remainder of the system follows; skepticism, which is the negative conclusion following from the requirement to base knowledge on a foundation if this cannot be done; and ungrounded, circular view of knowledge, as in Fichte's theory.[99] As illustrated in the previous paragraph, foundationless does not mean without justification or argument of any kind. Even though there is no final ground in the Cartesian sense, there is a justification for Fichte's theory. In this way, he anticipates the attempt to provide philosophy with a systematic form while refusing any vestige of foundationalism. Fichte rejects both foundationalism and skepticism and perceives a circular relation between the first principle and the theory that follows from it. The first principle underlies the latter, and the latter returns to the former. Hegel says that the result is a circle—what Fichte sees as the unsurpassable circle of the human mind: Either knowledge constitutes itself within the framework of this necessary circularity, or knowledge is not possible.[100]

Fichte's project is to construct a theory of subjectivity, an explanation of what it is to be an "I." To this end, Fichte wants to develop a unified account of subjectivity, one that explains the apparently diverse activities of the subject in terms of a single structure that underlies and informs them.[101] More importantly for Hegel, by showing that the capacities for knowledge and free agency both depend upon one distinctive subjective feature of the "I," Fichte tries to unify the theoretical and practical aspects of subjectivity that Kant keeps separate. He is motivated by practical concerns, particularly the intelligibility of human freedom. Fichte's theory aims to improve upon Kant's by providing a unitary account of the subject, one that would bring unity and coherence into the human being by demonstrating that there are not two distinct faculties of reason but only one.[102] Fichte claims that a faculty of theoretical reason is only possible if the capacity for practical reason is presupposed. Simply put, theoretical reason is grounded in practical reason. For Fichte, the subject comes into existence as it acts, and prior to the act of instituting norms, there is no self, no subject. The "I" simply posits [*setzen*] itself: "There can be no ultimate criteria for positing except that which is entailed by the necessity of such positing in the first place, by whatever is necessary to maintaining a normative conception of ourselves."[103] By "posit" Fichte refers to a non-temporal, causal activity that is formed only by the mind and emphasizes the "unconditioned" nature of the "I:"

Hence what is *absolutely posited*, and *founded on itself*, is the ground of one particular activity (and, as the whole Science of Knowledge will show, of *all* activity) of the human mind, and thus of its pure character; the pure character of activity as such, in abstraction from its specific empirical conditions. The self's own positing of itself is thus its own pure activity. The *self posits itself*, and by virtue of this mere self-assertion it exists; and conversely, the self *exists* and *posits* its own existence by virtue of merely existing. It is at once the agent and the product of action.[104]

Since the "I" posits a normative status to itself, Fichte goes on to argue that this activity of self-consciousness is the manner through which the "I" constitutes itself as a cognitive thinking subject. The empirical world appears to offer a series of "checks" or "stimuli" in the form of experimental data whose status is not posited by us. Nevertheless, everything that has been said to exist, from natural objects to political regimes, is to be regarded as a posit, and what we ultimately take to exist has to do with which set of inferences are necessary in order to make the most of those empirical checks [Anstoss] found in our consciousness.[105] Therefore, all consciousness is conditioned on the ability to make inferences, and the ability to make inferences is conditioned on self-authorization, where we freely posit ourselves.

With the *Foundations of Natural Right*, Fichte writes that self-consciousness requires positing other self-conscious entities. He establishes the basic principles of a liberal political order by considering the problems of legitimacy from a Kantian perspective. Fichte defends the claim that all individuals possess a set of natural rights and that the central purpose of the state is to protect these rights from infringement. The *Foundations of Natural Right* inquires into the conditions under which individual subjects can achieve self-consciousness and argues that right [*Recht*] constitutes one of those conditions.[106] For Fichte, free agency requires that individuals be conscious of themselves as free and rational. A subject could not be self-conscious without ascribing a free efficacy [*Wirksamkeit*] to itself, an activity whose ultimate ground lies purely within itself. The existence of a world independent of our conscious activities and experience of it is a condition of self-consciousness, and is therefore one of the necessary "posits" that the thinking subject is required to make:

> The concept of right should be an original concept of pure reason; therefore, this concept is to be treated in the manner indicated. This concept acquires necessity through the fact that the rational being cannot posit itself as a rational being with self-consciousness without positing itself as an *individual*, as one among several rational beings that it assumes to exist outside itself, just as it takes itself to exist. . . . I posit myself as rational, i.e. as free. In doing so, the representation of freedom is in me. In the same undivided action, I simultaneously posit other free beings. . . . In appropriating freedom for myself, I limit myself by leaving some freedom for others as well. Thus the concept of right is the concept of the necessary relation of free beings to one another.[107]

As indicated above, positing is both a theoretical and practical activity. "What is being claimed is that the practical I is the I of original self-consciousness; that a rational being perceives itself immediately only in willing, and would not perceive itself and thus would also not perceive the world (and therefore would not even be an intelligence), if it were not a practical being."[108] Fichte notes that self-consciousness requires the positing of an independent world as a place where freedom can be realized. Moreover, Fichte concludes that the freedom of one subject requires the freedom of other subjects. That is, free individuality is possible only in relation to other subjects, and so intersubjectivity is a necessary condition of self-consciousness.

Given the fact that an individual shares the external world with other free subjects, this is possible only if individuality is recognized by those other beings as setting limits to their own free agency.[109] This mutual recognition [*Anerkennung*] is an important influence on Hegel's move from subjectivity to intersubjectivity. Mutual recognition, or social authorization, is a philosophical requirement of personal individuality. In other words, without such mutuality, there are no selves; subjectivity requires intersubjectivity. Furthermore, rights cannot be deduced from ethical individualism but require intersubjectivity. In a sense, Fichte is criticizing all previous philosophies, particularly those dealing with rights, for not first demonstrating the need for intersubjectivity, or the impossibility of thinking of the individual as isolated, which he sees as the same thing.[110] For Fichte, intersubjectivity is a necessary condition for the very existence of individuality and self-awareness. In addition, the idea of natural rights outside of a community is a fiction:

> There is no condition in which original rights exist; and no original rights of human beings. The human being has actual rights only in community with others, just as—according to the higher principles noted above—the human being can be thought of only in community with others. An original right, therefore, is a mere *fiction*, but one that must necessarily be created for the sake of a science of right.[111]

Thus, it is impossible to think of rights without thinking of an individual in relation to other individuals. Hegel's attempt to reconcile individual liberty with community follows Fichte's lead. Nor, for Fichte, can we think of free beings as existing together unless their rights mutually limit each other.

Like Fichte, Friedrich Schelling (1775–1854), Hegel's friend and college roommate, tries to clarify Kantian philosophy. In addition, he attempts to unite Kant and Baruch de Spinoza (1632–1677). He combines his newly found Spinozism with a rejection of what he took to be Fichte's error. In the *System of Transcendental Idealism*, Schelling puts forward the view that nature is the unconscious product of subjectivity.[112] Schelling rejects Fichte's argument that the distinction between subjective and objective is subjective, and holds that the distinction is relative to something called "the absolute." This absolute straddles the boundary between subjective experience and the objective world. He takes the Fichtean idea that subjectivity posits the world and extends it into a view of subjectivity as the underlying principle that expresses itself in nature.[113] Schelling gives shape to the vision of a cosmic spiritual principle and develops it into a philosophy of nature.[114] Nature has an inherent bent to realize subjective life. By conceiving of Spinoza's substance as living force, Schelling lays the ground for seeing the absolute as subject. Thus, according to Schelling, life manifests subjectivity in the objective world directed towards its own goals. Since this nature is teleological, a harmony is realized between necessity and freedom. However, the most that nature can do on its own is life, not consciousness.

Schelling thinks that history consists of a successive movement that strives to realize an ideal. History provides a continuous demonstration of God's presence. "Philosophy is thus a history of self-consciousness, having various epochs, and by means of it that one absolute synthesis is successively put together."[115] Like Hegel, Schelling argues that philosophy has a history that consists in the development of self-consciousness. Furthermore, Schelling sees history as process: "That the concept of history embodies the notion of an infinite *tendency to progress*, has been sufficiently shown above."[116] For Schelling, the goal of history is the union of law and freedom. Schelling's "absolute" bears a strong resemblance to Hegel's *Geist*. When conscious subjectivity reaches out to incorporate nature there must be a higher unity, and, for Schelling, this is only attained in art.[117] Schelling concludes in his *System of Transcendental Idealism* that the "absolute" could only be the object of imagination—in particular, artistic imagination:

> For if aesthetic production proceeds from freedom, and if it is precisely for freedom that this opposition of conscious and unconscious activities is an absolute one, there is properly speaking but one absolute work of art, which may indeed exist in altogether different versions, yet is still only one, even though it should not yet exist in the most ultimate form. . . . If aesthetic intuition is merely transcendental intuition become objective, it is self-evident that art is at once the only true and eternal organ and document of philosophy, which ever and again continues to speak to us of what philosophy cannot depict in external form, namely the unconscious element in acting and producing, and its original identity with the conscious. Art is paramount to the philosopher, precisely because it opens to him, as it were, the holy of the holies, where burns in eternal and original unity. . . .[118]
>
> The one field to which absolute objectivity is granted, is art. . . . Philosophy attains, indeed, to the highest, but it brings to this summit only, so to say, the fraction of a man. Art brings the whole man, as he is, to that point, namely to

a knowledge of the highest, and thus is what underscores the eternal difference and marvel of art.[119]

Thus, the work of art discloses the absolute in a non-discursive way that is more authentic than either scientific or philosophical knowledge can ever be. This is an important difference with Hegel, who refuses to subordinate philosophy to art.

Since traditional metaphysics sought after a realm of being outside experience, Kant concluded that the entire project of rational knowledge of reality is doomed to failure. Hegel joins with Fichte and Schelling in their effort to transform Kant's critical philosophy into a new idealism. Like them, he rejects Kant's contention that there is an unknowable "thing-in-itself." While he accepts Kant's need to examine critically the categories of reason, Hegel rejects Kant's claim that philosophy cannot formulate a meaningful overall view of reality: "But Kantian philosophy does not go on to grapple with the fact that it is not things that are contradictory, but self-consciousness itself."[120] Instead, Hegel asserts that a knowledge of things is discoverable through reflection on experience. Every object is also knowable, since it is a product of the mind. While Kant assumes that the forms of knowledge receive their material content from the given of experience, Hegel also argues that content as well as the forms of knowledge must be the product of one's mind. It is on the basis of his early Schellingian critique of Fichte that Hegel is able to elaborate a coherent account of objective subjectivity that allows him to pursue the Copernican turn much more fully than Kant or Fichte had been able to.[121]

This explains Hegel's claim that every reality is rational and that the rational is real. However, if all objects of our knowledge are the product of mind, but not our minds, it must be assumed that they are the products of an intelligence other than that of a finite individual. Thus, all objects of knowledge, and therefore all objects, and indeed the entire universe, are the products of *Geist*, an Absolute Mind.[122] While Kant's categories represent the mental process of an individual and provided for a critical explanation of the limits of knowledge, Hegel holds that they possess a mode of being independent of any individual's thought and have their being in *Geist*.[123] To put it differently, Hegel argues that a type of ultimate knowledge is possible because *Geist* is embedded into experience. Moreover, while Kant sees the categories that govern experience as being rigidly juxtaposed to one another, Hegel views them as dialectical—as intimately connected, mutually dependent and mutually defining.[124] That is, whatever exists, exists in relationship to other things, and these relationships make it what it is. The point is that Hegel thinks that a knowledge of things can be properly established by reason. He further believes that reason can overcome the dualism of subject and object, which is one of the tasks of his philosophy.

In his Jena years, Hegel revises the Romantic tendencies of his youth with a Kantian faith in reason. He redefines *Geist* as the dynamic self-embodiment of reason rather than the Romantic self-expression of infinite life. The theoretical basis for this new confidence in the capabilities of philosophy is Hegel's reformulation of Kantian reason [*Vernunft*]. "The structure of speculative thinking or Reason—the necessary dialectical self-movement of the 'concept' from the abstract, unmediated, and implicit to the concrete, fully mediated, and explicit—was thus identical with the structure of ultimate reality or 'Being'."[125] For Hegel, the reconstruction of the self-development of the categories of thought into a speculative logic provides a fully determinate "absolute" knowledge of ultimate reality. As is discussed in the next section, this fusion of logic and ontology allows Hegel to construct a conception of reconciliation between man and God, finite and infinite spirit, that affirms man's essential nature as a free, rational being. Like his Romantic contemporaries, Hegel holds that *Geist* embodies and reveals itself in the natural and historical world. However, unlike the Romantics, he also claims that this embodiment and revelation is a necessary logical process, the self-explication of speculative reason. In addition, Hegel argues that human beings are active not only as understanding beings who interpret the world through concepts but also as living beings.

## THE DIALECTICAL METHOD: *GEIST* AND *AUFHEBUNGEN*

For Hegel, philosophy is radically historical, and his dialectical method first becomes known by its application to history. Hegel's lectures on the philosophy of world history are based on the principle that reason rules the world and thus that world history advances rationally.[126] Moreover, the course of world history is a meaningful process with a definite purpose. He insists that the very idea of reason is already caught up in the world at every moment. Since *Geist* develops in time, all knowledge comes from experience. *Geist* also has a normative *telos*, and part of this *telos* is self-knowledge that it gains through human knowledge of the world.[127] His thought represents a conscious effort to bring together real life and philosophical theory to the point where they cannot be separated. "As thinking progresses, therefore, its object becomes progressively more determined and, therefore, more concrete, and the thinking, too, becomes more concrete."[128] Consequently, thinking is not a movement away from the concrete, but instead is the very process of concretion. Accordingly, philosophy cannot separate itself from its historical period and cannot discover timeless truths that are separate from the world. Since knowledge cannot be a priori, it emerges in and is the product of the collective effort of human beings over the course of history.[129] Thus, Hegel recognizes the contextual dependencies of philosophy and sees it as an expression of the spirit of the times.

Hegel's system is concerned with the theory of knowledge. In particular, he is interested in how knowledge-claims match up with their objects. Thus, he concentrates on the relationship of consciousness and object. In the introduction to *Science of Logic*, he says that his *Phenomenology of Spirit* exhibits consciousness in its movement onwards from the first immediate opposition of itself and its object to absolute knowing.[130] The result is achieved by an exhaustive enumeration of epistemological alternatives. Hegel's point is not only that alternative accounts of knowing are deficient in some respect, but that the deficiencies themselves must somehow lead to a proper account.[131] To fully grasp the development of consciousness is to climb for oneself what he refers to the "ladder" to the standpoint of science, or absolute knowing.[132] The rungs of the ladder are successive "appearings" on way to genuine knowing. The climber is liberated from the contradiction of consciousness and object, and thought emerges as subject and object are combined in pure thought. Hegel refers to this as the identity of subject and object. A central aim in the *Phenomenology* is to demonstrate that a properly constructed theory of knowledge requires realism about the objects of human knowledge.[133] This differentiates Hegel from Kant and Fichte. Despite their achievements, Hegel sees Kant and Fichte as skeptics, since "they undercut their own results by admitting that they have no way of establishing that the conditions for a possibly self-conscious experience of objects are genuinely objective."[134]

Hegel's *Phenomenology of Spirit* grounds this identity by demonstrating that all conceptions that treat the object as merely external to subject are untenable and need to be successively abandoned. His term for this way of looking at reason-giving activities is *dialectic*. It is important to note that it is not philosophers who refute the pretensions of the successive types of consciousness in a Hegelian manner; they refute themselves. Each form of consciousness uncovers problems with its own key ideas through some form of self-critical experience. Hegel analyzes these various forms of consciousness in order to illustrate known philosophical views and highlight their contradictions. Even though he seldom identifies other philosophers by name, he alludes to their contentions and illustrates the faults of their reasoning. Each type of consciousness proves to be unsustainable by immanent standards implied in its own self-understanding.[135] "The movement of consciousness doubting its own adequacy and consequently negating its inadequacy goes on."[136] In the *Phenomenology*, Hegel follows the progress from simple sense knowledge to absolute knowing. Epistemology has its dialectic—its inner dynamic. Hegel's dialectic examines various accounts of knowing and illustrates how they are transformed. His goal is to make it clear that the world is rational if it is looked at in the right sort of way. Such an approach would enable human beings to consciously achieve a fully rational comprehension of reality, realizing the purposes of human inquiry and leading to intellectual and practical satisfaction in the world.[137]

Hegel repeatedly refers to the idea of *Geist*, and it is crucial to understanding his philosophy. He says that the whole object of *The Philosophy of History* is to become acquainted with *Geist* in its guiding role in history.[138] The development of *Geist* in time is history. All existence is the manifestation, the actualization, of *Geist* as "idea." Only by being actualized does *Geist* receive its full reality, and only by containing *Geist* does the existing obtain its full existence. For Hegel, the movement of *Geist* explains epistemology, religion, nature, logic, and politics. In the *Phenomenology of Spirit*, Hegel claims that "the spiritual alone is the actual; it is essence. . . ."[139] His philosophy asserts that *Geist*, representing universal reason, shapes history through the actions of men. Human activity is nothing but the activity of self-conscious reason in the world.

Even though Hegel frequently integrates Christian doctrines into his writings, makes numerous references to God in all his works, and argues that Christianity is the most complete form of religion, he is much more than a Christian apologist. His mature writings express the view that philosophy, since it comprehends religion and subsumes its insights in form of pure concepts, surpasses religion and becomes the highest human attainment. In fact, he uses the term *Geist*, or Absolute, rather than God [*Gott*] to force his readers to think philosophically. Nevertheless, Hegel does see *Geist* as connected to God's providence. Human beings come to understand the true, dialectical character of reason in Christianity and Hegel's speculative philosophy. In the *Philosophy of Nature*, he talks about God as the creator of the world. His discussion there sheds some light on the relationship between God and *Geist*:

> God reveals Himself in two different ways: as Nature and as Spirit [*Geist*]. Both manifestations are temples of God which He fills, and in which He is present. God, as an abstraction, is not the true God, but only as the living process of positing His Other, the world, which, comprehended in its divine form is His Son; and it is only in unity with His Other, in Spirit [*Geist*], that God is subject. . . . The study of Nature is thus the liberation of Spirit [*Geist*] in her, for Spirit is present in her in so far as it is in relation, not with an Other, but with itself. This is also the liberation of Nature; implicitly she is Reason, but it is through Spirit that Reason as such first emerges from Nature into existence. . . . Thus God alone is the Truth, in Plato's words, the immortal Being whose body and soul are joined in a single nature.[140]

Human beings have a very special relationship with God. "God is the spirit of his community; he lives and is real in it. The world spirit is the system of this process whereby the spirit produces for itself the true concept of itself."[141]

*Geist* is frequently seen as a transcendent metaphysical construct lying beyond the bounds of possible experience. There can be no doubt, however, that Hegel's *Geist* lies within the experiences and activities of men:

> One word more about giving instruction as to what the world ought to be. Philosophy in any case always comes on the scene too late to give it. As the thought of the world, it appears only when actuality is already there cut and dried after its process of formation has been completed. The teaching of the concept, which is also history's inescapable lesson, is that it is only when actuality is mature that the ideal first appears over against the real and that the ideal apprehends this same real world in its substance and builds it up for itself into the shape of an intellectual realm. When philosophy paints its grey in grey, then has a shape of life grown old. By philosophy's grey in grey it cannot be rejuvenated but only understood. The owl of Minerva spreads its wings only with the falling of the dusk.[142]

*Geist* is entirely present or actual, and is not something that is over and above things. "The Hegelian Absolute is not realized in the supramundane consciousness, nor in a timeless comprehensive vision, but in the creative activities and products of the artist, the faith and worship of the religious person, and the systematic insights of the philosopher."[143] Again Hegel reminds us that: "It is just as absurd to fancy that a philosophy can transcend its contemporary world as it is to fancy that an individual can overleap his own age, jump over Rhodes."[144]

Although it underlies and manifests itself in all reality, *Geist* is necessarily embodied and cannot exist separately from the universe that it sustains.[145] It must necessarily be embodied in finite spirit. Moreover, *Geist* cannot be confined to the particular place and time of any one spirit. These finite beings must be living beings, since only living beings are capable of expressive activity. Thus, in order for *Geist* to exist, the universe must contain rational selves. Hegel's *Geist* can be understood teleologically as tending to realize reason, freedom, and self-consciousness. For Hegel the radical freedom of *Geist* is not incompatible with a necessary structure of things; on the contrary, the two notions are intrinsically linked. As Charles Taylor explains it:

> *Geist* in positing the world is bound by rational necessity, the necessary structure of things if *Geist* is to be. But this is no limit on his freedom. For *Geist* as subjectivity is quintessentially reason. And reason is most fully realized when one follows in thought and action the line of rational, that is, conceptual, necessity. If one had a line of action which was grounded entirely on rational, conceptual necessity, without reposing on any merely given premises, then we would have a pure expression of subjectivity as reason, one in which Spirit would recognize itself as expressed, and hence free, in a total, unadulterated way; something immeasurably greater than the freedom of finite spirits. This

is the freedom of *Geist*, which posits a world as its own essential embodiment according to rational necessity.[146]

Thus, the fact that *Geist*'s activity in positing the world follows entirely the line of rational necessity is not a restriction on its freedom. As a rational subjectivity, it is following nothing but its own essence in following rational necessity. There is neither an outside element nor a given that determines it.

The dialectical method is pervasive in Hegel's philosophy and governs all parts of his system. The dialectic contains Hegel's theory of human experience and cognition:

> Hegel's point is that the character and content of our experience—what is *for us*—is a function both of our conceptions and of the objects or events themselves that we grasp with our conceptions. Experience is our access to the world; it is rooted in the world even while it is also conditioned by what conceptions we use and how we use them in grappling with the world, both cognitively and practically.[147]

His philosophical inquiry takes all lower-level conceptions of knowledge and subjects them to criticism in order to establish the need for a logically higher perspective. When confronted with an object, human beings attempt to know the object. "Consciousness" is the subjective recognition of an object that is other than the knowing self, and "experience" is the moving process of cognition that generates a new conceptual object by discovering the contradiction of the one originally posited.[148] In other words, we arrive at a new conceptual standpoint by overcoming the skeptical aporia of the previous stage. Cognitive experience is the progressive discovery of truth. This moving process—Hegel's dialectic—will come to a halt when the posited concept agrees perfectly with the object as experienced. Hegel's dialectic is first fully developed in the *Phenomenology of Spirit*. It contains Hegel's science of experience, and its goal is not knowledge of God, but rather of human beings as knowers—that is, the logical science of being in the world. "Indeed, if we would look for a similar concept of experience we would find it not in classical epistemology but in the much more practical-minded writings of the American pragmatists William James and John Dewey."[149]

In order to understand how reason advances through history, it is necessary to grasp what Hegel means by dialectic. The concept goes back to ancient Greek philosophy, where Plato introduces it in describing the teachings of Socrates. Socrates' dialectic is a type of argumentation that proceeds by questioning and refuting the viewpoint of others by revealing their logical flaws. For Plato, the dialectic comes to represent a philosophical pathway to the highest truths—knowledge of the Forms [the eternal essence of things].[150]

Plato draws a distinction between material things and intellectual, or ideal, things. Intelligible things are only accessible through the use of dialectics. According to Plato, dialectics begins where mathematics ends—that is, it begins with theoretical theses that are derived as the conclusions of a process of hypothetical deduction, and then subjects these to systematic questioning, looking for the principles in which they are grounded. Dialectics leads one to a higher degree of understanding of true reality, Plato's intellectual Forms. For Plato, understanding true reality relies on pure reason, unaided by the senses.

Plato's dialectic requires that the validity of any hypothesis be verified. This validation demands that each hypothesis be measured and analyzed against other, and sometimes conflicting, hypotheses. Plato employs this technique in order to arrive at a unifying idea. In brief, it is used to discover some part of reality itself. For Plato, it is only at this highest level that we can find certainty, and it is here alone that we are in the realm of reality where truth might be discovered.[151] In order to find the essence of things and thus ultimate reality, one must go to the mind alone. Hegel acknowledges his philosophical debt to Plato regarding the dialectic, but he says that his own loftier dialectic of the concept veers off in a distinct direction from the negative mode that frequently appears in Plato:

> The concept's moving principle, which alike engenders and dissolves the particularization of the universal, I call "dialectic," though I do not mean that dialectic which takes an object, proposition, &, given to feeling or, in general, to immediate consciousness, and explains it away, confuses it, pursues it this way and that, and has as its sole task the deduction of the contrary of that with which it starts—a negative type of dialectic commonly appearing in Plato. Dialectic of this kind may regard as its final result either the contrary of the idea with which it begins, or, if it is as incisive as the scepticism of the ancients, the contradictory of this idea, or again, it may be feeble enough to be content with an "approximation" to the truth, a modern half-measure. The loftier dialectic of the concept consists not simply in producing the determination as a contrary and a restriction, but in producing and seizing upon the positive content and outcome of the determination, because it is this which makes it solely a development and an immanent progress.[152]

Unlike Plato, Hegel sees the world as characterized most fundamentally by change, becoming, and opposition. With the passage of time, each truth exists for only a limited period of duration. Borrowing from Kant, his dialectic includes a positive as well as a negative, and everything that exists is driven by conflicting tendencies. Hegel's dialectic of "forms of consciousness" [*Gestalten des Bewusstsiens*] is an attempt to think through our ideas about the world and about ourselves and to develop them to the point where we can

see their consequences and inadequacies.[153] Consciousness is capable of opposing points of view and feels the necessity to resolve them. By doing this,
our comprehension grows. Thus, unlike Plato, Hegel has a keen philosophical
interest in the physical world, as well as the intellectual world of idea.

Hegel's dialectic contains at least five dimensions.[154] The first is the process of becoming, or the need to apprehend the world and everything in it
as fluid. Instead of seeing the world and its reality as permanent essences, it
is seen as changeable and open ended. "Whatever is" is on its way to being
something else and is also on its way to perishing. While discussing the sublation of becoming, Hegel says that, on the one hand, to sublate [*aufheben*]
means to preserve, to maintain, and, on the other hand, it means to cause to
cease, to put an end to.[155] A description of reality must depict the fact that
existing things are constantly in transition. Hence, becoming not only affects
all existing things, but it also affects all human thought about things. Second,
oppositional relationships of any kind—whether in the physical or intellectual
world—are not a problem for Hegel. His philosophy sees beyond confrontation and contention to an equally important factor of dependency and comple-
mentarity, which opens the way to their possible resolution, or reconciliation.
Hegel argues that everything is constituted as much by what it suppresses or
excludes negatively as by what it expresses positively:

> Positive and negative are supposed to express an absolute difference. The two
> however are at bottom the same: the name of either might be transferred to the
> other. . . . Positive and negative are therefore intrinsically conditioned by one
> another, and are only in relation to each other.[156]

This is both an ontological claim about how things are and an epistemological
assertion regarding how human beings know things.

Third, the dialectic contains thought, a determination of how rival view-
points come to be resolved. Philosophical growth takes place when ideas are
negated and improved. For Hegel, truth emerges at each stage when previous
developments are superceded dialectically [*aufheben*]. Nevertheless, philosophical predecessors are still integral parts of a single system: "Speculative
Logic contains all previous Logic and Metaphysics: it preserves the same
forms of thought, the same laws and objects—while at the same time remodeling and expanding them with wider categories."[157] When something
is dialectally superceded, for Hegel, it is not only surpassed in a new result
where the old is implicit, it is transformed. When Hegel uses *aufheben*, we
are witnessing a process whose original elements are in one sense canceled, in
another sense preserved, but in an overall sense are transformed in such a way
as to reappear, metamorphosed, within a later stage of the process.[158] Hegel's
*Logic* demonstrates that the various categories of thought are dialectically

interrelated in such a way that conceptual oppositions are responsible for perplexities, which can be resolved by rethinking these fundamental notions.

Fourth, Hegel's dialectic sees truth, or knowledge, as something that develops over time. Truth is an achievement, not a fixed state. For Hegel, truth is like an organism in that it grows into what it is supposed to become. It is the outcome of a process of reflection in which we seek more adequate concepts for expressing what we know.[159] More importantly, an evolution of concepts is necessary for truth to emerge fully. Consequently, truth is accumulative and is gained through reflection on inadequate concepts in order to remedy them. Thought revises and is constantly opposing itself, and it overcomes its earlier formulations in a dialectical way. Fifth, all finite things are perishable:

> It is of the highest importance to ascertain and understand rightly the nature of the Dialectic. Wherever there is movement, wherever there is life, wherever anything is carried into effect in the actual world, there is Dialectic at work. . . . Everything that surrounds us may be viewed as an instance of Dialectic. We are aware that everything finite, instead of being stable and ultimate, is rather changeable and transient [perishable]; and this is exactly what we mean by that Dialectic of the finite, by which the finite, as implicitly other than what it is, is forced beyond its own immediate or natural being to turn suddenly into its opposite. . . . All things, we say—that is, the finite world as such—are doomed; and in saying so, we have a vision of Dialectic as the universal and irresistible power before which nothing can stay, however secure and stable it may deem itself.[160]

Thus, the dialectic is seen as a physical force in the world, and is the originator of all change and development. Dissolution and destruction occur too, and things perish. For Hegel, physical elements are also dialectical.[161] Everything embodies the principle of dialectical opposition with itself.

The distinctive subject matter of philosophy is thought, that is, the ideas or concepts by which human beings think about the world.[162] This thought is not a fixed state of being, but instead is a restless activity and a process of development from the indeterminate to the determinate, from the vague to clear, and from the abstract to the concrete. In sum, Hegel's dialectic is about movement, tension, and reconciliation. The fundamental premise behind his thought is that it is not possible to separate the object of thought from the activity of thinking about it, since it is only through thinking about an idea that it becomes clear, determinate, and concrete.[163] Like all activity, the activity of thought takes place not in an instance but throughout time. With this premise, Hegel is taking issue with the entire Platonic tradition of philosophy, which sees the object of thought as an eternal Form. In Hegel's view, the main problem with this Platonic conception of thought is that the meaning of ideas is never complete and given, as if it is only a question of perceiving their transparent essence. Rather, ideas become clear and distinct and take on determinate meaning only through the activity of thinking about them. It is only when the opposition between categories of knowledge is overcome that the tension in a conceptual scheme can be resolved and superceded by a more unified and rational worldview. Moreover, Hegel insists that art, religion, and philosophy are the self-consciousness of their age and that all the aspects of a culture form a single whole.

For Hegel, the object of thought is not given to, but created by thinking. To put it differently, thought is posited by the very act of discovering its meaning. Since the idea acquires its determinate meaning only through the activity of thinking about it, a sharp distinction between the object and the activity of thinking of thought cannot be made:

> As it is only in form that philosophy is distinguished from other modes of attaining an acquaintance with this same sum of being, it must necessarily be in harmony with actuality and experience. In fact, this harmony may be viewed as at least an extrinsic means of testing the truth of a philosophy. Similarly it may be held the highest and final aim of philosophic science to bring about, through the ascertainment of this harmony, a reconciliation of the self-consciousness of reason with the reason which *is* in the world—in other words, with actuality.[164]

Properly understood, philosophical thinking brings about reconciliation between idea and physical reality, or subject and object.

Hegel's dialectic is a method of exposition in which existing concepts are shown to be implicitly self-contradictory and to develop necessarily into the next, which forms a continuously connected hierarchical series culminating in an all-embracing category known as *Geist*, or Absolute Idea. The outcome of one dialectical stage directly paves the way for the next. In Hegel's technical language, the negation of each stage is a determinate negation:

> But when . . . the result is conceived as it is in truth, namely, as a *determinate* negation, a new form has thereby immediately arisen, and in the negation the transition is made through which the progress through the complete series of forms comes about of itself. But the *goal* is as necessarily fixed for knowledge as the serial progression; it is the point where knowledge no longer needs to go beyond itself, where knowledge finds itself, where Notion corresponds to object and object to Notion. Hence the progress toward this goal is also unhalting, and short of it no satisfaction is to be found at any of the stations on the way.[165]

With the dialectic, Hegel combines immanent self-movement with the necessity of transforming movement. Negation is the propelling force toward a more genuine knowledge, that is, a more adequate way to grasp the truth.

Hegel contends that the crucial issues of metaphysics, epistemology, ethics, politics, and religion are all associated with the dialectical way that the categories of universal and particular are conceived. Apparently insuperable philosophical difficulties will be generated unless these categories are brought together or mediated in the right way. Consequently, when Hegel talks about the failure of understanding to overcome the opposition between these categories, he points to a whole series of divisions in our view of the world, between abstract and concrete, ideal and real, one and many, necessity and freedom, state and citizen, moral law and self-interest, general will and particular will, reason and tradition, and God and man.[166] Hegel argues that the division between the universal and the particular lies behind all these dichotomies. Only dialectical thinking is capable of resolving philosophical and practical dichotomies by combining individuality with universality in the proper fashion.[167]

The dialectic is the dynamic principle of both the actual world and all genuine knowledge of that world. "Thus understood the Dialectical principle constitutes the life and soul of scientific progress, the dynamic which alone gives immanent connection and necessity to the body of science. . . ."[168] In a word, it constitutes the real and the true. After demonstrating the dialectical hierarchy in logic, Hegel goes on to interpret natural and spiritual phenomena as embodiments of this same dialectical hierarchy.[169] He tries to derive all known actuality—material or intellectual—by means of his dialectic. The dialectic is the general principle of all motion, all life, and all development in the existing world. "The main point of the whole contention is that the inner movement of the knowing process is one and the same with the inner movement of the object known. . . ."[170] It allows Hegel to establish the unity of thought and being. As discussed in the next chapter, he also interprets human history as a teleological process unfolding in a dialectical sequence of consciousness and freedom by escaping earlier contradictions. If history is to be brought into philosophy without its making philosophy into a new form of dogmatism or apology of the status quo, then the purely historical account of the contingencies that have made us who we are must be supplemented by a dialectical history of self-consciousness.[171]

## HEGEL'S CRITIQUE OF MODERNITY

The tension between liberalism's individual freedom and communitarianism's social-political bond is one of the most widely contested issues of political theory. Champions of individual freedom consider the essence of politics to be the defense of personal rights and liberties against the encroachments emanating from government. From this perspective, all community standards appear questionable and possibly repressive. Countering liberalism, communitarians are quick to point out corrosive effects that egotism and possessive individualism have on moral and political life. One of the appealing aspects of Hegel's thought resides precisely in its attempt to reconcile and transcend this conflict, by integrating and preserving facets of both liberalism and communitarianism.[172] Moreover, his political philosophy entails the dialectic of individuality and community, liberty and authority. In essence, his *Philosophy of Right* constitutes a multifaceted edifice that makes room for both free individual initiative and shared moral bonds. It provides a way to curb the excesses of global economic forces that are being pursued in the name of free trade. Moreover, in the American context, it would seem as if many of Hegel's worst fears have occurred, where an atomistic freedom has permeated social life, and an economic "bottom line" dominates most social decisions. As discussed in Chapter 10, champions of economic individualism have reduced trade barriers and created free trade zones that have contributed downward pressures on labor costs. Moreover, in the name of economic competitiveness, corporations have greatly reduced their contributions to health care plans, pensions, and other benefits.[173]

Hegel not only celebrates the achievement of modern freedom, he also worries about its effects and excesses. Civil society is based on a separation, but full freedom demands unity as well. Although the institutions of civil society embody self-determination, they do not do so fully.[174] Civil society requires that people respect others and choose goals that fit into the circulation of needs and commodities. It tells one a great deal about means but nothing about ends. Consequently, it leaves people free to choose their own goals. Hegel sees this as less than ideal. He argues against this type of individualism. In fact, civil society left to itself has harmful effects. His conception of *Sittlichkeit* raises the question of how far can a society tolerate public and corporate polices that give free rein to economic interests without undermining the moral legitimacy of the community? Modern modes of mutual recognition imply no natural limits on society's activity. As the system of production and exchange expands, Hegel says that the means of production grows more specialized. As discussed in Chapter 10, workers come to lead a more machine-like existence, while the rich live a more opulent life.[175]

Hegel designs his political institutions as a bulwark against the fragmenting institutions of economic self-interest and the overbearing influence of economic factors on politics. Substantively, he maintains that liberalism collapses the state into civil society. Historically, under pressure from economic interests, few of Hegel's institutions were ever used in actual existing states, much less in the specific form he described. By grounding legitimate law and institutions in social practices, including those that are part of the economy, he comes closer to historical materialism than Marx recognized.[176] Hegel's rational community is designed to ensure the freedom of its members, and he does not mean freedom in the political sense alone. Hegel is interested in freedom in a deeper, more metaphysical sense. His concern is with freedom in the sense that one is free when able to choose without being coerced either by other human beings, natural desire, or social circumstances. Like Kant, Hegel believes that freedom can exist only when one chooses rationally, which is in accord to universal principles. If these choices are to bring about individual satisfaction, the universal principles must be embodied in an organic community organized along rational lines.

Hegel's dialectic retains the classical notion of community and combines it with the modern notion of the individual. In this way, his political project is the reconciliation of the individual with the community. Furthermore, his dialectical criticism preserves what he finds of value in classical liberalism while reformulating it in ways that are more sensitive to the historical context of rights. The central feature of his theory of state is its respect for rights, including an intersubjective right to recognition.[177] While liberalism in one sense has liberated modern individuals from the tyranny of social custom and tradition, in another sense, it leaves them open to their passions and individual whims. Moreover, Hegel objects to empirical theories of natural rights, such as Hobbes' and Locke's, insofar as they cannot establish what they want to prove. If empiricism is to be more than a mere description of those rights that people happen to enjoy, it must be able to demonstrate that these rights are necessary and universal, that they are rooted in certain permanent features of human nature. However, empiricism cannot do this.[178] Since categories of necessity and universality are not given in experience, they must be discovered by other means. For Hegel, empiricism lacks all criteria for drawing the boundary between the accidental and necessary.

If Hobbes and Locke rely too much on experience for their approach, Kant is too abstract. Hegel's response to the abstract character of Kantian morality is to stress that moral duty has a history and that to conceive it as something apart from social and political circumstance is inaccurate.[179] In identifying moral conduct as part of ethical life, Hegel is returning to an Aristotelian conception of the community as a structure of relations within which moral powers can develop. As illustrated in Chapter 4, his goal is to combine the ancient emphasis on the dignity and architectonic character of political life with the modern conception for freedom, rights, and mutual recognition. Hegel's *Rechtsstaat* [Modern State] is a place where individual interests and the interest of the whole community are in harmony—in short, it is where the individual is reconciled with the community. Thus, in choosing one's duty one chooses freely because it is a rational choice; individual fulfillment is achieved in serving the objective form of the universal. By remedying one of Kant's defects, Hegel maintains that since universal law is embodied in the concrete institutions of the state, it ceases to be abstract and empty. It prescribes individual duties of one's role in the community. The next chapter examines the dialectic of freedom from the ancient to the modern world, which brings us a step closer toward the reconciliation of the individual with community.

## NOTES

1. Robertson Davies, *The Rebel Angels* (London: Penguin, 1981), 38–39.

2. See Eric Weil, *Hegel and the State*, trans. Mark A. Cohen (Baltimore: Johns Hopkins Press, 1998), for a criticism of this position. For instance, he notes that it is surprising that Marx and Engels—who are considered Hegel's most severe critics—strongly reject the idea that Hegel is a "royal-Prussian" reactionary (8).

3. Frederick C. Beiser, "Introduction: Hegel and the Problem of Metaphysics," in *The Cambridge Companion to Hegel*, ed. Frederick C. Beiser (Cambridge: Cambridge University Press, 1993), 1.

4. Fred R. Dallmayr, *G. W. F. Hegel: Modernity and Politics* (Newbury Park, Ca.: Sage, 1993), 1–2.

5. Beiser, "Hegel's Historicism," in *The Cambridge Companion to Hegel*, 270.

6. Georg W. F. Hegel, *Lectures on the History of Philosophy: Greek Philosophy to Plato, Volume 1*, trans. E. S. Haldane (Lincoln: University of Nebraska Press, 1995), 45.

7. Georg W. F. Hegel, *Lectures on the History of Philosophy: Medieval and Modern Philosophy, Volume 3*, trans. E. S. Haldane and Frances Simson (Lincoln: University of Nebraska Press, 1995), 444–445.

8. Georg W. F. Hegel, "Fragment of a System," in Georg W. F. Hegel, *Early Theological Writings*, trans. T.M. Knox (Philadelphia: University of Pennsylvania Press, 1948), 309–319.

9. Hegel, "Fragment of a System," 311.

10. Georg W. F. Hegel, *Phenomenology of Spirit*, trans. A. V. Miller (Oxford: Oxford University Press, 1952), 21.

11. Beiser, "Introduction," 20.

12. Richard Dien Winfield, *Overcoming Foundations: Studies in Systematic Philosophy* (New York: Columbia University Press, 1989), 26.

13. Winfield, *Overcoming Foundations*, 46.

14. Michael Sandel, *Liberalism and the Limits of Justice* (New York: Cambridge University Press, 1982), p. 11.

15. Timothy C. Luther, *Hegel and Marx: Economics and Democracy* (Boston: Houghton Mifflin, 2002), 26.

16. Benjamin Barber, *Strong Democracy: Participatory Politics for a New Age* (Berkeley: University of California Press, 2003), 11.

17. Beiser, "Hegel's Historicism," 276.

18. Hegel, *Lectures on the History of Philosophy, Volume 1*, 30.

19. Quentin Lauer, *Hegel's Idea of Philosophy* (New York: Fordham University Press, 1983), 13.

20. Hegel, *Lectures on the History of Philosophy, Volume 3*, 522.

21. Hegel, *Lectures on the History of Philosophy, Volume, 1*, 99.

22. Lauer, *Hegel's Idea of Philosophy*, 19.

23. Hegel, *Lectures on the History of Philosophy, Volume, 1*, 388.

24. Hegel, *Lectures on the History of Philosophy, Volume, 1*, 406.

25. Georg W. F. Hegel, *Lectures on the History of Philosophy, Volume 2: Plato and the Platonists*, trans. E. S. Haldane and Frances Simson (Lincoln: University of Nebraska Press, 1995), 14.

26. See Plato, *Sophist*, trans. N. White (Indianapolis: Hackett, 1993).

27. Hegel, *Lectures on the History of Philosophy, Volume 2*, 29.

28. Plato, *The Republic*, trans. R. Sterling and W. Scott (New York: W. W. Norton & Company, 1985), 201.

29. Hegel, *Lectures on the History of Philosophy, Volume 2*, 24.

30. Plato, *The Republic*, 273.

31. Hegel, *Lectures on the History of Philosophy, Volume 2*, 99.

32. Hegel, *Lectures on the History of Philosophy, Volume 2*, 131.

33. Aristotle, *Physics*, trans. W. Charlton (Oxford: Clarendon Press, 1970), 1.

34. Aristotle, *The Politics*, trans. C. Lord (Chicago: The University of Chicago Press, 1984), 131–132.

35. Hegel, *Lectures on the History of Philosophy, Volume 2*, 208.

36. Hegel, *Lectures on the History of Philosophy, Volume 2*, 262.

37. Hegel, *Lectures on the History of Philosophy, Volume 3*, 179.

38. Hegel, *Lectures on the History of Philosophy, Volume 3*, 224.

39. René Descartes, *Meditations*, trans. L Lafleur (Indianapolis: Bobbs-Merrill, 1960), 71.

40. Descartes, *Meditations*, 76.

41. Descartes, *Meditations*, 84.

42. Hegel, *Lectures on the History of Philosophy, Volume 3*, 227.

43. Christopher Falzon, *Foucault and Social Dialogue: Beyond Fragmentation* (London: Routledge, 1998), 20–21.

44. Hegel, *Lectures on the History of Philosophy, Volume 3*, 247.

45. John Locke, *An Essay Concerning Human Understanding* (Bergenfield: Meridian, 1964), 89–90.

46. Hegel, *Lectures on the History of Philosophy, Volume 3*, 300.

47. Hegel, *Lectures on the History of Philosophy, Volume 3*, 428.

48. Immanuel Kant, *Critique of Pure Reason*, trans. Norman Kemp Smith (New York: St. Martin's Press, 1929), 42.

49. Kant, *Critique of Pure Reason*, 152–153.

50. Thomas Hobbes, *Man and Citizen* (Indianapolis: Hackett, 1991), 31.

51. Hegel, *Lectures on the History of Philosophy, Volume 3*, 317.

52. Hegel, *Lectures on the History of Philosophy, Volume 3*, 318.

53. John Locke, *The Second Treatise of Government* (Indianapolis: Bobbs-Merrill, 1952), 58.

54. Timothy C. Luther, *The Political Philosophy of Democracy: Its Origins, Promises, and Perils* (Boston: Houghton Mifflin, 1998), 260.

55. Sandel, *Liberalism and the Limits of Justice*, 177.

56. Etienne Balibar, "Citizen Subject," in *Who Comes After the Subject?* Eds. E. Cadava, P. Connor, J. Nancy (New York: Routledge, 1991), 51.

57. Luther, *The Political Philosophy of Democracy*, 289–290.

58. Jean-Jacques Rousseau, *A Discourse on Inequality*, trans. Maurice Cranston (London: Penguin, 1984), 78.

59. Jean-Jacques Rousseau, *The Social Contract*, trans. G. Cole (Buffalo: Prometheus, 1988), 54.

60. Rousseau, *The Social Contract*, 54–55.

61. Ernst Cassirer, *The Question of Jean-Jacques Rousseau*, trans. Peter Gay (Bloomington: Indiana University Press, 1963), 126.

62. Hilail Gildin, *Rousseau's Social Contract* (Chicago: The University of Chicago Press, 1983), 3.

63. Cassirer, *The Question of Jean-Jacques Rousseau*, 55.

64. Rousseau, *The Social Contract*, 138.

65. Frederick Neuhouser, *Foundations of Hegel's Social Theory: Actualizing Freedom* (Cambridge: Harvard University Press, 2000), 57–58.

66. Paul Redding, *Hegel's Hermeneutics* (Ithaca: Cornell University Press, 1996), 1.

67. See Quentin Lauer, *Hegel's Idea of Philosophy* (New York: Fordham University Press, 1971), 2–3. To do this Hegel starts with no more than the common experience that in seeking to grasp reality more thoroughly we consult our ideas of reality rather than reality itself. The totality of awareness, called knowledge, is the awareness of a totality of reality; this realization means that man will find the very reality of reality only in the awareness of reality that is at the same time reality's progressive self-manifestation.

68. Galileo Galilei, *Discoveries and Opinions of Galileo*, trans. S. Drake (Garden City, NJ: Doubleday, 1957), 31.

69. Francis Bacon, *The New Organon* (Indianapolis: Bobbs-Merrill, 1960), 47–60.

70. Charles Taylor, *Hegel and Modern Society* (New York: Cambridge University Press, 1979), 7.

71. Friedrich Schiller, *On the Aesthetic Education of Man*, trans. L. Willoughby and E. Wilkinson (Oxford: Oxford University Press, 1967).

72. Schiller, *On the Aesthetic Education of Man*, 35.

73. Schiller, *On the Aesthetic Education of Man*, 33.

74. Schiller, *On the Aesthetic Education of Man*, 43.

75. Terry Pinkard, *Hegel's Phenomenology: The Sociality of Reason* (New York: Cambridge University Press, 1996), 208.

76. Frederick Beiser, *Hegel* (New York: Routledge, 2005), 35.

77. Hegel, *Phenomenology of Spirit*, 385.

78. See Walter Kaufmann, *Hegel: A Reinterpretation* (Notre Dame: University of Notre Dame Press, 1965), 6, where he says that Hegel sought to integrate Kant and romanticism in a single system. See also Robert B. Pippin, *Hegel's Idealism: The Satisfactions of Self-Consciousness* (Cambridge: Cambridge University Press, 1989), where he discusses the dependency of Hegel's idealism upon the revision of Kantian concepts.

79. Tom Rockmore, *Before and After Hegel: A Historical Introduction to Hegel's Thought* (Berkeley: University of California Press, 1993), 5. I discuss Kant's moral theory and Hegel's criticisms of it in Chapter 4.

80. Robert C. Solomon, *In the Spirit of Hegel: A Study of G. W. F. Hegel's* Phenomenology of Spirit (New York: Oxford University Press, 1983), 46.

81. "Ideal for a Universal History with a Cosmopolitan Purpose," in Immanuel Kant, *Political Writings*, ed. H. Nisbet (Cambridge: Cambridge University Press, 1991), 41–42.

82. Allen Wood, *Kant's Ethical Theory* (New York: Cambridge University Press, 1999), 208.

83. Hegel, *The Philosophy of History*, 33.

84. Immanuel Kant, *The Critique of Practical Reason*, trans. Lewis. Beck (New York: Macmillan, 1993), 4.

85. Immanuel Kant, *Groundwork for the Metaphysics of Morals*, trans. Allen. Wool (New Haven, Conn.: Yale University Press, 2002), 77–78.

86. Kant, *Political Writings*, 50.

87. Kant, *The Critique of Pure Reason*, 9.

88. Hegel, *Lectures on the History of Philosophy, Volume 3*, 426.

89. Kant, *The Critique of Pure Reason*, xiii.

90. Kant, *The Critique of Pure Reason*, 41.

91. Hegel, *Lectures on the History of Philosophy, Volume 3*, 428.

92. Terry Pinkard, *German Philosophy 1760–1860: The Legacy of Idealism* (Cambridge: Cambridge University Press, 2002), 35.

93. Rockmore, *Before and After Hegel*, 29.

94. Johann Fichte, *The Science of Knowledge*, trans. Peter Heath and John Lachs (Cambridge: Cambridge University Press, 1982), 3.

95. Hegel, *Lectures on the History of Philosophy, Volume 3*, 479. See also Fichte, *The Science of Knowledge*, 4.

96. Fichte, *The Science of Knowledge*, 93.

97. Fichte, *The Science of Knowledge*, 93–94. See Rockmore, *Before and After Hegel*, 36. The significance of the concept of foundationless system that Fichte proposes is that foundationless is not the same as groundless, if that is taken to mean without justification or argument of any kind. There is a justification in Fichte's theory, but there is not and cannot be a final ground in the Cartesian sense of the term. If a Cartesian ground is required for a successful theory of knowledge, then Fichte fails to provide one. If a theory of knowledge can dispense with the Cartesian ground, then perhaps Fichte offers the first successful post-Cartesian theory of knowledge.

98. Fichte, *The Science of Knowledge*, 38.

99. Fichte, *The Science of Knowledge*, 93. See Rockmore, *Before and After Hegel*, 38.

100. Hegel, *Lectures on the History of Philosophy, Volume 3*, 494. See Fichte, *The Science of Knowledge*, 93–94.

101. Frederick Neuhouser, *Fichte's Theory of Subjectivity* (Cambridge: Cambridge University Press, 1990), 2.

102. Neuhouser, *Fichte's Theory of Subjectivity*, 23.

103. Pinkard, *German Philosophy 1760–1860*, 115. "By focusing so straightforwardly on self-consciousness, Fichte was trying to get his readers to grasp the common Kantian-Fichtean point that the 'transcendental self' was not an 'item' within experience but a normative status that made conscious and self-conscious experience possible in the first place and could therefore not be found in any act of introspection" (118).

104. Fichte, *The Science of Knowledge*, 97.

105. Fichte, *The Science of Knowledge*, 191.

106. Johann Fichte, *Foundations of Natural Right: According to the Principles of the Wissenschaftslehre*, trans. Michael Baur (Cambridge: Cambridge University Press, 2000), 4.

107. Fichte, *Foundations of Natural Right*, 9.

108. Fichte, *Foundations of Natural Right*, 21.

109. Fichte, *Foundations of Natural Right*, 42.

110. Luc Ferry, *Political Philosophy, Volume 1: Rights—the New Quarrel between the Ancients and the Moderns*, trans. F. Philip (Chicago: The University of Chicago Press, 1990), 103.

111. Fichte, *Foundations of Natural Right*, 102.

112. Friedrich Schelling, *System of Transcendental Idealism (1800)*, trans. Peter Heath (Charlottesville: University of Virginia Press, 1978), 217.

113. Schelling, *System of Transcendental Idealism (1800)*, 11.

114. Friedrich Schelling, *Ideas for a Philosophy of Nature*, trans. E. Harris and Peter Heath (Cambridge: Cambridge University Press, 1988), 49–50.

115. Schelling, *System of Transcendental Idealism (1800)*, 50.

116. Schelling, *System of Transcendental Idealism (1800)*, 202.

117. Schelling, *System of Transcendental Idealism (1800)*, 12.

118. Schelling, *System of Transcendental Idealism (1800)*, 231.

119. Schelling, *System of Transcendental Idealism (1800)*, 233.

120. Hegel, *Lectures on the History of Philosophy, Volume 3*, 451.

121. Redding, *Hegel's Hermeneutics*, 13.

122. Hegel, *Phenomenology of Spirit*, 10–11.

123. Georg W. F. Hegel, *Logic*, trans. William Wallace (New York: Oxford University Press, 1975), 70–71.

124. Michael Allen Fox, *The Accessible Hegel* (Amherst, Mass.: Humanity Books, 2005), 61.

125. John Edward Toews, *Hegelianism: The Path Toward Dialectical Humanism, 1805–1841* (Cambridge: Cambridge University Press, 1980), 52.

126. Hegel, *Lectures on the History of Philosophy, Volume 1*, 1.

127. Kenneth R. Westphal, *Hegel's Epistemology: A Philosophical Introduction to the* Phenomenology of Spirit (Indianapolis: Hackett, 2003), 54. See Willem deVries, *Hegel's Theory of Mental Activity* (Ithaca, N.Y.: Cornell University Press, 1988), 44, where he says that Hegel's *Geist* determines nature's own existence because *Geist* is nature's *telos*.

128. Lauer, *Hegel's Idea of Philosophy*, 27.

129. Hegel, *Lectures on the History of Philosophy, Volume 1*, 29–32.

130. Georg W. F. Hegel, *Science of Logic*, trans. A. V. Miller (Amherst, Mass.: Humanity Books, 1969), 48.

131. Hegel, *Phenomenology of Spirit*, 51.

132. Hegel, *Phenomenology of Spirit*, 14.

133. Westphal, *Hegel's Epistemology*, 51. Hegel's epistemology is often overlooked because philosophers have too often supposed that combining realism with a social and historical epistemology is impossible. Consequently, anti-Cartesian epistemologists have much to learn from Hegel. By critically rejecting Kant's dichotomy between the *a priori* and the *a posteriori*, Hegel was able to extend Kant's transcendental strategy to show not only what our basic cognitive capacities are, but also to show that certain logically contingent, natural as well as social facts must obtain in order for us to have unified self-conscious experience at all (57).

134. Robert B. Pippin, *Hegel's Idealism: The Satisfactions of Self-Consciousness* (New York: Cambridge University Press, 1989), 92. Hegel thinks that his account accepts Kant's rejection of the Cartesian problematic without falling prey to Kantian skepticism.

135. Hegel, *Phenomenology of Spirit*, 54.

136. Quentin Lauer, *A Reading of Hegel's* Phenomenology of Spirit (New York: Fordham University Press, 1993), 17.

137. Hegel, *Phenomenology of Spirit*, 4.

138. Georg W. F. Hegel, *The Philosophy of History*, trans. J. Sibree (Buffalo, N.Y.: Prometheus Books, 1991), 9. See also Georg W. F. Hegel, *Reason in History: A General Introduction to the Philosophy of History*, trans. Robert Hartman (Indianapolis: Bobbs-Merrill, 1953), 11–12. See also Robert C. Solomon, *From Hegel to Existentialism* (New York: Oxford University Press, 1987), Chapter 1, for concise discussion of Hegel's concept of *Geist*. Solomon suggests that the notion of *Geist* that clearly emerges from Hegel's writings refers to some sort of general consciousness, a single "mind" common to everyone.

139. Hegel, *Phenomenology of Spirit*, 14.

140. Georg W. F. Hegel, *Philosophy of Nature*, trans. A. V. Miller (New York: Oxford University Press, 2004), 13.

141. Joseph McCarney, *Hegel: On History* (London: Routledge, 2000), 62.

142. Hegel, *Philosophy of Right*, 13. See also Alexandre Kojève, *Introduction to the Reading of Hegel: Lectures on the Phenomenology of Spirit*, trans. James Nichols (Ithaca, N.Y.: Cornell University Press, 1969), 210, where he asserts that "in order to discover the dialectical character of Being as such and of the Real in general, it was sufficient for Hegel to take the notion of the concrete seriously and to remember that philosophy must describe the concrete real instead of forming more or less arbitrary abstractions."

143. John N. Findlay, *Hegel: A Re-examination* (New York: Oxford University Press, 1958), 20. In fact, Findlay asserts that one could say that there has never been a philosopher by whom the transcendent has been more thoroughly done away with nor who has more thoroughly shown to exist only as revealed in human experience. See also Carl Friedrich, *The Philosophy of Hegel* (New York: Random House, 1953), xxviii, where he notes that Hegel's view is not concerned with the abstract and the non-real but the history of man in all manifold and variegated manifestations that constitutes the core of reality.

144. Georg W. F. Hegel, *Philosophy of Right*, trans. T. M. Knox (Oxford: Oxford University Press, 1952), 11.

145. Charles Taylor, *Hegel and Modern Society* (Cambridge: Cambridge University Press, 1979), 23. Also see Charles Taylor, *Hegel* (Cambridge: Cambridge University Press, 1975), 44–45, where he says that Hegel's spirit is not the God of traditional theism, although he claimed to be clarifying Christian theology. *Geist* is not a God who could exist quite independently of men, even if men did not exist. On the contrary, it is spirit who lives as spirit only through men. They are vehicles, and indispensable vehicles, of his spiritual existence, as consciousness, rationality, will. But at the same time *Geist* is not reducible to man and is not identical with the human spirit since he is also the spiritual reality underlying the universe as a whole. As a spiritual being he also has purposes and realizes ends which cannot be attributed to finite spirits, qua finite, but on the contrary which finite spirits serve. See also Michael O. Hardimon, *Hegel's Social Philosophy: The Project of Reconciliation* (Cambridge: Cambridge University Press, 1994), 43, where he discusses the necessity of *Geist* having its seat in embodied, living subjects: in rational animals, human beings. *Geist* must also be expressed in an external medium: language, custom, and institutions.

146. Taylor, *Hegel and Modern Society*, 29. Taylor also notes that: "Hegel is not saying that everything that exists and happens comes of necessity. He is talking about the basic structure of things, the chain of levels of beings, the general shape of world history; these are manifestations of necessity (31)."

147. Westphal, *Hegel's Epistemology*, 75.

148. Henry S. Harris, *Hegel: Phenomenology and System* (Indianapolis: Hackett, 1995), 13. Hegel claims that revolution and the generation of opposites have occurred a number of times in our quest for philosophical truth without our being clearly aware of what was happening. Empirically, our experience has been to give up some idea and find a new one. The giving up occurs because we have found a new idea.

149. Solomon, *In the Spirit of Hegel*, 10.

150. Plato, *The Republic*, 201.

151. See Plato, *Phaedo*, trans. F. Church (Indianapolis: Bobbs-Merrill, 1951), where he asserts that reality cannot be perceived through the body's sense organs. In fact, sense perceptions and opinions hinder the search for truth and distract us from acquiring truth.

152. Hegel, *Philosophy of Right*, 34.

153. Solomon, *In the Spirit of Hegel*, 25.

154. Fox, *The Accessible Hegel*, 38. Hegel's dialectic signifies becoming, opposing, thinking, truthing, and perishing.

155. Hegel, *Science of Logic*, 107.

156. Hegel, *Logic*, 173.

157. Hegel, *Logic*, 13. First, *aufheben* means to destroy or cancel; second, it means to preserve or maintain; and third, it means to elevate or transform. Hegel's dialectic includes all three.

158. Fox, *The Accessible Hegel*, 46.

159. Hegel, *Science of Logic*, 49.

160. Hegel, *Logic*, 116 and 118.

161. Hegel, *Logic*, 118.

162. Hegel, *Logic*, 4.

163. Beiser, "Hegel's Historicism," 276.

164. Hegel, *Logic*, 8.

165. Hegel, *Phenomenology of Spirit*, 51.

166. Stern, *Hegel and the* Phenomenology of Spirit, 20.

167. Hegel, *Science of Logic*, 605, and Hegel, *Logic*, 228–229.

168. Hegel, *Logic*, 116.

169. Michael Forster, "Hegel's Dialectical Method," in *The Cambridge Companion to Hegel*, 132.

170. Bauer, *A Reading of Hegel's* Phenomenology of Spirit, 40.

171. Pinkard, *Hegel's Phenomenology*, 11.

172. Dallmayr, *G. W. F. Hegel: Modernity and Politics*, 5.

173. Amitai Etzioni, *The New Golden Rule: Community and Morality in a Democratic Society* (New York: Basic Books, 1996), 81.

174. Hegel, *Philosophy of Right*, 23.

175. Hegel, *Philosophy of Right*, 150.

176. Kenneth Westphal, "The Basic Context and Structure of Hegel's *Philosophy of Right*," in *The Cambridge Companion to Hegel*, 263.

177. Steven B. Smith, *Hegel's Critique of Liberalism: Rights in Context* (Chicago: The University of Chicago Press, 1989), 6.

178. Smith, *Hegel's Critique of Liberalism*, 67.

179. Smith, *Hegel's Critique of Liberalism*, 71.

*Chapter Three*

# The Dialectic and History:
# The Odyssey of Liberty

What then shall we choose? Weight or lightness? Parmenides posed this very question in the sixth century before Christ. He saw the world divided into pairs of opposites: light/darkness, fineness/coarseness, warmth/cold, being/nonbeing. One half of the opposition he called positive (light, fineness, warmth, being), the other negative. We might find this division into positive and negative poles childishly simple except for one difficulty: which one is positive, weight or lightness?[1]

—Milan Kundera, *The Unbearable Lightness of Being*

Hegel takes history very seriously, and what distinguishes him from most previous philosophers is the exceptional historical sense underlying his mode of thinking. While his *Science of Logic* demonstrates the structure of reason, the *Philosophy of History* expounds reason's historical content:

The most general definition that can be given, is, that the Philosophy of History means nothing but the *thoughtful consideration of it*. Thought is, indeed, essential to humanity. It is what distinguishes us from the brutes. In sensation, cognition, and intellection; in our instincts and volitions, as far as they are truly human, Thought is an invariable element. . . . The only Thought which Philosophy brings with it to the contemplation of History, is the simple conception of *reason*; that Reason is the Sovereign of the World; that the history of the world, therefore, presents us with a rational process. This conviction and intuition is a hypothesis in the domain of history as such.[2]

In contrast to most of his predecessors who spoke on purely philosophical grounds, Hegel holds that the very foundations of the human condition can change from one historical era to another. This notion of historical change is fundamental to his view of the world. For him, history has meaning and significance. History follows according to providence, or God's plan: "God governs the world; the actual working of his government—the carrying out of his plan—is the History of the World."[3] Hegel's *Philosophy of History* is not a work of history in the traditional sense. His aim is not merely to record and comment on events of a particular time and place, but rather it is to contemplate the development of the conception of reason. The *Philosophy of History* is much more than a historical outline, it is a work of philosophy because in addition to taking the bare facts of history, it goes beyond these facts. His interest here is in a "philosophical world history," or "universal history" [*Weltgeschichte*].[4]

Universal history is exclusively interested in demonstrating how *Geist* [Absolute Spirit] comes to a recognition and an adoption of truth. For Hegel, world history enshrines the logic of *Geist*. Writing and advocating philosophical world history and the construction of philosophies of history to accompany it was a thriving enterprise in Hegel's day.[5] In fact, Immanuel Kant, Johann Gottfried Herder, Johann Gottfried Fichte, and Friedrich Schelling each devoted time to this task. As illustrated in previous chapters, Hegel is clearly a systematic thinker for whom truth is comprehensible only as a whole. The philosophy of history is understandably a crucial part of his system. Since the dialectic is the general principle of motion of all life and activities in the actual historical world, it is also the dynamic principle that helps us to understand all genuine knowledge of world history. Consequently, history follows a necessary dialectical plan.

Hegel's philosophy of history forms the sphere of what he calls objective spirit [*Geist*]. Just as the *Philosophy of Nature* sees that underlying rational necessity dialectically expresses itself in the general structures of the natural world, the *Philosophy of History* sees that the same logical necessity dialectically expresses itself in the phenomena of the human world. Insofar as these phenomena concern the existence of individual consciousness, they are also the matter of the sphere of *Geist*. For Hegel, this realm contains the entire domain of the social and political reality in the history of mankind. The very essence of *Geist* is activity.[6] As was noted in the previous chapter, the fulfillment of *Geist* requires the growth of a community that will fully express and embody reason. And because *Geist* posits that the world of space and time realizes itself, for Hegel, this fulfillment and the community of reason are the goal of history. To put it differently, history is understood teleologically as directed to realize *Geist*:

> It is only an inference from the history of the World, that its development has been a rational process; that the history in question has constituted the rational necessary course of the World-Spirit—that Spirit [*Geist*] whose nature is always one and the same, but which unfolds this its one nature in the phenomena of the World's existence. This must, as before stated, present itself as the ultimate *result* of history.[7]

*Geist* is worked out in historical time. History is a rational process, and it moves logically toward its goal. Self-conscious reason, which exists in the contemporary world, did not suddenly spring up but has developed slowly with time. Hegel insists that history is an empirical inquiry, and the distinctive principles of a people must be approached empirically and demonstrated in a historical fashion. *Geist* develops in a real, concrete world: "On the stage on which we are observing it—Universal History—Spirit [*Geist*] displays itself in the most concrete reality."[8]

Hegel's philosophy is not purely conservative; that is, he does not ignore difficulties in order to create a false reconciliation to the world. Rather, his dialectic aims to resolve those difficulties by removing them and finding new ways of looking at things. In fact, "the aim of knowledge is to divest the objective world that stands opposed to us of its strangeness, and, as the phrase is, to find ourselves at home in it. . . ."[9] Philosophy must take a reflective stance that guards against those forms of thought that prevent us from looking at the world properly. It must correct distorted outlooks that prevent reason from being seen in the world by showing how these outlooks arise as the result of some sort of distortion that can be overcome, as was illustrated in the last chapter. Only then will we overcome estrangement from the world and therefore have achieved freedom:

> The ignorant man is not free, because what confronts him is an alien world, something outside him and in the offing, on which he depends, without his having made his foreign world for himself and therefore without being at home in it by himself as in something his own. The impulse of curiosity, the pressure for knowledge, from the lowest level up to the highest rung of philosophical insight arises only from the struggle to cancel this situation of unfreedom and to make the world one's own in one's ideas and thoughts.[10]

Freedom, for Hegel, is determined by reason. "Indeed, dialectical reason and freedom go together, for the only subject matter that could be developed in a wholly immanent fashion would be self-determined determinacy, since it alone neither rests on giveness nor is determined by a distinct determiner."[11] *Geist*'s goal is the achievement and development of freedom within the context of world history: "Reason is Thought conditioning itself with perfect freedom."[12] For Hegel, freedom is only found within the confines of a political community. "Accordingly, freedom is not a natural or monological potential, but an actual structure of interaction consisting in the interdirected and mutually respected actions of a plurality of wills."[13] The dialectic of history is to be understood as reflecting the conceptually necessary stages in the self-unfolding of *Geist*.

Each specific historical state embodies a particular *Volksgeister* [Historical Civilization] with its particular beliefs, values, and practices, and each stage has its own particular form of self-consciousness.[14] Each stage embodies a specific type of people who works to bring forth the "idea" of that particular stage, represented by a certain level of freedom. Its people identify with its common purpose. Eventually things fall apart, and the historical civilization and its worldview breaks down. Having developed its particular form of freedom to the utmost of its ability, its inadequacies are brought to a head. Since no further development of freedom is possible, only inadequacy stands out. Although Hegel argues that the transition from one stage to the next is brought about by the fruition and natural death of each world-historical community, he recognizes that human beings do not fully grasp what they are doing in history. This is where Hegel introduces his conception of "the cunning of reason." Human beings are usually not aware of the historical significance of their individual acts. Like Kant, Hegel depicts reason as using the passions of human beings to fulfill its purposes:

> The special interest of passion is thus inseparable from the active development of a general principle: for it is from the special and determinate and from its negation, that the Universal results. Particularity contends with its like, and some loss is involved in the issue. *It* is not the general idea that is implicated in opposition and combat, and that is exposed to danger. It remains in the background, untouched and uninjured. This may be called the *cunning of reason*—that it sets the passions to work for itself, while that which develops its existence through such impulsion pays the penalty, and suffers loss.[15]

Even though particular human beings and their purposes carry on in battle and fall, the universal purpose of *Geist* prevails. As discussed in the previous chapter, human beings are vehicles of *Geist*, though they are not always aware of it. In this way, *Geist* uses the clash of individual ambitions to further its aims.

In *The Philosophy of History*, Hegel explains that great men have advanced the cause of *Weltgeist* [World Spirit]: "Historical men—*World-Historical Individuals*—are those in whose aims such a general principle lies."[16] As they follow their own interests and passions, they promote the process of *Geist*, that is, they perform a universal task that helps to actualize freedom by bringing a new political and social order. In short, they are a means of *Geist* achieving its end. This chapter examines the advance of liberty from the classical to modern world, and is organized into three sections. The first section discussed the dialectic role of *Geist* in perfecting freedom. Logic is the process by which categories that describe *Geist* are deduced from human experiences. He is interested in the real, existing world of concrete practices and human communities. The second section covers Hegel's long discussion of the dialectic of world history, tracing the progress of freedom from the ancient world through the middle ages, reformation, and Renaissance to the Enlightenment and the modern world of Hegel's day. *Geist* achieves freedom and self-understanding only through particular peoples and natural cultures that fit its dialectical pattern of world history. Hegel is concerned with demonstrating how *Geist* historically arrives at full consciousness through political and social institutions. The final section assesses the relationship between freedom and community. Human beings are truly free only when they are recognized as such by others. Subjectivity requires intersubjectivity. Consequently, the freest man is the one who most completely fulfills one's social obligation. Hegel discovers the synthesis of the individual's freedom and *Geist* in the concrete institutions of the state.

## *GEIST*, FREEDOM, AND CONFLICT

Hegel believes that the inner essence of *Geist* can be reached by human reason because Absolute Spirit is disclosed in nature as well as in the working of the human mind. It is thought itself that connects *Geist*, nature, and the human mind.[17] Things behave as they do because *Geist* is expressing itself through the structure of nature and mind. Therefore, a person thinks about nature the way *Geist* expresses itself in nature. Just as *Geist* and nature are dynamic processes, human thought is also a dialectic process. Like many earlier philosophers, Hegel lays great stress upon logic. His view resembles Descartes in that one can know the essence of reality by moving logically step by step and avoiding all self-contradictions along the way. However, unlike Descartes, whose emphasis was upon the relations of ideas to each other, Hegel argues that thought must follow the inner logic of reality itself. Since Hegel has identified the rational with the actual, he concludes that logic and logical connections must be discovered in the actual and not in some empty ratiocination.[18] Logic, thus, is the process by which categories that describe *Geist* are deduced from human experiences of the actual. His philosophy is clearly interested in the real, existing world of concrete practices and human communities. In this fashion, Hegel emphasizes the way in which abstract reason, which exists only on the theoretical plane, is transformed when it develops on the practical plane. This process of deduction is at the very heart of Hegel's dialectic.

For Hegel, one immense dialectical movement dominates world history from the past to present. He seeks to "derive all known actuality—whether actual categories or actual natural or spiritual phenomena—by means of his philosophy's dialectic."[19] Being vehicles of *Geist*, human beings have to school themselves in order to play their role in overcoming the opposition of the world by breaking away from a life sunk in nature and dominated by impulse:

> All revolutions, in the sciences no less than in world history, originate solely from the fact that Spirit [*Geist*], in order to understand and comprehend itself with a view to possessing itself, has changed its categories, comprehending itself more truly, more deeply, more intimately, and more in unity with itself. . . . Spirit [*Geist*] cannot remain at this stage of thinking.[20]

In brief, they must go beyond their immediate parochial perspectives to that of reason. The dialectic of identity and opposition in subjectivity is not merely of local interest but is of ontological import.[21] If *Geist* is subject and everything that is can only be in being related to this subject, then everything is caught up in the interplay of identity and opposition that makes up the life of this subject:

> The Absolute, what is ultimately real, or what is at the foundation of everything, is subject. And the cosmic subject is such that he is both identical and non-identical to the world. There is reality in that *Geist* cannot exist without the world; and yet also opposition, for the world as externality represents a dispersal, and unconsciousness which *Geist* has overcome to be itself, to fulfill its goal as self-conscious reason.[22]

The life of *Geist* as absolute subject is essentially a process, a movement, in which it posits its own conditions of existence then overcomes opposition inherent in these same conditions. *Geist* attains self-knowledge by developing successively more adequate interpretations of itself, that is, a series of increasingly more coherent interpretations accounting for an increasingly wide range of its activities.[23] Since the *Phenomenology of Spirit* is a study of the experiences of consciousness, it continually comes upon negative consequences. What consciousness takes to be truth is revealed to be illusory; consciousness must abandon its first belief and move on to another.[24] Thus, *Geist* cannot simply exist, but it can exist only by overcoming its opposition or by negating its own negation. Increasing self-knowledge requires *Geist* to overcome false dichotomies, negating its own negations and reconciling characteristics that, in ages past, seemed contradictory. In this respect, *Geist* can be said to be removing imperfections and clarifying its knowledge. In this way, *Geist* closely resembles the development of scientific knowledge with its continual push toward the unification of forces.

Contradiction, as illustrated in the last chapter, is the source of movement because whatever is in contradiction must pass over into something else. *Geist* is essentially movement and change, and the motor of Hegel's dialectics is contradiction. According to Hegel, the dialectic works as a method of exposition because the world works dialectically. *The Philosophy of History* is more than a list of historical facts. It takes the bare facts of history as its raw material, and it develops a philosophical progression from them. Thinking, for Hegel, has an inherent tendency to go beyond every limit and turn into its opposite. Dialectical paradoxes cannot be avoided:

> Hegel argues that the proper way to resolve dialectical paradoxes is not to suppress them, but to systematize them. If you become master of them, they can do positive philosophical work for you. Just as thought inevitably gives rise to contradictions, so it also inevitably reconciles them in a higher unity, as a human self that grows through self-conflict proves its growth by emerging from conflict into a higher self-harmony.[25]

Thus, contradictions need not disrupt thinking, since opposites are reconciled. In short, thought moves and contradiction, rather than bringing knowledge to a halt, acts as a positive moving force in human reasoning.[26]

A major conflict that Hegel tries to resolve is that between the substantial culture of the Greek world and the principle of the subjective freedom that reaches its culmination in the modern commercial order. The essence of *Geist* is freedom, and, as noted above, the advancement of freedom is the goal of history:

> All will readily assent to the doctrine that Spirit [*Geist*], among other properties, is also endowed with Freedom; but philosophy teaches that all the qualities of Spirit exist only through Freedom; that all are but a means for attaining Freedom; that all seek and produce this and this alone. It is the result of speculative Philosophy, that Freedom is the sole truth of Spirit.[27]

And since human beings are vehicles of *Geist*, Hegel has human freedom in mind even when he attributes freedom to *Geist*. As we will see in the following section, the freedom of *Geist* advances only through the actualization of freedom in human communities, which in fact, is a reciprocal relationship. *Geist* can only be free when *Volksgeist* is free, and *Volksgeist* can only be free when *Geist* is free. Consequently, *Geist* achieves freedom and self-consciousness only through particular *Geist* and historical cultures. The dialectical project of self-understanding and self-actualization is one in which individual human beings participate through the forms shaped by a cultural tradition.[28] Hegel's notion of freedom is neither a given nor an attribute of the self, but instead is an intersubjective process of reciprocal recognition that happens within the confines of a concrete culture.

## THE DIALECTIC OF WORLD HISTORY

History, for Hegel, is not a meaningless jumble of events but has meaning and significance. In the introduction to *The Philosophy of History*, Hegel clearly states his view of the direction and destination of all human history: "The History of the world is none other than the process of the consciousness of Freedom. . . ."[29] The more people develop spiritually, the more they become conscious of themselves; and the more they become conscious, the more they become free. Consequently, by conceiving freedom as interaction, Hegel is inexorably led to consider history as the domain in which freedom comes into being.[30] As the progress of the self-consciousness of *Geist*, world history is the progress of freedom. Freedom develops in the context of particular historical communities:

> One way of putting this would be to say that it is only in a certain form of *Volks-geist* [Spirit of a Particular People] that *Geist* as individual can be developed and sustained: it is only in the context of public culture of freedom, one in which certain ideas, practices, and self-understandings prevail, that the capacities for individual free and rational agency can be fostered and nourished. . . . A public culture of freedom does not create itself *ex nihilo* but is always, at least in part, the product of the historical process of development that draws on previous cultures and ways of living. . . . Hegel's thesis here, then, is that it is only in the context of a certain level of progress on the part of the *Weltgeist* [World Spirit] that any particular *Volksgeist* can develop and sustain itself. So, *Geist* as individual can be developed and sustained only in the context of a certain form of collective *Geist*, and the collective *Geist*, in turn, is determined as it is only in virtue of being a product of the labor of history or *Weltgeist*.[31]

*Geist* achieves freedom and self-understanding only through particular peoples and natural cultures that fit its dialectical pattern of world history. The spirit of a people [*Volksgeist*] is a determinate and particular spirit, and it is modified by the degree of its historical development.[32] Hegel further notes that universal history is exclusively concerned with demonstrating how *Geist* historically arrives at full consciousness through political and social institutions.

Understood teleologically, history's goal is to realize *Geist*.[33] Coming from a philosophy of intersubjectivity, Hegel applies his concept of *Geist* to the analysis of social relations in general. Hegel's conception of objective *Geist* includes social institutions and customs, which give content to the notion of freedom:

> Rather, we affirm, are Law, Morality, Government, and they alone, the positive reality and completion of Freedom. Freedom of a low and limited order, is mere caprice, which finds it exercise in the sphere of particular and limited desires. . . . In the history of the World, only those peoples can come under our notice which form a state. For it must be understood that the later is the realization of Freedom, i.e., of the absolute final aim, and that it exists for its own sake. It must

further be understood that all the worth which the human being possesses—all spiritual reality, he possesses only through the state.[34]

Thus, for Hegel, society and the state are the very conditions in which freedom is realized. "From the historical point of view this emergence of spirit [*Geist*] is intimately connected with the flowering of political liberty. . . ."[35] Philosophy only appears when there are free political institutions.

Human freedom is advanced through stages; and these stages are historical civilizations.[36] Freedom's principle is not mere subjective will or caprice, but is universal will. The forms of *Geist* are the achievement of intersubjectivity and essentially community:

> This development implies a gradation—a series of increasingly adequate expressions or manifestations of Freedom, which result from its Idea. The logical, and—as still more prominent—the *dialectical* nature of the Idea in general, viz. that it is self-determined—that it assumes successive forms which it successively transcends; and by this very process of transcending its earlier stages, gains an affirmative, and, in fact, a richer and more concrete shape. . . . In history this principle is idiosyncrasy of Spirit [*Geist*]—peculiar National Genius. It is within the limitations of this idiosyncrasy that the spirit of the nation, concretely manifested, expresses every aspect of its consciousness and will—the whole cycle of its realization. Its religion, its polity, its ethics, its legislation, and even its science, art, and mechanical skill, all bear its stamp.[37]

Thus, many generations of artists, religious believers, politicians, and philosophers have contributed to its traditions and practices. Each community is the result of successive phases of *Geist* manifest in its distinct political principles.[38] Put differently, the stages of history represent stages of consciousness that are objectified in a succession of cultures. In virtue of this, communities and their practices are historical through and through. The march of history is seen in the succession of communities, the earlier ones being very imperfect expressions of what later ones embody more and more adequately. The stages of history are represented by *Volksgeist*. One nation, or one culture, is dominant in each historical stage. The motor of the dialectic is historical contradiction between existing reality and what it is meant to realize. Each historical stage actualizes *Geist*'s freedom in a way that is limited, and thus is inadequate. Eventually it collapses due to the inherent contradiction and gives way to the next stage. The next stage actualizes freedom better than the previous one, but is still inadequate. Even though the next stage reconciles the contradiction of its predecessor, it eventually falls victim to its own contradiction, and so on through the whole of history. In this way, history demonstrates a dialectical movement.

The remainder of this section examines the specific steps and stages of Hegel's dialectic of history and the actualization of freedom. Universal history is the exhibition of *Geist* in the process of working out the potential of knowledge and freedom. And for Hegel, this is a slow and gradual process—one where the potential slowly develops into the actual: "As the germ bears in itself the whole nature of the tree, and the taste and form of its fruits, so do the first traces of Spirit virtually contain the whole of that History."[39] Thus, freedom first shows up in the real world in very incomplete forms, and only gradually and dialectically reaches its fruition. The dialectical advance of freedom occurs through the reconciliation of the contradictions within actual historical cultures:

> The Orientals have not attained the knowledge that Spirit—Man *as such*—is free; and because they do not know this, they are not free. They only know that one is free. But on this very account, the freedom of that one is only caprice . . . . That *one* is therefore only a Despot; not a *free man*. The consciousness of Freedom first arose among the Greeks, and therefore they were free, but they, and the Romans likewise, know that only *some* are free—not man as such. Even Plato and Aristotle did not know this. . . . The German nations, under the influence of Christianity, were the first to attain the consciousness, that man, as man, is free: that it is the *freedom* of Spirit which constitutes its essence. . . . The History of world is none other than the process of the consciousness of Freedom; a progress whose development according to the necessity of its nature, it is our business to investigate.[40]

Hegel's point is that freedom advances gradually and dialectically through history, moving from inadequate to more adequate forms of consciousness. The philosophy of history records the continued processes of growth in the structures and systems of human culture.[41] First, the Eastern nations thought that only one is free, and then the Greek and Roman worlds thought that only some are free. Finally, with the advent of modernity, we know that all men are absolutely free. For Hegel, freedom is the destiny of the world. Hegel's philosophy is an important aspect of his political philosophy. Through it, we can better understand the conflict between individual liberty and community interests. Furthermore, the odyssey of liberty leads to Hegel's reconciliation of the individual and community.

## The Oriental World

He begins with an account of the Oriental world, by which he means China, India, and the Persian Empire. Hegel is one of the first European thinkers to incorporate the Asian world into his scheme of history: "The first phase—that with which we have to begin—is the East. Unreflected consciousness—substantial, objective, spiritual existence—forms the basis. . . ."[42] China and India are seen as stationary civilizations that have reached a certain point in their development and progressed no further. According to Hegel, the principle of the oriental world is static and epitomized in the absolute power of a monarch who ascribes divine attributes to himself: "The glory of the Oriental conception is the One Individual as that substantial being to which all belongs, so that no other individual has a separate existence, or mirrors himself in his subjective freedom."[43] Thus, he sees them as being outside the movement of world history, which means that they are not part of the overall process of development that is the basis of the philosophy of history. Their seed does not grow: "In the political life of the East we find a realized rational freedom, developing itself without advancing to subjective freedom. It is the childhood of History."[44] In Eastern culture, since consciousness appears only in one individual, Hegel says that society cannot advance itself.

Hegel says that history begins with China, the oldest existing civilization according to historical record. "Early do we see China advancing to the condition in which it is found today; for as the contrast between objective existence and subjective freedom of movement in it, is still wanting, every change is excluded, and the fixedness of a character which recurs perpetually, takes the place of what we should call the truly historical."[45] Freedom is almost completely lacking in China. Authority is not questioned and obedience is automatic: "In China the Universal Will immediately commands what the Individual is to do, and the latter complies and obeys with proportionate renunciation of reflection and personal independence."[46] All subjective freedom and moral concernment with an action are ignored. As such, the distinction between slavery and freedom is necessarily not great, since all are equal before the Emperor, that is, all are alike and degraded.[47] Thus, Chinese society lacks any differentiation between objective existence and subjective consciousness. Hegel holds that there is little room for the development of independent personality in this society.

The Chinese state, according to Hegel, is organized on the principle of family. Its government is based upon the paternal management of the Emperor, and all others see themselves as children of the state:

> For although the Emperor has the right of a Monarch, standing at the summit of a political edifice, he exercises it paternally. He is the Patriarch, and everything in the State that can make any claim to reverence is attached to him. . . . This paternal care on the part of the Emperor, and the spirit of his subjects—who like children do not advance beyond the ethical principle of the family circle, and can gain for themselves no independent and civil freedom—makes the whole an empire, administration, and social code, which is at the same time moral, and

thoroughly prosaic—that is, a product of the Understanding without free Reason and Imagination.[48]

Both political freedom and rational thought are completely lacking. There is little room for the exercise of individual will, and government is conducted on the basis of ancient maxims that are internalized by its subjects. Furthermore, the Emperor is also the head of the state's religion. Thus, constant oversight is unnecessary. That is why China places such a strong emphasis on the honor and obedience one owes to parents.

Equality prevails in China, but it is without any freedom: "And though there is no distinction conferred by birth, and everyone can attain the highest dignity, this very equality testifies to no triumphant assertion of the worth of the inner man, but a servile consciousness—one which has not yet matured itself so far as to recognize distinctions."[49] This makes the Chinese empire into the model of an absolute monarchy. Individual morality is totally undifferentiated from political *Sittlichkeit* [Ethical Life], and the rulers do not respect any particular interests or opinions:

We have the first example of a subjugation of the mere arbitrary will, which is merged in this substantiality. Moral distinctions and requirements are expressed as Laws, but so that the subjective will is governed by these Laws as by an external force. Nothing subjective in the shape of disposition, Conscience, formal Freedom, is recognized. Justice is administered only on the basis of external morality, and Government exists only as the prerogative of compulsion.[50]

Since China is static, Hegel says that it has no real history, and, despite all the foreign conquests, it exists today in the same manner as it has existed for over four thousand years. In terms of the development of *Geist*, China had not changed between its beginning and Hegel's day. From its inception, only the Emperor is free.

India, like China, is a stationary and fixed society, according to Hegel, completely lacking freedom both as abstract will and as subjective freedom. In India, there is no conception of individual freedom whatsoever because the basic institution of Indian society, the caste system, which determines one's position and occupation for life and is not seen as a political institution, but as something natural and unchangeable:

Yet the distinctions which these imply are referred to Nature. Instead of stimulating the activity of a soul as their center of union, and spontaneously realizing that soul—as is the case in organic life—they petrify and become rigid, and by their stereotyped character condemn the Indian people to the most degrading spiritual serfdom. The distinctions in question are the *Castes*. . . . But the Indian culture has not attained to a recognition of freedom and inward morality; the distinctions which prevail are only those of occupations, and civil conditions.[51]

The caste system leaves no room for consciousness. People are reduced to their individual functions and the distinction between what is human and animal-like disappears. Moreover, individuals are bound to their caste for life. Since the Indian caste system combines political and religious authority, it is essentially totalitarian:

> In India the primary aspect of subjectivity—viz., that of the imagination—presents a union of the Natural and Spiritual, in which Nature on the one hand, does not present itself as a world embodying Reason, nor the Spiritual on the other hand, as consciousness in contrast with Nature. Here the antithesis in the [above-stated] principle is wanting. Freedom both as *abstract* will and as *subjective* will is altogether absent: there cannot therefore be any State in the true sense of the term. . . . In India, therefore, the most arbitrary, wicked, degrading despotism has its full swing.[52]

Thus, the governing power of India is not a human despot, but the despotism of nature, and free consciousness is completely absent.

History represents the path for social development. Laws and norms are by nature the permanent elements in a people's existence. Under a traditional caste system, Hegel says, people give their lives to an unyielding destiny. History presents a people with their own image in a condition which thereby becomes objective to them:

> Without History their existence in time is blindly self-involved—the recurring play of arbitrary volition in manifold forms. History fixes and imparts consistency to this fortuitous current—gives it the form of Universality, and by so doing posits a directive and restrictive rule for it. It is an essential instrument in developing and determining the Constitution—that is, a rational political condition. . . .[53]

According to Hegel, ancient India completely lacks this type of history. Thus, it has no potential for the growth and development of freedom. His discussion of the Oriental world contains many points of detail, all related to the idea that in these societies only one person, the ruler, is a free individual. All others are totally lacking freedom, since they must subordinate their will to that of the ruler.

Hegel thinks that this lack of freedom goes very deep. It is more than the subjects simply being aware that the despot could punish them cruelly for disobeying his will. This would require them actually having wills of their own and the ability to think about whether it is prudent or right to obey the despot. The truth is, for Hegel, that the Oriental subject has no will of his or her own in the modern sense. In the Oriental world not only law, but even morality, is a matter of external regulation:

> Now finitude of the will characterizes the orientals, because with them the will has not yet grasped itself as universal, for thought is not yet free for itself. Hence there can but be the relation of lord and slave, and in this despotic sphere fear constitutes the ruling category.[54]
>
> In the case of Eastern Religion . . . we are much more directly reminded of the philosophic conception, for since in the East the element of subjectivity has not come forth, religious ideas are not individualized. . . . The Orientals certainly have also individual forms, such as Brahma, Vishnu, and Civa, but because freedom is wanting the individuality is not real, but merely superficial.[55]

Thus, the modern conception of individual consciousness is absent. There is no sense of the possibility of individuals forming their moral judgments about right and wrong. For the subjects in the Orient, opinions on these matters come from the outside and are not to be questioned. Oriental subjects, therefore, are outside history since they lack understanding, the power of looking at an object in an independent light.[56]

Persia, as Hegel sees it, is different. True history, according to Hegel, begins with Persia:

> With the Persian Empire we first enter on continuous History. The Persians are the first Historical People; Persia was the first Empire that passed away. While China and India remain stationary, and perpetuate a natural vegetative existence even to the present time, this land has been subject to those developments and revolutions, which alone manifest a historical condition. . . . The principle of development begins with the history of Persia. This therefore constitutes strictly the beginning of World-History; for the grand interest of Spirit [*Geist*] in History, is to attain an unlimited immanence of subjectivity—by an absolute antithesis to attain complete harmony.[57]

Although at first glance the Persian Emperor seems to be an absolute ruler much like that in China, the basis of the Persian Empire is not merely family obedience extended to the entire state, but a general principle of law that regulates the rulers as well as the subjects. Persia was a theocratic monarchy, based on the religion of Zoroaster, which involved the worship of Light.

The Persians see the absolute symbolized in light. Hegel suggests that the idea of light as something pure and universal that, like the sun, shines on all and confers equally its benefits on all. Zoroaster's Light, which belongs to the world of consciousness, is equally approachable to all: "But here in Persia first arises that light which shines itself, and illuminates what is around; for *Zoroaster's* 'Light' belongs to the World of Consciousness—to Spirit [*Geist*] as a relation to something distinct from itself."[58] Zoroaster's Light establishes a form of universality, or unity:

> In the Persian principle this unity is manifested as Light, which in this case is not simply light as such, the most universal physical element, but at the same time also *spiritual* purity—the Good. Speciality—the involvement with *limited* Nature—is consequently abolished. Light, in a physical and spiritual sense, imports, therefore, elevation—freedom from the merely natural. Man sustains a relation to Light—to the Abstract Good—as to something objective, which is acknowledged, reverenced, and evoked to activity by his Will. . . . The Unity recognized therefore, now first becomes a principle, not an external bond of soulless order. The fact that everyone has a share in that principle, secures each's personal dignity.[59]

Of course this does not mean that Persia was in any sense egalitarian. The Emperor was still an absolute ruler and hence the only free man in the Empire. However, the fact that his rule was based on a general principle and was not seen as a natural fact meant that development was possible. Thus, for Hegel, the idea of rule based on an intellectual or spiritual principle signifies the beginning of the growth of the consciousness of freedom: "But in becoming objective, this Universal Essence acquires a positive nature: man becomes free, and thus occupies a position face to face as it were with the Highest Beings, the latter being made objective for him."[60] In the Persian Empire, the potential for growth in the consciousness of freedom existed, but this potential could not be realized within the structure of the Empire. Insofar as consciousness appears in Eastern culture, it is expressed only in one individual person who heads the political structure and not in the totality of the society, such a culture cannot change from within. Since true individuals are lacking, they are not yet properly reconciled with the community.

In its efforts to expand, the Persian Empire came into conflict with the Greek city-states. An enormous army and fleet of ships were sent by the Persians and were famously defeated by Greeks at Salamis. Hegel sees this epochal battle as a contest between a despot who sought a united world under one lord and separate states that recognized the principle of free individuality. The Greek victory means that the tide of world history passes from the despotic oriental world to the world of the Greek *polis* [City-State]. Having resolved the contradiction of its predecessor, it falls victim to its own contradiction; the first iteration of history's dialectical cycle. With the defeat of Persia history begins to follow a necessary dialectical course. The Greek *polis* is the first home of freedom.[61] For Hegel, political liberty, moral freedom, pure consciousness, and thinking are absent in the Oriental world.

## Ancient Greece

The next cultural sphere of Hegel's dialectic of history is ancient Greece. The Greek *Volksgeist* is distinguished by the multitude of forms and is represented by the plurality of city-states:

> This is the *elementary character* of the Spirit of the Greeks, implying the organization of their culture from independent individualities—a condition in which individuals take their own ground, and are not, from the very beginning, patriarchally united by a bond of *Nature*, but realize a union through some other medium—through Law and Custom having the sanction of Spirit [*Geist*]. . . . The history of Greece exhibits at its commencement this interchange and mixture of partly homesprung, partly quite foreign stocks; and it was Attica itself—whose people was destined to attain the acme of Hellenic bloom—that was the asylum of the most various stocks and families. Every world-historical people, except the Asiatic kingdoms—which stands detached from the grand historical catena—has been formed this way.[62]

Hegel briefly discusses the development of Greek culture from Homer to Thucydides. Its ancient philosophers aid the development of reason, and its artists help advance the notion of individuality.[63]

Unlike oriental states, Greek democracy is not patriarchal. The Greeks lived in democratic states and shared the responsibilities of general administration and rule. Although Hegel asserts that the Greek world is animated by the idea of free individuality, it is his view that this freedom is by no means developed fully at this stage: "In Greece, viz., we have the freedom of the Individual, but it has not yet advanced to such a degree of abstraction, that the subjective unit is conscious of direct dependence on the [general] substantial principle."[64] He has two different reasons for regarding the Greek freedom as a limited one. First, only those who were citizens, legal members of the *polis*, were so reflected in public reality.[65] Slaves and resident aliens, for example, were not. Freedom was only the appanage of citizens. In fact, Hegel suggests that slavery was necessary for Athenian democracy to function. Since every citizen has the right to take part in public affairs, it was necessary that there is a category of workers who do the daily work of providing the necessities of life. All the menial economic tasks were taken over by non-citizens:

> This was a necessary condition of an aesthetic democracy, where it was the right and duty of every citizen to deliver or to listen to orations respecting the management of the State in the place of public assembly, to take part in the exercise of the Gymnasia, and to join in the celebration of festivals. It was a necessary condition of such occupations, that the citizens should be freed from handicraft occupations; consequently, that what among us is performed by free citizens—the work of daily life—should be done by slaves.[66]

Although this is an improvement on the Oriental world where only one was free, in the Greek world, due to slavery, only some are free. Thus, one of the essential conditions of Greek democracy was it exclusiveness. The citizenry then had the necessary leisure to see to the affairs of state.

Second, freedom was limited in the Greek city-state in another respect, according to Hegel. Even those who were free are free only in an incomplete way. He claims that the Greeks had no concept of individual conscience:

> Of the Greeks in the first and genuine form of their Freedom, we may assert, that they had no conscience; the habit of living for their country with further [analysis or] reflection, was the principle dominant among them. . . . When reflection once comes into play, the inquiry is started whether the Principle of Law (*das Recht*) cannot be improved. Instead of holding by the existing state of things, *internal* conviction is relied upon; and thus begins a subjective independent freedom, in which the individual finds himself in a position to bring everything to the test of his own conscience, even in defiance of the existing constitution.[67]

Even though subjective freedom does appear in Greece, it is still embedded in the substantial unity of the polis. The Greeks are totally identified with the whole. The *polis* is a given, not a willed entity. Whereas the people of the Orient simply obey the external authority of the despot without reflection, for the Greeks motivation for obedience comes from inside themselves. They have, Hegel suggests, the habit of living for their polis without any reflection. They would live or die for their *polis*. The Greek state worked because people are immediately identified with it.[68] The Greeks possess an internal readiness to do what is best for the community as a whole. In this condition, Hegel notes that ethical behavior is imbued in the individual naturally and is not the outcome of a conscious moral choice.

Compared to the Oriental world, the Greeks were free in that they did as they wished to do, not as an external decree required them to do. The Greeks simply thought of themselves as so indissolubly linked with their own particular *polis* that they did not distinguish between their own interests and the interests of the community in which they lived:

> Their grand object was their country in its living and real aspect—*this actual* Athens, this Sparta, these Temples, these Altars, this form of social life, this union of fellow-citizens, these manners and customs. To the Greek his country was necessary of life, without which existence was impossible.[69]

In short, they could not conceive of themselves as living apart from their community with all its customs and forms of social life. For Hegel, this is an incomplete freedom because its motivation comes so naturally. If people do something from habit, they have not deliberately chosen to do it, and their actions are still governed by forces external to their will, such as the social forces that give rise to the habits. For example, Hegel notes that the Greeks tended to consult an oracle for guidance before undertaking any important venture.[70] Genuinely free people would not allow their most important decisions to be determined by such events; they would use their capacity to reason before making important decisions. For the Greeks, living democratically meant living traditionally and not being faced with the agonizing choices of modern life, where the tension between the private and the public is at the core of civil life. "The ancient Greeks know nothing of this; they still lived in a totally unmediated political structure."[71]

Hegel also makes it clear why in his view Greek democracy is inappropriate as a model for the modern world. Ancient democracy was possible in part because societies were so small and its populations were so homogeneous:

> It must also be remarked . . . that such democratic constitutions are possible only in small states—states which do not much exceed the compass of cities. The whole Polis of the Athenians is united in the one city of Athens. . . . Only in such cities can the interests of all be similar; in large empires, on the contrary, diverse and conflicting interests are sure to present themselves. The living together in one city, the fact that the inhabitants see each other daily, render a common culture and a living democratic polity possible.[72]

Thus, a relatively small size is necessary in order to ensure that all citizens could take part and be really present when decisions are taken. It also requires that a homogeneity of the population be attained to an extent not possible in the larger modern state. Thus, the heterogeneity of the modern state further disqualifies the possibility of pure democracy. Since individual consciousness is lacking, individuals in Greece were not reconciled properly with their community.

The unity of the Greek state is doomed. It is destined to be overcome because of its limitations and parochialness. *Geist* must march on. The Greek's beautiful harmony is disrupted, first by the Sophists and later by Socrates. Critical thought and reflection are the key to further progress in the development of self-consciousness and freedom. Once the *polis* is realized, the cunning of reason calls world-historical individuals to look beyond it.[73] According to Hegel, Socrates was such a rational figure. He turns his allegiance away from the *polis* toward universal reason:

> Socrates—in assigning to insight, to conviction, the determination of men's actions—posited the Individual as capable of final moral decision, in contraposition to Country and to Customary Morality. . . . The principle of Socrates manifests a revolutionary aspects towards the Athenian State; for the peculiarity of

this State was, that Customary Morality was the form in which its existence was moulded, viz.—an inseparable connection of Thought with actual life. When Socrates wishes to induce his friends to reflection, the discourse has always a negative tone; he brings them to the consciousness that they do not know what the Right is.[74]

The summons to free inquiry, untrammeled by customary beliefs, is taken up by Socrates and subsequent Greek philosophers. Even though he wanted to remain obedient to the laws of Athens, he also wanted them to be founded upon reason. For example, Socrates is typically engaged in a dialogue with someone who thinks he knows what justice is. Socrates then leads his audience to critical reflection upon the customary morality they have always accepted. Critical reflection makes reason, as opposed to social custom, the final judge of right and wrong.[75] There is a price paid for the advent of individual critical reflection, however: Men turn to universal reason and turn away from the parochial state.

In this way, Socrates' teachings undermined the immediate identification with the public life on which the *polis* rests. The birth of the individual with universal reason, for Hegel, led to the dissolution of the *polis*. "Thus because Socrates makes the truth rest on the judgment of inward consciousness, he enters upon a struggle with the Athenian people as to what is right and true."[76] The principle of independent thought was the ultimate cause of the downfall of Athens and marks the beginning of the end of the world-historical role played by Greek civilization. What Socrates began was continued by Plato, who transforms the question of justice into an investigation of the state.[77] The dissolution of the *polis* is the birth of the individual with universal consciousness, an individual who defines herself as a subject of universal reason. Since he finds no identification with the public life of the *polis*, he now turns toward a larger community. For Hegel, *Geist* thus moves from the realm of the *polis* to that of the empire.

## The Roman Empire

The individual is once again cast into a world that is ruled by the arbitrary will of a sovereign. In contrast to the unreflective customary unity of the Greeks, Hegel sees the Roman Empire as built up from a collection of diverse peoples. Lacking all natural patriarchal or customary bonds, the Roman Empire thus requires the most severe discipline, backed by force, to hold it together:

Abstract universal Personality had not yet appeared, for Spirit [*Geist*] must first develop itself to that form of abstract Universality which exercised the severe discipline over humanity now under consideration. Here, in Rome, then, we find that free universality, that abstract Freedom, which on the one hand sets an abstract state, a political constitution and power, over concrete individuality.[78]

It is this peculiarity in the founding of the State which must be regarded as the essential basis of the idiosyncrasy of Rome. For it directly involves the severest discipline, and self-sacrifice to the grand object of the union. A State which had first to form itself, and which is based on force, must be held together by force.[79]

This dominance is not a reversion to the Persian Empire. While history is not a smooth and steady progression, it does not go backwards either. In dialectical fashion, the gains made in a previous epoch are not lost entirely. The Greek idea of individuality has not disappeared. The Roman world rests upon a political constitution and legal system that has individual rights as one of its most fundamental notions and recognizes individual freedom in a way that the Persian Empire never could.[80]

Roman society, according to Hegel, is the place of origin of the idea of the "person," an individual defined as a subject of rights in abstraction from his relation to the substance of his culture. The person is the bearer of abstract rights, which are unconnected to one's social and political role: ". . . Person, which involves the recognition of the independent dignity of the social unit—not on the ground of the display of the life which he possesses—in his complete individuality—but as the abstract *individuum*."[81] For example, an individual is a bearer of certain specific rights, such as the right to property. This is one of the dimensions of the modern state and Hegel's sees its origin in Rome. Nevertheless, the individual freedom recognized by the Roman state is purely legal or formal. Hegel calls it an "abstract" freedom of the individual:

> The Romans then completed this important separation, and discovered a principle of right, which is external—i.e., one not dependent on disposition and sentiment. While they have thus bestowed on us a valuable gift, in point of *form*, we can use and enjoy it without becoming victims to that sterile Understanding—without regarding it as the *ne plus ultra* of Wisdom and Reason. They were its victims, living beneath its sway; but they thereby secured for other Freedom of Spirit—viz., that inward Freedom which has consequently become emancipated from the sphere of the Limited and the External.[82]

Concrete individuality, the freedom to develop a diversity of ideas and ways of living, is ruthlessly crushed by the brute power of Rome. No real reconciliation occurs. Thus, the real difference between the Persian and Roman Empires seems to be that in the former the principle of despotism is unbridled and in the latter there is a constant tension between absolute power of the state and the ideal of individuality. For Hegel, we also owe the Roman world for the origin and development of positive law.[83]

The Roman world, as Hegel describes it, is not a particularly pleasant place. While his critical account of ancient Greece is accompanied by an obvious admiration for certain aspects of Greek culture, as discussed in Chapter 4, Hegel shows little sympathy for Roman culture. The joyous free spirit of the Greek world has been lost.[84] The Roman state is the ultimate end, not the totality that it was for the Greeks. Rome stands for sheer arbitrary power. Although the ideal of individuality makes some advances in Rome, the individual is a mere instrument in the hands of the state and the *polis* is turned into a universal empire, which becomes the sphere of hard work and servitude.[85] In the face of demands by the Emperor for outward conformity, freedom can only be discovered by retreating into oneself through philosophy:

> He either recognized his destiny in the task of acquiring the means of enjoyment through the favor of the Emperor, or through violence, testamentary frauds, and cunning; or he sought repose in philosophy, which alone was still able to supply something firm and independent: for the systems of that time—Stoicism, Epicureanism, and Scepticism—although within their common sphere opposed to each other, had the same general purport, viz., rendering the soul absolutely indifferent to everything which the real world had offer. . . . But the inward reconciliation by means of philosophy was itself only an abstract one—in the pure principle of personality; for Thought, which, as perfectly refined, made itself its own object, and thus harmonized itself, was entirely destitute of a real object.[86]

Although the specifics of these philosophies vary, Hegel stresses their common tendency to disqualify everything that the real, physical world offers and substitutes an internal dimension. Hegel's *Phenomenology* demonstrates the inadequacies of stoicism and skepticism. This inward reconciliation is abstract in that the individual is absolutely indifferent to the outside world. Adherents of this type of philosophy tend to retreat from the concerns of everyday life, detaching themselves from their own subjective views and trying to take a neutral, universalistic point of view. Freedom in thought has only pure thought as its truth, and, therefore, is a truth lacking the fullness of life; freedom is bought at the price of excessive abstractness and formality.[87]

## Medieval Christianity

Hegel views the spread of these philosophical schools as resulting from the helplessness that an individual who sees himself as a free being must feel in the face of a domineering power he is unable to influence. The retreat into philosophy is, however, a negative response to this situation.[88] A more positive solution is necessary, which is then provided by Christianity, which emerges as an answer to the utter lack of mediation between the subject and political power. Since the emergence of Christianity, history has been a continuous unfolding of the principle of subjective freedom in the world.[89] Hegel, like Thomas Aquinas, sees human beings as more than just very clever animals. Although people live in the natural world, as animals do, they are also spiritual beings. Until human beings recognize themselves as spiritual beings, they are trapped in the natural world of material forces. Since in the Roman state the natural world was implacably resistant to the aspiration for freedom, there was no escape within the natural world, aside from the already mentioned retreat into a philosophy.[90] Once human beings recognize themselves as spiritual beings, however, the hostility of the natural world ceases to be all-important. It can be transcended in a positive manner because there is something positive beyond the natural world. In other words, at this early stage, Christians see the spiritual world, not the natural world, as their true home.

Christianity introduces the element of subjective consciousness and passes through a number of stages that culminate in the Lutheran Reformation. Christianity comes to answer the yearning of the individual, who also cannot be reconciled with the political and social world, that the finite subject and absolute be fully united. They become fully united in the person of Christ:

> Man himself there is comprehended in the Idea of God, and this comprehension may be thus expressed—that the unity of Man with God is posited in the Christian Religion. But his unity must not be superficially conceived as if God were only Man, and Man, without further condition, were God. Man, on the contrary, is God only in so far as he annuls the merely Natural and Limited in his Spirit and elevates himself to God. . . . This implicit unity exists in the first place only for the thinking speculative consciousness; but it must become an object for the World—it must *appear*, and that in the sensuous form appropriate to Spirit, which is the human. Christ has appeared—a Man who is God—God who is Man; and thereby peace and reconciliation have accrued to the World.[91]

"The embodiment of God, the figure of the historical Christ—which the unity of the universal and the specific, of immutable consciousness and changeable consciousness—is therewhich produced for consciousness."[92] Thus, the Christian religion is special because Jesus Christ is both a human being and the Son of God. Nevertheless, this unity must be overcome in its immediate form. Christ must die, rise again, go to the Father, and return in spirit to animate the community:

> Its first realization is the formation by the friends of Christ, of a Society—a
> Church. It has been already remarked that only after the death of Christ could the
> Spirit come upon his friends; that only then were they able to conceive the true
> idea of God, viz., that in Christ man is redeemed and reconciled: for to him the
> idea of eternal truth is recognized, the essence of man acknowledged to be Spirit,
> and the fact proclaimed that only by stripping himself of his finiteness and sur-
> rendering himself to pure self-consciousness, does he attain the truth. . . . (This
> is a) history which every man has to accomplish in himself, in order to exist as
> Spirit, or to become a child of God, a citizen of his kingdom. The followers of
> Christ, who combine on this principle, form the *Church*, which is the Kingdom
> of God.[93]

Hence, the birth of Christ, for Hegel, realizes this unity in principle only; the
Church, which represents the external realization of the new community, is
necessary for the full realization of unity. "The Church is a real present life
in the Spirit of Christ."[94]

The historical task now becomes making this reconciliation externally,
politically real; the church community must become one with society. Early
Christianity did not yet connect to government in a meaningful way. So although freedom advanced, it existed only in the supersensible world and was
too abstract. This still left mankind separated from the social world:

> Consequently he has his true home in a super-sensuous world—an infinite subjec-
> tivity, gained only by a rupture with mere Natural existence and volition, and by
> his labor to break their power within him. This is religious self-consciousness.[95]

At this stage, Christianity achieves an awareness that the spiritual nature of
human beings is essential to their existence. The subjective freedom of religious self-consciousness, however, must be reconciled with the brute political
reality of the time. Christianity's religious freedom needs to become manifest
in the political world:

> Thus Freedom in the State is preserved and established by Religion, since moral
> rectitude in the State is only the carrying out of that which constitutes the funda-
> mental principle of Religion. The process displayed in History is only the mani-
> festation of Religion as Human Reason—the production of the religious principle
> which dwells in the heart of man, under the form of Secular Freedom. Thus the
> discord between the inner life of the heart and the actual world is removed.[96]

Unfortunately, as Hegel sees it, this does not happen right away but takes time.
Freedom cannot yet actualize itself. Under the Roman Empire, Hegel says that
Christianity cannot find a ground on which it may become actual and develop.

Christianity comes to the fore under the Roman Empire and becomes its official religion with Constantine. Although the western half of the Empire fell to barbarian invasions, the Byzantine Empire remains Christian for more than a thousand years.[97] During this period, the Church becomes a political power with political motives. For Hegel, however, this is a period of stagnant, decadent Christianity:

> The Byzantine Empire is a grand example of how the Christian religion may maintain an abstract character among a cultivated people, if the whole organization of the State and of the Laws is not reconstructed in harmony with its principle. At Byzantium Christianity had fallen into the hands of the dregs of the population—the lawless mob. Popular license on the one side and courtly baseness on the other side, take refuge under the sanction of religion, and degrade the latter to a disgusting object. In regard to religion, two interests obtained prominence: first, the settlement of doctrine; and secondly, the appointment to ecclesiastical offices. The settlement of doctrine pertained to the Councils and Church authorities; but the principle of Christianity is Freedom—subjective insight. These matters therefore, were special subjects of contention for the populace; violent civil wars arose, and everywhere might be witnessed scenes of murder, conflagration and pillage, perpetrated in the cause of Christian dogmas.[98]

It was merely an attempt to put a Christian veneer over structures that were already rotten to the core. "The Idea of Spirit contained in this doctrine was thus treated in an utterly unspiritual manner."[99] It takes a new people to carry the Christian principle to its ultimate destiny.

This involves an extremely slow transformation of social and political institutions. A religious self-consciousness also needs to be developed.[100] This is the realization that it is the spiritual world, not the natural world, that is our true home. In order to achieve this awareness human beings have to break the hold that natural desires, and the whole of natural existence, has over them. It is the role of the Christian religion to achieve this awareness.[101] This does not take place all at once, since it entails more than inner piety. The change that takes place in the pious heart of the Christian must then transform the real external world into something that satisfies the requirement of humans as spiritual beings.[102] This is the task of the next eighteen centuries, and it is undertaken by a new world-historical people, the Germanic peoples [*germanische Völker*]. According to Hegel, the role of the Germanic peoples in history is due solely to the fact that they destroyed the Roman Empire and received Christianity from the Romans and absorbed it into their culture.

## The Reformation and the Renaissance

With the Protestant Reformation and the Renaissance, the German world is the new home of *Geist*, and the place for freedom's next advance:

The German Spirit is the Spirit of the new World. Its aim is the realization of absolute Truth as the unlimited self-determination of Freedom—*that* Freedom which has its own absolute form itself as its purport. The destiny of the German peoples is, to be the bearers of the Christian principle. The principle of Spiritual Freedom—of Reconciliation (of the Objective and Subjective), was introduced into the still simple, unformed minds of those peoples; and the part assigned them in the serve of the World-Spirit was that of not merely possessing the Idea of Freedom as the substratum of their religious conceptions, but of producing it in free and spontaneous developments from their subjective self-consciousness.[103]

Hegel's Germanic world [*die germanische Welt*] entails more than Germany proper, it also includes a number of other Western European nations.[104] He uses Germanic people very broadly, encompassing all the Christian nations of Europe. His primary reason for designating the era as the Germanic world is that he takes the Reformation as the single key event of history since Roman times.

Hegel paints a gloomy picture of Europe during the thousand of years that passed after the fall of Rome. Social morality was lacking during the Middle Ages, and the embodiment of "the Divine" was wanting in actual life.[105] During that time, the Church became a perversion of the true religious spirit, inserting itself between man and the spiritual world, and insisting on blind obedience from its followers. In fact, the medieval Church exhibits itself as a manifold contradiction: "its acquisition as an outward existence, of possessions and an enormous property—a state of things which, since that Church despises or professes to despise riches, is none other than a Lie."[106] Another contradiction is that even though the Church repudiates political power, it has acquired considerable political power through feudalism. He sees the Crusades as secular conquest:

Through the Crusades the Church reached the completion of its authority: it had achieved the perversion of religion and the divine Spirit; it had distorted the principles of Christian Freedom to a wrongful and immoral slavery of men's souls; and in doing so, far from abolishing lawless caprice and violence and supplanting them by a virtuous rule of its own, it had even enlisted them in the service of ecclesiastical authority. In the Crusades the Pope stood at the head of the secular power: the Emperor appeared only in a subordinate position, like the other princes, and was obliged to commit both the initiative and the executive to the Pope.[107]

Papal authority extended deeply into the political realm. This finally ends with a renaissance, or a revival of learning and flourishing of the fine arts, which:

may be compared with that *blush of dawn*, which after long storms first betokens the return of a bright and glorious day. This day is the day of Universality, which breaks upon the world after the long, eventful, and terrible night of the

Middle Ages—a day which is distinguished by science, art and inventive impulse—that is, by the noblest and highest, which Humanity, rendered free by Christianity and emancipated through the instrumentalities of Church, exhibits as the eternal and veritable substance of its being.[108]

Thus, the Renaissance frees reason from the medieval dungeon, and helps to push consciousness beyond the spiritual realm.

It is the Reformation, however, not the Renaissance, that Hegel sees as the "all-enlightening *Sun*, following on that blush of dawn which we observed at the termination of the medieval period."[109] The Reformation resulted from the corruption of the Church, which in Hegel's view was not an accidental development but a necessary consequence of the fact that the Church does not treat God as a purely spiritual thing, but as material things. The Catholic Church was based on ceremonial observances, rituals, and other outward forms. According to Hegel, the spiritual element in human beings is fettered to mere material objects, since compliance to them was taken as being essential to the religious life. The ultimate expression of this deep-seated corruption is the practice of selling the spiritual peace brought by the remission of sins, something that concerns man's deepest and inmost nature:

> The Church whose office it is to save souls from perdition, makes this salvation itself a mere external appliance, and is now degraded so far as to perform this office in a merely external fashion. The *remission of sins*—the highest satisfaction which the soul craves, the certainty of its peace with God, that which concerns man's deepest and inmost nature—is offered to man in the most grossly superficial and trivial fashion—*to be purchased for mere money*; while the object of this sale is to procure means for dissolute excess.[110]

Hegel sees this practice of selling indulgences as the impetus that motivates Martin Luther's protest. In order for *Geist* to progress, there had to be a recovery of the spiritual meaning of the presence of *Geist* in the world, a setting aside of the gross sensuous meaning this had with Catholicism.

The Reformation, for Hegel, is an achievement of the Germanic people, arising from "the honest truth and simplicity of its heart."[111] Simplicity and heart are seen as the keynotes of the Reformation, which began with Luther and took root in the Germanic nations. Its result was to do away with the pomp and circumstance of the Catholic Church and to substitute the idea that each individual human being has, in his own heart, a direct spiritual relationship to Christ:

> Luther's simple doctrine is that the specific embodiment of Deity—infinite subjectivity, that is true spirituality, Christ—is in no way present and actual in an outward form, but as essentially spiritual is obtained only in being reconciled to

God—*in faith and spiritual enjoyment.* . . . Christ is an actual presence, though only in faith and in Spirit. He maintained that the Spirit of Christ really fills the human heart—that Christ therefore is not to be regarded as merely a historical person, but the man sustains *an immediate relation to him as Spirit.*[112]

With the Reformation, and the freeing of spirituality from its imprisonment in gross external things, the way was free for the task of making God's presence objective and real in the external world, not in the inadequate external rites of Catholicism, but by building a real earthly community. In brief, the unity of God and man has to be externally realized.

The Reformation is seen in Hegelian terms as being more than some isolated religious occurrence. Hegel always stresses the interrelatedness of different aspects of our historical development. In addition, as indicated above, human beings must make the world in which they live into something suitable for free spiritual beings, since fulfilling their spiritual nature requires more than perfecting their religious life. Thus, the Reformation is much more than an attack on the old Church and the replacement of Roman Catholicism by Protestantism. People's salvation is their own affair, and they enter into relationship with their conscience and into immediate connection with God, requiring no mediation of priests.[113] It proclaims that every human being can recognize the truth of his or her own spiritual nature and can achieve his or her own salvation. No outside authority is necessary to interpret the scriptures or perform outside rituals.[114] The individual conscience is the ultimate judge of truth and goodness. Through this assertion, the Reformation unfurls "the banner of the Free Spirit" and proclaims as its essential principle: "Man is in his very nature destined to be free."[115] This gives depth to the modern conception of selfhood.

Since the Reformation, Hegel sees the role of history as the transformation of the world in accordance with this essential principle. This is no simple task since if every human being is freely able to use his powers of reasoning to judge truth and goodness, the world can only receive universal assent when it conforms to rational standards:

The development and advance of Spirit from the time of the Reformation onwards consist in this, that Spirit, having now gained the consciousness of its Freedom, through that process of mediation which takes place between man and God—that is, in the full recognition of the objective process as the existence [the positive and definite manifestation] of the Divine essence—now takes it up and follows it out in building up the edifice of secular relations. . . . Obedience to the laws of the State, as the Rational element in volition and action, was made the principle of human conduct. In this obedience man is free, for all that is demanded is that the Particular should yield to the General. Man himself has a conscience; consequently the subjection required of him is a free allegiance.

This involves the possibility of a development of Reason and Freedom, and of
their introduction into human relations; and Reason and Divine commands are
now synonymous. The Rational no longer meets with contradiction on the part
of the religious conscience; it is permitted to develop itself in its own sphere
without disturbance, without being compelled to resort to force in defending
itself against adverse power.[116]

Hence, all social institutions—such as law, property, social morality, and
government—must be made to conform to general principles of reason. Only
then will individuals freely choose to accept and support these institutions,
and only then will law, morality, and government cease to be arbitrary rules
and powers that free agents must be compelled to obey. Only then will people
be truly reconciled with their community. Human beings will be both free
and fully reconciled with the world in which they live.[117] Thus, the attempt to
realize the rational state comes from Reformed Europe.

## The Enlightenment

The Enlightenment is the next dialectical event in Hegel's account of world
history, which brings his theory of history up to his time. The spiritualization
process begun by the Reformation carries on and brings about the Enlightenment. With the reconciliation of self-consciousness brought forth by the
Reformation:

> Man has attained to confidence in himself and in his thought, in sensuous nature
> outside of and within him; he has discovered an interest and pleasure in making
> discoveries both in nature and the arts. In the affairs of this world the under-
> standing developed; man became conscious of his will and his achievements,
> took pleasure in the earth and its soil, as also in his occupations, because right
> and understanding were there present.[118]

The physical world is once again present and of interest to mankind. New
knowledge can be discovered by penetrating beyond the superficial appearance of things. The new scientific method paves the way for a new conception
of man and nature.

Human beings become more and more aware of themselves as at one with
the universal and thus come to recognize that they are inwardly free with the
freedom of pure thought. This is not the inner freedom of the ancients, however, since modern human beings have come to realize that they are at one
with the very foundation of things:

> Man is not free, when he is not thinking; for except when thus engaged he sustains
> a relation to the world around him as to another, an alien form of being. . . . Thought

is the grade to which Spirit [*Geist*] has now advanced. It involves the Harmony of Being in its purest essence, challenging the external world to exhibit the same Reason which Subject [the Ego] possesses. Spirit perceives that Nature—the World—must also be an embodiment of Reason, for God created it on principles of Reason. . . . Thus, *Experimental Science* became the science of the World; for experimental science involves on the one hand the observation of phenomena, on the other hand also the discovery of the Law, the essential being, the hidden force that causes those phenomena—thus rendering the data supplied by observation to their simple principles. Intellectual consciousness was first extricated from that sophistry of thought, which unsettles everything, by *Descartes*.[119]

Descartes' "knowing subject" forms true representations of the so-called objective reality of the world. Hegel reads Descartes' *cogito ergo sum* as meaning that thought and being are one.[120] Furthermore, Descartes ushers in the age of reason and represents the advance of scientific reason. Consequently the Enlightenment not only defines man as thought, but it also holds that the whole of external reality conforms to thought. This is Hegel's reading of the new scientific consciousness that strives to understand the world as law-governed order. Nature can be understood and rationally explained, since God created it on principles of reason.[121]

The Enlightenment advances the cause of secular knowledge and its place in the human world. Nature becomes liberated from divine mysteries and privileged authorities, and confidence shifts to human discovery. The natural world is subject to empirical observation and scientific reasoning:

We thus see the finite, the inward and outward present, becomes a matter of experience, and through the understanding is elevated into universality; men desire to understand laws and forces, i.e., to transform the individual of perceptions into the form of universality. Worldly matters demand to be judged in a worldly way; the judge is thinking understanding.[122]

Data from experience becomes a source of knowledge. The thinking mind is, once again, capable of action. While Isaac Newton uncovers universal laws that explain the physical phenomena of the empirical world, Thomas Hobbes develops laws of the political and social world. Social and moral laws can be discovered through reason.[123] Enlightenment thinkers, such as Voltaire and Diderot, hold to the notion that all social institutions should conform to the principles of reason. Enlightenment philosophy conceives of the human self as a free and rational individual, one that possesses natural rights. Its goal is to emancipate mankind from the bonds of ignorance and superstition and to rescue people from intolerance, cruelty, and oppression.

The rational subject is constituted by freedom in its capacity to transcend the constraints of sensuous nature or tradition. The free will is an advancement of Enlightenment thought, and plays a central role in the social and moral world:

> The Will is Free only when it does not will anything alien, extrinsic, foreign to itself (for as long as it does so, it is dependent), but will itself alone—wills the Will. This is absolute Will—the volition to be free. . . . The Freedom of the Will, *per se*, is the principle and substantial basis of all Right—is itself absolute, inherently eternal Right, and the Supreme Right in comparison with other specific Rights; nay, it is even that by which Man becomes Man, and is therefore the fundamental principle of Spirit [*Geist*].[124]

The conception of free will represents an advance of the principle of individuality that was initiated by Protestantism. For Hegel, however, even with this development, consciousness is still incomplete:

> Hence the Enlightenment distinguishes clearly and has a vision of men as individuals, independent of each other, but it loses sight of the community in which they are set. Its political theory is atomistic. Hence, too, the Enlightenment sees merely external, individual objects in the world that surrounds us; it does not also see the world as an order posited by God, *Geist*, or reason. What the Enlightenment sees is true, but fatally partial. Thus it desacralizes, for it only sees the world as a heap of objects, open to human scrutiny and use; it does not see it as the manifestation, the emanation of reason.[125]

This is why the value theory of the Enlightenment is utilitarian. The notion of individual will is still abstract, and the will in question appears as an isolated individual will; consequently, the state is an aggregate of many wills.[126] This problem helps explain what went wrong with the French Revolution.

## The French Revolution

"Hegel was deeply stirred by the French Revolution's call to make politics a sphere of freedom, and then equally dismayed by its eventual failure to institutionalize political freedom in actual organs of self-government."[127] The French Revolution, according to Hegel, is the result of the criticisms of the existing order made by French philosophers. Before the Revolution, France had a nobility with a confused mass of privileges but without real power. Hegel justifies the French Revolution as having been caused by the greed and wealth of the dominant class, and by its insistence on continuing to plunder government funds and the people's hard work.[128] The popular discontent was the result of a tension between the terrible weight on the people's shoulders and the governmental means to sustain its opulence and dissipation. Rousseau's conception of the "rights of man" asserted itself and triumphed against the utterly irrational situation in France.[129] Hegel conceives of the French Revolution as the world-historical event that, for the first time, had conferred real existence and validity on abstract right.[130] He leaves no doubt as to his view of the significance of this event:

> Never since the sun has stood in firmament and the planets revolved around it had it been perceived that man's existence centers in his head, i.e., in thought, inspired by which he builds up the world of reality. Anaxagoras had been the first to say that [reason] governs the World; but not until now had man advanced to the recognition of the principle that Thought ought to govern spiritual reality. This was accordingly a glorious mental dawn. All thinking beings shared in the jubilation of this epoch.[131]

However, the immediate result of this world-historical event was the Revolutionary Terror, which inflicted punishment as the quick death of the guillotine without legal formalities.[132] For Hegel, the excesses and failure of the Revolution illustrate the root inadequacy of the Enlightenment. The French Revolution fails to ground empirically the subjective wills of the many into the general will:

> Not satisfied with the establishment of rational rights, with freedom of person and property, with the existence of a political organization in which are to be found various circles of civil life each having its own functions to perform, and with that influence over the people with is exercised by the intelligent members of the community, and the confidence that is felt in them, "*Liberalism*" sets up in opposition to all this the atomistic principle, that which insists upon the sway of individual wills; maintaining that all government should emanate from their express power, and have their express sanction. Asserting this formal side of Freedom—this abstraction—the party in question allows no political organization to be firmly established.[133]

The mistake was attempting to put into practice purely abstract philosophical principles without regarding the concrete disposition of the people. For Hegel, the collision between the individual and the community is something whose solution has to be worked out in the future, that is, the problem with which history is now occupied.

This attempt was based upon a misunderstanding of the role of reason, which must not be applied in isolation from the existing community and the people that make it up. Even though the Revolution was a failure, it is a world-historical event because its principles were passed on to other nations: "As regards outward diffusion its principle gained access to almost all modern states, either through conquest or by express introduction into their political life."[134] For instance, the short-lived victories of Napoleon were sufficient to

bring a code of rights, establish liberty and the right to property, and abolish
most feudal obligations in Germany:

> *Germany* was traversed by the victorious French hosts, but German nationality
> delivered it from this yoke. One of the leading features in the political condition
> of Germany is that code of Rights which was certainly occasioned by French op-
> pression, since this was the especial means to bringing to light the deficiencies
> of the old system. The fiction of an Empire has utterly vanished. It is broken up
> into sovereign states. Feudal obligations are abolished, for freedom of property
> and of person have been recognized as fundamental principles. Offices of State
> are open to every citizen, talent and adaptation being of course the necessary
> conditions.[135]

Thus, "Hegel welcomes in Napoleon both the conqueror of the French Revolution and the protector of the revolutionary order, the general who is actually victorious over Robespierre and the patron of the new bourgeois code of
law."[136] Hegel's account of world history reaches his own day. He concludes
with the reminder that all history is nothing but the development of the idea of
freedom.[137] This requires that both individuals should government themselves
according to their own conscience and also that the objective world with its
social and political institutions should be organized rationally.

It is not enough to have individuals governing themselves according to
their own conscience, which would merely be subjective freedom. As long
as the objective world is not rationally organized, individuals acting on their
own will inevitably come into conflict with law and morality. Existing law
and morality would, therefore, be seen as a limit upon their freedom. Hegel's
goal is the rational organization of the objective world in order to allow individuals to follow their own conscience and freely choose to act in accordance
with the law and morality of the objective world, which is necessary for the
reconciliation of individuals to their community. The goal is for freedom to
exist on both the subjective and objective level:

> But Objective Freedom—the laws of *real* Freedom—demand the subjugation of
> the mere contingent Will—for this is in its nature formal. If the Objective is in
> itself Rational, human insight and conviction must correspond with the Reason
> which it embodies, and then we have the other essential element—Subjective
> Freedom—also realized.[138]

Hegel's ideal is clearly ambitious—perfect harmony between the free choices
of individual and the needs of the society as a whole. "A man is free only
when he himself has made himself free."[139] In brief, the idea of freedom will
become a reality and *Geist* will have achieved its goal. As is illustrated above,
Hegel's philosophy of history is founded on a general logic—specifically a

dialectic of consciousness. All determinate vehicles of *Geist*, from individual to collective centers of consciousness, participate in this logic. Since this brings us up to Hegel's day, the next section examines his life and intellectual development.

## HEGEL'S LIFE AND TIMES

Georg Wilhelm Friedrich Hegel was born in Stuttgart on August 27, 1770 to Georg Ludwig and Maria Hegel. His father, educated as a lawyer, was a secretary in the revenue office and then later an expeditionary councilor for the Duchy of Württemburg. He was one of six children born to his parents, but only three survived into adulthood: of these, Hegel was the oldest, followed by his sister, Christine Louis, and his brother, Georg Ludwig. He survived several life-threatening illnesses during his youth, and poor health was a problem his entire life. His mother died when he was eleven. Hegel's brother, Georg Ludwig, had a brief career as a military officer, rising to the rank of captain; he was part of Napoleon's Russian campaign in 1812, but never returned. His sister, Christine, never married and stayed home to care for her father; she died a few months after Hegel in 1831. Hegel's life spanned the French Revolution and the bloody aftermath of the terror, the rise and fall of Napoleon, the Revolution of 1830, and the demise of the Holy Roman Empire and the reorganization of political and social life as the tide of liberal reform ebbed and flowed in various German states. Several generations of Hegels had been ministers in the Protestant Church, and, from his earliest years, Hegel developed a strong sense of religious identity.[140]

Germany was still divided into numerous political entities and the spirit of modern German nationalism had not yet been born. Hegel's home life was marked by Protestant Pietism, which meant that he was steeped in its theosophy and mysticism from childhood.[141] Hegel's mother taught him Latin at home; when he was ten, his father hired K. A. Duttenhofer, a noted local mathematician, to give Hegel private lessons in geometry.[142] Young Hegel attended the primary school in Stuttgart, and from 1780, the *Gymnasium*, or secondary school there. Its curriculum gave top priority to the study of Greek and Roman classics, while also imparting the values of the Enlightenment. The *Gymnasium* also stressed theology, which is illustrated by the fact that more than fifty percent of the graduates went on to pursue some kind of career that involved theological studies.[143] Hegel received an Enlightenment [*Aufklärung*] education and was qualified for theological training. He was a conscientious student, devoting himself to classical studies and graduated first in his class. His diary entries show him to be a voracious reader of all

types of contemporary and classical literature. His youthful commitment to
the moral, rational, and pedagogical ideals of the *Aufklärung* was not superficial, but remained an important component of his cultural outlook in later
years.

As a result of his academic achievements, he won a scholarship to a well-
known Protestant seminary at Tübingen, where he studied philosophy and
theology. The University of Tübingen was one of the numerous state univer-
sities whose primary aim was to prepare young men for service in the government, the church, or teaching. Hegel, as recipient of a ducal scholarship, lived
in the Theological Seminary. Seminary scholars had a special uniform and the
hours for study, recreation, and going out were strictly regulated. Attendance
at lectures was monitored by assistants. His father promised to mortgage his
property to enable Hegel to work diligently toward the goal of becoming a
clergyman.[144] While at the seminary, Hegel met the poet Friedrich Hölderlin
and the philosopher Friedrich Schelling. The three became fast friends and
roommates. They jointly resolved not to become pastors, and Schelling and
Hölderlin came to be the chief catalysts for Hegel's ultimate turn away from
the clergy and his turn toward a career in philosophy.[145] With his two com-
panions, he read and discussed Rousseau and Schiller and started an exploration of Kant, Greek poetry, and philosophy. Although Hegel read Kant, when
the Kantians at the Seminary formed a club, he did not join, claiming that he
was too involved in the study of Rousseau.[146] Hegel was early suspicious of
Kantian thought, which seemed to rely too much on intellectual reason and
neglected the moral force of passions, thus failing to give a complete account
of the living human agent. The three friends became open to prospects of
political reform and to new ideas that might transform the social situation in
Germany.

The French Revolution in 1789 had a great impact upon Hegel, Hölderlin, and Schelling. They cheered the Revolution and followed the events in
France closely. They hoped for something similar in Germany. They were
disillusioned with the corruption and provinciality of Württemberg. The Revolution seemed to promise fulfillment of their hopes that the retrograde forces
of the old empire were not long for the world.[147] Hegel joined a political club
to discuss the Revolution and read revolutionary tracts. Like many German
intellectuals of the time, he tended to see the emerging French Revolution as
a new version of the older Protestant Reformation, destined to lead society to
a better ethical condition. He was influenced as well by the Pietist idea that
reform of the church had not been enough and that a thorough-going reform
of the world was equally required, and that the French Revolution would lead
to this reform. During this time, young Hegel became endowed with a sense
of constitutionalism and with the idea that political rights have to be anchored

in some kind of social practice.[148] It may be important, given later charges that he is a reactionary, to note that from a young age Hegel is an advocate of political reform and change and not a defender of the status quo.

By the 1790s, while reading the works of F. H. Jacobi, Hegel became enthralled with the "pantheism controversy" surrounding Jacobi's *Uber die Spinoza in Briefen an Herrn Moses Mendelssohn.*[149] It challenged the Enlightenment faith in natural religion and morality. Jacobi argues that reason, if honest and consistent, undermines morality and religion. His attack on reason rests in his identification of rationalism with a complete scientific naturalism, and more specifically with the mechanistic paradigm of explanation. Jacobi sees Spinoza as the paragon of this new scientific naturalism, because Spinoza banishes first causes and holds that everything in nature happens according to mechanical laws.[150] Spinoza also rejects the dualism of the soul and body in favor of the view that soul and body are only aspects of the same underlying substance. The charge of Spinozism was a serious one in Germany at that time, since it bordered on religious heresy. Many Germans, including Jacobi, felt Spinoza's denial of a personal God undermined Christianity and moved toward atheism. Schelling was impressed by this debate, and a few years later confided to Hegel that he had become a Spinozist.[151] In addition to their heretical political ideas, clearly Hegel and his friends were beginning to entertain religious thoughts quite different from those taught at the seminary. (Conservatives eventually charge that Hegel's conception of *Geist* is pantheism.) Jacobi's challenge leaves the Enlightenment with a dilemma: either a rational atheism or an irrational leap of faith. Although he is initially sympathetic to Jacobi's challenge, Hegel ultimately tries to find a middle path between the two.

For the young Hegel, who was under the influence of Rousseau, it was unreasonable to think that the idea of Enlightenment reason is the sole motivator of human action. Moreover, he identifies a genuine *Volksreligion* with the religion of ancient Greece.[152] While Christianity trains people to be citizens of heaven, Hegel believes that Greek religion teaches and honors citizenship. From his reading of Herder, Hegel picks up the idea that the modern fragmentation of society makes modern life incapable of forming any conception of a common interest. From Herder, he learns also that reason has to be supplemented by emotion and argumentation by enthusiasm. At that time, Hegel holds that "subjective religion" is a means for overcoming this fragmentation. While Hegel's solution is far from being fully developed, this illustrates that Hegel's interest in reconciling fragmentation of modern life goes back to his days as a theology student.

Hegel studied at the theological seminary from 1788 to 1793. A two-year study of philosophy at Tübingen led to the *pro magistro* disputation, or master's degree. "This was followed by a three-year course in theology, terminating with the *Dissertation pro candidatura examinis consitorialis.*"[153] After passing his examinations, Hegel returned to Stuttgart in 1793. In the fall of that year, he took up a post as a private tutor with a patrician family of Berne, Switzerland, where he felt somewhat cut off and isolated. It was quite customary for young scholars without money or patronage to become private tutors [*Hofmeister*] before planning their doctoral *habilitation*, and many famous university professors, such as Kant and Fichte, spent their first post-graduate years in this capacity. The position of private tutor was a good way for a young man to make contacts, be introduced into society, and have time for his own scholarly work. Specifically, Hegel worked for Carl Friedrich von Steiger as a tutor for his son and two daughters. During this period Hegel continued his reading and philosophical pursuits. He had access to an excellent library of philosophical, historical, and political works. He spent many hours reading Grotius, Hobbes, Hume, Leibniz, Locke, Machiavelli, Montesquieu, Shaftsbury, Spinoza, and Voltaire.[154] In Hegel's mind, the new revolutionary order would bring about a state of affairs in which men of learning, taste, and cultivation, would be running things instead of the undereducated, pompous, corrupt aristocracy represented by families such as the von Steigers.[155] During the Berne years, Hegel also studied the Scottish political economists, which aided the development of his conception of civil society.[156]

While at Berne, he also wrote a book-length manuscript, "The Positivity of the Christian Religion," which was published after his death.[157] In it, Hegel tries to synthesize the basic influences on his thought at the time, such as bringing Gibbon's account of the decline of the Roman Empire and the role of Christianity played in it to bear on Kant's reconstruction of Christian religion as the religion of morality. Hegel shows how these two accounts can be reconciled in an examination of Christianity. Positivity in religion relies on the dictates of authority rather than the dictates of reason. Hegel argues that Jesus never intended to institute a positive religion. Hegel draws a contrast between Jesus, who is portrayed as an ethical-religious Kantian, who only wanted people to be free and to develop their own powers to impose moral laws on themselves, and the founders of Christianity, the disciples and early church fathers, who are portrayed as corrupting Jesus' teachings and setting up Christianity as a positive religion.[158] Jesus' own teachings are not "positive" and are not meant to substitute a new authoritarian system for the old authoritarian system. For Hegel, Christianity must first motivate people to be free, which is something that "positive" Christianity cannot do. Furthermore, he fuses Kant's idea of a religion of morality with his own critique of the fragmentation of modern life. In this work, he also discusses justice and rights and makes his first attempt to reconcile individuals with the community.[159] He argues that the state has the duty to protect political rights, such as freedom of speech and conscience and property.

In early 1797, Hegel accepted a similar position in Frankfurt in the Johann Gogel household, which was secured by Hölderlin. On his way, Hegel stopped off in Stuttgart to visit his family. Frankfurt provided a rich literary library, greater leisure, and more contact with friends. Hegel wrote more essays on religion, not for publication but to clarify his thoughts.[160] While in Berne Hegel criticizes religion from the standpoint of the Enlightenment, in Frankfurt he defends religion against such criticism. Under Hölderlin's influence, Hegel worked on a completely new manuscript on Christianity—"The Spirit of Christianity and Its Fate." This work is animated by the notion that the fate of a people cannot be understood as the result of contingent factors; rather, it is the logical outcome of principles inherent in their common life.[161] Departing from his early manuscript, Hegel argues that Kant's conception of the categorical imperative was a form of "self-coercion," which is only another expression of the alienation of people from nature and each other. Although the Kantian conception of morality as autonomous legislation is an advance over Judaism, it still does not overcome domination in general. In the Kantian conception of virtue, "the universal becomes the master and the particular to the mastered."[162] The spirit of Christianity was understood as love, which transcends both the allegedly slavish obedience of the Judaism and Kant's rigid moralism. Hegel also notes that people are individually free when they act according to the principles that follow from the free spirit of the people as whole, not as isolated individuals.[163] Hence, with this emphasis on the community as a whole, he is already reacting against the excessive individualism of liberalism.

According to Hegel, Christianity developed from Catholicism through Protestantism, to philosophy, from the witnessing of revelation to ascertainment and intellectual knowledge; the mediation of philosophy will bring about a higher form of religion through the "sublation" and reconciliation of opposites.[164] Although this early work does not present the dialectical method in detail, Hegel is beginning to think in terms of dialectics and historical development, and he sees a union, reconciliation, and sublimation as their ultimate destiny. In "The Spirit of Christianity and Its Fate," Hegel first formulates his idea of *Geist*, his conception of dialectic, theme of reconciliation, and organic conception of the world. Religious practices can instill life and sense of community into its members. Furthermore, even in his early theological writings, he deals extensively with the problems of political philosophy. For instance, on one hand, he wants to call for some way of overcoming the fragmentation of modern life and establishing some form of community without at the same time violating individual liberty of conscience; on the other, he wants to praise the reliance on individual insight and understanding taught by Socrates without letting such self-reliant individuals go on to fragment themselves from the social whole and from each other.[165] He wrote a manuscript on the need for political reform in Württemberg.[166] Hegel also devotes himself to a thorough investigation of Kant's moral and legal philosophy.

When his father died in 1799 Hegel received a modest inheritance, to which he added his savings. This enabled him to give up tutoring and prepare for an academic career; so in 1801, he moved to Jena, in Weimar, where he joined his friend, Schelling, who was at the University of Jena. Schelling invited Hegel to come directly to Jena and live at his place for the time being. The years in Jena allowed Hegel to work out the basis of his own philosophical system and became known to the philosophical world through some of his minor publications. Over a few months, Hegel wrote his first philosophical work: *Difference Between Fichte's and Schelling's Systems of Philosophy*.[167] It furnished a critique of Kant, Fichte, and Jacobi. His early work sided with Schelling in every case of difference. However, in trying to become a systematic philosopher, Hegel defends Schelling in his own way. The result is a highly original Hegelian text that nonetheless offers itself to the public as a piece of Schellingian philosophy.[168] Specifically, there are already important differences between Hegel's use of the "absolute" and that of Schelling. In the *Difference*, Hegel says that Schelling's philosophy is the only one that constructs a sketch of a harmonious whole. Schelling's philosophy aims to overcome the basic conceptual dichotomies and antinomies that evolved in modern metaphysics from Descartes to Kant and bring them into a systematic unity. During this period, Hegel begins to see the history of philosophy as a progression of increasingly developed positions and the possibility of the ultimate culmination and synthesis.[169]

At the end of the summer, Hegel submitted a dissertation—*De Orbitis Planetarum*—to the faculty and passed the qualifying examination. He then received his *venia legendi*, the right to lecture at a German university. Hegel became a *Privatdozent*, an unsalaried lecturer, at the University of Jena. Throughout the Jena years, he struggles to formulate his own system of philosophy, and his lectures are preliminary accounts of part of his system. These lectures include logic and metaphysics, the philosophy of nature, and the philosophy of *Geist*. His lecturers on the history of philosophy were extraordinary and demonstrated that from the very first, he included the historical development of philosophical consciousness as a decisive factor in his nascent system.[170] Due to increasing philosophical differences, the friendship between Hegel and Schelling cooled down. In 1803, Schelling accepted an offer from the new university at Würzburg and left Jena. And, in 1805, Hegel became an associate professor and was granted an annual salary.

After Schelling's departure, Hegel begins to criticize Schelling's view more openly and to rethink his own metaphysics. During these critical years, Hegel worked out his central concept of *Geist*, or Absolute Spirit. *Geist* does not just appear but germinates slowly over the years, beginning with his efforts to grapple with the problems of religion.[171]

Although Hegel began work on "The German Constitution" in 1798, he did not finish the manuscript until 1802. In it, he argues that Germany is not a state in the true sense. For Hegel, a state is more than an authority or a body possessing a monopoly of force. Instead, it is only a state when it has united its citizens in a common project with which they can freely identify.[172] In developing this commentary on contemporary German life, Hegel is dealing with issues that motivated his early efforts at outlining the conditions for modern religion by asking what might provide the basis for moral, spiritual, and social reform. Specifically, he is interested in the failures of the Holy Roman Empire in light of the challenges posed by the French Revolution. While German principalities are individual and fragmented, the French rallied the people by means of the Revolution to the cause of the nation of France. To realize the potential open to Germany, Hegel argues that *Geist* must be understood—"the original, untamed character of the German nation determined the iron necessity of its fate."[173] Even at this early stage, Hegel maintains that *Geist* has to do with freedom. His understanding of feudal representation leads him to conclude that the system of original German freedom develops into the system of representation, which in turn becomes the system of all modern European states:

> Most of the above states were founded by Germanic peoples, and their constitutions have developed out of the spirit of these peoples. Among the Germanic peoples, reliance was originally placed on the arm of every free man, and his will was involved in the nation's deeds. . . . This system of representation is the system of all modern European states.[174]

Hegel says that the universal shape of the world spirit [*Weltgeist*] was born from this. That is, Germanic freedom along with the principle of representation mark an epoch in world history. Ironically, although Germany gives the idea of modern representation to the rest of the world, it is itself incapable of realizing that ideal.[175] Hegel will be concerned with this question for the rest of his life, as will be seen in the later writings.

During this period, Hegel began to prepare his first major work, the *Phenomenology of Spirit*. His inheritance was exhausted and he badly needed money. He accepted a cash advance from a publisher that contained heavy penalty clauses if he failed to post the manuscript by October 13, 1806, which turned out to be the day the French occupied Jena after their victory over the Prussians. Hegel had to rush the final sections of the book in order to meet the deadline and then had to send off the only copy of the manuscript amidst the confusion. Fortunately for Hegel, the manuscript traveled undisturbed and the work was published in early 1807. Its criticisms of Schelling closed the final door on their friendship. Life in Jena was disrupted by French occupation and the University was closed. While at Jena, he fathered an illegitimate son, Ludwig, with the wife of his landlord. The *Phenomenology of Spirit* is his first attempt to lay out the basis for his entire system of philosophy, and Hegel claims that it serves as an introduction to systematic philosophy. Equally important, it is Hegel's first work to present the dialectic directly. It is also his first try at developing a method for reconciling the apparently irreconcilable.[176] He starts with the most elementary notion of consciousness and shows that it cannot stand up to self-critique and must thus give way to another higher one. This higher notion of consciousness is also shown to be contradictory and passes to another. The process is repeated until we come to a true understanding of consciousness as self-knowing *Geist*, which represents absolute knowledge, grounded in the concrete questions of life. The *Phenomenology* further demonstrates that being free is not simply expressing oneself in isolation, but instead is to stand in a complex, mediated relationship to other self-conscious entities.[177] Its publication marks the beginning of Hegel's emergence as a distinctive figure within the post-Kantian movement.

Hegel is forced to accept an offer from a friend to work as an editor of a newspaper, the *Bamberger Zeitung*, and he moves to Bamberg in March of 1807. The newspaper is pro-Napoleonic in its outlook, which suits Hegel, given his sympathies for the French cause. Since Germany is without *Geist*, the old institutions no longer sustain themselves and have to give way to new, modern institutions. During this period, he often complains about being under the "newspaper yoke," feeling like a galley-slave, and chafing under Bavarian censorship.[178] Nevertheless, his time in Bamberg helps form his political ideas. His political views are confirmed by his journalist observations: Without an anchoring in social practice, in the self-identities of the people in the reformed communities, the reforms could not have authority; they would only appear, indeed would only be, the imposition of one group's preferences and ideals on another.[179] Without a local *Sittlichkeit* to serve as a collective identity, the reformers could only be masters. Nonetheless, despite the nice salary and social status, newspaper life was not what Hegel wanted for himself.

In November of 1808, Hegel accepts a position as *Rector* [headmaster] of a *Gymnasium* [an academic high school] at Nuremberg and teaches philosophy there for nine years. Niethammer—a friend of Hegel and the commissioner of education in Bavaria—in effect makes Hegel his agent in Nuremberg; he is supposed to make sure that the educational reforms succeeded.[180] Accepting this position is a better stepping stone to a university appointment than being a newspaper editor. By the end of 1810, he is doing well in the community and his efforts of reform at the *Gymnasium* are met with approval. Hegel manages to put the *Gymnasium* on a successful footing. His domestic life settles down in Nuremberg. In 1811, Hegel, at the age of forty-one, marries Marie von Tucher, the twenty year-old daughter of an old Nuremberg family, and despite the difference in age, the marriage appears to have been a happy one. Their first child died soon after birth. They have two sons, Karl and Immanuel, and after the death of the mother of Hegel's illegitimate son, Ludwig is taken into the household.

During these years, he completes and publishes the *Science of Logic*, which appears in three volumes in 1812, 1813, and 1816. This project began as reworking of the structures of Kant's three *Critiques*.[181] Although making judgments requires one to distinguish between subject and object, Hegel holds that the division should not be primary. To do so is to fall into the mistaken path the leads to the gulf between empiricism and rationalism that haunts modern philosophy. His argument is that the simple act of thinking involves trying to articulate the sense of the unity of thought and being.[182] In making judgments, one literally articulates the original unity of experience and the world. With the *Science of Logic*, Hegel finds a structure that allows him to develop his thoughts on the possibilities for modern life in the investigation of nature, social life, art, religion, philosophy, and history. Furthermore, it establishes Hegel's position as the non-Schellingian successor of the post-Kant era. Even though it is strikingly un-Schellingian in character, the German public still sees it as a Schillingian work.[183]

Hegel's works were gaining wider appreciation, and in 1816, he was offered a position as Professor of Philosophy at the University of Heidelberg. He delivered his inaugural lecture, which discussed the *Weltgeist*, on October 28, 1816. During this time, Hegel often is involved with political controversies and reform movements. He lectures on aesthetics, anthropology, psychology, political philosophy, and the history of philosophy. His lectures on political philosophy become the basis for his later *Philosophy of Right*. While at Heidelberg, he publishes his *Encyclopedia of the Philosophical Sciences* in 1817, which consists of three volumes: the *Logic*, the *Philosophy of Nature*, and the *Philosophy of Mind*. By that time his professional reputation is so high that he is asked by Karl Altenstein, the Prussian Minister of Education, to take up the prestigious chair of philosophy at the University of Berlin, which has been vacant since the death of Fichte. Altenstein knew that Hegel was sympathetic to the Prussian reform. Due to the reforms of von Stein and von Hardenberg, the Prussian educational system had become the intellectual center of all the German states.[184] Hegel gave his inaugural speech on October 22, 1818, which discusses the relationship between *Geist* and Germany.[185] He admires the way Germany has awakened to historical awareness as well as cognizance of her cultural mission and her task of teaching the people national consciousness. *Geist*, and thus philosophy, has taken flight to the Germans. However, shortly after Hegel's arrival, the reform movement suffers a serious setback. In 1819, fearing radical conspiracies, the government of Friedrich Wilhelm III revokes its plan to establish a new constitution and endorses the repressive Karlsbad Decrees, which introduces censorship of all publications with political content. It also created a special commission to investigate and prosecute university faculty. Suspected of subversive activity, some of Hegel's students are banished and imprisoned, and Hegel himself is placed under police surveillance for some time.[186]

Hegel teaches at the University of Berlin from 1818 until his death on November 14, 1831, from cholera. He rapidly becomes a major figure in German philosophy, and his influence spreads to other fields, such as law, political thought, theology, history, and aesthetics. For example, in 1821, he begins to lecture in natural law, political science, and the philosophy of law. While in Berlin, he writes his last published book, the *Philosophy of Right*, in 1821. In its preface, Hegel asserts that philosophy grasps its current era in thought.[187] Philosophy's vocation, in other words, is not to make reality, but rather to cognize prevalent and present-day reality. This *Philosophy of Right* contains his mature writings on modern *Sittlichkeit* and *Rechtsstaat*. Moral individuals exercising their rights require a proper location, which includes family, civil society, and the constitutional state. Although the *Philosophy of Right* was criticized both during and after Hegel's lifetime as being an apology for Prussian absolutism, it is in fact an attempt by Hegel to articulate the rational form of the kind of reformed, modern European state and society that people like von Stein had tried to establish in Prussia, a fact that most of his friends and students understood.[188] Simply put, the core idea of the book is that what counts as "right" in general is what is necessary for the realization of freedom. Furthermore, the constitutional protection of basic rights must be insured if people are to identify with the collective aim of such a political society. In short, he reconciles the individual within the context of a community, which in contemporary language means trying to steer between the extremes of liberalism and communitarianism.

Hegel's lectures on history, aesthetics, the philosophy of religion, and the history of philosophy were published posthumously, since they contain valuable philosophical contributions.[189] World history is fundamentally about the development of the "idea" of freedom. "Thus it is with the Spirit of a people; it is a Spirit having strictly defined characteristics, which erects itself into an objective world, that exists and persists in a particular religious form of worship, customs, constitution, and political laws—in the whole complex of its institutions—in the events and transactions that make up its history."[190] The history of actual existing states is the history of humanity in its social and political existence, not a providential narrative written by God.

Hegel's last written piece is his essay *On the English Reform Bill*.[191] It attacks the weakness of the royalist principle against Parliament, the peculiarity of English civil law, and the cruel treatment of Ireland. Equally important, his commenting on the English Reform Bill allows Hegel to obliquely criticize the current proposals for reform in Prussian. By pointing out the shortcomings in the English solutions, he could indirectly point out similar problems in Prussian proposals, which ran the danger of repeating many of the same errors.[192] The forces of modernization, seen most clearly in England, atomize the populace, and since each citizen understands himself in the modern way as a free, self-ruling agent, each necessarily feels that freedom can only be limited by public institutions rather than being underwritten by them. True freedom can only be possible if some common projects are articulated and developed into a set of properly mediating, concrete institutions of a modern civil society and a constitutional state. The English Reform Bill, according to Hegel, threatened to reform the English constitution by creating an institutional setup that did not counteract the atomizing tendencies of modern life but instead underwrote and promoted them.[193] In 1829, Hegel is elected Rector of the University of Berlin, but he dies suddenly and unexpectedly within two years. Hegel is buried next to Fichte, who had earlier held the chair of philosophy at Berlin.

## FREEDOM AND THE COMMUNITY

All the events of the past are leading up to the goal of freedom. The dialectical process is constantly moving toward a greater harmony between the objective and the subjective. This realization, for Hegel, has to occur within the limits of a community. Human beings are truly free only when they are recognized as such by others. Subjectivity requires intersubjectivity. The truly human person, radically different from an animal, always searches for recognition and can therefore be truly human only by living in society.[194] In this sense, the freest man is the one who most completely fulfills one's social obligation, or duty to one's community. Thus, it seems inevitable that Hegel should discover the synthesis of the individual's freedom and *Geist* in the concrete institutions of the state. As illustrated in the section above, historical consciousness revolves around the political sphere because in this sphere a community is created that is conscious of its continuity over time and requires and produces an enduring record of its actions. Hegel believes that history as history of states is the guiding, central thread around which any comprehensive historical account must be organized.[195]

Since Medieval times, traditional political philosophy has not recognized the historical change as fundamental to a discussion of the normative order. Hegel attempts to answer the problem of historicity by relating political philosophy to history and making his understanding of history into a vantage point from which problems of political philosophy could be viewed. It is in this sense that Hegel can be seen as the first major political philosopher of modern society: The break in historical continuity ushered in by the historical developments leading to the French Revolution made the traditional paradigms of classical political philosophy totally unresponsive to the new needs.[196] Thus, while political philosophy prior to Hegel was preoccupied with questions of legitimacy, he introduces the dimension of change and historicity that has become central to political thought.

Although *The Philosophy of History* gives a glimmering of what Hegel takes freedom to be, one must turn to the *Philosophy of Right* for the further illumination of his more explicit comments on freedom. This work expresses Hegel's philosophical ideas about ethics, jurisprudence, society, and the state, and since freedom is always central to his concerns, this book contains his most detailed discussion of freedom in the social and political sphere. In most general terms, the Hegelian concept of right [*Recht*] concerns free will and its realization, which requires a transition to practice. Philosophy is concerned with reason in a concrete form, and no one—not even a philosopher—can jump over his or her own historical moment. All knowledge, even philosophical knowledge, is perspectival. For Hegel, human beings can only know on the basis of the world in which they live.

The concept of the state is at the heart of Hegel's political philosophy. Although in "The German Constitution" he defines the state as merely a union of men for communal self-defense, it is already clear that even at this early stage in his thinking he is quite clear that such a political union is not a contract of previously independent individuals motivated by fear or enlightened self-interest.[197] The state is the result of an evolution of generations of individuals forming a historical community:

> The organization of that body known as the German constitution took shape in [the context of] a life quite different from that which later invested it and does so now. The justice and power, the wisdom and valor of times gone by it, the honor and blood, the well-being and misfortune of long-deceased generations and of the manners and relationships which perished with them, are [all] expressed in the forms of this body.[198]

Thus, a state is the product of the peoples' communal life, developed gradually in response to changing circumstances, and bearing the stamp of past crises. The formation of the state is not an act of will by human beings at any one point of time, whether driven by fear or rational self-interest. A nation, in the course of history, develops and perfects a machinery for common defense and for the regulation of its internal affairs. Thus, Hegel clearly does not support a social contract theory on the origin of the state.[199]

Hegel becomes deeply dissatisfied with the individualistic conceptions of natural law and morality of his predecessors who are unable to do justice to important aspects of social and political life. He turns to the philosophy of Plato and Aristotle. The insight that he gains from the analysis of ancient Greek philosophy, history, and literature is that human beings form genuine communities only when they share the same conception of the good and identify themselves wholeheartedly with the basic moral ideas of their country or culture. These shared and universally accepted conceptions and values, which are alive and operative in actions and attitudes of community members, are incapsulated in the customs, laws, and institutions. Hegel calls this *Sittlichkeit*, which is usually translated as "ethical life" or "social ethics."[200] Hence, a people, or nation, form a genuine community insofar as their interrelations are animated and pervaded by *Sittlichkeit*.

In Hegel's more mature writings, *Sittlichkeit* no longer refers paradigmatically to a lost Greek ideal, but rather means a modern ethical life, which is characterized by the uniquely modern institutions of civil society. His ethical theory can be seen as an attempt to reconcile traditional Aristotelian ethical theory with the Kantian and Fichtean emphasis on free selfhood. From Aristotle, Hegel draws the idea that ethics must be founded on a conception of the human good, regarded as the actualization of the human essence; but from Kant, he has learned the lesson that this good is not to be identified with human happiness, or with any other good answering to what is merely given in human nature.[201] Following Fichte, Hegel views the human self as free in the radical sense that its identity and the content of its self-realization are the result of its own activity. Hegel's dialectic of history builds toward the major crux of his political philosophy, the reconciliation of the individual with the community. His *Philosophy of Right* is an attempt to present modern society as an ethical life in which distinctively modern self-conceptions are made concrete and actualized. The following chapter examines Hegel's conception of *Sittlichkeit* and assesses its place in Hegel's system.

# NOTES

1. Milan Kundera, *The Unbearable Lightness of Being*, trans. M. Heim (New York: HarperPerennial, 1984), 5.

2. Georg W. F. Hegel, *The Philosophy of History*, trans. J. Sibree (Buffalo, N.Y.: Prometheus Books, 1991), 8–9.

3. Hegel, *The Philosophy of History*, 36.

4. Hegel, *The Philosophy of History*, 53.

5. Joseph McCarney, *Hegel on History* (New York: Routledge, 2000), 12.

6. Hegel, *The Philosophy of History*, 73.

7. Hegel, *The Philosophy of History*, 10.

8. Hegel, *The Philosophy of History*, 16.

9. Georg W. F. Hegel, *Logic*, trans. William Wallace (Oxford: Oxford University Press, 1975), 261.

10. Georg W. F. Hegel, *Hegel's Aesthetics: Lectures on Fine Arts, Volume 1*, trans. T.M. Knox (Oxford: Oxford University, 1975), 98.

11. Richard Dien Winfield, *Overcoming Foundations: Studies in Systematic Philosophy* (New York: Columbia University Press, 1989), 245.

12. Hegel, *The Philosophy of History*, 13.

13. Richard Dien Winfield, *Freedom and Modernity* (Albany: State University of New York Press, 1991), 99.

14. Hegel, *The Philosophy of History*, 14.

15. Hegel, *The Philosophy of History*, 32–33. He also discusses the cunning of reason in Hegel, *Logic*, 272.

16. Hegel, *The Philosophy of History*, 29. Alexander the Great, Julius Caesar, and Napoleon are examples of world-historical individuals. Although their actions spring from personal ambition, their behavior still coincides with the universal interest. However, for Hegel, these historical individuals are not the actual subjects of history. They are merely executors of its will, or agents of *Geist*.

17. Georg W. F. Hegel, *Lectures on the History of Philosophy: Greek Philosophy to Plato, Volume 1*, trans. E. S. Haldane (Lincoln: University of Nebraska Press, 1995), 33–34.

18. Georg W. F. Hegel, *Philosophy of Right*, trans. T. M. Knox (Oxford: Oxford University Press, 1975), 10.

19. Michael Forster, "Hegel's Dialectic Method," in *The Cambridge Companion to Hegel*, ed. Frederick Beiser (Cambridge: Cambridge University Press, 1993), 138.

20. Georg W. F. Hegel, *Philosophy of Nature*, trans. A. V. Miller (Oxford: Oxford University Press, 1975), 11.

21. See Hans-Georg Gadamer, *Hegel's Dialectic: Five Hermeneutical Studies* (New Haven, Conn.: Yale University Press, 1976), 36, where he asserts that when describing the phenomenon of consciousness in his phenomenology of spirit, Hegel assumes from the start that in which knowing will fulfill itself, that in which alone the concurrence of certainty and truth can be given, cannot merely be consciousness of the objective world which becomes conscious of itself. Rather it must transcend the ontological status of individual subjectivity. It must be spirit.

22. Charles Taylor, *Hegel* (Cambridge: Cambridge University Press, 1975), 104.

23. Hegel, *Philosophy of Nature*, 21.

24. Jean Hyppolite, *Genesis and Structure of Hegel's Phenomenology of Spirit*, trans. Samuel Cherniak and John Heckman (Evanston, Ill.: Northwestern University Press, 1974), 12.

25. Allen Wood, *Hegel's Ethical Thought* (New York: Cambridge University Press, 1999), 2.

26. See Gadamer, *Hegel's Dialectic*, for an excellent account of the dialectic of motion, which dominates Plato's and Aristotle's philosophy, and its coinciding with that of Hegel. Gadamer notes that Hegel claims to have vindicated Plato's way of justifying belief, the dialectical scrutinizing of all assumption, with his own dialectical method. He also argues that Hegel "worked out his own dialectical method by extending the dialectic of the Ancients and transforming it into a sublimation of contradiction into ever higher syntheses" ( 31).

27. Hegel, *The Philosophy of History*, 17.

28. Wood, *Hegel's Ethical Thought*, 19.

29. Hegel, *The Philosophy of History*, 19.

30. Winfield, *Freedom and Modernity*, 110.

31. Alan Patten, *Hegel's Idea of Freedom* (New York: Oxford University Press, 1999), 22.

32. Hegel, *The Philosophy of History*, 53.

33. Georg W. F. Hegel, *Reason in History*, trans. Robert Hartman (Indianapolis, Ind.: Bobbs-Merrill, 1953), 20–25.

34. Hegel, *The Philosophy of History*, 39.

35. Georg W. F. Hegel, "Introduction to the History of Philosophy," in Quentin Lauer, *Hegel's Idea of Philosophy* (New York: Fordham University Press, 1983), 124.

36. Hegel, *The Philosophy of History*, 48.

37. Hegel, *The Philosophy of History*, 63–64.

38. Hegel, *The Philosophy of History*, 47.

39. Hegel, *The Philosophy of History*, 18. "The principle of *Development* involves also the existence of a latent germ of being—a capacity or potentiality striving to realize itself. This formal conception finds actual existence in Spirit; which has the History of the World for its theatre, its possession, and the sphere of realization. . . . So Spirit is only that which it attains by its own efforts; it makes itself *actually* what it always was *potentially*" (54–55).

40. Hegel, *The Philosophy of History*, 18–19.

41. Hegel, *The Philosophy of History*, 56.

42. Hegel, *The Philosophy of History*, 105. See also McCarney, *Hegel on History*, 142. McCarney says that the paucity and poverty of Hegel's anthropological sources with regard to Africa should be noted. For the most part, Hegel had to rely on the tales of travelers, officials, and missionaries eager to highlight the primitive and exotic. It was to be nearly a century before the results of the scientific study of African traditional societies and, hence, a proper appreciation of their cultural achievements, were to be widely available to Europeans.

43. Hegel, *The Philosophy of History*, 105.

44. Hegel, *The Philosophy of History*, 105.

45. Hegel, *The Philosophy of History*, 116.

46. Hegel, *The Philosophy of History*, 120.

47. Hegel, *The Philosophy of History*, 130–131.

48. Hegel, *The Philosophy of History*, 123.

49. Hegel, *The Philosophy of History*, 138.

50. Hegel, *The Philosophy of History*, 111.

51. Hegel, *The Philosophy of History*, 144.

52. Hegel, *The Philosophy of History*, 160–161.

53. Hegel, *The Philosophy of History*, 163.

54. Hegel, *Lectures on the History of Philosophy, Volume 1*, 96.

55. Hegel, *Lectures on the History of Philosophy, Volume 1*, 118.

56. See Hegel, *The Philosophy of History*, 162.

57. Hegel, *The Philosophy of History*, 173–174. See also Kojève, *Introduction to the Reading of Hegel*, 232, where he says that "for history to exist, there must be not only a given reality, but also a negation of that reality and at the same time a preservation of what has been negated. For only then is evolution creative; only then do a true continuity and a real progress exist in it."

58. Hegel, *The Philosophy of History*, 173.

59. Hegel, *The Philosophy of History*, 175.

60. Hegel, *The Philosophy of History*, 174.

61. Hegel, *Lectures on the History of Philosophy, Volume 1*, 100.

62. Hegel, *The Philosophy of History*, 225–226, and Hegel, *Lectures on the History of Philosophy, Volume 1*, 149–157.

63. Hegel, *The Philosophy of History*, 238.

64. Hegel, *The Philosophy of History*, 250.

65. Hegel, *Lectures on the History of Philosophy: Volume 1*, 153.

66. Hegel, *The Philosophy of History*, 254–255.

67. Hegel, *The Philosophy of History*, 253.

68. Hegel, *The Philosophy of History*, 252.

69. Hegel, *The Philosophy of History*, 253.

70. Hegel, *Lectures on the History of Philosophy, Volume 1*, 423.

71. Shlomo Avineri, *Hegel's Theory of the Modern State* (Cambridge: Cambridge University Press, 1972), 226.

72. Hegel, *The Philosophy of History*, 255.

73. Hegel, *Lectures on the History of Philosophy, Volume 1*, 384.

74. Hegel, *The Philosophy of History*, 270.

75. Hegel, *Lectures on the History of Philosophy, Volume 1*, 406.

76. Hegel, *Lectures on the History of Philosophy, Volume 1*, 426.

77. Georg W. F. Hegel, *Lectures on the History of Philosophy: Plato and the Platonists, Volume 2*, trans. E. S. Haldane (Lincoln: University of Nebraska Press, 1995), 91.

78. Hegel, *The Philosophy of History*, 278–279.

79. Hegel, *The Philosophy of History*, 284.

80. Hegel, *The Philosophy of History*, 279.

81. Hegel, *The Philosophy of History*, 317.

82. Hegel, *The Philosophy of History*, 289.

83. Hegel, *The Philosophy of History*, 289.

84. Hegel, *Lectures on the History of Philosophy, Volume 2*, 235. "In a wave of adversity which came across the Roman world, everything beautiful and noble in

spiritual individuality was rudely swept away. In this condition of disunion in the world, when man is driven within his inmost self, he has to seek the unity and satisfaction, no longer to be found in the world, in an abstract way."

85. Hegel, *The Philosophy of History*, 317. See also, Avineri, *Hegel's Theory of the Modern State*, 227. This universal entity engulfs individuals and they disappear in it—persons, peoples, all particular and distinct units. This is the abstraction of power, and with the growth of the empire the struggle for power within Rome itself becomes worse, since nothing could satiate the infinite drive for more and more power.

86. Hegel, *The Philosophy of History*, 317–318.

87. Hegel, *Phenomenology of Spirit*, 122.

88. Hegel, *Lectures on the History of Philosophy, Volume 2*, 276.

89. Hegel, *The Philosophy of History*, 319.

90. Hegel, *The Philosophy of History*, 320.

91. Hegel, *The Philosophy of History*, 324.

92. Hyppolite, *Genesis and Structure of Hegel's Phenomenology of Spirit*, 201.

93. Hegel, *The Philosophy of History*, 328.

94. Hegel, *The Philosophy of History*, 328.

95. Hegel, *The Philosophy of History*, 333.

96. Hegel, *The Philosophy of History*, 335.

97. Georg W. F. Hegel, *Lectures on the History of Philosophy: Medieval and Modern Philosophy, Volume 3*, trans. E. S. Haldane and Frances Simson (Lincoln: University of Nebraska Press, 1995), 46. "Hence in the Roman as in the Byzantine world, Christianity has triumphed as a Church; but neither of these worlds was capable of effectuating the new religion in itself and of bringing forth a new world from this principle."

98. Hegel, *The Philosophy of History*, 338–339.

99. Hegel, *The Philosophy of History*, 339.

100. Hegel, *Lectures on the History of Philosophy, Volume 3*, 50.

101. Hegel, *The Philosophy of History*, 333. For Hegel, man is truly at home in a super-sensuous world gained only by a rupture with mere natural existence. This is religious self-consciousness.

102. Hegel, *The Philosophy of History*, 335.

103. Hegel, *The Philosophy of History*, 341.

104. See Georg F. W. Hegel, "The German Constitution," in *Political Writings*, ed. Laurence Dickey and H. B. Nisbet (Cambridge: Cambridge University Press, 1999), 62–63.

105. Hegel, *The Philosophy of History*, 380.

106. Hegel, *The Philosophy of History*, 379.

107. Hegel, *The Philosophy of History*, 394.

108. Hegel, *The Philosophy of History*, 411.

109. Hegel, *The Philosophy of History*, 412.

110. Hegel, *The Philosophy of History*, 414.

111. Hegel, *The Philosophy of History*, 414.

112. Hegel, *The Philosophy of History*, 415–416.

113. Hegel, *Lectures on the History of Philosophy, Volume 3*, 147.

114. Hegel, *The Philosophy of History*, 417

115. Hegel, *The Philosophy of History*, 416–417.

116. Hegel, *The Philosophy of History*, 422–423.

117. Hegel, *The Philosophy of History*, 423–427.

118. Hegel, *Lectures on the History of Philosophy, Volume 3*, 158.

119. Hegel, *The Philosophy of History*, 439.

120. Taylor, *Hegel*, 400. Man is reason, and he is as such one with the principle of things; so he will find reason in the external world if he only looks for it.

121. Hegel, *The Philosophy of History*, 439.

122. Hegel, *Lectures on the History of Philosophy, Volume 3*, 159.

123. Hegel, *The Philosophy of History*, 441.

124. Hegel, *The Philosophy of History*, 443.

125. Taylor, *Hegel*, 401. The only way that the Enlightenment can accommodate *Geist* is by emptying it of all content. Since God can no longer be an active subject, there is only room for a law-governed nature. God thus must be reduced to the impersonal supreme being of Deism.

126. Hegel, *The Philosophy of History*, 445.

127. Winfield, *Freedom and Modernity*, 111.

128. Domenico Losurdo, *Hegel and the Freedom of Moderns*, trans. Marella and Jon Morris (Durham, N.C.: Duke University Press, 2004), 106.

129. Hegel, *The Philosophy of History*, 446.

130. Jürgen Habermas, *Theory and Practice*, trans. John Viertel (Boston: Beacon Press, 1973), 122.

131. Hegel, *The Philosophy of History*, 447.

132. Hegel, *The Philosophy of History*, 450.

133. Hegel, *The Philosophy of History*, 452.

134. Hegel, *The Philosophy of History*, 452.

135. Hegel, *The Philosophy of History*, 455–456.

136. Habermas, *Theory and Practice*, 123. Robespierre is ensnared in the contradiction of the absolute freedom entertained by a consciousness which remains merely subjective. Hegel sees Jacobin Terror as a negation of abstract freedom exaggerated to the point of absolute freedom.

137. Hegel, *The Philosophy of History*, 456.

138. Hegel, *The Philosophy of History*, 456.

139. Kojève, *Introduction to the Reading of Hegel*, 220.

140. Frederick Beiser, *Hegel* (New York: Routledge, 2005), 8.

141. Franz Wiedmann, *Hegel: An Illustrated Biography*, trans. Joachim Neugroschel (New York: Pegasus, 1968), 14.

142. Terry Pinkard, *Hegel: A Biography* (Cambridge: Cambridge University Press, 2000), 4.

143. Pickard, *Hegel*, 8.

144. Wiedmann, *Hegel*, 15.

145. Pinkard, *Hegel*, 21.

146. Wiedmann, *Hegel*, 19.

147. Pinkard, *Hegel*, 23.

148. Pinkard, *Hegel*, 26.

149. Pinkard, *Hegel*, 30.

150. Beiser, *Hegel*, 26.

151. "Schelling's Reply to Hegel, February 2, 1794," in Georg W. F. Hegel, *Hegel: The Letters*, trans. C. Butler and C. Seiler (Bloomington: Indiana University Press, 1984), 32.

152. Pinkard, *Hegel*, 42.

153. Wiedmann, *Hegel*, 22–23.

154. Wiedmann, *Hegel*, 25.

155. Pinkard, *Hegel*, 49. For Hegel, the idea a of *Bildung*—a multipurpose term that includes the ideals of education, art, culture, and the formation of cultivated taste—fused into the revolutionary Greek ideal; it was thought that a revolution in Germany would lead to the displacement of people like the von Steigers from leadership and their replacement with people like Hegel, men of *Bildung*.

156. Horst Althaus, *Hegel: An Intellectual Biography*, trans. M. Tarsh (Malden, Mass.: Polity Press, 2000), 19.

157. Georg W. F. Hegel, *Early Theological Writings*, trans. T. M. Knox (Philadelphia: University of Pennsylvania Press, 1948). The primary aim of this essay is to explain how Christianity, whose message consists in moral autonomy, degenerates into a positive religion that is commanded by civil authority.

158. Hegel, "The Positivity of the Christian Religion," in *Early Theological Writings*, 71.

159. Hegel, "The Positivity of the Christian Religion," in *Early Theological Writings*, 97.

160. Peter Singer, *Hegel* (Oxford: Oxford University Press, 1983), 5.

161. See Hegel, "The Spirit of Christianity and Its Fate," in *Early Theological Writings*.

162. Hegel, "The Spirit of Christianity and Its Fate," in *Early Theological Writings*, 214.

163. Hegel, "The Spirit of Christianity and Its Fate," in *Early Theological Writings*, 245.

164. Wiedmann, *Hegel*, 28.

165. Pinkard, *Hegel*, 59.

166. See "The Magistrates should be Elected by the People," in Hegel, *Political Writings*.

167. Georg W. F. Hegel, *The Difference Between Fichte's and Schelling's System of Philosophy*, trans. Henry Harris and W. Cerf (Albany: State University of New York Press, 1977).

168. Pickard, *Hegel*, 154.

169. Robert C. Solomon, *In the Spirit of Hegel: A Study of G. W. F. Hegel's* Phenomenology of Spirit (New York: Oxford University Press, 1983), 150.

170. Wiedmann, *Hegel*, p. 33.

171. See Hegel, *Early Theological Writings*, 18–19, where Richard Kroner notes in the "Introduction" that at an early stage in his development Hegel saw clearly that the intellect, trying to conceive things divine, necessarily encountered contradictions

and that these contradictions, far from being fatal to comprehension, make it possible to grasp knowledge.

172. Hegel, "The German Constitution," in *Political Writings*, 22–23.

173. Hegel, "The German Constitution," in *Political Writings*, 51.

174. Hegel, "The German Constitution," in *Political Writings*, 62–63.

175. Hegel, "The German Constitution," in *Political Writings*, 66.

176. Althaus, *Hegel*, 98.

177. Georg W. F. Hegel, *Phenomenology of Spirit*, trans. A. V. Miller (Oxford: Oxford University Press, 1952), 110.

178. Wiedmann, *Hegel*, 40.

179. Pinkard, *Hegel*, 252.

180. Pinkard, *Hegel*, 270. "In accepting the post of rector, Hegel told Niethammer that 'I am daily ever more convinced that theoretical work accomplishes more in the world that practical work. Once the realm of ideas is revolutionized, actuality will not hold us back.' Hegel wanted to shape the new world, and to his mind, nothing shaped it better than the power of thought and *Bildung*."

181. Georg W. F. Hegel, *Science of Logic*, trans. A. V. Miller (Amherst, Mass.: Humanity Books, 1969), 63–64.

182. Hegel, *Science of Logic*, 75.

183. Pinkard, *Hegel*, 351.

184. Pinkard, *Hegel*, 419. A reform government was installed in 1807 under the leadership of Baron von Stein as chief minister. Stein, while wanting to reshape Prussian life around his vision of a mixture of English free-market economic theory, aristocratic liberalism, and preservation of some of the old corporate structure in Germany, also brought a firm belief that the key to success lay in a well-educated administrative bureaucracy that could bring off these reforms in a disciplined, rational manner. He was succeeded by Karl August Prince von Hardenberg in 1810. By the defeat of Napoleon and the Congress of Vienna, the momentum was sapped out of the reform process.

185. Hegel, "Inaugural Address," in *Political Writings*, 181–185.

186. Beiser, *Hegel*, 16.

187. Hegel, *Philosophy of Right*, 12–13.

188. Pinkard, *Hegel*, 473.

189. See Georg W. F. Hegel, *Introductory Lectures on Aesthetics*, trans. Bernard Bosanquet (London: Penguin, 1993).

190. Georg W. F. Hegel, *The Philosophy of History*, trans. J. Sibree (Buffalo, N.Y.: Prometheus, 1991), 17.

191. See Georg Hegel, "On the English Reform Bill," in *Political Writings*.

192. Pinkard, *Hegel*, 641.

193. Hegel, "On the English Reform Bill," in *Political Writings*, 269–270.

194. Kojève, *Introduction to the Reading of Hegel*, 236.

195. See Harry Brod, *Hegel's Philosophy of Politics: Idealism, Identity, and Modernity* (Boulder, Colo.: Westview Press, 1992), 14.

196. See Shlomo Avineri, *Hegel's Theory of the Modern State* (Cambridge: Cambridge University Press, 1972), x. See also Walter Kaufmann, ed., *Hegel's Political*

*Philosophy* (New York: Atherton, 1970), for a collection of ten essays that criticize Hegel as a political philosopher.

197. Hegel, "The German Constitution," 15–16.

198. Georg W. F. Hegel, "The German Constitution," in *Political Writings*, 9.

199. Georg W. F. Hegel, "On the Scientific Ways of Treating Natural Law, on Its Place in Practical Philosophy, and Its Relation to the Positive Sciences of Right," in *Political Writings*, 112–113.

200. See Allen Wood, *Hegel's Ethical Thought* (Cambridge: Cambridge University Press, 1990), Chapter 11, where he notes that Hegel uses *Sittlichkeit* to signify two apparently distinct things. First, it refers to a kind of social order, one that is differentiated and structured in a rational way. Thus *Sittlichkeit* is Hegel's name for an entire set of institutions, the ones anatomized under the heading in the *Philosophy of Right* as the family, civil society, and the modern political state. Second, the term also refers to a certain attitude or subjective disposition on the part of individuals toward their social life, an attitude of harmonious identification with its institutions. In using the term to refer both to subjective attitudes and to social institutions, Hegel means to suggest that there is a close connection between the two. Institutions may foster certain attitudes on the part of the individuals who live under them, and conversely, social institutions depend on the prevalence of certain determinate attitudes on the part of individuals.

201. Allen Wood, "Hegel's Ethics," in *The Cambridge Companion to Hegel*, 217.

## Chapter Four

# Hegel's *Sittlichkeit*:
# Individual Freedom in Ethical Life

I didn't want to stake everything on Rasputin, for only too soon it became
clear to me that in this world of ours every Rasputin has his Goethe, that
every Rasputin draws a Goethe or if you prefer every Goethe a Rasputin in
his wake, or even makes one if need be, in order to be able to condemn him
later on. . . . A bit of madness with Rasputin and a bit of rationality with
Goethe. The extremists with Rasputin, the forces of order with Goethe.[1]

—Günter Grass, *The Tin Drum*

Hegel's ethical theory is a branch of rational inquiry that lies in demonstrating how ethical conceptions and a theory of human good can be grounded in
human self-understanding. This knowledge allows us to determine that some
modes of life are appropriate for human beings and others are not. In this
way, ethical theories can be regarded as theories of human self-actualization,
which have historically been approached a number of ways. Plato grounds
his ethics in psychology and the proper ordering of the human soul, whereas
Aristotle identifies the good life with an actualization of the human essence
in accordance with its proper excellences. More recently, Kant conceives of
human nature as finite rational will, and utilitarian theorists, such as Jeremy
Bentham and John Stuart Mill, see human beings as bundles of desires and
preferences. A common pitfall of ethical theories is that their conceptions of
human nature are too thin, one-sided, or abstract. Hegel's theory, which is
based on a more complex conception of human nature, systematizes a number
of different human self-images.[2] As the last two chapters clearly illustrate,
Hegel grounds human nature on his theory of history, which demonstrates
how different elements of human nature arose dialectally through a process of
cultural development. Hence, Hegel's ethical theory is culturally and historically specific in a way that most ethical theories are not.

117

Although Hegel's ethical theory is historical, it is necessary to stress that he tries to avoid cultural relativism. He does this by defending a conception of human nature that is the outcome of a process in which human beings acquire genuine self-knowledge through the development and self-actualization of *Geist*. His account of the historical process through which this human self-knowledge has been acquired is grounded in a modern theory of human selfhood and self-awareness, which is indebted to Kant and Fichte. While Descartes focuses primarily on the internal processes of the thinking subject and John Locke and David Hume on empirical perception, Kant sees thinking as the activity of synthesizing them. As demonstrated in Chapter 2, for Hegel, self-awareness is essentially practical. Thinking is not the awareness of human desires, but rather is the awareness of a system of abiding concerns and projects with which human beings actively identify.[3] Kant identifies the will with practical reason, and self-concern is indispensable for one's sense of identity, since it determines the content of one's self-interest. Self-concern helps people to modify or inhibit desires, and it also serves as a basis for rational judgments about what is in their own good.

Kant sees a person's identity, or selfhood, as a rational construct. Fichte's way of expressing this idea is to say that the self "posits itself," and the self is "not a being but a doing."[4] Although the self is an object of awareness, it is not a detached contemplation. For Fichte, it is a practical activity, that is, self-awareness is an activity of reflection on another activity that is already given.[5] Since self-awareness reflects on will and intuits its own identity, it is always self-concern. Self-awareness transforms desires into self-interests. Therefore, self-awareness connects with practical activity—to be a self is simultaneously to be both aware of something and to do something. A self-conception involves simultaneously what one is and what one is striving to become.[6] Fichte's ideas are absorbed by Hegel's theory of self-awareness; the will's individuality results from its own activity of self-determination, proceeding from universality through particularity.[7] Even though one can speak of a self only in relation to an actively willed system of practical concerns, these concerns have a dimension that goes beyond particularity—the traits, desires, and qualities that distinguish one person from another.

The Fichtean self is not a metaphysical entity that is distinct from your or my self, but instead is a transcendental structure that is exemplified by a particular self. Accepting this, Hegel insists that one "moment" of the will—that which enables me to apply the word "I" to myself—is the moment of universality in which I identify myself with what is common to all beings capable of calling themselves "I."[8] However, as we saw in the last chapter, self-concern is always socially and culturally situated. For Hegel, the individual self is an expression of its culture's historically developed understanding of human nature and its practical possibilities. Although self-concern is a universal concern, it is a social and historically situated concern, one that expresses a collective project of fashioning a human world.[9] By carrying out the practical project whereby they define themselves, human beings acquire a deeper knowledge of themselves. *Geist* advances, and human nature develops. For Hegel, the dialectical project of self-understanding and self-actualization is one in which individuals participate through the forms shaped by a cultural tradition. *Volkgeist* [Spirit of the People] binds the population of a state spiritually, which forms it into an ethical community.

Human determination is freedom.[10] For Hegel, freedom is neither a faculty given by nature nor a capacity of the self, but rather is a structure of interaction between individuals wherein the self-determination of each is constitutively related to that of others through mutual recognition and respect. Hegelian, like Kantian, ethics is founded on freedom. For instance, Hegel regards the state as the actuality of the ethical idea, only because the state is the "actuality of concrete freedom."[11] The ethical world really exists. He draws a striking parallel between nature and politics. Just as there is a science of nature, there is a science of the state, and reason is no harder to discern in the productions of human consciousness than it is in the natural phenomena.[12] Hegel's view that the state is fundamentally an ethical institution distinguishes him from virtually all other modern social theorists. In short, as he sees it, the state is not founded on coercion but on freedom. The source of the state's strength is not in force, but instead is in the way its social structure organizes the rights—the subjective freedom—and the welfare of individuals into a harmonious whole. Furthermore, each individual's identity as a free person depends on the rational unity of the whole. As discussed more thoroughly in Chapters 5 and 10, this recognition allows him to reject excessively narrow views of freedom, such as that of classical economics, and it provides a foundation for criticisms of globalization. Hegel is known for claiming that a worthy or good life involves achieving some sort of identification with modern social institutions. "It is only by participating in such institutions, by adopting and affirming the central modern social roles, that a good life with others can be led."[13] In ethical action, individuals find that their fulfillment, which includes subjective freedom, is grounded on the universal, or the state. Persons are abstractions—incomplete or one-sided images of the individual will—that are overcome only when considered in relation to *Sittlichkeit* [Ethical Life], which is "the objective ethical order."[14]

Hegel's ethical project is to demonstrate the intersection between participation in *Sittlichkeit* and individual freedom. *Sittlichkeit* is crucial notion in Hegel's political philosophy, encapsulating the crux of his critique of liberalism and of modern political philosophy in general. His view is that individuals can be fully self-actualized and concretely free only if they are devoted to ends beyond their own individual welfare to universal or collective ends. It is only as social participants that people can be free subjects and truly self-determining:

> The rational state is an end in itself only because the highest stage of *individual* self-actualization consists in participating in the state and recognizing it as such an end. This means that Hegel's ethical theory is after all founded on a conception of individual human beings and their self-actualization. Even the state's rationality is grounded on the fact that the individual will is actualized through participating in it and contributing to it as a universal end.[15]

In order for individual wills to particularize themselves, their self-determination must be a reciprocal interaction in which each wills its own objectification and relation to others in virtue of honoring their particular self-determination and relation. At this point, willing gains a self-consciousness that is no longer exclusively tied to private preferences but reconciled with broader, universal aims.[16] Through this line of reasoning, Hegel concludes that freedom is not a natural endowment or structure of the self, but instead is an interaction of a plurality of individuals, that is, intersubjectivity. By conceiving freedom as interaction, Hegel is inexorably led to consider history as the domain in which freedom comes into being. The state is not a mechanism for keeping peace, enforcing rights, or promoting any interest beyond its own existence. Rather, it is most fundamentally the locus of the higher collective ends, which, by rationally harmonizing the rights and welfare of individuals, liberate people by providing their lives with meaning.[17]

Few rights are more fundamental than the right of people to create communities and control the means of livelihood. Hegel recognizes that these rights depend upon the proper cultural values. A globalized economy denies these rights and violates Hegelian principles by transferring the power to make decisions to global corporations and financial institutions. As Hegel sees it, state control of individuals is not external coercion, but is the internal, ethical disposition that fulfills their rational nature and thus makes them free. He does not, however, deny the coercive functions of the state, and he also assigns them to civil society [*bürgerliche Gesellschaft*], that is, to the economic realm where people need external protection. In other words, the state appears as a coercive power only from the fragmented and self-interested perspective of individuals as members of civil society. The state's real power always rests on a deeper ethical harmony, and only through this can it retain the loyalty and support of its members. His conception of ethical life underwrites a conception of modern social life that is unique among modern theories in its emphasis on spontaneous harmony and free community as a condition for the possibility of all social institutions and relationships.[18]

Freedom can only be understood as an intersubjective structure in which the self-determinations of individuals stand indissolubly linked in a reciprocal relation in which each will autonomously determines itself in accord with the realization of others. As discussed in Chapter 2, recognition is not simply the act of a pre-existing subject; in being an act that constitutes the other in a determinate way, and in being by necessity reciprocal, it is an act that simultaneously constitutes the agent as such.[19] A free society is not only one that protects personal rights and provides for the subjective freedom and welfare of individuals. As illustrated in previous chapters, the concepts of freedom and of right develop in historical stages, a dialectical process whereby the concept of freedom develops its own determinations in the form of rights.[20] A free society is also one in which the individual good of its members is brought into rational harmony and grounded in a collective end, which its members understand and pursue both spontaneously and rationally for its own sake. Hegel would not be pleased with the direction recently taken by the United State. Democratic government is being stripped of its ability to regulate the economy responsibly and to protect the public. Globalization is exacerbating the gulf between individualism and community, and excessive privatization is threatening the public realms and commons. Hegel recognizes that self-interest exists and is important; nonetheless, self-interest is not all that exists and should not be given free rein. While free enterprise must be given room to work, it also needs to be limited at times and channeled for the public good.

Hegel is a dialectical thinker whose task is to reconcile the wisdom of the ancient Greeks with the truths of Christianity, reinterpreting both in terms of the claims of free subjectivity and Enlightenment reason. He views himself neither as a builder of a new system or method from scratch, like Descartes, nor a destroyer of tradition, like Nietzsche. Rather, he sees himself as a restorer of an ancient building in need of repair:

> In the case of the present part, I may claim their indulgence rather for the opposite reason; for the logic of the *Notion*, a completely ready-made and solidified, one may say, ossified material is already to hand, and the problem is to render this material fluid and to re-kindle the spontaneity of the Notion in such dead matter. If the building of a new city in a waste land is attended with difficulties, yet there is no shortage of materials; but the abundance of materials presents all the more obstacles of another kind when the task is to remodel an ancient city, solidly built, and maintained in continuous possession and occupation.[21]

Thus, Hegel's contribution consists in buttressing an ancient city in need of repair with newly available materials and engineering techniques. His philosophical system is merely the Western philosophical system, appropriated by the spirit of modernity. Therefore, the aim of his ethical philosophy is a remodeling of classical ethical theory, and adapting it to the content of modern self-understanding—that is, to reconcile the harmony of Greek culture with the reflective spirit of the Enlightenment.[22]

For Hegel, a proper moral culture is both an essential part of *Geist*'s development and is necessary for the proper reconciliation of the individual and community. Furthermore, the modern *Sittlichkeit*, or ethical life, is Hegel's attempt to remedy the abstract and atomistic notion of freedom embodied in the French Revolution with properly constructed political institutions and an ethical community. Hegel's ethical theory tries to mediate between the tensions and shortcomings of the ancient Greeks with Kantian liberalism—that is, a reconciliation of the individual freedom with community interests:

> Whereas Kant collapsed all right into morality and legality, Plato and Aristotle excluded the subjective reflection of moral conscience from their concept of ethical institutions. By contrast, Hegel . . . introduces an ethical life irreducible to abstract right and morality, which nevertheless incorporates their respective freedoms in its ethical order.[23]

To this end, the chapter is organized into four sections. The first section examines Hegel's analysis of ancient Greek culture, identifying both its strengths and weaknesses. The next section discusses Kant's moral theory, which, for Hegel, represents modernity's most developed form of self-consciousness and individual freedom to date. Hegel's criticisms of Kant's moral theory are covered in the following section. The final section of the chapter addresses Hegel's notion of modern *Sittlichkeit*, which comes from his dialectical confrontation of Greek culture and Kantian moral theory. To put it another way, he tries to mediate between the Greek world and the modern principle of subjective freedom, which reaches its culmination in today's commercial order. For Hegel, modern *Sittlichkeit* is proper home of fully developed political freedom. It preserves what is good from both the Greeks and Kant's modern theory.

## GREEK *SITTLICHKEIT*

An important feature of Hegel's thought is his distinction between *Moralität* [Morality], typically associated with Kantian ethics, and *Sittlichkeit* [Ethical Life].[24] Human beings are embedded in the practices and institutions of their particular, historical society. For Hegel, these institutions and practices express certain ideas that reflect particular stages in development of *Geist*. To use Hegelian language, the institutions and practices are the "spirit" of the society objectified. These institutions and practices make up the public life of the particular society. Implicit social norms are lived out by the people in the community. The norms of the society's public life are the content of its *Sittlichkeit*. Hegel initially identifies *Sittlichkeit* with ancient Greek society and its attitude of unthinking, pious devotion to the traditional laws and customs of one's culture. Like many of his contemporaries, Hegel admired ancient Greece. He felt that its art, philosophy, religion, and culture were unsurpassed in many respects. Nevertheless, Hegel's dialectical analysis of Greek life dispels the Romantic view that idealizes ancient Greek life.

As covered in Chapter 2, Hegel's generation was disturbed by Rousseau's critique of the inauthenticity of modern life, and for many ancient Greek life offered a viable alternative, attractive to many of Hegel's romantic contemporaries, especially as the conception of Greek life was mediated in German literature, such as that seen in Goethe. Greek *Sittlichkeit* was thought to have produced a fully harmonious, non-alienated social order and self-understanding. As social and cultural beings, the ancient Greeks understand the basic elements of their social and cultural order as both natural and necessary. For them, the cultural world embodies a kind of natural necessity, and cultural norms and practices are part of part of the eternal order of things. Thus, the Greeks have a rigid understanding of social roles—men do one thing, women another, and rulers do one thing, subjects another. That is simply the way things are supposed to be if the social world is to function properly. What one is ultimately supposed to do is determined by his or her social and cultural order.

Hegel holds that the members of ancient Greek *Sittlichkeit* identified wholly and completely with their particular community.[25] That is, Greeks enjoy the satisfactions of community without the pain of alienation. The *polis*'s "happiness" consists precisely in that absence of separation and division between community members and their community. In short, it is the happiness of unity. It is by sacrificing their particularity, abandoning any conception of themselves as individuals apart from their cultural identity and subordinating their separate and particular interests to the shared interests of the community, that the members of this ancient *Sittlichkeit* come to see themselves as the kind of beings they are—individual instantiations of the shared spirit of their community. Hegel is clearly attracted to this, and he finds it a dramatic contrast to the division and fragmentation of modern social life. Even though he feels a yearning for a return to this more harmonious way of relating to the social world, it is nevertheless equally true that he rejects the idea of returning to ancient *Sittlichkeit*. To do so would be both impossible and undesirable. Insofar as *Sittlichkeit* exists only unreflectively, as habit or custom, ethical life is *Geist*'s lowest, or least developed form.[26] Within Hegel's dialectic, this means that *Geist* also will exist in later, more developed forms. Thus, Greek

*Sittlichkeit* represents a starting point for the development of morality as a higher form of *Geist*.

As noted in the last chapter, the Greek *Sittlichkeit* is the first home of freedom. Even though the Greek world is animated by the idea of freedom, Hegel holds that freedom is not fully developed at this point. Greek freedom is limited in two regards. First, only those who are citizens are free, and Greek democracy depends on slavery. Since every citizen has the right and duty to take part in the democratic assembly, it is necessary that there be a category of workers to take care of the necessities of life.[27] Besides slaves, women and aliens are also disenfranchised. So, in ancient Greece, only a few are free, and even their freedom is incomplete. For Hegel, freedom in Greek *Sittlichkeit* is limited in another important respect; the Greeks have no conception of individual conscience: "Of the Greeks in the first and genuine form of their Freedom, we may assert, that they had no conscience: the habit of living for their country without further reflection, was the principle dominant among them. . . ."[28] Since the Greeks are totally identified with the whole, even those who are free are free only in an incomplete way. In Greek *Sittlichkeit*, people have the habit of living for their *polis* without further reflection. Greek citizens are so immersed in the politics and ethos of their *polis* that they care little for themselves.

Since the Greeks are not capable of differentiating between their own interests and those of the community, they could not conceive of themselves as living apart from their particular *Sittlichkeit*. If people do something solely from habit and have not deliberatively chosen to do, they are not free because their actions are controlled by an external force. They are not guided by self-interest or happiness, but by the traditional ideal of the *polis* that they accept without question. Hegel further notes that the Greeks tend to consult oracles on most important matters before any venture is undertaken.[29] Genuinely free people would not allow their most important decisions to be determined in this way; they would use their capacity to reason prior to making their decisions. Critical thought and reflection are the keys to further progress of *Geist*. In the *Phenomenology of Spirit*, Hegel examines some of the Greek tragedians in order to illustrate that Greek life cannot be understood in its own terms to be as harmonious as many of his contemporaries thought it. Hegel is trying to demonstrate that the idealized view of Greek life—shared by many Romantics of his day—is fatally flawed. Different aspects of Greek *Sittlichkeit* are in potential conflict with one another.[30]

For the Greeks, cultural norms and social values are what define groups as distinct communities apart from all others. There is a recognition of the *Sittlichkeit* fully shared by the community's members, and it determines one's social roles and duties. The institutions and practices furnish the various ways that people reflect both as individuals and collectively on who they are. As indicated above, there is no discontinuity between how individuals understand themselves as individuals and how they understand the Greek community. Unlike modern individuals, Greek individuals do not step back and reflect on whether what they are doing is really right.[31] As Hegel demonstrates, this is because individuals do not understand themselves individually in the modern sense. In one sense, Greek *Sittlichkeit* is characterized by a certain type of clarity of knowledge about what is to be done and believed by its people. Ancient Greeks are not plagued by the reflective doubts of modern actors. Because they *know* ultimately what to believe and do, they do not need to reflect upon the reason for their actions because the reasons are embodied in their norms and ethics, and human law is just one more way that customs [*Sitten*] are put into effect.

For the Greeks, government is supposed to preserve justice in the community, which means apportioning benefits and punishments in a way that maintains the equilibrium [*Gleichgewicht*] of the community.[32] Self-conscious reflective life occurs within the context of a shared understanding of the *Sittlichkeit*. In its political institutions, the public life of the community is always presupposing and confronting deeper assumptions that are simply taken for granted and accepted. The community sees these as divine law.[33] Since divine law is given and immutable, it must simply be accepted as the way that things are to be done. Thus, government embodies the social institutions that are necessary to preserve the *Sittlichkeit*, and human law is constructed to reflect and maintain the eternal order, or divine law. While government embodies the kind of self-conscious reflection on what the community is to do to maintain itself as a particular and determinate people, the family is the Greek institution in which most basic assumptions about the natural or immediate character of individuals are realized.[34] The family has its basis in nature, in the natural facts of reproduction. The Greeks attach specific ethical significance to natural facts, and the social roles embodied in the Greek family seem to be a special feature of the way things are done: "This moment which expresses the ethical sphere in this element of immediacy or [simple] being, or which is *immediate* consciousness of itself, both as essence and as this particular self, in an 'other,' i.e., as a *natural* ethical community—this the Family."[35] Family members have their particular social roles.

For Hegel, what is striking about the Greeks is the way that their two basic institutions—government and family—together delineate how a self-sustaining *Sittlichkeit* might be possible. In Hegelian terms, Greek *Sittlichkeit* consists of the unity of self-consciousness and immediacy. "The problem for the Greek understanding of family life had to do with how it could combine this conception of family life as *natural* with a conception of it as *ethical*, as embodying a set of norms rather than just being a natural fact about people."[36] Hence, it needed to construct a set of duties that would define the family as a social institution and not simply as a natural institution. These duties would hold the family together as a social unit; but as a natural unit for the propagation and rearing of children, it would be contingent in many respects. Holding the Greek family together as a social unit means holding and respecting the memory of one's ancestors. Death is a natural fact; in performing the proper burial rites, the family transforms this natural fact into one charged with social meaning.[37]

Hegel's dialectical analysis of Greek *Sittlichkeit* proceeds through an interpretation of Greek tragedy and uncovers its shortcomings. The importance of performing the proper burial rites for the deceased plays an important role in Sophocles's *Antigone*. Through the burial rights, the family protects the standing of the deceased in the public community [*Gemeinwesen*] and signal that his or her self-identity remains important.[38] They also perform these rights in order to satisfy the divinities of the underworld, since it constitutes an absolute duty. This allows the family to maintain its social, normative status. The duties of the family toward the deceased constitute divine law, and must be performed without further reflection.[39] Furthermore, human law cannot replace or supplant divine law, which attempts to make sense of an otherwise irrational natural fact, death. Human law is intended to coerce individuals when the ethical harmony of the community is threatened. In order to hold the community together, divine law and human law apportion duties accordingly. "The normativity of *human* law falls completely within the domain of human decision and action; *divine* law, on the other hand, has to do with those natural facts governing basic and universal questions of self-identity and humanity's most basic interests, namely, the facts of birth, death, and sexuality."[40]

Greek *Sittlichkeit* is a mixture of natural and social ideas, which establish rigid gender roles. Men are destined for public life, and women for only family life. While men participate in the self-conscious life of public affairs, women hold the family as a unity of feeling together.[41] For the Greeks, the natural differences between men and women determine the social differences of their roles. As illustrated in Chapter 3, the process of mutual recognition bestows the status of free individuality on Greek citizens as equals. However, the type of free individuality that is the hallmark of idealized Greek life can only be attained in the public sphere, and not within the family because the relationship among husbands, wives, and children is not equal. Within the context of Greek understanding, the only possible relationship within which a woman can develop a sense of herself as a self is in the familial relationship of brother and sister, which is crucial for Hegel's interpretation of *Antigone*.[42]

For purposes of Hegel's dialectic, the crucial issue is whether the Greek understanding is rational in its own terms.

Hegel uses *Antigone* to analyze the way in which Greek self-understanding must develop contradictions within itself. The social structure is marked by important divisions—between human law and divine law, between *polis* and family, between man and women. Sophocles' play presents us with Oedipus's family—his sons, Polyneices and Eteocles, and daughters, Antigone and Ismene. Believing that the crown of Thebes belongs to him, Polyneices attacks the city ruled by his brother. When both brothers are killed, their uncle, Creon, assumes power. He quickly orders Eteocles's body to be given proper burial rites, and denies these rites to Polyneices, whom he sees as a traitor. In defiance to the royal edict, Antigone performs the burial rites on Polyneices and is arrested and convicted for it. What makes this tragic is that both Creon and Antigone do what they have to do, and both are right: As ruler, Creon has the absolute duty to protect the city from traitors, and Antigone, as family member, has the absolute duty to perform the proper burial rights. Both are ethical characters in that each act according to their proper role with Greek *Sittlichkeit*, and since each is ethical, they are both compelled to do what they do.

Thus, the dialectical tension is that the clash between Antigone and Creon is not something that could be negotiated away or might have been avoided if one of the characters had controlled his or her feelings:

> Everything in this tragedy is logical; the public law of the state is set in conflict over against inner family love and duty to a brother; the women, Antigone, has the family interest as her "pathos," Creon, the man has the welfare of the community as his. . . . But this command, which concerned only the public weal, Antigone could not accept, in the piety of her love for her brother, she fulfils the holy duty of burial. In doing so she appeals to the law of the gods. . . .[43]
>
> The collision between the two highest moral powers is set forth in a plastic fashion in that supreme and absolute example of tragedy, *Antigone*. In this case, family love, what is holy, what belongs to the inner life and to inner feeling, and which because of this is also called the law of neither gods, comes into collision with the law of the State. Creon is not a tyrant, but really a moral power; Creon is not wrong, he maintains that the law of the State, the authority of government, is to be held in respect, and that punishment follows the infraction of the law. Each of these two sides realizes only one of the moral powers and has only one of these as its content; this is the element of one-sidedness here. . . . Both are recognized as having a value of their own in the untroubled course of morality. Here both have their own validity, but a validity which is equalized. It is only one-sidedness in their claims which justice comes forward to oppose.[44]

Instead, it is a discord within Greek *Sittlichkeit* itself—that is, between the two ethical powers of Greek life, human law and divine law. Since both characters

are ethical, each knows what has to be done.[45] For Creon and Antigone, it is
the other person who is in the wrong. From Antigone's perspective, Creon
is defying the divine law that requires proper burial, and Creon thinks that
Antigone has willfully violated the conditions and laws under which the community can exist and flourish. Both Creon and Antigone are guilty of violating
Greek law: Antigone breaches human law and Creon divine law. Since neither
of the two ethical powers of Greek life can claim to more important than the
other, both agents are equally guilty.[46] Hegel's point is that the important
conflict is Antigone's and Creon's clash with Greek *Sittlichkeit*. Since divine
law and human law are both essential to Greek life, this conflict is not merely
a conflict between two contingent individuals. Rather, it is an institutional
conflict between men and women, which is itself an expression of a conflict
between equally essential principles of Greek life.[47]

With the arrest and conviction of Antigone, the public sphere swallows
up the familial sphere. For Hegel, this antagonistic situation reveals the deep
contradictions at work in idealized Greek *Sittlichkeit*. The public sphere frequently has to intervene in the lives of members in order to hold Greek life
together. With this constant battling for the satisfaction of consciousness in
Greek life, individuals are shaken free of their social identities and the living
unity of the *polis* is "shattered into a multitude of separate atoms."[48] Hegel
thinks that this proves that Greek *Sittlichkeit* is not a viable alternative to
modern life. Although Greek ethical life was supposed to lead individuals to
the necessary ends in the life of their community, they ultimately discovered
that those ends clashed with each other in irreconcilable ways. Nevertheless,
the equality of Antigone and Creon as self-assertive free agents who express
the absolute right of self-consciousness is essential to the transition that Hegel
thinks we must make to the world of legal individuals.[49] This transition is necessary for the move toward modern *Sittlichkeit*. For Hegel, Sophocles' tragedy illustrates that allegiance to either sphere of the Greek world—the divine
or the human—must ultimately prove irreconcilable to the other. The Greek
world also collapsed because it had insufficient space for the individual, since
neither Antigone nor Creon was able to rise above their social spheres and see
value in the other's position.[50] As discussed in a later section, Hegel's aim is
to integrate the profound forms of self-understanding and affirmation found
in Greek *Sittlichkeit* with the explicit, self-conscious articulation of our world
and the self-understanding that characterizes modernity.[51]

## KANT'S METAPHYSICS OF
## MORALS AND MODERN FREEDOM

Immanuel Kant's philosophy impacts not only epistemology but also ethics.
Accordingly, he transforms practical philosophy by providing a new founda-

tion for morals. Before Kant, the origin of morals was sought in the order or nature of society, in the desire for happiness, in God's will, or in moral sentiments. He argues that morals cannot be conceived of in any of these ways. In the practical sphere, as in the theoretical, objectivity is only possible through the subject. His new foundation for ethics comes from the critical examination of practical reason.[52] For Kant, practical reason means being able to choose one's actions independent of sensible determinations, such as desires, sensations, and passions. Moral action requires being able to conceive of law, to accepts its principles, and act accordingly. His critique attempts to refute both ethical empiricism and moral skepticism. With the categorical imperative, Kant develops an ultimate criterion for judging personal morality. It demands that human beings act morally. With the autonomy of the will, he finds an a priori synthesis that gives the concept of freedom an objective, determined reality by linking it to practical reason.

The limitation of the foundational principles of the scientific worldview to appearance is necessary not only to explain certainty, but also to allow human beings to conceive of themselves as rational agents who are not constrained by the deterministic grip of nature but can freely govern themselves by moral law as practical reason.[53] Moral action presupposes freedom. For Kant, the only kind of being that is capable of understanding the concept "good" is a practically reflective being, a being with a will, a being that must choose what to aim at and what to do. Being a member of a moral world does not make the person good or bad; it only makes one capable of being good or bad. Moral philosophy's task is to discover principles of behavior that are binding on all mankind. Just as empirical theory fails to discover knowledge, moral knowledge is not ascertained by simply examining the actual behavior of people. Although an empirical study would provide interesting anthropological information about how people do behave, it would not properly describe how they ought to behave.[54] Kant is more interested in mankind standing outside of time, as unvarying moral and rational beings, than mankind as phenomenal creatures.

Kant believes that moral philosophy can establish principles of proper human action. Moral judgments, like the scientific judgments of the *Critique of Pure Reason*, come from reason and are not objects from experience.[55] Put differently, just as theoretical reason brings the category of causality to visible objects and explains the process of change, so too does practical reason bring the concept of duty to any given moral situation. Thus, Kant uses a priori concepts in both science and moral philosophy. In both cases, experience is understood only when the mind thinks in universal terms. In the context of human relations, practical reason is able to discover how one should behave at any given moment. Kant calls these principles practical synthetic a priori judgments.

Moral aptitudes, according to Kant, are proper subjects of philosophical inquiry. While theoretical reason is concerned with knowledge of the world, practical reason seeks to understand human aims and intentions in action.[56] The claim that normal adults are capable of being fully self-governing in moral matters is at the center of Kant's ethical theory. Setting goals is the internal exercise of freedom; and using the natural faculties and external things to achieve these ends is the external exercise of freedom. Since each individual possesses a will, Kant believes that all individuals are capable of acting in a moral way. Freedom is a transcendental idea, and it is one without application in the empirical world. Human freedom derives from the individual's ability to be self-determining. So, the free will is the appropriate object of practical reason:

> A will which can be determined independently of sensuous impulses, and therefore through motives which are represented only by reason, is entitled *freewill* (*arbitrium liberum*), and everything which is bound up with this will, whether as ground or as consequence, is entitled *practical*. . . . Reason therefore provides laws which are imperatives, that is, *objective laws of freedom*, which tell us *what ought to happen*—although perhaps it never does happen—therein differing from *laws of nature*, which relate only to *that which happens*. These laws are to be entitled practical laws.[57]
>
> The concept of freedom is the key to the definition of autonomy of the will. The will is a species of causality of living beings, insofar as they are rational, and freedom would be that quality of this causality by which it can be effective independently of alien causes determining it; just as natural necessity is the quality of all beings lacking reason, of being determined to activity through the influence of alien causes. The proposed definition of freedom is negative, and hence unfruitful in affording insight into its essence; yet from it flows a positive concept of freedom, which is all the more rich in content and more fruitful. . . . Thus if freedom of the will is presupposed, then morality follows together with its principle from mere analysis of its concept.[58]

Thus, the will is the source of human freedom. His conception of freedom of will is comprised of two aspects—free choice as independence from determination by sensuous impulse and practical reason as the determining ground of purposive activity. Therefore, for Kant, the basis of duty [*Pflicht*], or moral obligation, is found neither in human nature nor circumstances but in an a priori concept of reason. Hence, no external authority is necessary to constitute or inform of the demands of morality. Kant holds that the faculty of reason must be rooted in human nature as things in themselves, so people are free to act without constraint by the causal laws governing mere appearance. For Kant, duty is not tied to social expectations or laws; rather, duty is that which one would do if one were fully rational.[59]

Morality is an aspect of rationality that has to do with mankind's consciousness of rules. Human beings exist not only as self-conscious centers of knowledge, but also as agents. Free rational beings are bound by principles of practical reasoning, since acceptance of them is a presupposition of freedom without which practical reason is impossible.[60] To be a moral agent, one must be capable of recognizing both what morality demands and acknowledging the value of complying with those demands. Thus, the metaphysics of morals investigates the idea and principles of a possible pure will, not the actions and conditions of actual human volition.[61] This leads Kant to investigate the rational aspects of human behavior. The human will can make an independent impact on the world because it is rational. This ability of the will to be an independent effect upon the dictates of nature is freedom. Therefore, being free, people elevate themselves above natural necessity and do not solely follow their passions, but do what they think is right.

His account of moral action is most stringent. Moral considerations weigh heavily upon human relations. In fact, Kant sets standards that would appear, for the most part, to be unattainable. "There is nothing it is possible to think of anywhere in the world, or indeed anything at all outside it, that can be held to be good without limitation, excepting only the good will."[62] Moreover, whatever is good without qualification is not good in any relative sense, but is good absolutely. Although others recognize additional human goods, such as wealth, honor, health, and happiness, Kant does not think that any of these things possess a lasting ethical value. Since desires are not rational and often arise with bodily needs, if there is to be rationality in action, the human will must be its source. His main point is that the essence of the morally good act is the principle that a person affirms when willing the act.[63]

The use of practical reason means that the rational agent engages in conscious thought about how he or she should actually behave. Therefore, moral laws become universally valid, since in order to be valid for one human being, they must be valid for all human beings. In this context, Kant distinguishes a rational being, who strives to do what he or she should do, from a person who acts based on either inclination or self-interest.[64] If a particular decision to act stems from human emotions or feelings, then reason has no part in determining them. So goodness can only be a property of the human mind, not heart. An action is good without qualification only if it fulfills duty for the sake of duty.[65] Rational beings have the capacity to resist impulses; decisions are never determined mechanically, there is always choice. Kant rejects moral theories, such as Hume's, which identify moral motive with natural feeling.

So, for Kant, being moral consists of knowing what to do and when to do it. However, knowing what to do must be based solely on knowing that it is the right action, not doing it because of social pressure or the expectation of reward or personal benefit.[66] In short, a moral action is one done solely from duty. As one observer notes:

Although benevolent actions are obligatory, their moral value lies in submitting
to the obligation, not in actually achieving the end. If the end of the benevolent
action were the root of the obligation, failure to achieve it would nullify the
morality of the action regardless of the intention. . . . Kant's conception of the
nature of man would not permit him to derive man's obligation from anything in
the world of sense. By doing so, he would surrender the *a priori* of duty.[67]

Basing actions on moral obligation is the key to the universality, and moral
precepts would be variable and contingent if they depended on particular ends
for justification. In short, Kant attempts to establish an objective guide to
human behavior. Through duty and freedom, people gain awareness of themselves not as they appear but as they intrinsically are.[68] Although ethics starts
with freedom, moral agents act because they recognize the objective worth of
the claim made on them. Hence, only autonomous beings have genuine ends
of action, as opposed to objects of desire, and their actions are the only ones
deserving of esteem for being the embodiment of rational choice.

Since human desires are only contingent empirical facts, true moral necessity makes an act necessary regardless of what agents want. So, a rational
being strives to do what ought to be done. Since everything in nature works
according to laws, rational beings alone have the faculty of acting according
to the conception of law.[69] Thus, the pre-eminent good consists solely in the
"conception of law" itself, which is only possible in a rational being with a
free will. Since Kant deprives the will of every impulse that might arise, there
is nothing left to serve the will as principle except the universal conformity
of its actions to law as such: "So act as if the maxim of your action were to
become through your will a universal law."[70] When confronted with a decision, an individual only has to ask whether he would desire that his decision
be adopted as a universal law; and if he cannot will this, then the decision
must be rejected. A moral agent has a duty to moral law. Duty implies some
kind of obligation, and Kant suggests that rational beings are aware of this
obligation, which comes to them in the form of an imperative. As he sees it,
the ordinary reason of mankind conforms completely to this imperative when
rendering practical judgments.

Imperatives respond to the practical question of "What I ought to do?" and
constitute practical necessities. There are two kinds of imperatives, according to Kant: the hypothetical and the categorical. Hypothetical imperatives
presuppose an end. If people wish to achieve a certain end, they must employ
the appropriate means. Categorical imperatives, however, lay claim to universal validity; for this reason, moral imperatives are categorical.[71] Kant's
categorical imperative applies to everyone, and it is valid not merely under
contingent conditions and with exceptions but must be absolutely necessary.[72]
It demands certain conduct immediately, without having any other purpose as

a condition. It is categorical because it instantly applies to all rational beings, and it is imperative because it is the principle on which one ought to act:

> All imperatives are expressed through an *ought* and thereby indicate the relation of an objective law of reason to a will which in its subjective constitution is not necessarily determined by that law (a necessitation). They say that it would be good to do or refrain from something, but they say it to a will that does not always do something just because it is represented to it as good to do. . . . The categorical imperative, which declares the action for itself as objectively necessary without reference to any aim, i.e., also without any other end, is valid as an apodictically practical principle.[73]

Kant believes that everything in nature works according to the "conception of laws," and the categorical imperative is viewed as nature's conception of law as it applies to human behavior. "The categorical imperative is thus only a single one, and specifically this: "Act only in accordance with that maxim through which you can at the same time will that it become a universal law."[74] In doing the right thing, Kant thinks that people act in a law-like manner. Since the categorical imperative requires impartiality, people are not permitted to make exceptions for themselves. As the product of practical reason, the categorical imperative is an a priori synthetic judgment.[75] These moral principles are formal; they do not say anything about the content of an action, but supply rules to which one can appeal to in order to judge actions. Hence, ethical law borrows nothing whatsoever from experience. Nevertheless, abstract as the categorical imperative may sound, it represents a supreme form of obligation and the consummation of practical rationality.

Autonomy is living by the principles of reason; and reason is nothing but the principle that informs practices of autonomy in thinking and acting.[76] Kant shows that reason, correctly understood, is the principle of thinking and acting on principles that all can freely adopt.[77] He understands that individuals are members of a community. His moral litmus test asks how individuals would like other people to react when confronted with the same situation. If the consequences of everyone's sharing the same motives are compatible with their well-being and freedom, then the action is moral. It can be seen as a rational self-constraint on one's own liberty. Rational beings are capable of exercising civil liberties in harmony with the common good. In brief, a practical law is a principle that each rational being has an overriding and a priori reason to obey.

The categorical imperative is intended to give substantive reality to human freedom. It specifies the concept and law governing the autonomous will. Autonomy allows people to fulfill the requirements of categorical imperative. Purposes come from people's plans, and the categorical imperative serves to test these purposes in order to determine if acting on them would be morally permissible. Kant supposes that every action, as an intentional act of a rational agent, involves the adoption of a maxim. If human beings are to be free, they must always treat others with the proper respect:

> Now I say that man, in general every rational being, exists as an end in himself and not merely as a means to the discretionary use of this or that will, but in all its actions, those directed toward itself as well as those directed toward other rational beings, it must always at the same time be considered as an end. . . . If, then, there is supposed to be a supreme practical principle, and in regard to the human will a categorical imperative, then it must be such from the representation of that which, being necessarily an end for everyone, because it is an end in itself, constitutes an objective principle of the will, hence can serve as a universal practical law. . . . The practical imperative will thus be the following: Act so that you use humanity, as much as in your own person as in the person of every other, always at the same time as end and never merely as means.[78]
>
> It follows that, in the order of ends, man (and every rational being) is an end himself, i.e., he is never to be used merely as means for someone (even for God) without at the same time being himself an end, and that humanity in our person must itself be holy to us, because man is subject to the moral law and there for subject to that which is holy.[79]

Since people are rational, they should never be regarded as merely a means to anything else. Subsequently, as an end in themselves, people are only bound by self-made laws. Hence, Kant is one of the first to address the charge that utilitarianism is incompatible with justice. The interests of the few cannot be sacrificed to satisfy the greater good of the greater number. Objective ends, for Kant, are not ends that rational beings happen to desire as a matter of fact but are ends that rational beings should seek to promote. Each person shares responsibility for promoting the ends of moral reason within the community.

Practical reason seeks its unifying order in what Kant calls the highest good, and this can be realized only in the notion of a perfect community, which is found in the kingdom of ends.[80] Kant's political philosophy grows out of his moral theory, and is divided into two parts: the theory of justice or jurisprudence [*Rechtslehre*] and ethics [*Tugendlehre*]. Practical reason also sets up the standards for political life. Moral norms, derived from the categorical imperative, should measure the fundamental acts of public policy. Nonetheless, he is fully aware that politics cannot mirror his moral vision. Although he recognizes that politicians act from all sorts of motives other than moral ones, this is not an excuse for abandoning all thought of principled action in the political realm.[81] Even though moral theory establishes the necessary principles of freedom, not everyone actually follows them. So, political authority is necessary. Since the rules of justice and the fate of civilized society hang together, the use of legal force to maintain or establish sovereignty has an ethical underpinning.

## HEGEL'S CRITIQUE OF KANT'S MODERNISM

Since the advent of modern political philosophy, great thinkers have identified the inherent tension between individual freedom and social responsibility. Rousseau's general will and Kant's categorical imperative try to reconcile this tension. Hegel continues this effort with his attempt to reconcile the particular and the universal. For Hegel, people are free when their determinations have their source in "thinking intelligence." Kant represents an important advance over previous liberal thinkers. The advance consists in Kant's recognition that freedom cannot be conceived as an act choice. Hegel comes to conceive freedom as interaction by thinking through the problems of Kant's practical reason.[82] Hegel accepts the argument of Rousseau and Kant that true self-determination requires rational self-legislation, but he cannot accept that such rational self-determination involves an identification with the general will, or a subjection to the categorical imperative. One is a false harmony, the other, a permanent dualism.[83] Hegel does think that individuals must act on what they believe are good reasons. However, the reasons that justify their participation in an ethical community are more than simply prudential for achieving their particular wants or even some end viewed as an objective good for all human beings. Hegel wants to show that the true realization of freedom, or the achievement of genuine subjectivity, occurs when "I see myself in an other."[84] This means that taking others into account is not limited to coordinating actions successfully; it means that the force of an ethical reason requires that I have already come to identify myself and my good with others and with some collective good.

So long as human beings regard liberty as the freedom to pursue selfish whims, society is only possible if external checks are placed on liberty. The classical liberal conception of liberty sees freedom as the absence of restrictions. Government, in Hobbes' view, is then an external organization to meet men's necessities. But if they realize that their true freedom consists in the acceptance of principles and laws that are there, a synthesis of universal and particular interests becomes possible.[85] Hegel's introduction to the *Philosophy of Right* consists of an explication of the concept of the will, designed to show that the fully developed concept of the will generates a fully developed concept of freedom, including elements that ensure that this freedom has both objective and subjective reality. Like Kant, Hegel thinks that the task of subjectivity is bringing one's will into conformity with a universal rational principle, so that it accords with the will itself. The universal side of subjectivity takes the form of an "ought," legislating to a particular side.[86] Ethical principles are universal and objective and thus have universal applicability within the community.

Hegel is very familiar with the liberal conception of freedom, but unlike Locke and other liberals, he refers to it as formal or abstract freedom, meaning that it has form but no substance. Freedom, for Hegel, is not the ability to do whatever one pleases. His objection to this notion of freedom is that it takes the choices of the individual as the basis from which freedom must begin. Individual choice, considered in isolation from everything else, is the outcome of arbitrary circumstances. Hence, it is not genuinely free. Due to his historical perspective, Hegel never loses sight of the fact that human wants and desires are shaped by the society one lives in, and that this society in turn is a stage in the historical process. Thus, abstract freedom, the freedom to do as one pleases, is effectively the freedom to be pushed to and fro by the social and historical forces of one's time. Furthermore, Hegel argues that individual autonomy can be achieved only within a communal context. It is a fundamental insight of *Phenomenology of Spirit*, as discussed in Chapter 2, that an individual subject necessarily exists within a structure of intersubjective recognition. Freedom is realizable only in a modern, law-governed commercial society. While freedom is a necessary feature of human agency, for Hegel, it is one that must be socially achieved. "What leads Hegel beyond practical reason to interaction is his realization that the will can particularize itself only in relation to other wills, and indeed, only by willing that relation as well."[87] Being a free, self-determining subject means being a social participant in a community, which means recognizing oneself as in both deeds and practices.

Some desires are the product of nature, such as the desire for food or sexual desire, which people are born with or have the potential to develop. Other desires are formed by one's upbringing, education, or cultural environment. Regardless of whether a desire is biological or social in origin, Hegel notes that they are not chosen. Because individuals do not choose their desires, they are not free when they act from particular innate or socially conditioned desires. He holds that individuals are fundamentally social practitioners. Everything that one does, says, or thinks is formed in the context of social practices. No one acts on the general, merely biological needs for food, safety, or companionship; rather, one acts on much more specific needs for much more specific kinds of objects that fulfill those needs, and one acts to achieve them in very specific ways.[88] One's society deeply conditions one's ends because it provides specific objects that meet those ends, and specific procedures for obtaining them. Like Kant, Hegel sees reason as being essentially universal, and, therefore, holds that freedom is found in what is universal:

> Like Kant's, Hegel's interest is in the general principles or criteria of evaluation presupposed in any deliberation and choice, however implicit or rarely formulated as such. *These* principles are mine only if genuinely self-imposed, prompting the question under what conditions such self-imposition could occur.[89]

Both philosophers see a connection between freedom and the development of the individual conscience, and both believe duty appears as a restriction on man's natural or arbitrary desires. Both think that the appropriate relationship is what it means to be free. In fact, the individual only truly finds his liberation from mere natural impulse in duty.[90]

Kant argues that true moral worth belongs only to actions done from duty. Doing one's duty for its own sake is held by Hegel to be a notable advance on the negative idea of liberty as doing whatever one pleases.[91] Despite this crucial advance by Kant, he never gets beyond the abstract notion of doing duty for its sake. Although Hegel sees its positive elements, at the same time he is one of its most trenchant critics. *The Philosophy of Right* contains a significant criticism of Kant's ethical theory. Hegel has three main objections. First, he argues that Kant's theory never gets down to specifics about what one ought to do. This is not due to Kant's lack of interest in practical questions, but because his entire theory insists that morality must be based upon pure practical reasoning, free from any particular motives beyond duty. As a result, Kant's theory can only yield the bare, universal form of the moral law. It cannot tell people what their specific duties are. According to Hegel, this universal form is simply a principle of consistency or noncontradiction:

> However essential it is to give prominence to the pure unconditioned self-determination of the will as the root of duty, and to the way in which knowledge of the will, thanks to Kant's philosophy, has won firm foundation and starting-point for the first time owing to the thought of its infinite autonomy, still to adhere to the exclusively moral position, without making the transition to the conception of ethics, is to reduce this gain to an empty formalism, and the science of morals to the preaching of duty for duty's sake. From this point of view, no immanent doctrine of duties is possible. . . . Kant's further formulation, the possibility of visualizing an action as a *universal* maxim, does lead to the more concrete visualization of a situation, but in itself it contains no principle beyond abstract identity and the "absence of contradiction" already mentioned. . . . But if duty is to be willed simply for duty's sake and not for some content, it is only a formal identity whose nature it is to exclude all content and specification.[92]

Since the universalization test of the categorical imperative is incapable of generating any particular duty, Kantian ethics is guilty of empty formalism. Hegel claims that any desire could be put into universal form, and once the introduction of particular desires are allowed, the requirement of universal form is powerless to prevent the justification of whatever immoral conduct takes one's fancy. Hegel tries to give dialectical form to the historical move from Kant to Fichte and beyond.[93]

Hegel's second major objection to Kant's ethics is that it offers no solution to the opposition between morality and self-interest. In his view, Kant fails to show why an individual would choose to be moral. Kant merely says that we should do our duty for its own sake. Although Hegel agrees with Kant that duties ought to be done because they are duties, he disagrees with Kant that duties ought to be done solely because they are duties. Hegel does regard the Kantian conception of duty as an advance, however, for it helps to make modern man free in a way the Greeks, embedded in their narrow customary horizons, never could be.[94] Hegel tries to demonstrate that moral reflection is not sufficient, of itself, to generate a substantive set of moral norms by criticizing the ethics of conscience.[95] He therefore seeks to unit the natural satisfaction of the Greek form of life with the free conscience of the Kantian idea of morality. For Hegel, the individual in his or her subjectivity and moral autonomy is concerned within the state and generally within the objective relations and institutions of society.[96]

Third, Hegel thinks that Kant's conception of moral intention is flawed. For Kant, the morality of one's actions is based solely on intention. While Hegel does not deny that intentions are important, he notes that people may fail to achieve what they intend due to unfavorable circumstances. In other word, the results of one's moral act are equally important. This means that we should judge an individual's inner willing by the overall pattern of outward deeds. Good intentions require serious action and effort toward implementation. People get no moral credit for mere wishes. In this respect, Hegel's position goes further than Kant's. For Hegel, the good will is supposed to consist in a purposeful striving toward a good end. He questions the consistency of feeling contentment when one has failed to achieve the end that the person was supposedly so devoted to. Hegel sees this as a misuse of virtuous consciousness.[97] Although there are often complex external circumstances, Hegel further holds that human beings are responsible for whatever belongs to their action by its very nature. If the nature of their actions is such that they do not produce good results, then they cannot save the goodness of their will by hiding behind the profession of their good intentions:

> What the subject is, is the series of his actions. If these are a series of worth-
> less productions, then the subjectivity of his willing is just as worthless. But if

the series of his deeds is of substantive nature, then the same is true also of the individual's inner will.[98]

While Kant says that the good will without any results shines like a jewel, having full value in itself, Hegel says that the "laurels of mere will are dry leaves that never have been green."[99]

Hegel rejects the view that presupposes a gap between what is objective in action and what is subjective in its motives.[100] Intentions have actuality only as embodied in the external world. The subjective will does not exist without external deeds—that is, the significance of one's intentions can only be grasped in light of its consequences. Hegel's theory of responsibility allows for a degree of moral luck, since the contingency is inevitable in the external world:

> The realized good is good by virtue of what it already is in the subjective end, in its Idea; realization gives it an external existence; but since this existence is determined merely as an intrinsically worthless externality, in it the good has only attained a contingent, destructible existence, not a realization corresponding to its Idea. . . . From the side of the objective world presupposed for it, in the presupposition of which the subjectivity and finitude of the good consists, and which as a different world goes its own way, the very realization of the good is exposed to obstacles, obstacles which may indeed even be insurmountable. The Idea of the realized good is, it is true, an *absolute postulate*, but it is no more than a postulate, that is, the absolute afflicted with the determination of subjectivity.[101]

Moral agents who understand the nature of subjectivity do not try to flee from contingency; they accept it as a condition of the possibility of expressing their subjectivity.[102]

Hegel believes that Kant's moral theory is itself a particular historical practice. While not false, Kant's notion of a universally binding requirement to respect all others as ends in themselves is simply too abstract. In order to appreciate Hegel's effort at a reconciliation of freedom and moral duty, it is necessary to see that the realization of freedom takes place only within the institutions and social rules that essential to the exercise of social agency:

> Hegel argues that such reason, or self-imposed principles of action, cannot be understood in the way suggested by his famous competitor [Kant], as moral demands I make on myself, as obligations, duties, or moral reasons. Ethical reasons are not, like these, radically discontinuous with my sensible, natural being; nor are they expressions of my real or pure or better self or part. . . Hegel claims that the rational institutions of right, property, contract, morality, ethical life are all implicit in an original natural will, that such a will implicitly aims at becoming a fully free will, and so realizes itself in the institutions that make possible and realize such freedom.[103]

This immediate, or natural, will is ultimately free, or fully actualized, within *Sittlichkeit*.[104] Human beings are free only when they determine their actions as universal subjects, not merely particular egos:

> And, coming again to the sort of claim paradigmatic for Hegel's understanding of ethical reasons, he claims that an individual's "dignity" and the "stability of his particular purposes" are understood to be "grounded" in such ethical substantiality, that he "knows" this and knows that his purposes and dignity become "actual" in such an ethical life [*Sittlichkeit*]. There is thus good reason for him to participate actively in such institutions and practices. He is an autonomous, self-determining agent, *himself*: only by virtue of such participation, but not because pure practical reason demands this of him, nor because it is prudentially wise for him to participate.[105]

For Hegel, this only occurs when agents understand themselves as ethical beings, that is, in being members of an ethical community with social institutions and practices. Hegel accepts important aspects of Kant's moral subjectivity, but he does not conceive of it as an inner determination of the self. Rather, he develops an intersubjective structure consisting in action toward others which is recognizably related to the inner intention of its author.[106] While Hegel thinks that the Greeks stood in an unthinking and unreflective relation to custom, Kantian modernism refuses to recognize any obligation as valid that it does not see as rational.[107] Such a system of integrated principles, practices, and morally developed agents is *Sittlichkeit*, or ethical life. Hegel's dialectic approach tries to remedy modern alienation and atomism through the reconciliation of ancient Greek culture with Kantian moral theory. As will be discussed in Chapter 6, this is also an important step in reconciling liberalism and communitarianism.

## MODERN *SITTLICHKEIT*

Usually translated as ethical life, Hegel uses *Sittlichkeit* to signify two distinct aspects of social life. First, it refers to a certain type of social order, one that is differentiated and structured in a rational way. For instance, in the *Philosophy of Right*, it is Hegel's name for an entire set of social institutions—the family, civil society, and the state.[108] Second, *Sittlichkeit* also refers to a certain attitude, or "subjective disposition," on the part of individuals toward their social life, an attitude of harmonious identification with society's institutions.[109] In the first section on *Sittlichkeit* in the *Philosophy of Right*, Hegel emphasizes the double use of this term:

Ethical life [*Sittlichkeit*] is the Idea of freedom in that on one hand it is the good become alive—the good endowed in self-consciousness with knowing and willing and actualized by self-conscious action—while, on the other hand self-consciousness has in the ethical realm its absolute foundation and the end which actuates its effort. Thus ethical life is the concept of freedom developed into the existing world and the nature of self-consciousness.[110]

*Sittlichkeit* refers both to subjective attitudes and particular social institutions in order to focus on the close connection between the two, that is, it refers to a single reality that has two complementary sides. "Institutions may foster certain attitudes on the part of the individuals who live under them—attitudes toward themselves and other individuals, and attitudes toward the institutions. Conversely, social institutions depend on the prevalence of certain determinate attitudes on the part of individuals."[111] Without individuals, social institutions could not arise, function, or perpetuate themselves. For Hegel, the substance of the ethical life is living because it is recognized and sustained by the individual subjects. *Sittlichkeit* has an objective side, in the form of a particular social order, and a subjective side, in the form of individual self-consciousness.

*Sittlichkeit* connects to Hegel's conception of *Geist*, and thus it advances in a dialectical fashion through the progress of *Geist* in history.[112] As part of *Geist*, *Sittlichkeit* is a unity of the subjective and the objective. As noted in Chapter 3, *Geist*'s activity only takes a self-sufficient form in a particular people or nation. The ethical is spiritual because it rises above nature. In the ethical, custom becomes a second nature:

But when individuals are simply identified with the actual order, ethical life [*das Sittliche*] appears as their general mode of conduct, i.e., as custom [*Sitte*], while the habitual practice of ethical living appears as a second nature which, put in the place of the initial, purely natural will, is the soul of custom permitting it through and through, the significance and the actuality of its existence. It is mind living and present as a world, and the substance of mind thus exists now for the first time as mind.[113]

Hence, *Sittlichkeit* actualizes freedom because it is not natural. Individuals who participate in ethical life are conscious of laws. Unlike nature, *Sittlichkeit* imposes its laws on itself and is therefore free.

As discussed above, Hegel holds that the members of ancient Greek *Sittlichkeit* identified wholly and completely with their particular community.[114] They enjoyed the satisfactions of community without the pain of alienation. The Greek *polis*'s "happiness" consists precisely in that absence of separation and division between people and their community. In short, it is the happiness of unity. It is by sacrificing their particularity, abandoning any conception of themselves as individuals apart from their cultural identity, and subordinating their separate and particular interests to the shared interests of the community that the members of ancient *Sittlichkeit* come to see themselves as the kind of beings they are, individual instantiations of the shared spirit of their community.[115] As noted above, Hegel is clearly attracted to this, and he finds it in dramatic contrast to the division and fragmentation of modern social life.

Although at times Hegel's writings seem to reveal a feeling of loss and even a yearning for a return to this more harmonious way of relating to the social world, it is nevertheless equally true that he rejects the idea of returning to the ancient *Sittlichkeit*. To do so would be both impossible and undesirable. It is impossible because of the movement of *Geist* in history, through which humanity has attained the "principle of particularity," which recognizes the importance of the separate and particular interest of human beings and their right to develop and pursue them:

> Since the subjective satisfaction of the individual himself . . . is also part and parcel of the achievement of ends of absolute worth, it follows that the demand that such an end alone shall appear as willed and attained. . . . The right of the subject's particularity, his right to be satisfied, or in other words, the right of subjective freedom, is the pivot and center of the difference between antiquity and modern times. This right in its infinity is given expression in Christianity and it has become the universal effective principle of a new form of civilization. Amongst the primary shapes which this right assumes are love, romanticism, the quest for the eternal salvation of the individual . . . , next come moral convictions and conscience; and, finally, the other forms, some of which come into prominence in what follows as the principle of civil society.[116]

The "principle of particularity" and the "principle of subjective freedom" are irreversible for Hegel. Also, the undivided unity of ancient *Sittlichkeit* is primitive and undesirable, since it leaves no room for particularity, subjectivity, or individuality. Thus, Greek *Sittlichkeit* is merely a starting point for the development of morality as a higher form of *Geist*. Modern *Sittlichkeit* provides the dispositions that make a social world hospitable to subjective freedom.[117]

Hegel's aim is therefore not to reconstruct the harmony of ancient *Sittlichkeit* but rather to find a way of grasping modern *Sittlichkeit* as combining the fruits of modernity, the principle of particularity, with community membership, the principle of universality.

> In this regard, Hegel's move entails a clear break with the traditions of Kantian and classical Greek theories of justice. Whereas Kant collapsed all right into

morality and legality, Plato and Aristotle excluded the subjective reflection of moral conscience from their concept of ethical institutions. By contrast, Hegel here introduces an ethical life irreducible to abstract right and morality, which nevertheless incorporates their respective freedoms in its ethical order.[118]

In true dialectical fashion, his goal does not require the suppression of individuality; it is a project of reconciliation. The idea of reconciliation is an idea of unity with the social world, which involves regarding oneself as a member of the social world in some very strong sense.[119] Hegel argues that a rational society makes the civil, legal, and political structure of the community known to its members, along with how individual activities contribute to and benefit from this structure. In this way, he expects to combine individual satisfaction and freedom in conformity to the social ethos of the community. "The claim that freedom is achieved through modern Sittlichkeit, then, amounts to the claim that the duties and virtues of modern Sittlichkeit are what have come to count as good reasons for us moderns and have a certain rational, historical superiority vis-à-vis pervious attempts to formulate good reasons."[120] Since our needs and desires are shaped by society, a community can foster the development of those desires that most benefit the community.

Like Rousseau's general will, the community teaches its members that their own identity consists in being a part of the community so that they will not pursue interests that might damage the community:

Individuals in their capacity as burghers in this state are private persons whose end is their own interest. This end is *mediated* through the universal which thus *appears* as a *means* to its realization. Consequently, individuals can attain their ends only in so far as they themselves determine their knowing, willing, and acting in a universal way and make themselves links in this chain of social connections.[121]

This relationship is reciprocal; the community cannot disregard the interests of its members anymore than a body would disregard an injury to its left arm. In the *Philosophy of Right*, he calls "civil society" [*bürgerliche Gesellschaft*] the positive creation of individualism, and it is seen as the achievement of modern *Sittlichkeit*. It is comprised of the institutions and practices involved in the production, distribution, and consumption of products that meet a variety of needs and wants. As Hegel sees it, freedom is only realizable in a commercial society. Put differently, a subject must acquire an external sphere of freedom in order to exist as idea. The relationship between subject and external things is a connection of external possession and ownership, that is, a relation of property. It also represents the growing recognition by the community that its members have legitimate rights and interests as particular, private individuals.

"Personality essentially involves the capacity for rights. . . . Hence the imperative of right is: 'Be a person and respect others as persons.'"[122]

Hegel's ethical order means systematically allowing for social diversity and enabling different individuals to actualize various possibilities. The subjective freedom of modern life leads people to demand that they choose their own way for themselves.[123] Being a site of self-actualization, modern *Sittlichkeit* is a realm of "concrete freedom," which combines subjective and objective freedom in the proper relationship:

> Roughly speaking an agent (or 'will') enjoys subjective freedom to the extent that he reflects on, and is able to find some subjective satisfaction in, his actions and relationships (his 'determinations'). He enjoys objective freedom, by contrast, to the extent that his determinations are prescribed by reason: they are the determinations to which a fully rational agent, in the circumstances, would be committed. The subjectively free agent, then, is the agent who stands back from his determinations, reflects on them critically and independently, and is able both to endorse them and to find some subjective satisfaction in them. The objectively free agent, on the other hand, is the agent who, quite independently of whether he engages in reflection, has the correct determinations—the determinations that are prescribed by reason. The fully free agent—the agent who enjoys what Hegel terms 'concrete' or 'absolute' freedom—is free in both the subjective and objective senses.[124]

Hegel claims that agents enjoy both subjective and objective freedom in modern *Sittlichkeit*. He stops well short of the individualism of modern liberalism, however. His point is that one does not find his authentic self or true individuality by detaching himself from social responsibility, or by adding quirks and peculiarities to it.[125] To be an individual is always to have a determinate standing in society. True individuality, thus, consists in fulfilling in one's own way a determinate social function. Individuality degenerates into alienation unless it is supported socially by solidarity. Hegel's social thought reflects an organic as opposed to a mechanic metaphor for society. Like Herder, he infers from this metaphor that each culture is a self-contained whole that must be understood and appreciated in terms of its own internal laws.

Hegel's ethical theory is not relativist, however; it attempts to articulate some sort of standard for ethical conceptions and the social orders that embody them. *Sittlichkeit* does not refer to just any community but only to the community that has a rational or universal content, which has freedom for its content.[126] The laws and institutions of such a community are determined by the concept of freedom and together they compose a rational system. Hegel's ethical theory also is a self-actualization theory whose object is plural in the sense that the human spirit forms different conceptions of itself at different

times and places.[127] He notes that economic need, utility, and production owe
are shaped by social interaction. In other words, even though members of a
given society related to one another through their needs, Hegel does not think
that they do so as a natural condition. Societies are built on a historically
emergent framework in which individuals act to satisfy, not their physical
requirements or psychological desires, but those freely chosen needs whose
means of satisfaction can only be had through other analogously needy individuals.[128] Even though the particular content of these economic needs are a
matter of personal preference, they are predicated on the social context, that
is, the culture.

Modern *Sittlichkeit* is his remedy for the tension between the individual
and society, the particular and the universal. It is a home for people who are
both individuals and social members. Hegel's conception of modern *Sittlichkeit* offers a remedy for modern homelessness and alienation. It provides a
social anchor for individuals who feel lost and alone in the modern world.
But it is important to recognize that he does not conceive of reconciliation as
a state of perfect harmony, or a circumstance in which absolutely no conflicts
remain. Reconciliation need not be a state of perfect harmony. For example,
when two individuals become reconciled it might be recognized that conflict
can be a healthy part of their relationship. In a similar vein, Hegel maintains
that conflict is an integral component of reconciliation in the social world.[129]
He contends that people will inevitably come into conflict in the modern
social world, even if it is well ordered and even if they are reconciled. More
specifically, they experience conflict between the separate and particular interests that they have as individuals. Modern *Sittlichkeit* is not a Utopia.

It is no accident that such conflicts occur. Hegel argues that in a well-
ordered society people will be raised to have separate and particular interests,
some of which inevitably come into conflict with the demands of their social
roles.[130] In his view, reconciliation essentially involves accepting, even embracing, tensions. The tension between separate and particular interests and
the demands of community are a necessary by-product of one's individuality. The conflict is found between one's individual, family, and community
roles. Human beings need separate spheres in which they can find intimacy,
actualize their individuality, and enjoy political community. For Hegel, civil
society is the sphere of *Sittlichkeit* in which human beings actualize their individuality, but the price of differentiation is conflict. The roles social members
occupy within *Sittlichkeit* are constitutive of their identities.[131] Civil society
is the part of modern life that meets the private interests of individuals, but
it is also a network of spontaneous, private relations established within the
framework of law by individuals pursuing their own ends.[132]

Hegel makes a basic distinction between civil society and state. The complex of activities, attitudes, rules, and institutions that make up civil society is only an aspect of political and social life abstracted from the wider, more concrete state.[133] In this realm, a person's movement toward universality is shown by the very multiplication of wants. As will be discussed in more depth in Chapter 5, with the specialization of labor, wants are refined and extended. Consciousness cannot be developed without the material base implied in the multiplication of material wants.[134] The specialization required to meet mankind's material needs and wants leads to the development of different categories of workers, also known as classes or estates [*Stände*]. The different classes have different particular interests that they actively pursue. But the very conflict of interests always present gives rise to the consciousness of a possible general interest under which administration of justice can be subsumed:

> When men are thus dependent on one another and reciprocally related to one another in their work and the satisfaction of their needs, subjective self-seeking turns into a contribution to the satisfaction of the needs of everyone else. That is to say, by a dialectical advance, subjective self-seeking turns into the mediation of the particular through the universal, with the result that each man in earning, producing, and enjoying on his own account is *eo ipso* producing and earning for the enjoyment of everyone else.[135]

Law arises to objectify right [*Recht*], and it presumably reflects reason unaffected by particularized interests. *Bildung* [Education and Socialization] is also of paramount importance, since the process of becoming reconciled to the social world involves a transformation of consciousness through which one moves from an atomic individual to an individual societal member.[136]

It is Hegel's contention that modern individuality and social membership are not only compatible but also intertwined and inextricable. In fact, it is precisely through one's social membership that a person is able to actualize oneself as an individual, and through individuality that people are able to actualize themselves as social members. People, for Hegel, are individuals in the minimal sense; his conception of individuality is minimal in three respects.[137] First, it is a necessary condition for being a human individual. A person must regard himself as distinct from other persons in order to be an individual. One becomes an individual through a process of differentiation from others.[138] Second, it states the weakest conception of individuality that can still intuitively be regarded as a genuine conception of human individuality. One can be an individual without stepping back from one's social roles and institutions. In short, Hegel's minimal conception of individuality represents a form of individualism that makes no reference to the contrast between the individual and society. However, his conception of individuality is clearly much stronger than the virtually nonexistent one in ancient Greece. Hegel's individuals possess political rights. It is the strong, not minimal, conception of individuality that Hegel regards as distinctively atomistic and excessive.

With his conception of social membership, Hegel maintains that human beings are essentially social. First, they depend on society for the satisfaction of biological, social, and cultural needs. Second, they depend on society for the realization of their distinctly human capacities, such as thought, language, and reason. In this respect, he resembles the Aristotelian notion that man is a political animal. People are formed by their national culture.[139] For example, the roles of family member, member of civil society, and citizen figure strongly in the psychological makeup of human beings. Hegel says that the attitudes, habits, and ideals internal to these roles constitute core features of personality.[140] Being a member of a particular state means participating in its central institutions. In fact, Hegel contends that people need and desire the sort of intimacy that these roles entail. Hence, his moral psychology is rooted in his social psychology.

Whereas Kant left autonomy without reality by restricting ethics to the inner legislation of moral duty while relegating all external relations (including property, family, civil government, and world law) to the nonethical sphere of legality, Hegel here conceives the family, civil society, and the state as ethical interactions precisely insofar as they give subjective freedom actuality by being the existing framework of its realization. . . . Hegel recognizes that it is no more self-evident how the special unity of ethical community works itself out than how the family, society, and the state can provide the modes of its existence.[141]

Individuals, according to Hegel, need society in the strong sense. This claim is grounded in his notion that in order to realize themselves fully as *Geist*, people must participate in social life. Human social life is found within the social arrangements constituted by *Sittlichkeit*—the family, civil society, and the state.[142] Hence, when people participate in these arrangements, they are realizing themselves as *Geist* precisely by exercising their roles of family member, member of civil society, and citizen. One of the central aims of the *Philosophy of Right* is to stress that individuals are also members of the *Sittlichkeit*.[143] It argues that a full-fledged form of individuality and a full-fledged form of social membership can be reconciled. Hegel argues that conceptions of the self as a bearer of separate and particular interests, a possessor of individual rights, and a subject of conscience are all internal to the role of member of *Sittlichkeit*.[144] Critics, and some of his communitarian supporters, think that Hegel reduces ethical life to the unreflective submission of individuals to a community's customs. "What is not sufficiently understood is that the content of this ethical substance embraces rights and freedoms that have been established in the preceding moments of abstract right and morality."[145]

In addition to arguing for the compatibility of modern individuality and social membership, Hegel contends that social membership makes modern individuality possible. For instance, he maintains that the conception of the individual as bearing separate and particular interests and rights belongs to the self-conception people have as members of *Sittlichkeit*.[146] Modern *Sittlichkeit* is seen as the proper sphere for the exercise of these self-understandings. In fact, these self-understandings are engendered by the practices of one's culture. It is through participation in civil society that people come to think of themselves as bearers of separate and particular interests. Participating in civil society is a matter of abstracting oneself from one's role of family member or citizen and pursuing one's separate and particular interests in the world of work.[147] As discussed in the next chapter, it is through participating in civil society, through actualizing oneself as a member of *Sittlichkeit*, that one actualizes oneself as an individual and is truly free:

> Ethical life [*Sittlichkeit*] is the Idea of freedom in that on one hand it is the good become alive—the good endowed in self-consciousness with knowing and willing and actualized by self-conscious action—while, on the other hand self-consciousness has in the ethical realm its absolute foundation and the end which actuates its effort. Thus ethical life [*Sittlichkeit*] is the concept of freedom developed into the existing world and the nature of self-consciousness.[148]

## NOTES

1. Günter Grass, *The Tin Drum*, trans. R. Manheim (New York: Vintage, 1961), 93 and 412.

2. Allen Wood, *Hegel's Ethical Thought* (New York: Cambridge University Press, 1990), 17.

3. Wood, *Hegel's Ethical Thought*, 17.

4. Johann G. Fichte, *The Science of Knowledge*, trans. Peter Heath and John Lachs (Cambridge: Cambridge University Press, 1983), 66 and 99.

5. Fichte, *The Science of Knowledge*, 232–233.

6. Wood, *Hegel's Ethical Thought*, 18.

7. Georg W. F. Hegel, *Philosophy of Right*, trans T. M. Knox (London: Oxford University Press, 1952), 23.

8. Hegel, *Philosophy of Right*, 21.

9. Georg W. F. Hegel, *Lectures on the History of Philosophy, Volume 1: Greek Philosophy to Plato*, trans. E. S. Haldane (Lincoln: University of Nebraska Press, 1995), 45.

10. Hegel, *Philosophy of Right*, 21.

11. Hegel, *Philosophy of Right*, 160. The true giving of content to morality cannot occur at the level of conscious inwardness; it demands a surrender to *Sittlichkeit*, the concrete ways of a well-organized society.

12. Eric Weil, *Hegel and the State*, trans. Mark Cohen (Baltimore: Johns Hopkins University Press, 1998), 21.

13. Robert B. Pippin, *Idealism as Modernism: Hegelian Variations* (Cambridge: Cambridge University Press, 1997), 92.

14. Hegel, *Philosophy of Right*, 105.

15. Wood, *Hegel's Ethical Thought*, 21.

16. Fred Dallmayr, *G. W. F. Hegel: Modernity and Politics* (Newbury Park, Calif.: Sage, 1993), 103.

17. Allen Wood, "Hegel's Ethics," in *The Cambridge Companion to Hegel*, ed. Frederick Beiser (Cambridge: Cambridge University Press, 1993), 230.

18. Allen Wood, "Hegel's Ethics," 231

19. Georg W. F. Hegel, *Phenomenology of Spirit*, trans. A. V. Miller (Oxford: Oxford University Press, 1977), 110.

20. Paul Franco, *Hegel's Philosophy of Freedom* (New Haven: Yale University Press, 1999), 190.

21. Georg W. F. Hegel, *Science of Logic*, trans. A. V. Miller (Amherst: Humanity Books, 1969), 575.

22. Wood, *Hegel's Ethical Thought*, 7.

23. Richard Dien Winfield, *Freedom and Modernity* (Albany: State University of New York Press, 1991), 123.

24. Georg W. F. Hegel, *Faith and Knowledge*, trans. W. Cerf and Henry Harris (Albany: SUNY Press, 1977). Hegel first develops the distinction between *Sittlichkeit* and *Moralität* in 1802 in this work.

25. Georg W. F. Hegel, *The Philosophy of History*, trans. J. Sibree (Buffalo: Prometheus, 1991), 252.

26. Hegel, *Philosophy of Right*, 109.

27. Hegel, *Lectures in the History of Philosophy, Volume 1*, 100.

28. Hegel, *The Philosophy of History*, 253.

29. Hegel, *The Philosophy of History*, 254.

30. Michael J. Inwood, "Hegel, Plato and Greek *Sittlichkeit*," in *The State and Civil Society: Studies in Hegel's Political Philosophy*, ed. Z. Pelczynski (Cambridge: Cambridge University Press, 1984), 41.

31. Terry Pinkard, *Hegel's Phenomenology: The Sociality of Reason* (New York: Cambridge University Press, 1996), 138.

32. Hegel, *Phenomenology of Spirit*, 268.

33. Hegel, *Phenomenology of Spirit*, 268.

34. Pinkard, *Hegel's Phenomenology*, 139.

35. Hegel, *Phenomenology of Spirit*, 268.

36. Pinkard, *Hegel's Phenomenology*, 140.

37. Hegel, *Phenomenology of Spirit*, 270.

38. Hegel, *Phenomenology of Spirit*, 270–271.

39. Hegel, *Phenomenology of Spirit*, 271.

40. Pinkard, *Hegel's Phenomenology*, 141–142.

41. Hegel, *Phenomenology of Spirit*, 274–275.

42. Pinkard, *Hegel's Phenomenology*, 143.

43. Georg W. F. Hegel, *Hegel's Aesthetics: Lectures on Fine Art, Volume 1*, trans. T. M. Knox (Oxford: Oxford University Press, 1975), 464.

44. Georg W. F. Hegel, *Lectures on the Philosophy of Religion, Volume 2*, trans. E. Spiers and J. Sanderson (New York: Humanities Press, 1962), 264–265.

45. Hegel, *Phenomenology of Spirit*, 284.

46. Hegel, *Phenomenology of Spirit*, 285.

47. Pinkard, *Hegel's Phenomenology*, 145.

48. Hegel, *Phenomenology of Spirit*, 289.

49. Henry S. Harris, *Hegel: Phenomenology and System* (Indianapolis: Hackett Publishing, 1995), 95.

50. Robert Stern, *Hegel and the* Phenomenology of Spirit (New York: Routledge, 2002), 142. It is because each individual identifies him or herself wholly with one overriding ethical imperative that Hegel sees the clash between Antigone and Creon as tragic.

51. Kenneth R. Westphal, *Hegel's Epistemology: A Philosophical Introduction to the* Phenomenology of Spirit (Indianapolis: Hackett Publishing, 2003), 34.

52. Immanuel Kant, *Critique of Practical Reason*, trans. Lewis Beck (New York: Macmillan, 1933), 3.

53. Immanuel Kant, *Groundwork for the Metaphysics of Morals*, trans. Allen Wood (New Haven, Conn.: Yale University Press, 2002), 77–78.

54. Kant, *Groundwork for the Metaphysics of Morals*, 28–29.

55. Immanuel Kant, *Critique of Pure Reason*, trans. Norman Kemp Smith (New York: St. Martin's Press, 1929), 28–29, and Kant, *Critique of Practical Reason*, 17.

56. Kant, *Critique of Practical Reason*, 16–18.

57. Kant, *Critique of Pure Reason*, 633–634.

58. Kant, *Groundwork for the Metaphysics of Morals*, 63.

59. Marcia Baron, "Acting from Duty," in Kant, *Groundwork for the Metaphysics of Morals*, 95.

60. Kant, *Critique of Practical Reason*, 83.

61. Kant, *Groundwork for the Metaphysics of Morals*, 9.

62. Kant, *Groundwork for the Metaphysics of Morals*, 9.

63. Kant, *Critique of Practical Reason*, 115.

64. Kant, *Groundwork for the Metaphysics of Morals*, 23.

65. Kant, *Groundwork for the Metaphysics of Morals*, 17.

66. Kant, *Critique of Practical Reason*, 164.

67. Lewis Beck, *Studies in The Philosophy of Kant* (Indianapolis: Bobbs-Merrill, 1965), 23.

68. Karl Jaspers, *Kant*, trans. R. Manheim (New York: Harvest, 1962), 76. For Kant, only the doctrine of the phenomenology of objective existence stands in the way of any denial of freedom. If phenomena are things-in-themselves, freedom cannot be saved. For then nature is the complete cause of every event. The awareness

of freedom is demonstrated by the concept of duty. Freedom is the point where the supersensible is present in this world, where we can grasp it in our hands though we can never know it as something in the world. Through the unconditioned practical law, human reason knows itself to belong to the supersensible world.

69. Immanuel Kant, *Fundamental Principles of the Metaphysics of Morals*, trans. T. Abbott (Buffalo, N.Y.: Prometheus Books, 1987), 40.

70. Kant, *Groundwork for the Metaphysics of Morals*, 38.

71. Kant, *Critique of Practical Reason*, 18.

72. Kant, *Groundwork for the Metaphysics of Morals*, 45. Since it is imperative it requires duty, and right or duty is used to define some ends as obligatory. According to Kant, without some such ends, rationality could assess many actions only insofar as they might be instrumentally good for obtaining desired things. This would make relevant policies only hypothetical and thus fail to discover discernable moral worth.

73. Kant, *Groundwork for the Metaphysics of Morals*, 30–31.

74. Kant, *Groundwork for the Metaphysics of Morals*, 37. See J. B. Schneewind, "Autonomy, Obligation, and Virtue: An Overview of Kant's Moral Philosophy," in *The Cambridge Companion to Kant*, ed. Paul Guyer (Cambridge: Cambridge University Press, 1992), 328–329, where he notes that Kant's freedom is more than the absence of determination. A will wholly underdetermined would be random and chaotic. It would not allow for responsibility, nor consequently for praise or blame. So Kant argues that for a will to be rational and free, it is also essential that it act only on universalizable maxims. The free will is one whose choices are determined by a law internal to its nature.

75. Kant, *Groundwork for the Metaphysics of Morals*, 37.

76. Kant, *Critique of Practical Reason*, 33.

77. Kant, *Groundwork for the Metaphysics of Morals*, 42–43. See also Onora O'Neill, "Vindicating Reason," *The Cambridge Companion to Kant*, 299. Reason is sketched not as abstract principle, but as lawlike guidance of thinking and doing in a dynamic process that neither submits to outside control nor fails to acknowledge differences of opinion and practice, and which treats resulting contradictions and tensions as an indefinitely extended demand for revision.

78. Kant, *Groundwork for the Metaphysics of Morals*, 45–47.

79. Kant, *Critique of Practical Reason*, 138.

80. Kant, *Critique of Practical Reason*, 116.

81. Immanuel Kant, "Perpetual Peace," in *Political Writings*, trans. H. Nisbet (Cambridge: Cambridge University Press, 1991), 116.

82. Winfield, *Freedom and Modernity*, 111. "For Hegel, the ethical import of Kant's conception is clear: With individuality barred from objective existence and reason relegated to an external ordering of given particulars, practical reason cannot possibly provide freedom the self-determined reality it requires" (115).

83. Pippin, *Idealism as Modernism*, 101.

84. Pippin, *Idealism as Modernism*, 103.

85. See Hegel, *Philosophy of Right*, 21–35.

86. Hegel, *Philosophy of Right*, 78.

87. Winfield, *Freedom and Modernity*, 117.

88. Kenneth Westphal, "The Basic Context and Structure of Hegel's *Philosophy of Right*," in *The Cambridge Companion to Hegel*, 236. In this respect, Hegel is acknowledging the force of Romantic criticisms of the Enlightenment's a-historical, a-social, individualist account of reason.

89. Pippin, *Idealism as Modernism*, 98.

90. Hegel, *Philosophy of Right*, 107. Hegel notes that the bond of duty can appear as a restriction only on indeterminate subjectivity or abstract freedom. The truth is that in duty individuals find their liberation: First, liberation from dependence on mere natural impulse, and second, liberation from indeterminate subjectivity. Thus, substantive freedom is acquired in duty.

91. Hegel, *Philosophy of Right*, 253. "I should do my duty for duty's sake, and when I do my duty it is in a true sense my own objectivity which I am bringing to realization. In doing my duty, I am by myself free. To have emphasized this meaning of duty has constituted the merit of Kant's moral philosophy and its loftiness of outlook."

92. Hegel, *Philosophy of Right*, 89–90. See Franco, *Hegel's Philosophy of Freedom*, 215, where he notes that Hegel focuses exclusively on the first and most formalistic foundation of the categorical imperative, neglecting the second and third formulations, which go some distance toward providing the content that Hegel claims is missing from Kant's ethics. Nevertheless, though Hegel's critique of Kantian ethics may not be the tour de force he imagined, the charge of Kant's ethics are ultimately empty and formalistic is not unwarranted since it is difficult to determine what we ought to do in any particular ethical situation using the categorical imperative alone.

93. Franco, *Hegel's Philosophy of Freedom*, 216.

94. Joachim Ritter, *Hegel and the French Revolution: Essays on* The Philosophy of Right, trans. Richard Winfield (Cambridge: MIT Press, 1982), 168. Whereas Kant collapsed all right into morality and legality, Plato and Aristotle excluded the subjective reflection of moral conscience from their concept of ethical institutions. Hegel, by contrast, introduces an ethical life irreducible to abstract right and morality, which nonetheless incorporates their respective freedoms in its ethical order.

95. Westphal, "The Basic Context and Structure of Hegel's *Philosophy of Right*," 253.

96. Ritter, *Hegel and the French Revolution*, 152.

97. Hegel, *Phenomenology of Spirit*, 231.

98. Hegel, *Philosophy of Right*, 83.

99. Hegel, *Philosophy of Right*, 252.

100. Hegel, *Philosophy of Right*, 251–252.

101. Hegel, *Science of Logic*, 820.

102. Wood, *Hegel's Ethical Theory*, 145.

103. Pippin, *Idealism as Modernism*, 99. See Karl-Otto Apel, "Kant, Hegel, and the Contemporary Question Concerning the Normative Foundations of Morality and Right," in *Hegel on Ethics and Politics*, eds. Robert Pippin and O. Höffe (Cambridge: Cambridge University Press, 2004), 59, where he notes that Hegel claims to identify the mediation and integration of the subjective freedom and an ethical substance that is not longer simply natural but has been sublated, that is negated and preserved, in

self-conscious form. For Hegel, this is the sphere of state in which the ethical idea properly manifests itself as such.

104. Hegel, *Philosophy of Right*, 20. See also, John N. Findlay, *Hegel: A Re-Examination* (Oxford: Oxford University Press, 1958), 318.

105. Pippin, *Idealism as Modernism*, 109.

106. Winfield, *Freedom and Modernity*, 122.

107. Georg W. F. Hegel, *Philosophy of Mind*, trans. A. V. Miller (New York: Oxford University Press, 1971), 249.

108. Hegel calls the third part of the *Philosophy of Right* ethical life, or *Sittlichkeit*. His discussion of *Sittlichkeit* is divided into three parts—The Family, Civil Society, and The State. The family and civil society are examined more thoroughly in Chapter 5, and Hegel's conception of the state is discussed in Chapter 6.

109. Hegel, *Philosophy of Right*, 104.

110. Hegel, *Philosophy of Right*, 105.

111. Wood, *Hegel's Ethical Thought*, 197.

112. Hegel, *Philosophy of Mind*, 253. *Sittlichkeit* is the perfection of objective *Geist*—the truth of subjective and objective *Geist* itself.

113. Hegel, *Philosophy of Right*, 108–109.

114. Hegel, *The Philosophy of History*, 252.

115. Michael Hardimon, *Hegel's Social Philosophy: The Project of Reconciliation* (New York: Cambridge University Press, 1994), 34.

116. Hegel, *Philosophy of Right*, 83–84.

117. Alan Patten, *Hegel's Idea of Freedom* (New York: Oxford University Press, 1999), 37.

118. Winfield, *Freedom and Modernity*, 123.

119. Hardimon, *Hegel's Social Philosophy*, 32.

120. Patten, *Hegel's Idea of Freedom*, 31.

121. Hegel, *Philosophy of Right*, 124

122. Hegel, *Philosophy of Right*, 37.

123. Hegel, *Philosophy of Right*, 132–133.

124. Patten, *Hegel's Idea of Freedom*, 35.

125. Wood, *Hegel's Ethical Thought*, 200.

126. Franco, *Hegel's Philosophy of Freedom*, 224. Individuals do not relate to the laws and institutions of *Sittlichkeit* as a child does to the commands of its parents, but rather as a self-conscious adult who recognizes the rationality of those laws and institutions. Hegel does not see the ethical disposition of its members as simply a throwback to the ethical attitude that characterized premodern societies.

127. Wood, *Hegel's Ethical Thought*, 203; and Hegel, *Philosophy of Right*, 216–223.

128. Winfield, *Freedom and Modernity*, 126.

129. Hegel, *Philosophy of Right*, 107–108.

130. Hegel, *Philosophy of Right*, 126–134.

131. Frederick Neuhouser, *Foundations of Hegel's Social Theory: Actualizing Freedom* (Cambridge: Harvard University Press, 2000), 95.

132. Hegel, *Philosophy of Right*, 122–123.

133. Hegel, *Philosophy of Right*, 123.

134. Hegel, *Philosophy of Right*, 127–128.

135. Hegel, *Philosophy of Right*, 129–130.

136. Neuhouser, *Foundations of Hegel's Social Theory*, 149. For Hegel, *Bildung* is inseparably connected to freedom. It is not simply the formative experience of any type but formative experience that has a specific end, that is, self-determination. *Bildung* refers to the kind of formative experience that results in the transformation of unformed, natural individuals into subjects who aspire to be free and who possess the capacities necessary to realize their freedom.

137. See Hardimon, *Hegel's Social Philosophy*, 146–153.

138. Hegel, *Philosophy of Right*, 133.

139. Hegel, *Philosophy of Right*, 108. See Neuhouser, *Foundations of Hegel's Social Theory*, 101, where he says that despite an infinite variety among the concrete circumstances that enter into the particular identities acquired within *Sittlichkeit*, they are also, at a fundamental level, shared identities that secure a significant degree of commonality among the basic self-conceptions, and hence the substantive interests, of social members.

140. Hegel, *Philosophy of Right*, 105–106, 109, and 163–164.

141. Winfield, *Freedom and Modernity*, 124.

142. These three institutions are discussed in the next two chapters. See Patten, *Hegel's Idea of Freedom*, 37. Modern *Sittlichkeit* contributes to the realization of subjective freedom, because a community containing the family, civil society, and the state is the minimum self-sufficient institutional structure in which agents can develop, maintain, and exercise the capacities and attitudes involved with subjective freedom. For Hegel, a free society is a fragile construction that can be sustained only if certain institutional structures are in place.

143. Hegel, *Philosophy of Right*, 110. See Neuhouser, *Foundation's of Hegel's Social Theory*, 98, where he notes that membership in *Sittlichkeit* involves a recognition of individuals' particularity—of their worth as the particular beings they are.

144. Hegel, *Philosophy of Right*, 124–145.

145. Franco, *Hegel's Philosophy of Freedom*, 221. Ethical life is the third of the three large moments that constitute the basic structure of the *Philosophy of Right*, and it is in ethical life that the one-sidedness of the two earlier moments, abstract right and morality, are synthesized and overcome. It is only in ethical life that the objectivity of abstract right is brought together with the subjectivity of morality to form a concrete whole.

146. Hegel, *Philosophy of Right*, 126–130 and 134–145.

147. Hegel, *Philosophy of Right*, 127–129.

148. Hegel, *Philosophy of Right*, 105.

# Chapter Five

# The Family and
# *Bürgerliche Gesellschaft*:
# The Realm of Particular Freedom

Human beings could expect to be forsaken by the rain clouds, and all the animals and plants would disappear. All over the world Europeans had laughed at indigenous people for worshiping the rain clouds, the mountains, and the trees. But now Calabazas had lived long enough to see the white people stop laughing as all the trees were cut and all the animals killed, and all the water dirtied or used up. White people were scared because they didn't know where to go or what to use up and pollute next.[1]

—Leslie Marmon Silko, *The Almanac of the Dead*

With *Sittlichkeit* [Ethical Life], Hegel distinguishes his ethical theory from the earlier modern standpoints of abstract right and morality by virtue of its concreteness. Formal right and morality were shown to be abstract and unable to stand on their own as independent realities. A concrete standpoint is achieved only by uniting these two abstract points of view into a single whole.[2] Hegel accomplishes this in the three parts of *Sittlichkeit*—the Family, Civil Society [*bürgerliche Gesellschaft*], and the State [*Rechtsstaat*]. Each is a concrete unity of objectivity and subjectivity, and therefore each is capable of actual existence, as demonstrated in the previous chapter. Hegel argues that we no longer have to settle for pure abstractions but can have concrete forms of social life. Ethical life develops from the family, through civil society, to the modern state.[3] Individual rights achieve their fulfillment, since it is here that individuals come into true possession of their own essence, their inner universality:

The right of individuals to be subjectively destined to freedom is fulfilled when they belong to an actual ethical order, because their conviction of their freedom

155

finds its truth in such an objective order, and it is in an ethical order that they are actually in possession of their own essence or their own inner universality.[4]

This chapter focuses on the family and civil society and leaves Hegel's treatment of the state for the next chapter.

The development of ethical life mirrors the dialectical "movement of the logical concept from immediacy to differentiation or reflectedness to a synthesis of these two moments, identity that contains difference."[5] To put it in less technical vernacular, *the family* represents ethical life in its simplest form, since the ethical unity of the family is an immediate one based on love. Family members do not relate to one another as self-sufficient personalities but as parts of a larger whole to which they immediately identify.[6] However, the family also exists in a larger context in which individuals are not bound together by the natural sentiment of love. For Hegel, this larger context is the realm of *civil society*, the sphere of economic or market relationships. In this realm, the individuality and self-interest that were submerged by the family become liberated. Even though individuals are driven primarily by self-interest in civil society, they are implicitly governed by the universal and are invisibly led to serve one another's interests through the mechanism of the market.[7] The universality that is implicit in civil society—which operates as unconscious necessity there—becomes the explicit goal of individuals in *the state*. In the *Rechtsstaat* [Modern State], individuals once again become conscious of their unity with others, but it is no longer on the plane of immediate feeling as in the family. This unity is on the plane of law and reason.[8]

It is important to note that the family and civil society are not moments in the development of *Sittlichkeit* to be cast away once the state is reached. For Hegel, they constitute crucial elements of a properly developed political system. Hegel's political philosophy allows both to develop themselves freely and to achieve a degree of independence from the state. Hegel contrasts *Rechtsstaat* with the purely substantial states of antiquity, such as Plato's *Republic*, which tries to suppress the individuality and subjective freedom that are embedded in the family and civil society.[9] Nonetheless, the family and civil society are not only important because they embody the principle of subjective freedom, Hegel argues that they also play a crucial educative function by ensuring that individuals are not merely self-interested in their relation to the state but are already ethical in themselves. Hegel therefore refers to the family and civil society as the ethical roots of the state: Their importance "is due to the fact that although private persons are self-seeking, they are compelled to direct their attention to others. Here then is the root which connects self-seeking to the universal, i.e., to the state. . . ."[10] The family and civil society help purge people of their raw individuality. This transformation of subjectivity into ethical intersubjectivity is an aspect of Hegel's mediation between the ancient and modern world.

Hegel recognizes that economic need is not satisfied with natural things; rather, it is satisfied with commodities, goods expressly owned by other members of civil society who are willing to exchange them to satisfy their own social wants.[11] Unlike with both classical economists and Marxists, he notes that commodities carry utility that is social not natural. According to Hegel, participating in commodity exchange is an ethical right, since it realizes the particular self-determination of the individual with the existing system of the economy. To be sure, Hegel also concludes that civil society cannot restrict itself to economic relations or let them have free sway. This is particularly important, especially given today's neoliberal justification of globalization and unrestricted free trade. For Hegel, the economy cannot guarantee the realization of the very needs its interactions generates: "Precisely because the economy consists in commodity relations resting on mutual agreements of exchange, it is a matter of contingency whether its members encounter other willing parties whose respective needs and good correlate with their own."[12] Thus, Hegel finds that as long as the economy is left to its own logic, there is nothing to prevent economic crises, overproduction, unemployment, and extreme economic inequality. In a word, deregulation is not always a good policy.

Hegel's dialectic claims that reason, as the governing principle of *Geist*, is actualized in the structures of will that compose the social world, which is manifested as structures of freedom. This chapter examines Hegel's conception of the family and civil society, which constitute two parts of modern *Sittlichkeit*. This continues Hegel's attempt to ground individual liberty within an intersubjective moral framework. The chapter is divided into three sections. The first section discusses the important role played by the family in the development and maintenance of ethical life. Although the family is an important realm of particular freedom on its own, Hegel sees it as intrinsic to the development of universal freedom and community. The second section examines Hegel's conception of civil society, which is the realm of subjective freedom and particularity. It includes subsections devoted to Hegel's system of needs and political economy, the administration of justice and property, police and the regulation of community welfare, and the corporation. The final section addresses Hegel's conception of particularity and subjective freedom and marks the transition to the modern state, which is dealt with in the following chapter. Subjective freedom, for Hegel, is attained when individuals recognize the validity of substantive ethical norms and identify with the social institutions and their constitutive principles that compose a realm of objective freedom.

## THE FAMILY

Hegel's theory of family is important for both its own sake and for the light it throws on his understanding of the state. It represents the simplest example of what Hegel means by ethical life. It is a substantial whole—or universal—that does not stand over against the individual. Hegel "provides a basic conceptual anatomy of family, social, and political association that permits differentiating the modes of ethical freedom independently of extraneous factors."[13] The family is the institution where human beings first experience non-heteronymous priority of the whole over the part. Family members do not relate to each other as independent persons but rather as members of a larger whole where they find their essential identity. For Hegel, this nonindividualistic dimension of the family is important:

> The family, as the immediate substantiality of mind, is specifically characterized by love, which is mind's feeling of its own unity. Hence in a family, one's frame of mind is to have self-consciousness of one's individuality within this unity as the absolute essence of oneself, with the result that one is in it not as an independent person but as a member.[14]

The submersion of individual personality in the family does not constitute a regression from the individualistic standpoints of abstract right and morality. Although Hegel recognizes that the family historically preceded the institution of property and the awareness of subjective freedom, the family represents a higher stage of development and a more concrete embodiment of freedom than either abstract right or morality.[15] Hegel focuses on the small bourgeois family and not the extended traditional family. With the development of the modern economy, the extended family is replaced by the smaller bourgeois family.[16]

The family is a form of an ethical community of self-determination. In the family, the particular will of the individual is no longer contingently related to the universal in the form of either abstract right or the good. Hegel asserts that it instead wills the universal as such. In the family, we no longer have to do with the arbitrary will of the individual but with a genuinely universal will; the family is founded on an identity of will.[17] The family represents the substantiality of ethical spirit and embodies substantive freedom in an immediate, natural way, that is, in the form of feeling and love. Thus, the family is not only a fact of nature; it is an ethical substance that has a spiritual meaning that transcends the natural moment.[18] For Hegel, love is one of the most immediate examples of "being with oneself in the other."[19] He further stresses the significance of family love in overcoming independent personality:

> Love means in general terms the consciousness of my unity with another, so that I am not in selfish isolation but win my self-consciousness only as the renunciation of my independence and through knowing myself as the unity of myself with another and of the other with me. Love, however, is feeling, i.e., ethical life in the form of something natural. . . . The second moment is that I find myself in another person, that I count for something in the other, while the other in turn comes to count for something in me.[20]

Nevertheless, it is necessary to stress that the identity of the self and other in the family is only immediate, based on feeling. This allows Hegel to distinguish it from the unity found in the state, which is based on law and reason. However, since both the family and the state are substantial wholes in which individuals are subordinated to the universal, neither can be understood in terms of the individualistic model of a contract.

Even though Hegel sees the state as resting on different principles from the family, it does not mean that he regards the family as irrelevant to the state. To the contrary, Hegel suggests that the family plays a crucial role in transforming individuals into something more than merely self-interested persons. This lays the ethical foundations needed to form a rational state: "The family is the first precondition of the state. . . ."[21] More specifically, the family helps to build a foundation of trust between its members and the state.[22] Hegel argues that the ethical relationships found in the family are passed on to the state and serve as a needed ethical foundation, since each person feels united with the totality. The value of the family does not consist solely in this political function. The family is just as necessary for an individual's subjective freedom as is property. Important individual needs and interests are met through family life.

*The Philosophy of Right* offers an analysis of the three essential aspects of family life—marriage, family property, and the upbringing of children. The key to Hegel's understanding of marriage is his view that it is essentially an ethical relationship.[23] The family achieves its ethical purpose on the basis of natural relations that involves these three aspects of life. By this he means that marriage is a substantive unity in which the individuality of marriage partners is subordinated to the whole. This substantive unity is the self-conscious goal of marriage partners: "The ethical aspect of marriage consists in the parties' consciousness of this unity as their substantive end, and so in their love, trust, and common sharing their entire existence as individuals."[24] This emphasis on consciousness is important, since consciousness is what distinguishes the ethical relationship of marriage from the mere natural relationship of animal generation. While marriage contains aspects of animal generation, the preservation of the species is only an external universal, devoid of self-consciousness. "In self-consciousness the natural sexual union—a union purely inward or implicit and for that very reason *existent* as purely external—is changed into a union on the level of mind, into self-conscious love."[25]

By seeing marriage as an ethical relationship, Hegel differentiates his viewpoint from three other conceptions of marriage—the naturalistic, the contractual, and the romantic. Hegel identifies the naturalistic conception with the tradition of natural law, in which marriage is considered only in its physical aspect or natural character. "Consequently, it was treated only as a sex relationship, and this completely barred the way to its other characteristics."[26] The naturalistic conception has at least two versions with their own distinguishing characteristics. The first involves the claim that the primary purpose of marriage is the procreation of children and the reproduction of the species. As noted above, Hegel rejects this as the chief end of marriage, which would reduce marriage to the animal level. A second version of the naturalistic interpretation involves the claim that marriage exists primarily for the satisfaction of natural sexual desire. Hegel dismisses this because it makes marriage indistinguishable from concubinage: "The distinction between marriage and concubinage is that the latter is chiefly a matter of satisfying natural desire, while this satisfaction is made secondary in the former."[27] Human sexuality is raised from something that is merely biological and natural to something that is ethical and spiritual.

It is equally mistaken, according to Hegel, to view marriage as a contractual relationship. He associates the contractual interpretation with Kant's understanding of marriage. In a contract, the parties relate to each other as self-sufficient persons and form a common will with respect to a specific object, but they never lose their independence with respect to one another: "On this view, the parties are bound by a contract of mutual caprice, and marriage is thus degraded to a level of a contract for reciprocal use."[28] Consequently, they do not form a complete unity. Their independent personalities do not coalesce to form a single person, which is exactly what is involved in marriage as an ethical relationship for Hegel.[29] While Hegel accepts the fact that marriage originates in the arbitrary will like a contract, he does not think that this constitutes its essential basis:

> On the contrary, though marriage begins in contract, it is precisely a contract to transcend the standpoint of contract, the standpoint from which persons are regarded in their individuality as self-subsistent units. The identification of personalities, whereby the family becomes one person and its members become its accidents . . . , is the ethical mind.[30]

Thus, marriage begins with the point of view of a contract, but it quickly supercedes this condition. For Hegel, contractual relationships are abstract, contingent, and self-centered.[31]

The third mistaken conception of marriage that Hegel rejects is the romantic view that simply equates marriage with love. This is the conception that becomes very popular in Romantic thought toward the end of the eighteenth century. Like Kierkegaard after him, Hegel finds romantic love to be too insecure as a basis for marriage.[32] Since love is subjective, transient, and completely contingent, it totally conflicts with the ethical character of marriage. In contradistinction to the contingency and subjectivity of romantic love, Hegel uses rightful ethical love [*rechtlich sittliche Liebe*] to describe the appropriate disposition of marriage.[33] For Hegel, this eliminates the transient, fickle, and purely subjective aspects of love from marriage. In this context, he defends the public marriage ceremony as a bond that expresses and confirms the ethical quality against the contingency of feeling of Romantic thinkers, such as Friedrich von Schlegel who dismiss the marriage ceremony as an empty formality.[34]

It is necessary to note that Hegel does not completely obliterate the principle of subjective freedom. He insists that marriage must be based on the free consent of the individuals involved:

> On the subjective side, marriage may have a more obvious source in the particular inclination of the two persons who are entering upon the marriage tie. . . . But its objective source lies in the free consent of the persons, especially in their consent to make themselves one person, to renounce their natural and individual personality to this unity of one with the other.[35]

Thus, marriage is a determinate intersubjectivity, since it originates in free consent. Even though he recognizes that parents often arrange marriages, he never implies that parents can arrange a marriage without the consent of the parties. In his Heidelberg lectures, Hegel also says that the opposition of the parents cannot be an absolute obstacle to marriage.[36]

Since the ethical love animating the family is bound up with the activities of honoring the rights and duties of spouses and children, the imperatives of family freedom can fall within the scope of the law.[37] Hegel believes that marriage is indissoluble in principle, since the *telos* of marriage is the formation of an enduring ethical union. However, while marriage as such aims in principle to be an enduring ethical union, particular marriages may break down.[38] Because marriage is based on subjective feeling to a significant extent, divorce can occur when feelings radically change. Hegel recognizes that two people cannot be compelled to stay together in the total absence of love. According to its ethical character, Hegel argues that marriage ought to be indissoluble; but since marriage contains the moment of feeling, it is not absolute but unstable, and thus has the possibility of dissolution.[39] Even though the modern notion of subjective freedom must grant the right to divorce, Hegel does not believe that this right should be exercised arbitrarily. Having granted the right to divorce, Hegel adds: "Legislators, however, must make its dissolution as difficult as possible and uphold the right of the ethical order against caprice."[40] Hegel also derives other features of marriage, including the requirement of monogamy and prohibition that it not take place between blood relatives. Marriage is essentially monogamous because it is entered into by two self-sufficient persons who then surrender their personalities in a mutual and undivided way.[41] Unless the surrender is mutual, the rights of one of the partners is infringed. Polygamy, for Hegel, enslaves women. The ethical justification of marriage is monogamy, because only in monogamy do women receive recognition and therefore equal rights.[42]

The dialectical tension is evident in marriage. On one hand, marriage presupposes free personality, and on the other hand, it transcends free personality:

> Further, marriage results from the free surrender by both sexes of their personality—a personality in every possible way unique in each of the parties. Consequently, it ought not to be entered by two people identical in stock who are already acquainted and perfectly know to one another; for individuals in the same circle of relationship have no special personality of their own in contrast with that of others in the same circle.[43]

Marriage does not constitute a retreat from free personality to the more primitive standpoint of natural existence; instead, it begins with free personality and supercedes it. It is precisely because marriage begins with free and direct personalities that the unity to which it gives rise is strong and vital.[44] In dialectical fashion, Hegel holds that all strength rests on the opposition from which unity arises.

One of the most controversial aspects of Hegel's writings concerning marriage is what he has to say about the different roles of men and women. Like most people during his time, Hegel thinks that there are important natural differences between men and women. For the most part, he expresses these differences in terms of conventional dichotomies—men are objective while women are subjective, men are active and women are passive, men are thinking and women are feeling. Because he perceives important differences, Hegel asserts that men and women have different spheres. For example, men have their actual substantive life in the state, science, and otherwise struggle in the external world, and women have their substantial vocation in the family.[45] Although Hegel grants women juridical equality and the rights of free personality, he is emphatic that they restrict themselves to the family and not trespass into the male spheres of civil society, politics, and science:

> A girl is destined in essence for the marriage tie and for that only. . . . Women are capable of education, but they are not made for activities which demand a universal faculty such as the more advanced sciences, philosophy, and certain

forms of artistic production. Women may have happy ideas, taste, and elegance, but they cannot attain to the ideal. The difference between men and women is like that between animals and plants. . . . When women hold the helm of government, the state is at once in jeopardy, because women regulate their actions not by the demands of universality but by arbitrary inclinations and opinions.[46]

In Hegel's view, gender identification and roles are hardly equal. On one hand, his concept of reciprocal recognition implies coequality. On the other hand, his conception of marriage exhibits a fundamental inequality between men and women. Even the question regarding natural differences is far from resolved, and Hegel's opinion is not likely to find much support today. Women now excel in all these areas.

It should be noted that Hegel does not regard women as inferior per se, but that natural differences suit them for different social roles and functions. "The difference in the physical characteristics of the two sexes has a rational basis and consequently acquires an intellectual and ethical significance."[47] For Hegel, the differences are rational because they correspond to the two fundamental moments of the concept—immediate substantiality and thinking universality. Hegel formulates the fundamental difference between men and women in terms of this logical opposition.[48] He contends that these two moments represented by men and women must both be explicitly present in a fully developed ethical life [*Sittlichkeit*]. Hegel holds that men and women have different but complementary capacities. The moment of immediate substantiality, for Hegel, corresponds to family existence. People cannot live their entire lives in the competitive world of civil society or the public realm of the state with its universal demands. Men need a retreat from these strenuous occupations that involve struggle with the world, and this retreat is the private realm of the family over which women preside: "In the family, he has a tranquil intuition of this unity, and there he lives a subjective ethical life on the plane of feeling."[49] Family life affords mental and emotional refreshment for men so they can rejoin social and political interactions. The family allows individuals to find a haven from the harsh struggles of civil society by participating in the bonds of unity.

The fundamental question raised by Hegel's argument is whether the state requires a class of people who, as a matter of principle, cannot realize their freedom in the fullest possible sense in civil society and politics. The problem is not only that there are individuals—women—who are incapable of freedom in the fullest and most rational sense, it is that a fully developed ethical life requires that there be such individuals.[50] This clearly clashes with the liberal conception of individual self-actualization. Hegel argues that there must be an immediately substantial gender because he believes that such a gender exists. His argument rests on the belief that women are inherently limited in their ability to fully and rationally actualize themselves as individuals.[51] Although Hegel is wrong in this belief, it is something that he shares with most nineteenth-century philosophers. The issue of equality is addressed more fully in Chapter 10.

The two other aspects of family life that Hegel discusses are family property and the upbringing of children. Since the family constitutes a single person over and above its individual members, the family gives itself existence in property:

> The family, as person, has its real external existence in property; and it is only when this property takes the form of capital that it becomes the embodiment of the substantial personality of the family. . . . The arbitrariness of a single owner's particular needs is one moment in property taken abstractly; but this moment, together with the selfishness of desire, is here transformed into something ethical, into labor and care for a common possession.[52]

This property does not belong to any single family member, rather is held in common. The father, or husband, is the head of the household and administers property.[53] A more spiritual objectification of the unity of the family comes into being with the children. For Hegel, children are the genuine existence or objectification of the love between parents.[54] The principle duty of parents has to do with their upbringing. Hegel says that the goal of education is for the family to raise the children out of the immediacy in which they originally exist to self-sufficiency and freedom of personality.[55]

School plays an important transitional role for Hegel. It helps prepare children to leave the family and enter civil society. In the *Philosophy of Mind*, Hegel discusses school as the transitional phase between the family and civil society:

> This is done in a much higher degree in the school than in the family. In the latter, the child is accepted in its immediate individuality, is loved whether its behavior is good or bad. In school, on the other hand, the immediacy of the child no longer counts; here it is esteemed only according to its worth, according to its achievements, is not merely loved but criticized and guided in accordance with universal principles, molded by instruction according to fixed rules, in general, subjected to a universal order which forbids many things innocent in themselves because everyone cannot be permitted to do them. The school thus forms the transition from the family into civil society.[56]

The goal of the education that children receive in the family, in conjunction with the education received in school, is to raise them to be free and self-sufficient personalities. For Hegel, the achievement of this goal marks the dissolution of the family and the transition to civil society.[57]

## CIVIL SOCIETY

Civil society [*bürgerliche Gesellschaft*], as Hegel conceives it, is a social sphere, distinct from family and state, the other two parts of modern Sittlichkeit. More specifically, it is the sphere of private, social, and primarily economic relationships situated between the family and the state. It is the realm where people pursue their separate and particular interests. Civil society "establishes the framework within which ethical claims of a purely economic kind can be realistically raised for the first time, without eliminating the distinct ethical norms of other coexisting spheres, such as the family and state."[58] In distinguishing civil from political society, Hegel recognizes the emergence of a new social configuration: a separate, private social sphere, within which agents live for themselves, without participating in public affairs.[59] Hegel recognizes that the economy is an integral domain of justice. Although the idea of a separate social sphere beyond the patriarchal ties of the family and below the universal claims of the state is quite familiar today, in Hegel's time it was still an emergent reality, especially in Germany. While other theorists, such as John Locke and Adam Smith use the concept of "civil society" [*societas civilis*] interchangeably with "political society" to designate the condition of human beings entered upon leaving the state of nature, Hegel is widely regarded as the first to use civil society to refer exclusively to a nonpolitical social-economic realm.[60] Civil society refers to the modern recognition of subjective freedom, specifically finding freedom in labor and property.

The heart of this sphere is the modern market economy. Economic relations proceed through acts of commodity exchange, where individuals acquire what they need from someone else by voluntarily giving in return some good of their own that another individual wants. In commodity exchange, the goods through which individuals interact are not things but social objects of the will bearing value in virtue of the interdependent self-determinations of their values.[61] That is, in pursuing the satisfaction of their own ends, individuals inevitably the needs of each other. Furthermore, commodity exchange only takes place insofar as the participating individuals recognize one another as free persons, objectively owning their respective goods and satisfying needs of their own choosing:

> The concrete person, who is himself the object of his particular aims, is, as a totality and a mixture of caprice and physical necessity, one principle of civil society. But the particular person is essentially so related to other particular persons that each establishes himself and finds satisfaction by means of the others, and at the same time purely and simply by means of the forms of universality, the second principle here.[62]

Thus, "the interaction theory of justice established by Hegel has admitted the economy into the reality of right, and in so doing, has undertaken to conceive an economic order determined entirely in nonnatural, nonmonlogical terms of free relations between agents."[63] Economic justice requires a social dimension that consists of the complementary pursuit of interest by a plurality of individuals.

In this way, human beings use commodities to interact as independent bearers of need and enjoy the recognized freedom to pursue their particular ends in public. Accordingly, engaging in commodity exchange is an ethical right, since it realizes the particular self-determination of the individual within the existing system of the economy.[64] Seen as the embodiment of free will, the merit of property resides in the owner's freedom of disposition, not in the quantity of things owned. Individuals pursue their own self-interests without a concern for others. Civil society, for Hegel, constitutes the liberation of self-sufficient personality that remains underdeveloped within the immediate ethical unity of the family.[65] His understanding of this sphere is strongly influenced by the classical economists, such as Smith and Ricardo. In fact, what Hegel calls the "the system of needs" is a modern market economy of labor, production, and exchange.[66] He shares the belief that through the satisfaction of one's private ends within the system of needs, individuals inevitably satisfy the needs of one another:

> In the course of the actual attainment of selfish ends—an attainment conditioned in this way by universality—there is formed a system of complete interdependence, wherein the livelihood, happiness, and legal status of one man is interwoven with the livelihood, happiness, and rights of all. On this system, individual happiness, &c., depend, and only in this connected system are they actualized and secured.[67]

Subjective selfishness turns into a contribution toward the satisfaction of the needs of everyone else.

Hegel's conception of civil society includes a legal structure to support and regulate it in order to promote the public welfare. The public authority is the system of public administration concerned with the regulation and control of civil society. It is responsible for removing or remedying accidental hindrances to achieving individual ends. It also provides the legal structure necessary for the regulation of the system of needs, and includes a legal code and a judicial system.[68] Chief among its functions is the protection of property and contracts. Individuals respect one another as persons by making and honoring contracts. Public authority, for Hegel, is an all-purpose corrective mechanism.[69] It also provides a range of public goods, such as criminal justice, street maintenance, and education. In short, it furnishes the services that individuals need in their capacity as members of civil society. Through these services, the public authority gives birth to a common civic sphere within the private realm of civil society. On one hand, civil society represents the most dramatic expression of the principle of particular or subjective freedom; on the other hand, it represents only an incomplete actualization of human freedom and one that needs to be distinguished from and subordinated to the full realization of human freedom in the modern state.[70] As will be demonstrated in Chapter 6, civil society must be kept in check by being incorporated into a deeper community.

## The System of Needs and Political Economy

In civil society, people are united by the principle of self-interest, and individuals pursue their own self-interests without any direct reference to others. Nevertheless, they soon find that they cannot find satisfaction without simultaneously satisfying the welfare of others. In the realm of economics, individuals necessarily act in relation to other particular individuals. In this way, each particular individual with his own particular ends takes a form of universality:

> In civil society each member is his own end, everything else is nothing to him. But except in contact with others he cannot attain the whole compass of his ends, and therefore these others are means to the end of the particular member. A particular end, however, assumes a form of universality through this relation to other people, and it is attained in the simultaneous attainment of the welfare of others.[71]
>
> Here burghers are *bourgeois*, not *citoyens*. Individuals have their own welfare as their purpose, they are persons governed by right and the moment of right emerges in a universal form. But the individual's substance and welfare are conditioned by the welfare and preservation of all. Individuals care only for themselves, have only themselves as their purpose, but they cannot care for themselves without at the same time caring for all and without all caring for them. In pursuing their own self-interest they at the same time work for the others.[72]

With this account of civil society, Hegel borrows Adam Smith's conception of the "invisible hand" argument, the pursuit of individual self-interest leads to the general welfare of all.

> If we consider a people's economic life as a whole, we discover a hidden harmony which results from the interaction of the individual labor and the individual enjoyment of all the members of the people. Hegel had especially emphasized this dialectic of wealth in the Jena courses on "Philosophy of Spirit."

He had just read the German translation of Adam Smith's *Wealth of Nations* and had seen in that book an illustration of his own dialectic. From the point of view of being-for-itself, wealth corresponds to its development for-itself. Each labors and enjoys himself on his own behalf. This is the moment of multiplicity in the unity of substance. . . . But thanks to the division of labor, the labor of each serves the collectivity and is only a fragment of the total labor.[73]

Hegel sees political economy as one of the triumphs of modern science. The spectacle of modern economic activity is astonishing in its variety and vitality.[74] Even though it is not obvious with his distinction between civil society and the state, Hegel nonetheless retains a suspicion of unfettered economic activity and a desire to subordinate it to the higher, more universal aims of the state.

Civil society, however, is not merely a realm of selfish individualism opposed to the universalism of the state. Like the family, civil society plays an important educational role. In a crucial way, civil society educates the individual to universality too. Individuals attain their individual ends in civil society only by simultaneously satisfying the ends of others, since they are forced to surrender some of their natural particularity and to adopt the form of universality. Civil society does not mark a corruption of the original simplicity of the state of nature, as Rousseau would have it, but rather it is a necessary overcoming of it.[75] "In the individual subject, this liberation is the hard struggle against pure subjectivity of demeanor, against the immediacy of desire, against the empty subjectivity of feeling and the caprice of inclination."[76] This is what education [*Bildung*] consists of for Hegel:

By educated men, we may prima facie understand those who without the obtrusion of personal idiosyncrasy can do what others do. . . . Thus education rubs the edges off particular characteristics until a man conducts himself in accordance with the nature of the thing.[77]

Individuals are members of civil society and act accordingly.

Hegel asserts that one of the most important things about the nature of human needs is their non-natural character. While the needs of animals and their means of satisfying them are given and limited, the needs of human beings and their means of satisfying them are capable of almost infinite multiplication:

At the same time, the satisfaction of need, necessary and accidental alike, is accidental because it breeds new desires without end, is in thoroughgoing dependence on caprice and external accident, and is held in check by the power of universality. In these contrasts and their complexity, civil society affords a spectacle of extravagance and want as well as the physical and ethical degeneration common to both.[78]

> An animal's needs and its way and means of satisfying them are both alike restricted in scope. Though man is subject to this restriction too, yet at a time he evinces his transcendence of it and his universality, first by the multiplication of needs and means of satisfying them.[79]

Needs are created as new goods are invented. Unlike animal needs, human needs are never natural; instead, they are mediated by social opinion and peer pressure. "Finally, it is no longer need but opinion which has to be satisfied. . . ."[80] For Hegel, this also illustrates the social character of human needs. To an important extent, people must accept the opinions of others, since they depend upon others in order to satisfy needs. The generation of needs takes place within an element of universal recognition, which forces people to fit in with one another and adapt their activity to the form of universality.[81] Consequently, human needs are intersubjective to a considerable extent, that is, in the economic realms, subjectivity is also depended upon intersubjectivity.

Hegel's description of the socialization, multiplication, and refinement of human needs clashes with Rousseau's attack on the way that society creates artificial needs and distracts human beings from their natural needs. Hegel rejects Rousseau's view that people are freer in the state of nature, subjected only to their natural needs. For Hegel, Rousseau's argument is incompatible with a proper understanding of human freedom:

> The idea has been advanced that in respect to his needs man lived in freedom in the so-called "state of nature" when his needs were supposed to be confined to what are known as simple necessities of nature, what he required for their satisfaction only the means which the accidents of nature directly assured him. . . . And apart from this, it is false, because to be confined to mere physical needs as such and their direct satisfaction would simply be the condition in which the mental is plunged in the natural and so would be one of savagery and unfreedom, while freedom itself is to be found only in the reflection of mind into itself, in mind's distinction from nature, and in the reflex of mind in nature.[82]

Contrary to Rousseau, Hegel asserts that the social character of human needs does not lead to human dependence and unfreedom. In fact, it contains an "aspect of liberation, i.e., the strict natural necessity of need is obscured and man is concerned with his own opinion, indeed with an opinion which is universal, and with a necessity of his own making alone, instead of with an external necessity, an inner contingency, and mere caprice."[83] Hegel thinks that social needs carry the same importance and urgency as natural needs. It is a truth of the modern world that keeping up with others is thought to be a need, and relative deprivation is keenly felt by modern human beings.

Work is the means by which goods are produced that satisfy the particular needs of consumers. Hegel discovers socialization and universalization in human work. In this area, Hegel concentrates on the division of labor. Through practical education, people seek the understanding necessary to achieve their sophisticated objectives. Through developing the habit of being occupied, and by focusing their attention on the task at hand with an eye to its usefulness for others, human beings acquire transferable, universally applicable skills:

> The multiplicity of objects and situations which excite interest is the stage on which theoretical education develops. This education consists in possessing not simply a multiplicity of ideas and facts, but also a flexibility and rapidity of mind, ability to pass from one idea to another, to grasp complex and general relations, and so on. . . . Practical education, acquired through working, consists first in the automatically recurrent need for something to do and the habit of simply being busy; next, in the strict adaptation of one's activity according not only to the nature of the material worked on, but also, and especially, to the pleasure of other workers; and finally, in a habit, produced by this discipline, of objectively active and universally recognized aptitudes.[84]

As human beings get cleverer, production increasingly utilizes the division of labor. The development of specialized skills that are directed toward highly specific elements in the production process leads to increased productivity.

From his early Jena writings, Hegel is sensitive to the dehumanizing effects of the division of labor, noting that Adam Smith's example of the pin factory reduces the consciousness of the laborer to mindless toil.[85] While Hegel recognizes dehumanizing aspects of physical labor and factory life, he fails to discover an acceptable remedy. After indicating how the division of labor leads to the simplification and abstraction of human labor and to a greater interdependence between human beings, he simply concludes that the division of labor makes work increasingly mechanical:

> The universal and objective element in work, on the other hand, lies in the abstracting process which effects the subdivision of needs and means and thereby *eo ipso* subdivides production and brings about the division of labor. By this division, the work of the individual becomes less complex, and consequently his skill at his section of the job increases, like his output. At the same time, this abstraction of one man's skill and means of production from another's completes and makes necessary everywhere the dependence of man on one another and their reciprocal relation in the satisfaction of other needs. Further, the abstraction of one man's production from another's makes work more and more mechanical, until finally man is able to step aside and install machines in his place.[86]

Eventually human labor will be replaced by that of machines. He seems to think that mechanical progress will serve human freedom.

It would be a mistake to overemphasize Hegel's optimism, however. While he clearly believes that the division of labor and introduction of machinery make work easier, Hegel is also aware of the negative effects of the division of labor. From his earlier lectures to the *Philosophy of Right*, Hegel speaks of the deadening effect of factory work on individuals.

> Need and labor, elevated into this universality, form on their own account a monstrous system of community and mutual interdependence . . . a life of the dead body, that moves itself within itself, one which ebbs and flows in its motion blindly, like the elements, and which requires continual strict dominance and taming like a wild beast.[87]

Furthermore, the subdivision and restriction of particular jobs "results in the dependence and distress of the class tied to work of that sort, and these again entail inability to feel and enjoy the broader freedoms and especially the intellectual benefits of civil society."[88] Hegel concludes his analysis of the system of needs by assessing the impact of distribution on society. Civil society creates a pool of wealth that members have the opportunity to share and augment through their investment. He sees inequality as being socially necessary in civil society. A person's share of universal resources is based on a combination of their initial capital and the subsequent employment of their skills. The latter are conditioned on the former as well as on unequal natural aptitudes and other contingent circumstances.[89] The greater a family's wealth, the more it can invest in developing their children's skill by providing a good education, and the greater their skills, the more likely that they can accumulate capital. Hegel dismisses the demand for economic equality as abstract. The demand for equality ultimately fails to give the right of particularity that is enshrined in civil society its due.[90]

Hegel's system of needs does more than differentiate individuals according to their particular skills, aptitudes, and resources; it also knits them together into estates [*Stände*], or social groups based on common forms of work.[91] Estates are an important transition in Hegel's argument and the move toward the state. The gathering of individuals into estates begins to transcend the atomism of civil society. They serve an integrative function similar to the family, and they link individuals to something larger and more universal than their private self-interests. This type of universality is more than that of the invisible hand of the market and entails a more substantial and explicit identification of individuals with others. That is why Hegel holds that while the family is the primary basis of the state, estates are the second.[92] Estates are crucial, since private individuals, despite their selfishness, find it necessary to have recourse to others. This is therefore the root that links selfishness with the universal.

Hegel distinguishes three estates—the substantial, or immediate, estate made up of agricultural works and landlords; the formal, or reflective, estate made up of tradesmen, manufacturers, and businessmen; and the universal estate, made up of civil servants and public officials.[93] The estates are vertical segments of civil society. The form of capital is different in each case, as is the ethos of those who earn their living by them. The dialectical basis of the classification of the estates—substantial, formal, and universal—seems to segment society into those who do not think at all, those who think only of themselves and their customers, and those who think of everyone else.[94] Each estate has its distinctive mentality, which constitutes the rationale of the classification. This is the subjective particularity of the modern world that reflects individual aspirations and capabilities. For Hegel, a free labor market is an essential element of freedom. Members of civil society must commit themselves to a career and assimilate the ethos of an estate. Hegel holds that individuals attain actuality only by committing themselves to a particular estate. Individuals ultimately utilize their absolute wills to determine which estate they will pursue: "But the question of the particular class to which an individual is to belong is one on which natural capacity, birth, and other circumstances have their influence, though the essential and final determining factors are subjective opinion and the individual's arbitrary will."[95] For Hegel, this is most of what is meant by the general idea of freedom. Developing one's skill and working out one's aspirations are concrete elements in the process of self-determination.[96]

## The Administration of Justice and Property

The universality implicit in the system of needs becomes explicit for itself in the administration of justice [*die Rechtspflege*]. Human beings possess certain universal rights, such as the right to property, the right to live, and the right of physical integrity. The administration of justice articulates the requirement that peoples' rights are explicitly stated and effectively enforced. This type of justice is abstract right, or the right to property:

> As the private particularity of knowing and willing, the principle of this system of needs contains absolute universality, the universality of freedom, only abstractly and therefore as the right of property. At this point, however, this right is no longer merely implicit but has attained its recognized actuality as the protection of property through the administration of justice.[97]

When Hegel first discusses the right to property in the *Philosophy of Right*, it is merely abstract, without actuality in particular will of the individual. With civil society, the right to property takes on a concrete existence or actuality, ceasing to be only "in itself" and becoming "for itself:"

> The relatedness arising from the reciprocal bearing on one another of needs and work to satisfy these is first of all reflected into itself personality, as abstract right. But the very sphere of relatedness—a sphere of education—which gives abstract right the determinate existence of being something universally recognized, known, and willed, and having validity and an objective actuality mediated by this known and willed character.[98]

After the particular will sheds its immediacy and is educated into universality through the system of needs, abstract right takes on an existence in which it is universally recognized, known, and willed. In the administration of justice, the particular will explicitly wills the universal in the form of the right of property.

"Insofar as legality falls within ethical community, whose conception follows upon that of property rights and morality, legal affairs will presuppose property relations and moral subjectivity as necessary structural components."[99] For Hegel, it is precisely because abstract right is recognized and willed that it must be posited, and exist as law:

> The principle of rightness becomes law [*Gesetz*] when, in its objective existence, it is posited [*gesetzt*], i.e. when thinking makes it determinate for consciousness and makes it known as what is right and valid; and in acquiring this determinate character, the right becomes positive of law in general. . . . In becoming law, what is right acquires for the first time not only the form proper to its universality, but also its true determinacy.[100]

By posited, Hegel does not mean willed or commanded as Hobbes would have it with his positive conception of law; instead, Hegel means brought to consciousness, or recognized, as a universal. With his emphasis on the posited character of law, he is drawing contrast between the conscious way that human beings subscribe to law and the unconscious way in which animals and other natural things are governed by laws.[101] From his discussion of the posited and known character of law, Hegel goes on to defend the codification of law over those Romantic notions that argue in favor of customary law.

The distinction between law and custom is not absolute, since both contain an aspect of being known:

> Since it is only animals which have their law as instinct, while it is man alone who has law as custom [*Gewohnheit*], even systems of customary law contain the moment of being thoughts and being known. Their difference from positive law consists solely in this, that they are known only in a subjective and accidental way,

with the result that in themselves they are less determinate and the universality of thought is less clear in them.[102]

For Hegel, codifying the law simply develops the element of thought and universality that is implicit but underdeveloped in customary right. Codification does not necessarily destroy the living quality of customs, as Romantics assert. In fact, Hegel insists that the valid laws of the nation do not cease to be its customs merely because they are written and codified.[103] The problem with customary right is that it creates confusion in the administration of justice because it makes right the preserve of a few judges and experts. Hegel illustrates this problem by pointing out the chaos and inequality created by English common law and the failure to codify its precepts into actual law.[104] The positing of law overcomes the indeterminacies of custom.

For Hegel, the posited character of law does not imply, as it does for Hobbes, that it contains an authoritative element that is utterly opaque to speculative reason.[105] Because positive right contains both rational and contingent elements, philosophy's task is to penetrate beneath the surface: "Once that is granted, the great thing is to apprehend in the show of the temporal and transient the substance which is immanent and eternal which is present."[106] Nonetheless, Hegel still recognizes a "purely positive" aspect of the law, one that resists being penetrated by speculative reason and that cannot be derived from philosophy. This aspect involves the quantitative determinations involved in the application of a universal concept to individual cases, such as the amount of the fine or length of the prison sentence. For Hegel, these determinations are essentially contingent and cannot be deduced from speculative reason even though an injustice occurs when the penalty is too stiff for the particular crime. Law is a dynamic and open-textured system that needs to be pragmatically responsive to finite material: "Reason itself requires us to recognize that contingency, contradiction, and show have a sphere and a right of their own, restricted though it be, and it is irrational to strive to resolve and rectify contradictions within that sphere."[107] Hegel thinks that the recognition of the purely positive aspects of law is necessary because it keeps philosophy from getting tangled up in contingent considerations. Furthermore, it protects us from the illusion of a perfectly rational code of law and the futile perfectionism that goes along with it.[108]

The institutions and practices of justice that Hegel discusses in connection with the administration of justice relate to the requirement that the law be recognized by and willed by individuals. This requirement comes from the right of subjective insight or self-consciousness that Hegel deduces in his discussion of morality, where he restricted this right of subjective self-consciousness to what is generally recognized as right.[109] Now he elaborates on what this right of subjective self-consciousness requires with respect to the administration of justice. The right of subjective self-consciousness requires that laws be universally known: "If laws are to have a binding force, it follows that, in view of the right of self-consciousness they must be made universally known."[110] To be recognized, law requires an intersubjective moment. He further asserts that the application of the law in particular cases be revealed through the publicity of legal proceedings and that the verdict of guilt or innocence must be pronounced by a jury of one's peers in criminal trial:

> By taking the form of law, right steps into a determinate mode of being. It is then something on its own account, and in contrast with particular willing and opining of the right, it is self-subsistent and has to vindicate itself as something universal. This is achieved by recognizing it and making it actual in a particular case without the subjective feeling of private interest; and this is the business of a public authority—the court of justice.[111]

While these practices are common today, they were not widely available in Hegel's day.

For Hegel, the court of justice establishes the operation of impersonal and impartial legal authority. When the courts take over from wronged individuals the task of enforcing rights, right [*Recht*] is actualized and made positive with respect to particular cases. Objectively, the law that a particular crime has challenged is reaffirmed, and subjectively, the right of the matter is made clear by the criminal who is forced to acknowledge the validity of the law that is enforced against him. As Hegel puts it, the court of law:

> takes over the pursuit and avenging of crime, and this pursuit consequently ceases to be the subjective and contingent retribution of revenge and is transformed into the genuine reconciliation of right with itself, i.e. into punishment. Objectively, this is the reconciliation of the law with itself; by the annulment of the crime, the law is restored and its authority is thereby actualized. Subjectively, it is the reconciliation of the criminal with himself, i.e. with the law known by him as his own and as valid for him and his protection; when this law is executed upon him, he himself finds in this process the satisfaction of justice and nothing save his own act.[112]

Thus, prosecution and punishment are not arbitrary, since they are based on the due process of law and reconciliation. The verdict is supposed to be sustained by evidence and arguments relating to the law, and the accused has the right to stand in court and counter the arguments and evidence. Hegel further argues that all criminal proceedings should be public so that all citizens can recognize that the law is actualized in particular cases.[113] It is crucial that the legal system be transparent and intellectually accessible to all citizens.

As illustrated above, mutual recognition between individuals incorporates a sense of legitimate individuality in the rational form of property ownership. For Hegel, wrong [*Unrecht*] occurs when an individual breaks or violates legal arrangements. In an important sense, wrong consists in the violation of mutual recognition [*Anerkanntsein*]. Wrong appears as the self-aggrandizement of the individual and involves the self-assertion of one individual against an other, as well as against universal *Anerkanntsein*.[114] According to Hegel, the principle of abstract right, when pushed to the extreme of self-assertion, undermines abstract right and becomes the principle of wrong. Such individuals push aside universal laws and place themselves above the universal. Wrongs do more than violate artificially posted universals, they violate the basic requirement and fundamental condition of a community of freedom.[115] Consequently, wrongs must be unmasked and brought to light.

In order for right to achieve actuality and objectivity, Hegel holds that punishment restores right as a power over wrong. He conceives of right and wrong in terms of the logic of essence.[116] Right is what is essential, and is a condition of any community of freedom. Wrong is the contrary of essence, or what is nonessential. Thus, punishment is the overcoming [*Aufhebung*] of the inverted wrong:

> The principle of rightness, the universal will, receives its essential determinate character through the particular will, and so is in relation with something which is inessential. This is the relation of essence to its appearance. . . . In wrong, however, appearance proceeds to become a show. A show is a determinate existence inadequate to the essence, the empty disjunction and positing of the essence, so that in both essence and show the distinction of the one from the other is present as sheer difference. The show, therefore, is falsity which disappears in claiming independent existence; and in the course of the show's disappearance the essence reveals itself as essence, i.e. as the authority of the show. The essence has negated that which negated it and so is corroborated. Wrong is a show of this kind, and, when it disappears, right acquires the character of something fixed and valid.[117]

Wrong negates right and tries to set itself up as self-sufficient. In punishing wrong and making it disappear, essence shows itself as essence. Crime is a contradiction that is resolved in punishment.[118] Right is the essence that negates that which negated it, and is thereby confirmed. Therefore, "through the disappearance of wrong, right acquires the determination of something enduring and valid; it is actual as negation of a negation."[119]

Since in Hegel's system of right, freedom is made actual, it is necessary to assess the place of punishment as coercion in such a system. Hegel follows Kant in distinguishing between a first coercion or transgression and a second coercion or punishment. For Kant:

everything that is contrary to right is a hindrance to freedom based on universal laws, while coercion is a hindrance or resistance to freedom. Consequently if a certain use to which freedom is put is itself a hindrance to freedom . . . (i.e., if it is contrary to right), any coercion which is used against it will be a hindrance to a hindrance of freedom, and will thus be consistent with freedom according to universal laws—that is, will be right. It thus follows . . . that right entails the authority of anyone who infringes it.[120]

Primary coercion, or transgression, is contrary and injurious to freedom and right. Thus, transgression is a negation, since it negates the socially constructed order of right. Punishment, for Hegel, is not a coercion in this primary sense; rather, it is a coercion against coercion, a second coercion that cancels the first coercion. Consequently, "punishment is not an evil that is contrary to right but the realization of right, that is, the way in which right, the universal *Anerkanntsein* is which all, including the offender, have a stake, is maintained in spite of transgression."[121] The second coercion is not coercion for coercion's sake; rather it is relative to the first and a reaction to and cancellation of the original violation: "That coercion is in its conception self-destructive is exhibited in the world of reality by the fact that coercion is annulled by coercion; coercion is thus shown to be not only right under certain conditions but necessary, i.e. as a second act of coercion which is the annulment of one that has preceded."[122] The second coercion is justified because it defends freedom against coercion and upholds right. When a criminal commits a crime, the wrongdoing violates rights and reduces the particular right to a mere semblance [*Schein*], which means that the truth of the right has been denied.[123]

For Hegel, punishment is a reciprocal action, since it is the original coercion reciprocated. There are two ways in which this reciprocation can occur: revenge and retribution. Hegel says that revenge involves a particular subjective will in immediate opposition to and retaliation against another subjective will. Revenge is a "this-for-that" reciprocity. Because the retaliation is subjective, it does not aim for justice and right. Revenge aims at getting even. "Hence revenge, because it is a positive action of a particular will, becomes a new transgression; as thus contradictory in character, it falls into an infinite progression and descends from one generation to another *ad infinitum*."[124] Therefore, revenge does not end the cycle of coercive violence but merely perpetuates it. Retribution is the second form of reciprocation. Hegel conceives of retribution as an infringement of an infringement, that is, a coercion that cancels [*aufgehoben*] a coercion.

Because it implies an identity between transgression and punishment, Hegel's concept of retribution supports and articulates justice. Punishment, as the cancellation of the transgression, is not external to the transgression;

rather, punishment is inherent in transgression: "The annulment of the crime is retribution in so far as (a) retribution in *conception* is an 'injury of the injury,' and (b) since as existent a crime is something determinate in its scope both qualitatively and quantitatively, its negation as *existent* is similarly determinate."[125] This means that when the criminal meets with retribution, it has the appearance of an alien determination that does not belong to him. However, the punishment is merely the manifestation of the crime, that is, it is one half that is necessarily presupposed by the other.[126] Furthermore, Hegel sees punishment as the re-establishment of freedom:

> A criminal, when punished, may look upon his punishment as a restriction of his freedom. Really the punishment is not foreign constraint to which he is subjected, but the manifestation of his own act: and if he recognizes this, he comports himself as a free man.[127]
>
> Thus, the punishment is the restoration of freedom; and not only has the criminal remained (or rather been made) free, but the administrator of the punishment has acted rationally or freely. In this, its [proper] determination, the punishment is accordingly something in itself, genuinely infinite and absolute, which therefore carries its own respect and fear within it; it derives from freedom, even as a constraint [*Als Bezwingend*], it remains free.[128]

Punishment reconciles the contradiction within the criminal by revealing it as deficient form of freedom. Punishment is the negation of a negation, since it is a sublation [*Aufhebung*] of an infringement of right.

Hegel's concept of retribution implies that nothing happens in punishment except what already lies in the transgression. Retribution coincides with justice and fairness. Just punishment must add nothing to the transgression; retribution demands and asserts an equality between the crime and punishment and between offender and victim.[129] For Hegel, this equality means that the criterion of punishment must be derived from the offender's own action. This distinguishes it from the emotions of revenge. Punishment is necessary, since failing to punish transgression and allowing transgressions makes them part of the established order.[130] Hegel argues that this would be equivalent to recognizing wrong as right, injustice as justice. Considered as a whole, Hegel's conception of punishment is a form of retribution that is a negation of the criminal will through applied threat and conviction. At the same time, the deepest ground of punishment is the reconciliation of the criminal with humanity and is thereby brought to light as something that continues to remain a postulate that governs the actuality of existing positive law and right.[131] Punishment can only restore the right [*Recht*] if the institutions whereby punishment is affected constitute the means of public recognition of rights.[132]

## Police and the Regulation of Community Welfare

By itself, the administration of justice is incomplete insofar as it is only concerned with annulling violation of abstract right—infringements of personality and property. The livelihood and welfare of individuals are still left to contingency and chance. Even though the administration of justice makes the universal determinations of abstract right actual, it still remains a standpoint of abstract right and abstract personality. It fails to encompass the subjective particularity and welfare of the individual. Hegel argues that:

> Hence, the universal, which in the first instance is the right only, has to be extended over the whole field of particularity. Justice is a big thing in civil society. Given good laws, a state can flourish, and freedom of property is a fundamental condition of its prosperity. Still, since I am inextricably involved in particularity, I have a right to claim that in this association with other particulars, my particular welfare too shall be promoted. Regard should be paid to my welfare, to my particular interest, and this is done through the police and the Corporations.[133]

In Hegel's time, the term police [*Polizei*] means much more than the maintenance of public order through the enforcement of law; instead, it includes a wide range of government activity and market regulations and is probably better understood as public authority. For Hegel, it comprises of the regulation of commerce and industry, the provision of public goods such as bridges and streetlights, and the provision of necessities for the poor. At times, the differing interests of consumers and producers clash with one another and need to be reconciled. Public authority also includes policing in the narrower sense of preventing crimes and apprehending criminals.

With respect to policing in the narrower sense, Hegel asserts that there can be no fixed determinations or clear boundaries. What is considered harmful in some situations may not be in others. In general, the scope of police activity in this narrower sense will depend upon the customs of the community, the spirit of its constitution, the prevailing conditions, and current emergencies.[134] In refusing to draw boundaries, however, Hegel does not mean to give free reign to the police to search, detain, and otherwise harass individuals. Police supervision must go no farther than is necessary. For example, he is extremely critical of Fichte's "police state," in which no one is allowed to remain unknown to the police and everyone is required to carry their identity papers with them. Such a state would become a world of galley slaves, where each is supposed to keep his fellow under constant supervision.[135] Nevertheless, despite his interest in keeping police supervision to a minimum, Hegel's appreciation for circumstances prevents him from fixing this minimum in an abstract principle.

As noted above, police activity extends well beyond the narrow function of crime and punishment. One of its primary functions pertains to the provision and oversight of "public utility." For Hegel, public utility includes government regulation of commerce and industry, the inspection economic commodities, the provision of public services, the building and maintaining of public works, and so on. Hegel's conception of public authority navigates between the extremes of laissez-faire capitalism and communistic state control of everything:

> The oversight and care exercised by the public authority aims at being a middle term between an individual and the universal possibility, afforded by society, of attaining individual ends. It has to undertake street-lighting, bridge-building, the pricing of daily necessities, and care of public health. In this connection, two main views predominate at the present time. One asserts that the superintendence of everything properly belonging to the public authority, the other that the public authority has nothing at all to settle here because everyone will direct his conduct according to the needs of others. The individual must have a right to work for his bread as he pleases, but the public also has a right to insist that essential tasks shall be properly done. Both points of view must be satisfied, and freedom of trade should be such as to jeopardize the general good.[136]
>
> The differing interests of producers and consumers may come into collision with each other; and although a fair balance between them on the whole may be brought about automatically, still their adjustment also requires a control which stands above both and is consciously undertaken. The right to the exercise of such control in a single case (e.g. in the fixing of the prices of the commonest necessities of life) depends on the fact that, by being publicly exposed for sale, goods in absolutely universal daily demand are offered not so much to an individual as such but rather to a universal purchaser, the public. . . . But public care and direction are most of all necessary in the case of larger branches of industry, because these are dependent on conditions abroad and on combinations of distant circumstances, which cannot be grasped as a whole by the individuals tied to these industries for their living.[137]

Thus, government authority can be either too weak or it can go too far. However, it is essential to note that Hegel maintains that public authority does extend into the realm of economics in order to protect and promote the public welfare. As good as it may be in many respects, the free market has its shortcomings in regard to specific aspects of the public interest. Hegel clearly rejects arguments for complete laissez-faire. "Hegel understands that there is no invisible hand by which the self-regulating market guarantees equal economic opportunity to all."[138] At times, it is necessary to counter economic power with political power; that is, it is an imperative of economic justice that market institutions be supplemented by public administration. For instance, government should intervene when necessities are priced too high. Nonetheless, Hegel is also aware of the danger of too much public authority and regulation.[139]

For Hegel, a modern *Sittlichkeit* that is appropriate for human beings requires the proper balance between economics and politics. At times, government power is necessary to check excessive economic power. With globalization, what has taken place is a massive shift in power, out of the hands of nation-states and democratic governments and into the hands of multinational corporations. It is now the multinational companies that effectively govern the lives of the vast majority of the people on Earth, even though these new world realities are seldom reflected in the strategies of citizen movements for democratic social change. As illustrated in Chapter 10, the *Rechtsstaat* has lost its role protecting the lives and rights of its citizens through public regulation. Ironically, this is taking place under the name of democracy, where the advance of free markets is seen as the advance of democracy. The difficulty is that the most basic rule of corporate operation is that it must show a profit, regardless of everything else. For Hegel, "the just economy is only worthy of its title if it is subject to a continual political supervision that intervenes upon the market to prevent commodity relations from interfering with the equal political opportunity of citizens and the affairs of the state."[140]

Another governmental function that Hegel identifies is the responsibility to guarantee individuals a fair share in the universal resources of civil society. In order to fulfill this obligation, governments are supposed to educate its citizens, giving them skills to succeed economically in life. In the event that citizens fail in this endeavor, Hegel asserts that the state should provide them with the necessities of existence. The basis of this duty is that civil society had deprived individuals of their natural means of acquisition.[141] The family was originally the natural social structure that provided for the particular welfare of individuals. Civil society tears the individual away from family ties and substitutes its own structure:

> But civil society tears the individual from his family ties, estranges the members of the family from one another, and recognizes them as self-sufficient persons. Further, for the paternal soil and the external inorganic resources of nature from which the individual formerly derived his livelihood, it substitutes its own soil and subjects the permanent existence of even the entire family to dependence on itself and to contingency. Thus the individual becomes a son of civil society which has as many claims upon him as he has rights against it.[142]

Since individuals become dependent upon civil society to a considerable extent, civil society owes the meaningful possibility of a physical existence. In a way, civil society sort of assumes the role of "universal family." This includes the duty to educate children so that they can become productive members of civil society.[143] But most importantly, civil society assumes the duty to provide for those who cannot provide for themselves—to provide for the poor. "When the masses begin to decline into poverty, the burden of maintaining them at their ordinary standard of living might be directly laid on the wealthier class, or they might receive the means of livelihood directly from other public sources. . . ."[144]

Hegel's discussion of poverty in the *Philosophy of Right* is one of the most problematic parts of the book. "The important question of how poverty is to be abolished is one of the most disturbing problems which agitate modern society."[145] He recognizes that poverty is not just the result of individual laziness or incapacity, but is a necessary consequence of modern economic conditions. "It hence becomes apparent that despite an excess of wealth civil society is not rich enough."[146] Poverty appears to be a necessary consequence of modern capitalism. Thus, it seems that poverty arises from factors that are largely beyond the control of the individual. While Hegel recognizes the seriousness of the problem, he finds that there are no easy solutions. His discussion of poverty discloses a pessimism that sharply contrasts his dialectical reconciliation of contradictions. Hegel sees a correlation between "great wealth" and "great poverty." He suggests that the correlation between wealth and poverty has a lot to do with the division and mechanization of labor.[147] It appears that the social contraction between wealth and poverty cannot be overcome. Thus, the problem of inequality reveals a limitation of civil society. Some of the difficulties in Hegel's account of poverty are dealt with in Chapters 8 and 10.

It is not only poverty per se that Hegel is concerned about in modern society; he discusses the emergence of what he calls a "rabble" [*Pöbel*]. A rabble emerges when the feeling of right, integrity, and honor that comes from supporting one's activity and work is lost:

> When the standard of living of a large mass of people falls below a certain subsistence level—a level regulated automatically as one necessary for a member of the society—and when there is a consequent loss of the sense of right and wrong, of honesty and the self-respect which makes a man insist on maintaining himself by his own work and effort, the result is the creation of a rabble of paupers. At the same time this brings with it, at the other end of the social scale, conditions which greatly facilitate the concentration of disproportionate wealth in a few hands.[148]

The rabble is not only characterized by objective poverty but also by a subjective disposition. This condition leads to a bitterness—or inward rebellion—against the rich.[149] Without pride and a stake in society, the rabble becomes even more shameless and lazy. Economic deprivation threatens their membership in civil society and undermines their right to life. Corporations represent one of Hegel's solutions to the problem of poverty.

## Corporations

Corporations are civil bodies that are formed by the members of the various estates [*Stände*] of trade and industry whom share a certain skill, trade, or occupation to which all people working in that sector belong.[150] The Hegelian concept of corporation applies not only to the restrictive guilds of the Middle Ages but to the whole range of professional associations and voluntary organizations that grow out of the conditions of civil society.[151] In fact, he sees them as a central feature of modern freedom. The transition to the modern rational state is accomplished in the corporation, since by accepting responsibility for the welfare of its members the corporation removes the aura of personal opinion and contingency from life in civil society:

> The so-called "natural" right of exercising one's skill and thereby earning what there is to be earned is restricted within the Corporation only in so far as it is therein made rational instead of natural. That is to say, it becomes freed from personal opinion and contingency, saved from endangering either the individual workman or others, recognized, guaranteed, and at the same time elevated to conscious effort for a common end. As the family was the first, so the Corporation is the second ethical root of the state, the one planted in civil society. . . . In the Corporation these moments are united in an inward fashion, so that in this union particular welfare is present as a right and is actualized.[152]

Hence, the dichotomy between individual welfare and universal right is overcome in that particular welfare is actualized and present as right. Participants in the affairs of the corporation receive a concrete political education in that they see how particular interests depend upon the general welfare. That is to say, it affords members a material, political education. Hegel continuously refers to the "educative" effects of participation in civil society. Corporations are held to play an important integrating role because they are simultaneously situated at the apogee of the orbits of the particular interests of civil society and at the perigee of orbits of the universal interests of the state.[153] Since all citizens cannot directly participate in the affairs of state in the modern world, they play an essential role in investing private interests with a public character. In this way, corporations are a means to integrate independent branches of business into an ethical context.[154]

Corporations are associations of separate individuals who relate to one another as separate persons with a shared set of interests and concerns. Hegel suggests that they are like a second family.[155] Although corporations do not offer intimacy and love, they do provide an associated life of friendship, collegiality, and solidarity. By themselves, individuals are empty, indeterminate, and lack purpose. People must be something [*Etwas*], and they become something by entering a vocation or corporation. Hegel holds that then they can attain ethical substance, a consciousness of rectitude as a member of a corporation. In participating in its *esprit de corps*, individuals are a useful moment for the universal.[156] Corporations also offer their members objective recognition of their skills, abilities, and achievements. Corporations counteract the divisive tendencies of individual self-seeking in commerce by explicitly recognizing individual contributions to the corporate and social good. Furthermore, corporations resemble families in that they are structured to care for their members and look out for their own. Should members of a corporation become ill or lose their jobs as the result of an economic downturn, they can turn to their corporation as a second family for assistance.[157] The corporations are private, not public, bodies. Another crucial social task that corporations perform is providing members with a determinate socially recognized identity. Its members, Hegel maintains, have the standing of trained, competent practitioners of a socially useful particular trade or profession. Hence, becoming a member of a corporation is also a matter of making membership central to one's personal self-conception, which is basic to a person's identity.

In providing their members with the status of corporation membership, corporations expand the range of recognition that society gives to its members. Although the state recognizes people as members of the society, Hegel suggests that it is abstract since public authority does not recognize people in their "social particularity." This is to say, the state does not recognize them as occupants of a determinate social position and as bearers of a determinate social identity.[158] Corporations, therefore, serve a crucial political function. They mediate between individual members of society and the political apparatus of the state. With corporations, individuals begin to go beyond the individualism and selfishness that characterizes civil society and make the universal, a common good, their explicit purpose.[159] Modern *Sittlichkeit* needs a mediating institution like the corporation because ethics must exist not only in the universal form of the state but also in the form of particularity, that is, within civil society. Hegel believes that corporations can restrain and transform the ethos of self-seeking particularity into the pursuit of universal-social-ethical ends.[160] He further maintains that in a well-ordered society individuals do not vote for their political representatives directly. Each corporation elects its own deputy, whose task it is to represent the shared interests of the members of his corporation in the assembly of estates, which is the government's legislative body. In this respect, corporations serve as a democratic linkage institution.

One of the main reasons why Hegel advocates this form of corporately mediated representation is that he thinks it necessary for people to be represented in their social particularity—their identification with the ends and attitudes of the corporation—which he argues gives their individuality its content. Corporate representation is designed to guarantee that the corporation members' basic interests, values, and attitudes will be represented in the state in a systematic and explicit way.[161] Thus, above all, corporation membership provides individuals with a sense of concrete social identity. Corporations are a crucial bridge from the individualism of civil society to the universal life of the state. Hegel refutes the liberal conception of representation where individuals in a given geographic realm or district elect someone to a popular assembly. He suggests that institutionalizing the class relationships of civil society into the political structure is a way to overcome the atomism of civil society and integrate it into a comprehensive totality.

Through the various corporations, civil society consists in different estates. Each estate is to express what is common to its members. For Hegel, the modern state cannot be based on the direct identification of its citizens with the political system—a series of mediations are necessary:

> It is obviously of advantage that the deputies should include representatives of each particular main branch of society (e.g. trade, manufactures, &c., &c.)—representatives who are thoroughly conversant with it and who themselves belong to it. The idea of free unrestricted election leaves this important consideration entirely at the mercy of chance. All such branches of society, however, have equal rights of representation. Deputies are sometimes regarded as "representatives;" but they are representatives in the organic, rational sense only if they are representatives not of individuals or a conglomeration of them, but of one of the essential spheres of society and its large-scale interests. . . . As for popular suffrage, it may be further remarked that especially in large states it leads inevitably to electoral indifference, since the casting of a single vote is of no significance where there is a multitude of electors.[162]

Since direct representation and universal suffrage fail to achieve a totality, an institutionalized system of estates provides the needed mediation and unity. Furthermore, open elections do not guarantee that each important economic and civil branch of society is represented. A person's consciousness, for Hegel, is molded in accordance with one's membership in a particular class. The estates prevent individuals from becoming a mass or an aggregate. The real significance of the estates lies in the fact that it is through them that the state enters the subjective consciousness of the people and that people begin to participate in the state.[163] Hegel argues that mediating institutions, such as corporations, are necessary in order to prevent capitalist civil society from subverting itself by generating the extremes of wealth and poverty, creating a rabble. The need that corporations fulfill is ethical, social, and logical. Logically some mediating institution is needed to restore ethical order from the disintegration and chaos in civil society.[164]

## THE PARTICULAR AND SUBJECTIVE FREEDOM

The family and civil society afford individuals the opportunity to pursue their particularity. For Hegel, particularity is associated with the ideas of qualitative determinacy and difference from others. First, to be a particular being in this sense is to have at least one determinate quality that is not common to all other beings of the same species and that therefore distinguishes its bearer from a least some other members of that species.[165] Thus, a particular will possesses a determinate content that is not shared by all human beings and subsequently marks it as qualitatively distinct from other human wills. This is to say that the ends of particular will are not derived from some universal feature of human beings as such but from the determinate position that the bearer of that will occupies in the world, that is, a person's social context shapes the will. Second, another defining feature of a particular will is that particular wills are attached to their ends through inclination rather than abstract reason. This means that individuals have motivations for acting on their particular ends independently of any reflection for acting on those ends from a rational standpoint.[166] Through the family and civil society individuals differentiate themselves from others.

Human beings individualize themselves through their participation in the family and civil society. In fact, their positions within the institutions of *Sittlichkeit* help make up their identity as individuals—their roles as parents and place in civil society are central elements of the particular being that they take themselves to be. Nevertheless, it is important to note that Hegel does not mean that individuals are nothing more than bearers of the particular roles they occupy. As illustrated in Chapter 3 and 4, this is one of the problems with Greek *Sittlichkeit* where its inhabitants' relationship to their social roles is unmediated unity. With free will and subjective freedom, individuals in the modern world can not be reduced to their social roles. According to Hegel, individuals can realize themselves as free only if specific social conditions exist that make freedom possible. As discussed in the previous chapter, he asserts that *Sittlichkeit* is the unity of subjective freedom and objective freedom. This means that individuals must do more than merely conform to social norms and legal institutions; to be fully free, they must have the appropriate subjective relations to those laws and practices. A modern system of abstract rights recognized individuals as persons formally distinguishable from others, and membership in Hegel's *Sittlichkeit* involves a recognition of an individual's particularity—that is, of their worth as a particular being.[167]

While subjective freedom indirectly refers to non-interference, it directly refers to a kind of action that is reflective, conscious, and explicitly chosen by an agent. In short, freedom is self-determination. The idea of freedom is an intrinsic aspect of the *Philosophy of Right*, as it is in Hegel's entire system. Consequently, freedom is necessarily connected to Hegel's transition from the family to civil society. His argument for the transition from family to civil society is that this transition can be explained as the liberation of the individual into self-subsistent objective reality.[168] In the context of the development of freedom, civil society is a stage of development that leads beyond the actualization of freedom already attained in the family. For Hegel, freedom develops dialectically "from within itself," and this includes the transition from family to civil society.[169] Civil society gives people the opportunity to meet their particular aims and exercise their particular freedom. Human beings do this through their purposeful interactions with other human beings. In civil society, human beings achieve recognition on the basis of what they are as particular beings. They receive recognition and honor through their roles as productive, self-sufficient members of civil society; that is, they establish themselves as competent and conscientious practitioners of a socially useful occupation.[170] Hegel's conception of civil society represents a dialectical advance with the freedom of individuals within a system of complete interdependence. Mutual dependence forces individuals to step out of their particular point of view and adopt a more universal perspective. As is developed in the next chapter, "freedom for Hegel is conceived not in atomistic and negative terms but rather holistically, in positive, and intersubjective ones."[171]

*Bildung* [social education] is essential for freedom to flourish in the human world. *Bildung*, for Hegel, is the formative experience that is required for the transformation of unformed, natural beings into individuals that both aspire to be free and possess the capacities necessary to actualize freedom. Since human beings are not equipped by birth to realize the freedom that constitutes their essence, individual character must necessarily be formed socially, or intersubjectively. The institutions of Hegel's *Sittlichkeit*, especially family and civil society, are intended to carry out the process of *Bildung*. In the case of the family, the child-rearing is clearly one of the central aims of family life. As we saw above, this includes forming children into subjects who are capable of acquiring self-determined wills. The family is responsible for developing subjective capacities required for realizing freedom of personhood, moral subjectivity, and for acquiring the subjective disposition befitting for free citizenship.[172] Parents help children acquire the subjective capacity that instills the ability to say no to their immediate, unreflected desires. Hegel also says that familial trust serves as a foundation for the political trust that is required for citizenship: "In respect of his relation to the family, the child's education has the positive aim of instilling ethical principles into him in the form of an immediate feeling for which differences are not yet explicit, so that thus equipped with the foundation of an ethical life, his heart may live in its early years in love, trust, and obedience."[173]

Subjective freedom also means that individuals should voluntarily and rationally identify with their social institutions and practices. The voluntary unity of individuals with their social institutions requires the union of the particular will with the universal will. This kind of voluntary unity happens when individuals only have to pursue their own particular ends in order for universal ends to be achieved. Civil society contributes to the realization of freedom by providing its members with material incentives that enable them to participate uncoerced in an objectively rational and freedom actualizing practice.[174] Hegel borrows from Adam Smith's understanding of the harmony that exists between the individual and collective interests in a free market economy. He explicitly incorporates Smith's insight into his own account of how particular and universal wills relate to each other within market-governed relations of civil society. An economic exchange is an interaction within which two wills find concord without losing their particularity: "Yet this identity of their wills implies also (at this stage) that each will still is and remains *not* identical with the other but retains from its own point of view a special character of its own."[175] This arrangement both unites individual and collective ends and makes it possible for the collective good of the whole to be achieved through the free, uncoerced activity of its individual members. "The aim here is the satisfaction of subjective particularity, but the universal asserts itself in the bearing which this satisfaction has on the needs of others, and their free arbitrary wills."[176] Moreover, since the achievement of individuals' particular ends also depends upon the flourishing of the whole, the relations between individuals and the collective good with the market economy approximates Hegel's ideal.[177]

Smith's conception of the invisible hand does not completely capture the sense in which individuals objectively realize their identities and particularities, however. More importantly, particularity is actualized because people's social activities come from themselves in the sense that it is through such activities that they express and constitute their identities. Civil society represents the moment of difference:

> As the substance, being an intelligent substance, particularizes itself abstractly into many persons (the family is only a single person), into families or individuals, who exist independent and free, as private persons, it loses its ethical character: for these persons as such have in their consciousness and their aim not the absolute unity, but their own petty selves and particular interests. Thus arises the system of *atomistic*: by which the substance is reduced to a general system of adjustments to connect self-subsisting extremes and their particular interests. The developed totality of this connective system is the state as civil society, or state *external*.[178]

Individuals who participate in the economic sphere do so as independent beings who work and trade in order to satisfy their own particular needs. In carrying out their social roles, socially free individuals engage in activity that is self-determined in the sense that it is determined in accord with their understanding of their own practical identities. The social participation of individuals is free because it is successfully executed activity, undertaken for its own sake and informed by a conscious, voluntary adoption of universal ends, which at the same time is expressive of individuals' particular identities.[179] Thus, the family and civil society can be equated with objective freedom because they constitute a system of fully self-sufficient institutions that are capable of reproducing themselves. For Hegel, social institutions allow social members to realize more individualistic forms of freedom, especially those associated with personhood. Human beings cannot be themselves unless they achieve subjective freedom.

More than inner freedom is required for Hegel. Inner freedom is only a transitory stage in the process of achieving outer freedom.[180] To be objective and not merely abstract, freedom only exists externally where there are social institutions and practices. For Hegel, it is necessary that the social order attend to more than its members' rights. In fact, one of the conditions that allows members to embrace their social roles as constitutive of their own identities is that these roles enable them to satisfy their material needs. Anything less would be abstract. Being subjectively free means achieving personal freedom, and as persons, human beings require an external sphere in which to exercise their free choice. People cannot fulfill themselves as subjects unless they belong to civil society, and enjoy the freedom from state interference necessary to build their lives and livelihoods on their own work.[181] Actualizing subjective freedom requires that a person's self-image must include the conception of a subject that directs one's own life through one's own choices in concrete social practices, thus finding satisfaction in one's deeds as an expression of subjectivity.

While civil society gives existence to the principle of subjective freedom that distinguishes the modern world from the ancient, by itself it still represents an incomplete actualization of human freedom. Hegel's conception of freedom is complex and contains aspects of many historical approaches to freedom:

> It embraces freedom of action and social freedom, negative and positive freedom, freedom as self-knowledge and freedom as self-control. Most difficult of all to grasp, it embraces as the *subjects* of freedom individual persons, social groupings such as families, the rational state as a whole, as well as the quasi-divine, human spirit which is the subject of history.[182]

Consequently, Hegel distinguishes subjective freedom from the full actualization of human freedom in the modern state. Because free individuals are often so intent on pursuing their own private, selfish ends, they can lose respect for the common good. Thus, Hegel admits that the universal and particular tend to fall apart in civil society.[183] "Civil society on its own is not self-contained: it requires principles and institutions, different from and outside it, for its existence and continuation."[184] In brief, it needs a state to create and structure it. Although Hegel's rational state must allow freedom to particular individuals, particularity must be mediated, that is, particularity must be put in harmony with the unity of ethical life. In Hegel's dialectical method, the subjective freedom of civil society is sublated [*Aufgehoben*] in the state, which is the unity of the private person and the citizen. To sublate means both to preserve and to cause to cease.[185] Although civil society is transcended in the state, its essential features are preserved. The following chapter examines Hegel's attempt to reconcile individual freedom with community standards of justice in the modern state. For Hegel, the state is the *telos* of the dialectic of freedom insofar as individuals finally make the universal their explicit aim in the state. Consequently, we must move to the political institutions of the *Rechtsstaat* for the completion of freedom.

## NOTES

1. Leslie Marmon Silko, *The Almanac of the Dead* (London: Penguin, 1991), 628.
2. Georg W. F. Hegel, *Philosophy of Right*, trans. T. M. Knox (Oxford: Oxford University Press, 1967), 103.
3. Hegel, *Philosophy of Right*, 110. For Hegel, this transition did not transpire as a historical sequence. The family and the state existed prior to civil society.
4. Hegel, *Philosophy of Right*, 109.
5. Paul Franco, *Hegel's Philosophy of Freedom* (New Haven, Conn.: Yale University Press, 1999), 234.
6. Hegel, *Philosophy of Right*, 110.
7. Hegel, *Philosophy of Right*, 123.
8. Hegel, *Philosophy of Right*, 155.

9. Hegel, *Philosophy of Right*, 124.

10. Hegel, *Philosophy of Right*, 270. See also Robert R. Williams, *Hegel's Ethics of Recognition* (Berkeley: University of California Press, 1997), 207. "Ethical life is the accomplishment and realization of mutual recognition. In ethical life, what is my right is also my duty: the recognition I receive from the community as right, I also owe to the community as a duty."

11. Richard Dien Winfield, *Freedom and Modernity* (Albany, N.Y.: State University of New York Press, 1991), 126.

12. Winfield, *Freedom and Modernity*, 127.

13. Richard Dien Winfield, *The Just Family* (Albany, N.Y.: State University of New York Press, 1998), 32.

14. Hegel, *Philosophy of Right*, 110. See Siegfried Blasche, "Natural Ethical Life and Civil Society: Hegel's Construction of the Family," in *Hegel on Ethics and Politics*, ed. Robert Pippin and Otfried Höffe (Cambridge: Cambridge University Press, 2004), 188, where he notes that on the one hand, the family is only one field of social interaction produced between certain individuals who act toward one another in a particular fashion. One the other hand, the family is a form of social union that ultimately depends on the sensibility of human nature rather than exclusively—like the state—on explicit acts of will. Thus, the family is a form of natural ethical life.

15. Hegel, *Philosophy of Right*, 35.

16. Blasche, "Natural Ethical Life and Civil Society," 192. The structural economic changes are effectively responsible for the separation of the family from society.

17. Franco, *Hegel's Philosophy of Freedom*, 236.

18. Jean Hyppolite, *Genesis and Structure of Hegel's* Phenomenology of Spirit, trans. Samuel Cherniak and John Heckman (Evanston: Northwestern University Press, 1974), 342.

19. Hegel, *Philosophy of Right*, 228.

20. Hegel, *Philosophy of Right*, 261. See Williams, *Hegel's Ethics of Recognition*, 208, where he notes that Hegel's concept of love is both a speculative ontological principle and an account of intersubjectivity. His dialogical ontology and phenomenological account of recognition are two sides of the same coin.

21. Hegel, *Philosophy of Right*, 270. See also Hegel, *Philosophy of Right*, 154, where he says that the family is the first ethical root of the state.

22. Hegel, *Philosophy of Right*, 163.

23. Hegel, *Philosophy of Right*, 262.

24. Hegel, *Philosophy of Right*, 112.

25. Hegel, *Philosophy of Right*, 111.

26. Hegel, *Philosophy of Right*, 262.

27. Hegel, *Philosophy of Right*, 262–263.

28. Hegel, *Philosophy of Right*, 262.

29. Franco, *Hegel's Philosophy of Freedom*, 241.

30. Hegel, *Philosophy of Right*, 112.

31. Merold Westphal, "Hegel's Radical Idealism: Family and State as Ethical Communities," in *The State and Civil Society: Studies in Hegel's Political Philosophy*, ed. Z. Pelczynski (Cambridge: Cambridge University Press, 1984), 76. Hegel

calls it abstract because it is arrived at by abstracting from so much of what makes up the identity of each person. Contracts are contingent because they result from the arbitrariness of the parties united by them. Finally, people enter into contracts not in order to share themselves with someone else or to create some new reality larger than themselves, but for the sake of the personal advantages that they will gain. Since Hegel sees the family relation as an essential part of a person's identity, it is understandable that he would oppose any contractual approach that treats it as merely instrumental to the private ends of the individual.

32. See Søren Kierkegaard, *Either/Or, Volume 2*, trans. H. Hong and E. Hong (Princeton: Princeton University Press, 1987), 22–24.

33. Hegel, *Philosophy of Right*, 262.

34. Hegel, *Philosophy of Right*, 113 and 263.

35. Hegel, *Philosophy of Right*, 111.

36. Franco, *Hegel's Philosophy of Freedom*, 242.

37. Richard Dien Winfield, *Law in Civil Society* (Lawrence: University of Kansas Press, 1995), 63.

38. Williams, *Hegel's Ethics of Recognition*, 216. Hegel further notes that marriage in itself is not dissolved by adultery, willful desertion, incompatibility, bad economic management; it can only be dissolved if both parties consider these to be grounds for divorce and want the dissolution.

39. Hegel, *Philosophy of Right*, 263. See Winfield, *The Just Family*, 167.

40. Hegel, *Philosophy of Right*, 263. See also Franco, *Hegel's Philosophy of Freedom*, 242, where he notes that one can imagine that Hegel would object to the ease with which divorces are currently obtained in places such as the United States today. He further might side with those who wished to make divorce more difficult.

41. Hegel, *Philosophy of Right*, 115.

42. Williams, *Hegel's Ethics of Recognition*, 225.

43. Hegel, *Philosophy of Right*, 115.

44. Franco, *Hegel's Philosophy of Freedom*, 243.

45. Hegel, *Philosophy of Right*, 114.

46. Hegel, *Philosophy of Right*, 263–264.

47. Hegel, *Philosophy of Right*, 114.

48. Franco, *Hegel's Philosophy of Freedom*, 245. Hegel characterizes men as the spirituality that divides itself up into personal self-sufficiency with being for itself and the knowledge of free universality. He characterizes women in terms of the spirituality that maintains itself in unity as knowledge in the form of concrete individuality and feeling. See Alan Wood, *Hegel's Ethical Thought* (New York: Cambridge University Press, 1990), 245, where he says that Hegel believes that men and women think differently, that men are better at grasping abstract ethical principles, but women are more perceptive about particular ethical relationships, better at responding emotionally to them. See also, Hegel, *Philosophy of Right*, 114.

49. Hegel, *Philosophy of Right*, 114.

50. Franco, *Hegel's Philosophy of Freedom*, 246. For Hegel, the requirement that there be a private familial sphere differentiated and sheltered from the public spheres of civil society and the state seems to involve the requirement that there be a human

type or character—namely, women—who embodies and is exclusively devoted to this sphere. However, it is possible to agree with Hegel on the necessary role of the family without accepting that it implies anything about the nature and role of men and women. It could be suggested that the immediate domestic sphere could be looked after by either the male or female, or shared by both.

51. Franco, *Hegel's Philosophy of Freedom*, 246.

52. Hegel, *Philosophy of Right*, 116.

53. Hegel, *Philosophy of Right*, 116. This seems to conflict with his earlier point that the family is the realm of women, as civil society is the realm of men.

54. Hegel, *Philosophy of Right*, 117.

55. Hegel, *Philosophy of Right*, 117.

56. Georg W. F. Hegel, *Philosophy of Mind*, trans. William Wallace (New York: Oxford University Press, 1971), 61.

57. Hegel, *Philosophy of Right*, 118, and Hegel, *Philosophy of Mind*, 256.

58. Richard Dien Winfield, *The Just Economy* (New York: Routledge, 1988), 5.

59. Michael O. Hardimon, *Hegel's Social Philosophy* (New York: Cambridge University Press, 1994), 190.

60. Franco, *Hegel's Philosophy of Freedom*, 249.

61. Joachim Ritter, *Hegel and the French Revolution: Essays on* The Philosophy of Right, trans. Richard Winfield (Cambridge: MIT Press, 1982), 131–132. "Behind the seeming thinglike fixedness that property has as object of will, lies concealed for Hegel the movement, the often long historical process of the active preparation of nature, with which it gets transformed into an object of the will and taken into possession by man as an object of will."

62. Hegel, *Philosophy of Right*, 122–123.

63. Winfield, *The Just Economy*, 6.

64. Ritter, *Hegel and the French Revolution*, 140–141.

65. Hegel, *Philosophy of Right*, 262.

66. Hegel, *Philosophy of Right*, 126, and Hegel, *Philosophy of Mind*, 257.

67. Hegel, *Philosophy of Right*, 123.

68. Hegel, *Philosophy of Right*, 134–135.

69. Hegel, *Philosophy of Right*, 152.

70. Franco, *Hegel's Philosophy of Freedom*, 250. Hegel's account of civil society includes both a recognition of liberal individuality on the one hand, and a critique of a certain type of liberal individualism on the other.

71. Hegel, *Philosophy of Right*, 267.

72. This is from *Vorlesungen über Naturrecht und Staatswissenschaft* [*Lectures on Natural Right and Political Science*] quoted in Williams, *Hegel's Ethics of Recognition*, 232.

73. Hyppolite, *Genesis and Structure of Hegel's* Phenomenology of Spirit, 394.

74. Dudley Knowles, *Hegel and the* Philosophy of Right (New York: Routledge, 2002), 265. Farmers grow crops and raise cattle, people walk into factories and do a day's work, goods fill the roads as they are transported between units of production and to the point of sale, and the streets are full of consumers going in and out of shops, examining items for purchase discovering prices, and sometimes buying.

75. Franco, *Hegel's Philosophy of Freedom*, 254.

76. Hegel, *Philosophy of Right*, 125.

77. Hegel, *Philosophy of Right*, 268.

78. Hegel, *Philosophy of Right*, 123.

79. Hegel, *Philosophy of Right*, 127.

80. Hegel, *Philosophy of Right*, 269.

81. Hegel, *Philosophy of Right*, 127. "This abstract character, universality, is the character of being recognized and is the moment which makes concrete, i.e. social, the isolated and abstract needs and their ways and means of satisfaction."

82. Hegel, *Philosophy of Right*, 128.

83. Hegel, *Philosophy of Right*, 128.

84. Hegel, *Philosophy of Right*, 129.

85. Knowles, *Hegel and the* Philosophy of Right, 269.

86. Hegel, *Philosophy of Right*, 129.

87. "First Philosophy of Spirit," in Georg W. F. Hegel, *System of Ethical Life (1802/03) and First Philosophy of Spirit (1803)*, trans. Henry Harris (Albany, N.Y.: SUNY Press, 1979), 249.

88. Hegel, *Philosophy of Right*, 149–150. See Williams, *Hegel's Ethics of Recognition*, 237, where he notes that there is paradox: "As human beings become more self-reliant and specialized, at the same time they become increasingly dependent on others. This in turn exposes them to contingency. Their individual labor provides them only the *possibility* of satisfaction rather than satisfaction itself."

89. Franco, *Hegel's Philosophy of Freedom*, 257.

90. Hegel, *Philosophy of Right*, 130. Hegel writes that to oppose this inequality and right of particularity is a folly of understanding, which takes as real and rational its abstract equality and its "ought-to-be."

91. Hegel, *Philosophy of Right*, 130–131, and Hegel, *Philosophy of Mind*, 258.

92. Hegel, *Philosophy of Right*, 270.

93. Hegel, *Philosophy of Right*, 131. Determinacy and particularity are attained after a process of careful reflection.

94. Knowles, *Hegel and the* Philosophy of Right, 271.

95. Hegel, *Philosophy of Right*, 132.

96. Hegel, *Philosophy of Right*, 23.

97. Hegel, *Philosophy of Right*, 134.

98. Hegel, *Philosophy of Right*, 134.

99. Winfield, *Law in Civil Society*, 72.

100. Hegel, *Philosophy of Right*, 134–135.

101. Hegel, *Philosophy of Right*, 271. While the sun, planets, and cattle have their laws, they are unaware of them. It is mankind's privilege to know the law.

102. Hegel, *Philosophy of Right*, 135.

103. Hegel, *Philosophy of Right*, 135.

104. Hegel, *Philosophy of Right*, 272.

105. Franco, *Hegel's Philosophy of Freedom*, 264.

106. Hegel, *Philosophy of Right*, 10.

107. Hegel, *Philosophy of Right*, 137.

108. Hegel, *Philosophy of Mind*, 259–260.

109. Franco, *Hegel's Philosophy of Freedom*, 264.

110. Hegel, *Philosophy of Right*, 138. See also Hegel, *Philosophy of Mind*, 261.

111. Hegel, *Philosophy of Right*, 140.

112. Hegel, *Philosophy of Right*, 141.

113. Hegel, *Philosophy of Right*, 142. Hegel includes this among the rights of the subjective consciousness. "The reason for this is that a trial is implicitly an event of universal validity, and although the particular content of the action affects the interests of the parties alone, its universal content, i.e. the right at issue and the judgement thereon, affects the interests of everybody."

114. Williams, *Hegel's Ethics of Recognition*, 152.

115. Hegel, *Philosophy of Right*, 64. "If the particular will is explicitly at variance with the universal, it assumes a way of looking at things and a volition which are capricious and fortuitous and comes on the scene in opposition to the principle of rightness. This is *wrong*."

116. Hegel, *Philosophy of Right*, 64.

117. Hegel, *Philosophy of Right*, 244.

118. Wolfgang Schild, "The Contemporary Relevance of Hegel's Concept of Punishment," in *Hegel on Ethics and Politics*, 164.

119. Williams, *Hegel's Ethics of Recognition*, 157. "The actuality of right thus means not only that right is recognized in its other (wrong) but sustains itself in its otherness and contradiction; that is, it endures in spite of opposition."

120. Immanuel Kant, "Metaphysics of Morals," in *Political Writings*, eds. L. Dickey and H. Nisbet (Cambridge: Cambridge University Press, 1991), 134.

121. Williams, *Hegel's Ethics of Recognition*, 165.

122. Hegel, *Philosophy of Right*, 67

123. Hegel, *Philosophy of Right*, 64.

124. Hegel, *Philosophy of Right*, 73.

125. Hegel, *Philosophy of Right*, 71. See also, Schild, "The Contemporary Relevance of Hegel's Concept of Punishment," in *Hegel on Ethics and Politics*, 166, where he notes that punishment can be understood conceptually as a kind of repayment only to the extent that it is intrinsically ground in the act of crime itself. Hence, the criminal ultimately punishes himself and the justice of punishment can consist only precisely in this.

126. Hegel, *Philosophy of Right*, 72. See Knowles, *Hegel and the* Philosophy of Right, 149, where he notes that Hegel argues that the wrongdoing actually wills the punishment. Since the criminal is a person and persons claim and respect rights, it is the criminal's will that rights-claims be effective. It is also the criminal's freedom that effective rights-claims express and protect.

127. Georg W. F. Hegel, *Logic*, trans. William Wallace (New York: Oxford University Press, 1975), 220.

128. Georg W. F. Hegel, "On the Scientific Ways of Treating Natural Law," in *Political Writings*, 139.

129. Williams, *Hegel's Ethics of Recognition*, 168. Hegel believes that retribution is just because retributive punishment is simply the reversal of the offense, that

is, it demands that the principle of the transgression be applied to the offender. The equality between crime and punishment is the reason why punishment is capable of annulling the transgression.

130. Williams, *Hegel's Ethics of Recognition*, 171. Against pragmatic and utilitarian theories that view punishment as a protection of society, as a deterrent, or as rehabilitation, Hegel insists that justice requires that the criterion of punishment derive from the criminal himself and not from elsewhere. The basic question of punishment presents a striking and provocative combination of the seemingly offensive concept of retribution with a profound respect for freedom, dignity, and justice.

131. Schild, "The Contemporary Relevance of Hegel's Concept of Punishment," 176.

132. Knowles, *Hegel and the* Philosophy of Right, 147. Public recognition requires public institutions.

133. Hegel, *Philosophy of Right*, 275–276.

134. Hegel, *Philosophy of Right*, 146.

135. Franco, *Hegel's Philosophy of Freedom*, 267.

136. Hegel, *Philosophy of Right*, 276.

137. Hegel, *Philosophy of Right*, 147.

138. Winfield, *The Just Economy*, 157.

139. Georg W. F. Hegel, "The German Constitution," in *Political Writings*, 23.

140. Winfield, *The Just Economy*, 231.

141. Hegel, *Philosophy of Right*, 149.

142. Hegel, *Philosophy of Right*, 148.

143. Hegel, *Philosophy of Right*, 148.

144. Hegel, *Philosophy of Right*, 150.

145. Hegel, *Philosophy of Right*, 278.

146. Hegel, *Philosophy of Right*, 150.

147. Hegel, *Philosophy of Right*, 149–150. The universalization of labor through division and mechanization leads to greater profits and wealth for the owners of factories, but it also leads to the specialization and limitation of particular work and to the dependence and want of the class that is tied to such work.

148. Hegel, *Philosophy of Right*, 150. The problem of poverty has a lot to do with the efficiencies and tremendous increases in quantity of production brought about by the replace of labor by machines.

149. Williams, *Hegel's Ethics of Recognition*, 243. "The inequalities of wealth and poverty produce a potentially antagonistic social situation and threaten a return to the life and death struggle that precedes master and slave."

150. Hegel, *Philosophy of Right*, 153.

151. Steven B. Smith, *Hegel's Critique of Liberalism: Rights in Context* (Chicago: The University of Chicago Press, 1989), 142.

152. Hegel, *Philosophy of Right*, 154.

153. Hegel, *Philosophy of Right*, 153.

154. Fred R. Dallmayr, *G. W. F. Hegel: Modernity and Politics* (Newbury Park, CA: Sage, 1993), 133.

155. Hegel, *Philosophy of Right*, 154.

156. Williams, *Hegel's Ethics of Recognition*, 255. Individuals now have a cause larger than themselves, namely, the welfare of the corporation, and through it, the welfare of the state as a whole.

157. Hegel, *Philosophy of Right*, 152–153.

158. Hegel, *Philosophy of Right*, 200–201.

159. Franco, *Hegel's Philosophy of Freedom*, 275.

160. Williams, *Hegel's Ethics of Recognition*, 256. Corporations constitute an important ethical moment within civil society. For Hegel, corporations represent a turn toward ethical considerations that originates in the contradictions inherent in civil society itself, namely, its self-subverting atomism and its tendency to generate extremes of wealth and poverty.

161. See Hegel, *Philosophy of Right*, 200–201.

162. Hegel, *Philosophy of Right*, 202–203. Hegel opposes the system of direct suffrage because it would lead to atomization and apathy; instead, he favors a form of corporate representation in the legislature. The important issue of representation is social function, not geographical milieu. In this way, the corporation further serves as a link or mediation between civil society and the state.

163. Hegel, *Philosophy of Right*, 195.

164. Williams, *Hegel's Ethics of Recognition*, 260. Williams says that such ethical institutions exist today, at least to a degree. Churches and religious organizations, cooperatives, labor unions, environmental coalitions, and professional associations approximate Hegelian institutions. Although they have not come close to preventing poverty, they have probably mitigated poverty and its effects, and prevented them from being worse that they are.

165. Frederick Neuhouser, *Foundations of Hegel's Social Theory: Actualizing Freedom* (Cambridge: Harvard University Press, 2000), 89–90.

166. Neuhouser, *Foundations of Hegel's Society Theory*, 90.

167. Neuhouser, *Foundations of Hegel's Social Theory*, 98.

168. K.-H. Ilting, "The Dialectic of Civil Society," in *The State and Civil Society*, 214.

169. Hegel, *Philosophy of Right*, 34.

170. Hegel, *Philosophy of Mind*, 238.

171. William Maker, "Introduction," in *Hegel on Economics and Freedom*, ed. William Maker (Macon: Mercer University Press, 1987), 6.

172. Neuhouser, *Foundations of Hegel's Social Theory*, 151.

173. Hegel, *Philosophy of Right*, 117.

174. Neuhouser, *Foundations of Hegel's Social Theory*, 170–171.

175. Hegel, *Philosophy of Right*, 58.

176. Hegel, *Philosophy of Right*, 126.

177. Neuhouser, *Foundations of Hegel's Social Theory*, 88. Since individuals realize the ends of the whole by following only their own particular ends, they achieve the ends of the whole by following only their own will and, hence, freely.

178. Hegel, *Philosophy of Mind*, 256–257.

179. Neuhouser, *Foundations of Hegel's Social Theory*, 110.

180. Herbert Marcuse, *Reason and Revolution: Hegel and the Rise of Social Theory* (Atlantic Highlands, N.J.: Humanities Press, 1941), 199.

181. Hegel, *Philosophy of Right*, 126.

182. Knowles, *Hegel and the* Philosophy of Right, 75.

183. Hegel, *Philosophy of Right*, p. 267. See also, Marcuse, *Reason and Revolution*, 202, where he writes that "Hegel says that civil society cannot be an end in itself because it cannot, by virtue of its intrinsic contradictions, achieve true unity and freedom."

184. Peter Stillman, "Partiality and Wholeness: Economic Freedom, Individual Development, and Ethical Institutions in Hegel's Political Thought," in *Hegel on Economics and Freedom*, 80.

185. Georg W. F. Hegel, *Science of Logic*, trans. A. Miller (Amherst, Mass.: Humanity Books, 1969), 107.

## Chapter Six

# Autonomy and Solidarity: Hegel's *Rechtsstaat*

And yet I will venture to believe that in no time, since the beginning of Society, was the lot of those same dumb millions of toilers so entirely unbearable as it is even in the days now passing over us. It is not to die, or even to die of hunger, that makes a man wretched; many have died; all must die—the last exit for us all in a Fire-Chariot of Pain. But it is to live miserable we know not why; to work and yet gain nothing; to be heart-worn, weary, yet isolated, unrelated, girt-in with a cold universal Laissez-faire: it is to die slowly all our life long, imprisoned in a deaf, dead, Infinite Injustice, as in the accursed iron belly of a Phalaris Bull.[1]

—Thomas Carlyle, "Past and Present"

Political liberalism and unregulated capitalism overly stress private, individualistic aims. In fact, the classical ideal of the 'good life' is replaced by ever-increasing private wants and consumption. The economic practices of contemporary societies seem to rule out the very possibility of restraint of wants and desires in the interest of liberty. As public space is privatized, more and more dimensions of life are held to be outside the realm of politics in the name of property rights and economic efficiency, and cannot be touched by the public will. Hegel would likely view the contemporary situation as being one where civil society has infringed on the boundaries of the state and upset the balance of ethical life. Consequently, political action appears as necessarily futile, and, as the sense of efficacy shrinks, so too do the bounds of civic allegiance to the political community.[2] It is no wonder that voting turnout has declined sharply. Hegel correctly foresaw the danger of public apathy inherent within liberal models of representation, as well as the dangers of an unregulated—or even underregulated—civil society. In brief, liberalism provides a state that has lost its power and its capacity to form a coherent

199

community. Liberal society has become fragmented and atomistic, since its institutional structure is too weak to support a common sense of meaning and to generate a morally satisfying form of community. If government becomes impotent, democracy becomes a hollow façade. Hegel's political philosophy offers a viable alternative to liberalism. He recognizes that civil society cannot be reduced to economics alone; law and public administration are necessary in order to guarantee and enforce the rights of individuals to satisfy their needs through their own free association—after all, that is what democratic politics is all about.

Hegel believes that his speculative philosophy is able to comprehend the entire world of actuality. As noted in Chapter 4, he is a historical thinker who is oriented toward the history of constitutions and organized forms of social life in general. More specifically, his conception of world history is essentially a history of political constitutions. Hegel's speculative philosophy, and the *Philosophy of Right* in particular, culminate in an analysis of the *Rechtsstaat* [Modern State, Based on Rule of Law]. It is the third part of Hegel's *Sittlichkeit* [Ethical Life] and marks the ground of all the rights and institutions covered up to this point in our discussion. The content of practical reasoning is given by the duties and virtues embedded in the social institutions and practices of modern society. Hegel distinguishes the state from civil society. Whereas in civil society the universal is largely an unintentional byproduct of the pursuit of individual self-interest and thus appears as an unconscious necessity, in the state it becomes an end that citizens knowingly and willing acknowledge.[3] More to the point, the *Rechtsstaat* marks the *telos* of Hegel's dialectic of human freedom, insofar as it is in the *Rechtsstaat* that individuals finally make the universal their explicit purpose. Hegel's *Sittlichkeit* is the idea of freedom, as the living good that has its knowledge and volition in self-consciousness, and its actuality through self-conscious action.[4] A social order and its accompanying institutions are rational to the extent that they foster freedom.

Freedom is neither a faculty given by nature nor a capacity of the self, but rather is a structure of interaction between individuals wherein the self-determination of each is constitutively related to that of others through mutual recognition and respect.[5] Hegelian ethics is founded on freedom. For instance, Hegel regards the *Rechtsstaat* as the actuality of the ethical idea, only because the state is the "actuality of concrete freedom."[6] The ethical world really exists. He draws a striking parallel between nature and politics. Just as there is a science of nature, there is a science of the state, and reason is no harder to discern in the productions of human consciousness than it is in natural phenomena.[7] Hegel's view that the state is fundamentally an ethical institution distinguishes him from virtually all other modern social theorists.

As he sees it, the state is not founded on coercion but on freedom. The source of the state's strength is not in force, but instead is the way its social structure organizes the rights—the subjective freedom—and the welfare of individuals into a harmonious whole. Furthermore, each individual's identity as a free person depends on the rational unity of the whole. In ethical action, individuals find that their fulfillment, which includes subjective freedom, is grounded on the universal, or the state.[8]

Hegel's view is that individuals can be fully self-actualized and concretely free only if they are devoted to ends beyond their own individual welfare, to universal or collective ends. For individual wills to particularize themselves, their self-determination must be a reciprocal interaction in which each wills its own objectification and relation to others in virtue of honoring their particular self-determination and relation.[9] At this point, willing gains a self-consciousness that is no longer exclusively tied to private preferences but reconciled with broader, universal aims.[10] Through this line of reasoning, Hegel concludes that freedom is not a natural endowment or structure of the self, but instead is an interaction of a plurality of individuals, that is, it is intersubjective. Reciprocal recognition means a dialectical union between being-for-self and being-for-other.[11] By conceiving freedom as interaction, Hegel is inexorably led to consider history as the domain in which freedom comes into being. The state is not a mechanism for keeping peace, or the enforcement of rights. Rather, it is most fundamentally the locus of the higher collective ends, which, by rationally harmonizing the rights and welfare of individuals, liberate them by providing their lives meaning.[12]

At first glance, one might wonder why the state is necessary, since civil society seems to have everything that people need to be complete—a system of justice, a police force, and a public authority to regulate the market and take care of the poor. First, Hegel sees the need for a unifying authority or sovereign power above and beyond the particularistic institutions of civil society. As we saw in the last chapter, the specific transition from civil society to the state comes out of the corporations, which reflect the need to be subordinated to something higher and more universal. Even though corporations possess a relative universality, their ends remain limited and finite.[13] Only in the state is the universal, the common good, willed completely. Consequently, corporations must come under the supervision of the state, because otherwise they would become ossified and decline into a miserable guild system.[14] Second, in civil society, individuals only enjoy their particular freedom, while in a state they lead a universal life and are more fully free. "Since the state is mind [*Geist*] objectified, it is only as one of its members that the individual himself has objectivity, genuine individuality, and an ethical life."[15] Whereas the individual is merely a *bourgeois* in civil society, in the state he exists for universal life as a citizen, who is not a part but a member.

As Hegel sees it, the state's actions on individuals are not external coercion, but are the internal, ethical disposition that fulfills their rational nature and thus makes them free. He does not, however, deny the coercive functions of the state. In particular, people desperately need external protection in the form of coercion in the economic realm. In short, the state appears as a coercive power only from the fragmented and self-interested perspective of individuals as members of civil society.[16] The state's real power always rests on a deeper ethical harmony, and only through this harmony can it retain the loyalty and support of its members. His conception of ethical life underwrites a conception of modern social life that is unique among modern theories in its emphasis on spontaneous harmony and free community as a condition for the possibility of all social institutions and relationships.[17] As illustrated in Chapter 2, freedom can only be understood as an intersubjective structure in which the self-determinations of individuals stand indissolubly linked together in a reciprocal relation where each will autonomously determines itself in accord with the realization of others.

> Thus, unlike the Husserlian phenomenology of intersubjectivity which first discovers the self and then seeks to "constitute" a world of other selves, the Hegelian phenomenology finds that other selves are essential to the discovery of one's own self and that this "discovery" is actually a producing of oneself in relation to others. . . . The Hegelian self, then, cannot be simply posited as an object of its own observation; it must produce itself by its own activity, and this it can do only through the mediating activity of other selves which, as selves, also require the same mediating activity. Only in a community of selves, then, is self-consciousness possible.[18]

Recognition is not simply the act of a pre-existing subject; in being an act that constitutes the other in a determinate way, and in being by necessity reciprocal, it is an act that simultaneously constitutes the agent as such.[19] For Hegel, mutual recognition needs to be mediated by social institutions and practices. Two or more individuals can recognize each other as free and rational agents only through specific institutions and practices in which they are participating.[20] Human beings can only be free individuals within the context of a community. Thus, a free society not only protects personal rights and provides for the subjective freedom and welfare of individuals, it is also one in which the individual good of its members is brought into rational harmony and grounded in a collective end, which its members understand and pursue both spontaneously and rationally for its own sake.

This chapter develops the argument that while Hegel's philosophy is not fully ensconced in modern liberalism and contains important classical elements thus combining autonomy and solidarity. In short, Hegel's *Rechtsstaat* reconciles individual freedom and community—dialectally combining modern and classical political philosophy. In order to do this, the chapter is organized into five sections. The first section examines his criticism of social contract theory, which uncovers many of shortcomings of modern political philosophy. The second section explores Hegel's attempt to develop a moral culture that works toward reconciliation of individual interests within the moral fabric of community. The importance of a separation of church and state and religious toleration is covered in the third section. The following section reviews his idea of *Rechtsstaat*, including subsections of its three political institutions—Constitutional Monarchy, Universal Estate, and Legislative Assembly—as the place where the tensions solidarity and autonomy are finally overcome. This includes a brief analysis of Hegel's political institutions, noting how they differ from those of other modern theorists. The final section assesses Hegel's critique of modern liberalism, especially in light of recent postmodern criticisms.

## THE CRITIQUE OF SOCIAL CONTRACT THEORY

Like Rousseau, Kant, and Fichte, Hegel takes freedom to be the fundamental principle of his political philosophy, and as noted above, the state is the realm of actualized freedom. Although he recognizes different versions of social contract theory, Hegel says that its central claim is that the state is based on the individual will. More specifically, Hegel takes social contract theorists to be grounding the state in the *Willkür* [Choice or Discretion] of the individual as this is expressed in the decision to give or withhold consent to a social contract.[21] Thus, social contract theory conceives of the community as contingent and derivative from the antecedent will of independent individuals.[22] As described in Chapter 2, social contract theory typically begins with solitary, free individuals in a state of nature. While some contract theorists, such as Locke, see the state of nature as the original condition of human beings, others, such as Hobbes and John Rawls, see it as a hypothetical device to discern the characteristics of human nature and explain the origin of the state. Regardless of their differences, contract theorists tend to see individual will as the starting point of the state. Government can only be legitimately established through an uncoerced act of human will. Human beings freely choose to enter into a social contract because they perceive it to be in their self-interest to do so.

Furthermore, they specifically submit to political authority in order to protect
their lives, liberty, and property.

Hegel rejects the concept of the state of nature as a useful starting point
for political theory. Hobbes and Locke describe the state of nature as a place
of complete freedom, a place where people are under no political authority.
From this, they conclude that man is by nature free. Hegel holds that while
people are destined to be free, they could not be free in any meaningful way
in the state of nature:

> When man is spoken of as "free by Nature," the mode of his existence as well
> as his destiny is implied. His merely natural and primary condition is intended.
> In this sense, a "state of nature" is assumed in which mankind at large are in
> the possession of their natural rights with the unconstrained exercise and enjoy-
> ment of their freedom. The assumption is not indeed raised to the dignity of the
> historical fact; it would indeed be difficult, were the attempt seriously made, to
> point out any such condition as actually existing, or as having ever occurred.
> Examples of a savage state of life can be pointed out, but they are marked by
> brutal passions and deeds of violence. . . . What we find such a state of Nature
> to be in actual experience, answers exactly to the Idea of a *merely* natural condi-
> tion. Freedom as the *ideal* of that which is original and natural, does not exist
> *as original and natural*. Rather must it be first sought out and won; and that by
> an incalculable medial discipline of the intellectual and moral powers. The state
> of Nature is, therefore, predominately that of injustice and violence, of untamed
> natural impulses, of inhuman deeds and feelings.[23]

Individuals in the state of nature would clearly lack the capacity for rational
thought. Much like Hobbes, Hegel argues that the state of nature would be a
state of animal impulse and savagery. Thus, even if a state of nature actually
existed, it would not be a place where rational individuals could freely choose
to establish a proper political regime. For Hegel, the attributes and capacities
that make up free, rational agency cannot be developed and sustained in the
state of nature. They can only be developed and sustained in the context of
the institutions of *Rechtsstaat*.[24] "The freedom of nature, the gift of freedom,
is not anything real; for the state is the first realization of freedom."[25]

Although the state is the actuality of freedom, Hegel does not understand
freedom as the particular or arbitrary will of the individual. Rather, he sees
it in terms of the individual's substantial or rational will. So the state is not
merely a means to satisfy individual or particular wills.[26] Like the family, the
state consists of the common personality and interests of all its members, not
of the individual personality and its interests.[27] Unlike the family, however,
the individual's sense of unity with others in the state is not based on immediate feeling but rather on knowing and conscious will. "The state, there-

fore, knows what it wills and knows it in its universality, i.e. as something thought."[28] While family members are conscious of one's unity in feeling, members of the state are conscious of it as law, which must be rational and known by individual citizens. The state is not simply a means for individuals to satisfy their particularity; it is the objective embodiment of that universality or rationality that represents the deepest essence of human beings.[29] According to Hegel, social contract theory assumes that the universal can be separated from the individual—as if the individual could on its own be what it presently is, and the universal did not make it that which it is in truth.[30]

Hegel asserts that social contract theory misapplies the norms and principles of the *bourgeois* sphere of civil society to the normative theory of *Rechtsstaat*. "The intrusion of this contractual relation, and relationships concerning private property generally, into the relation between the individual and the state has been productive of the greatest confusion in both constitutional law [*Staatsrecht*] and public life."[31] Thus, applying the contractual relation to government is a complete distortion. For Hegel, there is an important distinction between *Staatsrecht* [Constitutional Law] and *Privatrecht* [Civil Law], since the norms and values that apply in one sphere are not appropriate for the other. Social contract theory ignores this distinction by treating the questions of membership, authority, and obligation as though they are essentially problems of bargaining and exchange.[32]

Although a contract theorist would argue that there is nothing wrong with applying the norms and principles of consensual exchange of civil society to the political sphere, Hegel holds that because social contract theory rests on individual choice [*Willkür*], it ends up treating membership, authority, and obligation as though they are optional. Under social contract theory, individuals can choose to enter the state or not, and they may or may not recognize political authority and assume certain obligations. Against this, Hegel cites Aristotle's dictum that a man living alone would be either an animal or a god. It is not a choice but rather it is the rational destiny [*Bestimmung*] of human beings to live within a state:

> It has recently become very fashionable to regard the state as a contract of all with all. Everyone makes a contract with the monarch, so the argument runs, and he again with his subjects. This point of view arises from thinking superficially of a mere unity of different wills. In contract, however, there are two identical wills who are both persons and wish to remain property-owners. Thus contract springs from a person's arbitrary will. . . . But the case is quite different with the state; it does not lie with an individual's arbitrary will to separate himself from the state, because we are already citizens of the state by birth. The rational end of man is life in the state, and if there is no state, reason at once demands that one be founded.[33]

For Hegel, it is not optional whether one lives under a state or not; it is one's absolute duty to do so. Since contracts are the product of individual choice, they are entered into at the discretion of the contracting parties. Hegel thinks that this would provide a too capricious and unreliable foundation for political authority. "Permission to enter a state or leave it must be given by the state; this then is not a matter which depends upon an individual's arbitrary will and therefore the state does not rest on contract, for contract presupposes arbitrariness."[34] Hegel holds that it is nearer to the truth to say that it is absolutely necessary for every individual to be a citizen. He is close to the Aristotelian position that people are by nature political animals. Hegel's claim is that the state is not based on a contract because individuals already have a duty to belong to and obey it, whether or not they have given their consent.[35] For Hegel, the state is systematic, a form of organization that blocks reduction.

Social contract theorists would likely object that Hegel's view of the state does not respect freedom enough, since it takes away individual choice. However, Hegel counters that contract theorists tend to hold on to an unacceptable analysis of freedom. To the extent that they equate freedom with the capacity of individual choice [*Willkür*], social contract theorists are working with a false conception of freedom.[36] Equating freedom with the capacity of choice allows the agent to follow his or her own unexamined desires and inclinations. Hegel argues that giving in to one's desires and inclinations is no more freedom that submitting to authority. In both cases, the person is allowing something external to determine what one should think or do. As noted above, Hegel's conception of freedom has an objective dimension—a condition of being free is that one must engage in rational choice. Thus, for Hegel, contract theory wrongly identifies freedom with *Willkür*.[37] Furthermore, as long as the state is based on rational principles of *Recht* [Right], it is not a limitation on freedom. For Hegel, objective freedom is tied to specific virtues and duties.

Even though Hegel accepts the idea that political authority must be grounded in the freedom of the individual, he does not think that this is possible only by the consent of the governed. Put differently, we should not ask whether or not political institutions enjoy the actual consent of social members; rather legitimacy should be measured by the reasonableness of an institution. For Hegel, a political theory starting from the principle of freedom should only be concerned with securing the freedom of all individuals, including the children and members of future generations.[38] Hegel maintains that working out the implications of individual freedom requires abandoning the standpoint of the individual in favor of an account of a community of individuals. The autonomous individual is an inadequate foundation for a concept of community and its ethical norms.[39] Like Aristotle, Hegel recognizes that the whole precedes its parts. Hegel argues that modern social institutions are necessary for the development and maintenance of free, rational agency. Like contract theorists, he is committed to freedom; but unlike them, he is sensitive to the social and political basis of freedom. This enables Hegel to view modern political institutions in a new light and to appreciate the relationship between members of a social community and their political rights in a way different from that of modern liberalism. Liberal theories of human nature define human beings in ways that deprive them of the strength of cooperation and common being. Hegel's *Rechtsstaat* is a complex form of mutual recognition that extends the sense of joint membership, participation, and shared self-identity throughout the social body.

## RECONCILING INDIVIDUALISM AND COMMUNITY

Since the advent of modern political philosophy, great thinkers have examined the inherent tension between individual freedom and social responsibility. Rousseau and Kant try to overcome this tension, and Hegel continues this effort with his attempt to reconcile the particular and the universal. His political theory provides a middle ground between the abstract atomic individualism of modern liberalism and abstract communitarianism. So long as human beings regard liberty as the freedom to pursue selfish whims, society is only possible if external checks are placed on liberty. The classical liberal conception of liberty sees freedom as the absence of restrictions. Government, in Hobbes's view, is an external organization to meet men's necessities. But if we realize that true freedom consists in the acceptance of principles and laws, a synthesis of universal and particular interests becomes possible.[40] Hegel's introduction to the *Philosophy of Right* consists of an explication of the concept of the will, designed to show that the fully developed concept of the will generates a fully developed concept of freedom, including elements that insure that this freedom has both objective and subjective reality.

Hegel is very familiar with the liberal conception of freedom, but unlike Locke and other liberals, he refers to it as formal or abstract freedom, meaning that it has form but no substance.[41] Freedom, for Hegel, is not the ability to do whatever one pleases. His objection to this notion of freedom is that it takes the choices of the individual as the basis from which freedom must begin. Individual choice, considered in isolation from everything else, is the outcome of arbitrary circumstances. Hence, it is not genuinely free. Due to his historical perspective, Hegel never loses sight of the fact that human wants and desires are shaped by the society one lives in, and that this society in turn is a stage in the historical process. Thus, abstract freedom, the freedom to do as one pleases, is effectively the freedom to be pushed to and fro by the social and historical forces of our time. Furthermore, Hegel argues that individual autonomy can be achieved only within a communal context. It is a fundamental insight of the *Phenomenology of Spirit* that an individual subject necessarily exists within a structure of intersubjective recognition.[42] Freedom is realizable only in a modern, law-governed commercial society. While liberty is a necessary feature of human agency, for Hegel it is something that must be socially achieved.

Some desires, such as hunger or sexual desires that people are born with and have the potential to develop, are the product of nature. Other desires are formed by one's upbringing, education, or cultural environment. Whether a desire is biological or social in origin, however, Hegel notes that in either case they are not chosen. Thus, since individuals do not choose their desires, they are not free when they act from particular innate or socially conditioned desires. He holds that individuals are fundamentally social practitioners. Everything that one does, says, or thinks is formed in the context of social practices. No one acts on the merely biological needs of food, safety, or companionship; rather, one acts on much more specific needs for much more specific kinds of objects that fulfill those needs, and one acts to achieve them in very specific ways.[43] Society deeply conditions personal ends because it provides specific objects that meet those ends, and specific procedures for obtaining them. Like Kant, Hegel sees reason as being essentially universal, and, therefore, sees freedom as being found in what is universal. Both philosophers see a connection between freedom and the development of the individual conscience, and both believe duty appears as a restriction on man's natural or arbitrary desires. In fact, the individual only truly finds his liberation from mere natural impulse in duty.[44]

As we saw in Chapters 3 and 4, Hegel holds that the members of ancient Greek culture identified wholly and completely with their particular community.[45] They enjoyed the satisfactions of community without the pain of alienation. This state's "happiness" consists precisely in that absence of separation and division between community members and their community. In short, it is the happiness of unity. It is by sacrificing their particularity, abandoning any conception of themselves as individuals apart from their cultural identity and subordinating their separate and particular interests to the shared interests of the community, that the members of ancient *Sittlichkeit* come to see themselves as the kind of beings they are—individual instantiations of the shared spirit of their community.[46] Hegel is clearly attracted to this, and he finds it in dramatic contrast to the division and fragmentation of modern social life.

As illustrated in Chapter 4, Hegel's aim is not to reconstruct the harmony of ancient *Sittlichkeit* but rather to find a way of grasping modern *Sittlichkeit* as combining the fruits of modernity, the principle of particularity, with community membership. His goal does not require the suppression of individuality, but is a project of reconciliation: "Particular interests should in fact not be set aside or completely suppressed; instead, they should be put in correspondence with the universal, and thereby both they and the universal are upheld."[47] The idea of reconciliation is an idea of unity with the social world, which involves regarding oneself as a member of the social world in some very strong sense.[48] Hegel argues that a rational society makes the civil, legal, and political structure of the community known to its members, along with how individual activities contribute to and benefit from this structure. In this way, he expects to combine individual satisfaction and freedom in conformity to the social ethos of the community. Since our needs and desires are shaped by society, a community can foster the development of those desires that most benefit the community.

Like Rousseau's general will, the community imbues its members with the sense that their own identity consists in being a part of the community so that they will not think of going off in pursuit of interests that might damage the community:

> Individuals in their capacity as burghers in this state are private persons whose end is their own interest. This end is *mediated* through the universal which thus *appears* as a *means* to its realization. Consequently, individuals can attain their ends only in so far as they themselves determine their knowing, willing, and acting in a universal way and make themselves links in this chain of social connections.[49]

This relationship is reciprocal; the community cannot disregard the interests of its members any more than a body would disregard an injury to its left arm. In the *Philosophy of Right*, he calls "civil society" the positive creation of individualism, and it is seen as the achievement of the modern world. As discussed in the previous chapter, it is comprised of the institutions and practices involved in the production, distribution, and consumption of products that meet a variety of needs and wants. As Hegel sees it, freedom is only realizable in a commercial society. Put differently, a subject must acquire an external sphere of freedom in order to exist as idea. The relationship between subject and external things is a connection of external possession and ownership, that is, a relation of property. This relationship also represents the growing recognition by the community that its members have legitimate rights and interests as particular, private individuals.

It is no accident that such conflicts occur. Hegel argues that in a well-ordered society people will be raised to have separate and particular interests, some of which inevitably come into conflict with the demands of their social roles.[50] In his view, reconciliation essentially involves accepting, even embracing, tensions. The tension between separate and particular interests and the demands of community are a necessary by-product of one's individuality. Conflict is found between one's individual, family, and community roles. Human beings need separate spheres in which they can find intimacy, actualize their individuality, and enjoy political community. For Hegel, civil society is the sphere in which human beings actualize their individuality. However, the price of this differentiation is conflict. Civil society is the part of modern life that is to meet the private interests of individuals. But it is also a network of spontaneous, private relations established within the framework of law by individuals pursuing their own ends.[51]

Hegel makes a basic distinction between civil society and state. The complex of activities, attitudes, rules, and institutions that make up civil society is only an aspect of political and social life abstracted from the wider, more concrete state.[52] In this realm a person's movement toward universality is shown by the very multiplication of wants. For example, with the specialization of labor, wants are refined and extended. Consciousness cannot be developed without the material base implied in the multiplication of material wants.[53] The specialization required to meet mankind's material needs and wants leads to the development of different categories of workers, also known as classes or estates [*Stände*]. The different classes have different particular interests that they actively pursue. But the very conflict of interests always present gives rise to the consciousness of a possible general interest under which administration of justice can be subsumed:

> When men are thus dependent on one another and reciprocally related to one another in their work and the satisfaction of their needs, subjective self-seeking turns into a contribution to the satisfaction of the needs of everyone else. That is to say, by a dialectical advance, subjective self-seeking turns into the mediation of the particular through the universal, with the result that each man in earning, producing, and enjoying on his own account is *eo ipso* producing and earning for the enjoyment of everyone else.[54]

Law arises to objectify right, and it presumably reflects reason unaffected by particularized interests. Education [*Bildung*] is also of paramount importance, since the process of becoming reconciled to the social world involves a transformation of consciousness through which one moves from an atomic individual to an individual social member.

It is Hegel's contention that modern individuality and social membership are not only compatible but also intertwined and inextricable. In fact, it is precisely through one's social membership that a person is able to actualize oneself as an individual, and through individuality that people are able to actualize themselves as social members. People, for Hegel, are individuals in the minimal sense.[55] First, it is a necessary condition for being a human individual. A person must regard himself as distinct from other persons in order to be an individual. In fact, one becomes an individual only through a process of differentiation from others.[56] Second, it states the weakest conception of individuality that can still intuitively be regarded as a genuine conception of human individuality. One can be an individual without stepping back from one's social roles and institutions. In short, Hegel's minimal conception of individuality represents a form of individualism that makes no reference to the contrast between the individual and society. However, his conception of individuality is clearly much stronger than the virtually nonexistent one in ancient times. It is the strong, not minimal, conception of individuality that Hegel regards as distinctively atomistic and excessive.

With his conception of social membership, Hegel maintains that human beings are essentially social. First, they depend upon society for the satisfaction of biological, social, and cultural needs. Second, they depend on society for the realization of their distinctly human capacities, such as thought, language, and reason. In this respect, he resembles the Aristotelian notion that man is a political animal. People are formed by their national culture.[57] For example, the roles of family member, member of civil society, and citizen figure strongly in the psychological makeup of human beings. Hegel says that the attitudes, habits, and ideals internal to these roles constitute core features of personality.[58] Being a member of a particular state means participating in its central institutions. In fact, Hegel contends that people need and desire the sort of intimacy that these roles entail. Hence, his moral psychology is rooted in his social psychology.

Individuals, according to Hegel, need society in the strong sense. This claim is grounded in his notion that in order fully to realize themselves as *Geist*, people must participate in social life, which is found within the social arrangements constituted by the family, civil society, and the state. Hence, when people participate in these arrangements they are realizing themselves as *Geist*, precisely by exercising their roles of family member, member of civil society, and citizen. One of the central aims of the *Philosophy of Right* is to stress that individuals are also members of the family, civil society, and state.[59] It argues that a full-fledged form of individuality and a full-fledged form of social membership can be combined. Hegel argues that conceptions of the self as a bearer of separate and particular interests, a possessor of individual rights, and a subject of conscience are all internal to the role of member of civil society.[60]

In addition to arguing for the compatibility of modern individuality and social membership, Hegel contends that social membership makes modern individuality possible. For instance, he maintains that the conception of the individual as bearing separate and particular interests, possessing individual rights belongs to the self-conception people have as members of civil society.[61] Civil society is seen as the proper sphere for the exercise of these self-understandings. In fact, these self-understandings are engendered by the practices of civil society. It is through participation in civil society that people come to think of themselves as bearers of separate and particular interests. Participating in civil society is a matter of abstracting oneself from one's role of family member or citizen and pursuing one's separate and particular interests in the world of work.[62] Thus, it is in participating in civil society by actualizing oneself as a member of civil society that one actualizes oneself as an individual.

## HEGEL'S *RECHTSSTAAT*

*The Philosophy of Right* culminates in a description of the rational state and represents Hegel's most comprehensive attempt to delineate the nature of the government in a systematic way. The state typically refers to a particular form of political society, characterized by the presence of institutions having the authority to coerce. Nevertheless, the essence of the state is not the law of force, but the law of reason. Furthermore, freedom is law to the extent that law is rational.[63] For Hegel, the modern state, as *Geist* objectified, satisfies the claims of the individual with those of society. His theory of the state, of the state as it really is, not the state of utopian dreamers, is the theory of reason as it is realized in mankind, realized for itself and by itself.[64] Hegel's idea of the state differs from Plato's in that the state is historical. In other words, it is not an idea that exists outside of becoming, but is an idea bound up with becoming itself.[65] Since legal arrangements and political institutions reflect the level attained by *Geist*, legal and constitutional provisions of earlier stages were bound to wither and be replaced. Like Montesquieu, Hegel stresses that a constitution is not simply made, but is a byproduct of the specific historical spirit of a people [*Volksgeist*]. Both argue that development is a vital aspect of political institutions. Unlike Montesquieu, however, Hegel's theory of the state does not lack the idea of an organic unity developing in and through itself. Thus, unlike most other political philosophers, Hegel does not engage in constructing political institutions, since the *Philosophy of Right* discusses institutions that he claims to find already existing to some extent. His organic theory of the division of powers in the state marks an important step beyond highly formalistic and mechanical doctrine of separation of powers found in the eighteenth century.[66]

As illustrated in the previous chapter, it is not possible to grasp completely the state's proper functions without understanding the functions of the family and civil society. Hegel's account of *Sittlichkeit* constitutes a unified theory that employs a single model to understand the essential character of both political and nonpolitical institutions.[67] The family, civil society, and the state each foster a particular type of identity that plays a role in actualizing freedom. The family furnishes society with human beings, civil society supplies the needed material goods, and the state coordinates the two other spheres. Thus, one of the primary duties of the Hegelian state is to ensure the survival and proper functioning of both the family and civil society. Hegel argues that individuals can be brought to will and work freely for the collective good insofar as doing so is an expression of their particular identity.[68] Since each identity requires thinking of oneself as having substantive attachments to other individuals, participation in the family, civil society, and the state is universally beneficial. Acting on one's identity as a family member, a professional, or a citizen is simultaneously to work for the collective good. However, one of the central tasks of a rational political order is to sustain political institutions and practices that enable individuals to escape alienation and atomism.

His conception of *Rechtsstaat* is a system of integration aimed at overcoming the threat of atomistic individualism that permeates the economic sphere. Put another way, civil society's egoism is transcended in the state, which signals a mode of relating to a universe of human beings not out of self-interest but out of solidarity. If the state is to realize *Sittlichkeit*, it must constitute a common life in which everyone finds their identity. Hegel's political theory can be seen as an attempt to achieve a universality that would not be, on the one hand, an aggregate of individual wills yet would not appear, on the other, as merely external coercive antithesis to the individual wills.[69] Thus, the state becomes necessary when civil society seems to be heading for disruption and chaos. It functions to re-integrate the self as a universal being after economic life has particularized and atomized the individual.[70] The Hegelian state can accomplish this without any mythic hypostasis because its reality is to be found in the consciousness of individual persons, who by virtue of this very consciousness cease to be purely private persons.[71] His philosophy interprets the whole of history in the same way—as the reconciliation of the individual with the universal. For Hegel, the ideals of individuality and social membership are not mutually exclusive values.

## Constitutional Monarchy

The political aspect of autonomy, however, is not achieved within civil society, but instead is a function of government. The state is identified with government. The state as a community embodying reason has to be lived as an organic whole. It cannot simply be an aggregation of its elements. For Hegel, pure democracy depends on citizens having a virtuous disposition by which they subordinate their particular interests to the universal interest. Once this public-spirited disposition is lost and the powers of particularity are unleashed in civil society, democracy would be destroyed.[72] His specifically modern form of government consists of a constitutional monarchy, which in its rational form contains three branches: the crown, the executive, and the legislature.[73] He argues that this constitution corresponds to the highest stage of historical development with respect to the idea of freedom. The kind of monarchy that Hegel has in mind is one that has moved away from the absolutist and authoritarian tradition toward a limited form of constitutional monarchy with republican features. The development of the state to constitutional monarchy is the accomplishment of the modern world, and is seen as reflecting the progress of *Geist*.[74] The Hegelian monarch represents the whole elevated above the special interests, which tend to prevail in civil society. It is intended to ameliorate the harsh aspects of individualism and make competition into a positive interest of the community.

Hegel sees the sovereignty of the state as the one principle that would bring unity to a competitive society based on the rational autonomy of the individual.[75] Sovereignty requires that all autonomous power centers of society converge toward a single point of authority. Hegel's state sovereignty is a necessary instrument for preserving society:

> For, the sovereign state would remove the destructive competitive element from the individuals and make competition a positive interest of the universal; it would be capable of dominating the conflicting interests of its members. . . . Conscious regulation of the social antagonisms, therefore, by a force standing above the clash of particular interests, and yet safeguarding each of them, could alone transform the anarchic sum-total of individuals into a rational society. The rule of law was to be the lever of that transformation.[76]

Hence, Hegel expects to find a reconciliation of the universal and the particular in the modern constitutional monarchy. The universal moment is represented by the legislative power, the particularization of the universal by the executive power, and the synthesis of both, as individual reality, by the constitutional monarchy.[77] A monarchy is required because somewhere there must be a power of ultimate decision, and in a free community he maintains that this power should be expressed by the free decision of a person. Only there does a political system come to be personified in an individual that is explicit and rational. However, it is essential to recognize that the sovereignty of the state not be identified with any single element. All three parts of the state possess sovereignty. For Hegel, the individual decision of the monarch presupposes the existence of the universally approved laws of particular organisms to enforce its execution. Nevertheless, the person of the monarch is uniquely suited to express the unity of the state.[78]

The basic feature of the abstract personality has developed itself through varied forms of subjectivity, and the complete concrete objectivity of the will develops within the personality of the state. An "I will" initiates all action and actuality. For Hegel, personality and subjectivity can only have absolute truth as a person. The personality of the state is only actual as a person, the monarch.[79] Hegel sees any attempt to substitute a republican assembly for this monarch as the mark of an undeveloped political state, where personality is an abstract moment. The function of the monarch is simply to make final decisions. When all sides of the issue have been offered, the last move is simple fiat of personal decision.[80] The monarch's authority resides in the complete groundlessness of final decisions. Sovereignty requires that all the autonomous power centers of a society converge toward a single point of public authority. The monarch's "I will" ends the search for a final word and makes possible the self-grounding of political obligation.[81] The monarch serves the purpose of institutionalizing the principle of human subjectivity.

In the same way, the decision of who shall be monarch is decided groundlessly by nature, and not by a process of choice. For Hegel, a hereditary monarchy is the only one that can be raised high above factions, and can give real unity to the society.[82] Like Plato and James Madison, Hegel is very concerned about the mischief of factions. Only a hereditary monarchy can be insulated from the shifting pressures and contingencies of society and provide the necessary substantiality and permanency.[83] In this way, the personal, contingent characteristics of the personality of the monarch are seen as being irrelevant. Hereditary monarchy allows for the expression of the will of the state in an immediate individual, one who is essentially characterized as this individual, in abstraction from all his other characteristics. Although the monarch may have the "individual moment" of making final decisions, he also has the "specific moment" represented by his advisors and the "universal moment" represented by the constitution and laws, which he cannot alter.[84] To a significant extent, the monarch is bound by the laws and the constitution, as well as the objective advice of his ministers.

## The Universal Estate

The second part of the constitution is the executive power, which is charged with applying laws. Hegel says that this function should be entrusted to a class of civil servants whose lives are dedicated to the goal of executing the law of the land. Administration must be the hands of a professional civil service that is independent of the interests of society.[85] The purpose of making the civil service a career is to assure the maximum independence and dedication to the function itself, the maximum freedom from private interests. The executive is the governmental body through which the community acts as a whole. Unlike other classes, they have the business of the oversight of the whole. For the same reason and in order to secure the most effective services, positions are filled based on merit.[86] The basis for eligibility for the civil service is not hereditary but knowledge and proof of ability. Anticipating Max Weber's ideal of modern bureaucracy, this branch is a body of highly trained civil servants and higher advisory officials, who are devoted to the common good of the community.[87] This power also consists of the judiciary and the police that were discussed in the previous chapter.

The central task of the executive is to implement the laws of the legislature and to execute the policies determined by the crown. The civil service makes up the greater part of the middle estate, which Hegel has called the universal estate:

> Civil servants and the member of the executive constitute the greater part of the middle class, the class in which the consciousness of right and the developed intelligence of the mass of people is found. The sovereign working on the middle class at the top, and Corporation-rights working on it at the bottom, are the institutions which effectively prevent it from acquiring the isolated position of an aristocracy and using its education and skill as means to an arbitrary tyranny.[88]

Like Aristotle, he stresses the importance of a strong middle class, describing it as the pillar of righteousness and intelligence necessary for a highly developed government. The civil service also serves as a mediating body that connects the political state to civil society. The dimension of total identification with the life of the state is not to be lived by everyone in the same way, but is the mode of life of a special group. Hegel's attempt to find a sphere that transcends private interests is similar to, although less radical than, Plato's Guardians. Civil servants are paid a salary and should also have tenure and be independent of immediate political pressure.[89] This shares the large life of the whole state with others in society, and is an organ in a greater organism. As noted above, the potential abuse of power is safeguarded by the answerability of civil servants to their superiors and the monarch.

## The Legislative Assembly

The legislature is the branch of government responsible for the formulation of law. Through the legislature, citizens make their complaints heard, express their needs, and participate in universal decisions. The legislative assembly passes laws that define and protect the rights of property and contract, thereby giving legal expression to the private sphere, conferring upon it the protection of the state.[90] Representation, for Hegel, is a system of mediation between the people and the government, between the particularism of civil society and the universalism of the state. As such, it is a necessary element of the political structure. The absence of mediation is despotism. The mediation brought about through representation is necessary if the attempt to integrate the contending particulars into a whole is to be successful:

> The Estates have the function of bringing public affairs into existence not only implicitly, but also actually, i.e. of bringing into existence the moment of subjective formal freedom, the public consciousness as an empirical universal, of which the thoughts and opinions of the Many are particulars. . . . Hence the specific function which the concept assigns to the Estates is to be sought in the fact that in them the subjective moment in universal freedom—the private judgement and private will of the sphere called "civil society" in this book—comes into existence integrally related to the state. . . . Regarded as a mediating organ, the Estates stand between the government in general on the one hand and the nation broken up into particulars (people and associations) on the other.[91]

The assembly of estates [*Stände*], therefore, is the aggregation and articulation of the interests of civil society; hence, its composition should reflect the divisions of civil society. In this way, the people deliberate according to the constitutive divisions that make up society, that is, through their respective estates.[92]

The estates and its representatives serve to express the needs and interests of the various classes, and its actions enter the popular consciousness. Hegel believes that a bicameral legislature is the best way to ensure proper representation.[93] The legislature should consist of an upper house, composed of members of nobility and landed aristocracy, and a lower house, elected by the commercial part of civil society. The electoral basis for the lower house should not be founded on merely direct, universal suffrage. Hegel maintains that undifferentiated suffrage causes atomization and political alienation.[94] If people vote according to their corporate affiliation, the gap between civil society and the state, which remains open with direct elections, can be narrowed:

> The circles of association in civil society are already communities. To picture these communities as once more breaking up into a mere conglomeration of individuals as soon as they enter the field of politics, i.e. the field of the highest concrete universality, is *eo ipso* to hold civil and political life apart from one another and as it were to hang the latter in the air, because its basis could then

only be the abstract individuality of caprice and opinion, and hence it would be grounded on chance and not on what is absolutely stable and justified.[95]

Thus, Hegel adds the integrative function to representation. Great acts by the estates have a deliberative character and should lead, not follow, public opinion. The legislature leads the empirical consciousness of the people beyond the sphere of private interests. Consequently, the public is educated by the legislative debates.

A legislature based on estates achieves a level of integration not possible with election through geographic districts. He sees this as a guarantee against atomization:

> Regarded as a mediating organ, the Estates stand between the government in general on the one hand and the nation broken up into particulars (people and associations) on the other. . . . Further, and more important, they prevent individuals from having the appearance of a mass or an aggregate and so from acquiring an unorganized opinion and volition and from crystallizing into a powerful bloc in opposition to the organized state.[96]

Hence, the estates are supposed to be the locus in which a common will, one which is that of the state, is crystallized out of the maze of private wills of civil society. The universal interest emerges from a process of rational deliberation in which all objective interests are adjusted. The real point of the estates is to incorporate civil society into the state. This cannot be done if the state is viewed primarily as a place where people come to protect their private interests and policy is merely some kind of pluralistic compromise essential to a functioning society. People must relate to the state not as individuals, but through their membership in the articulated components of the society.[97] Hegel is clearly not an advocate of modern pluralistic liberalism, which he describes as a mere aggregate or crowd. Since the state is an ethical institution, citizens should interact, not as private parties, but rather as members willing government policy as the end of their own free action.

Deliberations in the legislature have an additional function. In proper Hegelian fashion, truth comes out in a dialectical fashion and is never a priori. All objective interests are represented in the legislative deliberation. Debates in the assembly, with their quality of give and take, are a device through which truth, and the public interest, can emerge. The common view is that everyone knows from the start what is best for the state and the assembly merely discusses this knowledge. However, Hegel claims that the contrary is true:

> The opening of this opportunity to know a more universal aspect because by this means public opinion first reaches thoughts that are true and attains insight into the situation and concept of the state and its affairs, and so first acquires ability

to estimate these more rationally. By this means also, it becomes acquainted with and learns to respect the work, abilities, virtues, and dexterity of ministers and officials. While such publicity provides these abilities with a potent means of development and a theatre of higher distinction, it is at the same time another antidote to the self-conceit of the individuals singly and en masse, and another means—indeed one of the chief means—of their education.[98]

Thus, it is through the deliberations of the assembly that public virtues and abilities emerge. Hegel argues that legislative debates should be open to the public, since they are also an act of public education.[99] Political participation is important for Hegel not only because it brings subjective will to bear on universal interests, but also because it allows the universal interest of the state to enter the subjective consciousness of individuals. While unorganized public opinion threatens to become mob rule rendering governance impossible, the estates turn this potentially oppositional force into an integrating force in society.

Hegel's constitutional monarchy raises the problem of separation of powers. His view diverges from orthodox interpretation of the theory of separation of powers. Although he praises the principle of the division of powers as the guarantee of public freedom, he opposes any system that would achieve a separation of powers by investing each political institution with a separate and exclusive function.[100] Hegel rejects the mechanical doctrine of separation of power and the checks and balances found in Montesquieu, Madison, Kant, and Fichte, favoring instead an organic division of power within the modern state. Nonetheless, it would be a grave mistake to think that Hegel completely abandons the whole idea of governmental safeguards for the abuse of power, as his theory contains many safeguards by which one part of government monitors and checks another. "Thus, the power of the monarch will be checked by the constitution and the advice of his ministers, the ministers will be checked through their accountability to the Estates, the class of civil servants will be checked from above by the monarch and from below by the corporations, and the legislative power of the Estates will be organized and checked through the combined influence of all of the above institutions."[101]

Hegel dismisses the eighteenth-century model as an abstraction not worthy of reason. Instead, he seeks a system in which each power includes within itself all others as well:

The powers of the state, then, must certainly be distinguished, but each of them must build itself inwardly into a whole and contain in itself the other moments. When we speak of the distinct activities of these powers, we must not slip into the monstrous error of so interpreting their distinction as to suppose that each power should subsist independently in abstraction from the others.[102]

Such an organic interdependence ensures that the function of mutual limitation would not obliterate the function of integration. His classification of the various powers is different from the customary three powers as envisaged by Montesquieu.[103] Even though Hegel thinks that a rigid separation of power is overly mechanistic, he is aware of the real problems of the abuse of power that theories of separation were to address.

## SEPARATION OF CHURCH AND STATE AND TOLERATION

Hegel's conception of *Rechtsstaat* is based on a reciprocal unity of its members that presupposes their continued preservation and relative independence. Due to his tendency to see the state as organism, Hegel is frequently charged with totalitarian unity. Religious belief and practice obviously play an important part in determining the degree of unity within a given society. In the *Philosophy of Right*, he addresses the question of the relationship between religion and the state prior to his discussion of institutions of *Rechtsstaat*. Hegel's attitude toward church-state relationships is complex. On one hand, he rejects the Enlightenment idea that the church and state be completely separated. On the other hand, Hegel wants nothing to do with a theocracy. The issue of the proper relationship between church and state occupies Hegel from his earlier days. His *Early Theological Writings* reflect the dialectical tension between church and state.

In many of these early writings, Hegel draws a sharp line between church and state, relying heavily on Kant's distinction between morality and legality. Insofar as it is a sphere of coercion, legality should not be allowed to infringe on the freedom that is the essence of both morality and religion. Moral and religious obligations cannot be made into civil obligations:

> These characteristics are expedient, appropriate, and permissible in a small society of sectarian believers, but so soon as the society or its faith becomes more widespread and even omnipresent throughout a state, then either they are no longer appropriate (or rather, if nevertheless still retained, they acquire a different significance), or else they become actually wrong and oppressive.[104]

While he certainly recognizes the need for some separation of church and state, Hegel also advocates a more integrated relationship between religion and political life. This is illustrated clearly in Hegel's celebration of the unity of religion and politics in the Greek *polis*, against the unworldly and nonpolitical character of Christianity:

> Between these extremes of the multiple or diminished consciousness of friendship, hate, or indifference toward the world, between these extremes which

occur within the opposition between God and the world, between the divine and life, the Christian church has oscillated to and fro, but it is contrary to its essential character to find peace in a nonpersonal living beauty. And it is its fate that church and state, worship and life, piety and virtue, spiritual and worldly action, can never dissolve into one.[105]

In his youth, Hegel believed that if the state is a complete whole, then it cannot be entirely distinct from the church.

In the *Philosophy of Right*, Hegel tries to reconcile the two positions that he appeared to hold in his earlier writings. Religion, like family life, is associated with the sphere of immediate and subjective feeling. While religion has the same content as the state—absolute truth—its consciousness of this substantial content is in the form of subjective feeling or faith rather than determinate thought and knowledge.[106] Much of what he says about the relationship between church and state revolves around this difference in forms. While he certainly does not ignore the important unity between church and state, he emphasizes the difference between these two forms of spiritual existence. Hegel begins his discussion by complaining about Romantic and reactionary thinkers who maintain that religion is the foundation of the state:

> This is the place to allude to the relation of the state to religion, because it is often reiterated nowadays that religion is the basis of the state, and because those who make this assertion even have the impertinence to suggest that, once it is made, political science has said its last word. No doctrine is more fitted to produce so much confusion, more fitted indeed to exalt confusion itself to be the constitution of the state and the proper form of knowledge.[107]

He also rejects the idea that the state grows out of the church:

> Despite this, it is often said nowadays that the state must grow out of religion. The state is mind [*Geist*] fully mature and it exhibits its moments in the daylight of consciousness. . . . [T]he state seems to be the subordinate, and since what is finite cannot stand on its own feet, the state is therefore said to need the church as its basis. As finite, it lacks justification, and it is only through religion that it can become sacrosanct and pertain to the infinite. This handling of the matter, however, is supremely one-sided. . . . For the state has a life-giving soul, and the soul which animates it is subjectivity, which creates differences and yet at he same time holds them together in unity.[108]

Thus, church and state are not to be completely united, and the state's existence and justification does not depend upon religion.

Nevertheless, Hegel notes that there is an important degree of essential unity of religion and the state: "The state is the divine will, in the sense that it is mind [*Geist*] present on earth, unfolding itself to be the actual shape and organization of the world."[109] Furthermore, the content of both religion and the state is absolute truth, although it takes a different form in each. "It is philosophic insight which sees that while church and state differ in form, they do not stand opposed in content, for truth and rationality are the content of both."[110] Since the content of religion is absolute truth, religion is most important to the state:

> The essence of the relation between religion and the state can be determined, however, only if we recall the concept of religion. The content of religion is absolute truth, and consequently the religious is the most sublime of all disposi-tions. As intuition, feeling, representative knowledge, its task is concentrated upon God as the unrestricted principle and cause on which everything hangs. It thus involves the demand that everything else shall be seen in this light and depend on it for corroboration, justification, and verification. It is in being thus related to religion that state, laws, and duties all alike acquire for consciousness their supreme confirmation and their supreme obligatoriness, because even the state, laws, and duties are in their actuality something determinate which passes over into a higher sphere and so into that on which it is grounded.[111]

Consequently, the state receives its confirmation from religion. In this sense only, religion can be said to be the foundation of the state.

Hegel is careful to distinguish his position from the view that religion is the foundation of the state in that religion represents the infinite, while the state is only a finite entity. In this position, religion is an end in itself and the state is regarded solely as a means. This understanding of the state completely deprives the state of the ethical and spiritual character that Hegel has been trying to establish. The view that the state is merely a means whose "specific function consists in protecting and securing everyone's life, property, and caprice, in so far as these do not encroach upon the life, property, and caprice of others" is the view of the state that belongs to civil society.[112] For Hegel, the state is more than simply an organization to satisfy human necessities. An ethical understanding of the state requires more. He grants that religion and faith might be needed to inculcate a disposition of respect for the state. However, this must not be seen as the external provision of ethical and spiri-tual content that is completely lacking in the state. As cited above, the state is the divine will present in world as *Geist*. Thus, it is the march of God in the world.[113] The state consists of objective determinations in the form of political institutions and law, while religion is the relation to the Absolute in the form of feeling and faith.

Hegel warns that religious institutions must not impose their subjective at-titudes on the objective world of the state. This could lead to religious fanati-cism and the destruction of determinate laws and institutions:

In contrast with the truth thus veiled behind subjective ideas and feelings, the genuine truth is the prodigious transfer of the inner into the outer, the building of reason into the real world, and this has been the task of the world during the whole course of its history. . . . Those who "seek guidance from the Lord" and are assured that the whole truth is directly present in their unschooled opinions, fail to apply themselves to the task of exalting their subjectivity to consciousness of the truth and to knowledge of duty and objective right. The only possible fruits of their attitudes are folly, abomination, and the demolition of the whole ethical order, and these fruits must inevitably be reaped if the religious disposition hold firmly and exclusively to its intuitive form and so turns against the real world and the truth present in it in the form of the universal, i.e. of the laws.[114]

Hegel warns against religious fundamentalism and authoritarianism that reject critical reflection, demand conformity, and identify the state with a particular religion. Hence, the union of church and state is dangerous and would lead to the destruction of the ethical order. Religious fanaticism leads to a totalitarian suppression of difference.[115] The unexamined voice of the religious zealot can undermine the state. For Hegel, a proper ethical order requires a significant degree of separation of church and state. For these reasons, he boldly asserts that religion should not hold the reins of government.[116]

Even though religion and state diverge, Hegel does see some important areas of overlap between them. He therefore argues that the state's attitude toward the church should not be simply neutral. Since religion is the moment that integrates the state at the deepest level of disposition, the state must give religious communities every assistance and protection in the pursuit of their religions ends:

But if religion be religion of a genuine kind, it does not run counter to the state in a negative or polemical way like the kind just described. It rather recognizes the state and upholds it. . . . There thus arises a relation between the state and the church. To determine this relation is a simple matter. In the nature of the case, the state discharges a duty by affording every assistance and protection to the church in the furtherance of its religious ends; and, in addition, since religion is an integrating factor in the state, implanting a sense of unity in the depths of men's minds, the state should even require all its citizens to belong to a church—a church is all that can be said, because since the content of a man's faith depends on his private ideas, the state cannot interfere with it.[117]

By suggesting that the state might even force citizens to join a church, Hegel, like Locke, does not seem to extend toleration to the atheist. Nonetheless, he does not think that the state can compel its citizens to belong to a particular religion or denomination. Freedom requires that the decision to join a particular religious community should be left to the individual and that the state must exercise tolerance with individual choices. "A state which is strong because its organization is mature may be all the more liberal in this matter; it may entirely overlook details of religious practice which affect it, and may even tolerate a sect . . . which on religious grounds declines to recognize even its direct duties to the state."[118] Thus, since Hegel's state depends of the recognition of particularity, it should practice toleration toward religious minorities.

The right of freedom of conscience and toleration is an important political right that must be recognized by the state.[119] In this regard, Hegel goes well beyond most people in his day and many in ours in extending the right to worship according to one's conscience and extending toleration to different religions and sects. He argues against contemporary reactionaries of his time who would deny political rights to Jews.[120] The denial of civil recognition prevents Jews from being part of the community. He also supports the religious right of minorities such as Quakers and Anabaptists. Hegel concludes his discussion of church-state relations in the *Philosophy of Right* with a criticism of the Romantic notion of unity. Moreover, the state should not tolerate forms of worship that violate persons' rights. He reiterates his early statement that although both religion and state have the absolute truth as their content, they have different forms of consciousness of this absolute content:

> While state and church are essentially one in truth of principle and disposition, it is not less essential that, despite this unity, the distinction between their forms of consciousness should be externalized as a distinction between their special modes of existence. This often desired unity of church and state is found under oriental despotisms, but an oriental despotism is not a state, or at any rate not the self-conscious form of state which is alone worthy of mind [*Geist*], the form which is organically developed and where there are rights and a free ethical life.[121]

Thus, in spite of some overlap, church and state must be kept separate. His conception of freedom, rights, and *Sittlichkeit* require a certain level of separation. Religious belief and practice are essential components of freedom: "Freedom can exist only where Individuality is recognized as having its positive and real existence in the Divine Being."[122] Hegel further dismisses the idea that religion can be used simply to shore up the state and protect it from dissolution. Religion is more than civil religion that serves the interests of the state.[123]

Despite extending toleration to most religions, Hegel clearly privileges Protestantism. In *The Philosophy of History*, he points to the incompatibility of Catholicism with the rational state: "Here it must be frankly stated, that with the Catholic Religion no rational constitution is possible; for Government and People must reciprocate that final guarantee of Disposition, and can have it only in a Religion that is not opposed to a rational political constitution."[124] In Catholicism, unlike Protestantism, Hegel says that religious conscience is separate from—and is even opposed to—the sphere of secular right, which undermines the stability of secular right and the modern principle of individual free will. In fact, he sees this as one of the reasons that the French Revolution turned into a reign of terror. In France, the individual free will was forced to take on the abstract and atomistic form that led to fury and destruction.[125] According to Hegel, a similar thing happened in other Catholic nations where the principles of the Revolution spread. Liberalism remained an abstraction, without the stabilizing disposition nourished by Protestant religion:

> Thus Liberalism as an abstraction, emanating from France, traversed the Roman World; but Religious slavery had that world in the fetters of political servitude. For it is a false principle that the fetters which bind Right and Freedom can be broken without the emancipation of conscience—that there can be a Revolution without a Reformation.[126]

Hegel is also critical of the relationship between Catholicism and the state in his *Philosophy of the Mind*:

> And yet in Catholicism this spirit of all truth is in actuality set in rigid opposition to the self-conscious spirit. . . . Catholicism has been loudly praised and is still often praised—logically enough—as the one religion which secures the stability of governments. But in reality this applies only to governments which are bound up with institutions founded on bondage of the spirit (of that spirit which should have legal and moral liberty), i.e. with institutions that embody injustice and with a morally corrupt and barbaric state of society.[127]

Since the meaning of spirit is misconceived and perverted, he asserts that law and justice, morality and conscience, and responsibility and duty are corrupted at its source.

Hegel's last discussion of the relationship of church and state is found in the 1831 version of his *Lectures on the Philosophy of Religion*. Whereas this work focuses more on the connection between church and state rather than separation, he also stresses that in the modern world where the state is based on freedom, Protestantism supports this unity, while Catholicism thwarts it.[128] He further emphasizes the role of disposition in upholding the state and the importance of religion in sustaining the right disposition. His *Lectures* clearly reflect the uneasy relationship between church and state in Hegel's philosophy. His position stands between a complete unity and a thorough separation. On one hand, he dismisses the view that the state can be self-sustaining without the disposition of religion as being one-sided. On the other hand, Hegel is clearly aware of the dangers of too close an association between religion and government. Exclusive reliance on disposition can be one-sided.[129] In its proper place, religion is completely compatible with, and even necessary for, the rational state. Hegel steers a middle path between liberal secularism and theocracy.[130] The state, not the church, is Hegel's embodiment of social and political universal rationality. In conclusion, Hegel's view of church-state relations is that religion is valuable in inculcating an ethical spirit of society's members, though when misguided it can be a threat.

## HEGEL'S CRITIQUE OF MODERN LIBERALISM

Although Hegel is seen as being a defender of modernity, his thought still provides a basis for criticism. For instance, he clearly confronts modern subjectivity and liberalism's excessive individualism. The modern age was born in a series of events, i.e., the Protestant Revolution, the French Revolution, Cartesian and Kantian philosophy, and industrial capitalism. All of these events free individuality from previous restrictions, but it is in civil society that individual freedom finds itself taken into account in social institutions and politics. Although Hegel takes many points from Locke and the English economists, his use of the civil society is not identical to theirs.[131] As discussed in the previous chapter, civil society includes an economic system where members can work and trade to satisfy their needs, plus the civil institutions necessary to keep such a system going, such as markets, courts and administration of justice, public works, minimal welfare, and antimonopoly systems. His criticisms of modern subjectivity consist in the development of some additional spheres beyond the liberal, minimal government that is being advocated today in the name of globalization. In order to promote the common good, there has to be a free political domain that is separate from civil society. "It is the basic character of the state as an ethical institution incorporating all other relations of right within itself that sets the highest general bounds of the interaction of freedom and thus provides the ultimate measure for Hegel's judgment of modernity."[132]

Civil society encourages certain motivations and attitudes on the part of the individuals. Hegel's discussion of these motivations and attitudes differs from early descriptions in that for him all social institutions involve patterns and structures of mutual recognition through which a person achieves his own identity by recognizing others as persons who are recognizing him as a person. For Hegel, there is no self prior to this recognition—that is, there is no sovereign self as depicted by Hobbes and Locke: "It is therefore through culture that the individual acquires standing and actuality."[133] A human subject is a self-conscious being, which means being aware of oneself. He claims, however, that humans are not self-aware automatically and immediately from the start. Only in relation to other selves can the complex maneuver of self-awareness be possible.[134] As we saw in Chapter 2, interactions with objects alone cannot bring about the necessary reflexive movement of self-awareness, which happens only with mutual recognition. Human subjectivity is dependent upon an intersubjectivity that exists prior to individual acts of subjectivity.

Self-conscious mutual recognition is not an abstraction; it demands some structure of interactions, a set of roles and customs. For Hegel, the structure of interaction is not logically subsequent to the achievement of selfhood of individuals involved. The mutual recognition from others occurs within a field of appropriate roles and actions. It follows for Hegel that theories of politics and society that begin with atomized individuals are very much mistaken. On the contrary, individualism depends on mutual recognition. As we saw in Chapter 3, individualism is lacking in the pre-modern world, and Hegel traces this development through history to its culmination in modern time. Structures of mutual recognition are not vaguely general. They exist in particular, concrete forms. Modern society depends on structures of mutual recognition that are prior to the achieved selfhood of the individuals involved. Put simply, the individual depends upon a particular kind of mutual recognition, that is, intersubjectivity.

Civil society's definition of an individual as a free being, capable of property, connotes a whole framework of interaction and institutional roles that are quite formal in their nature. Being capable of property is not a quality that individuals can possess by themselves. For Hegel, individuals in civil society recognize one another as selves who recognize each other as people capable of putting their freedom into objects they can own.[135] This mutual recognition is supported by a whole system of contract and exchange. Although exchange exists in earlier historical epochs, Hegel notes that only in modern society are there no limitations of status required to be a person. The formality of the structures of mutual recognition in civil society defines a purified and formal individuality, distinct from a person's social roles. Modern persons recognize one another as individuals who can make choices and find a place in the world through property.

Hegel does not think that individualism has been a hidden truth about the foundations of society and culture. For him, the modern self is the achievement of a long dialectical process, and modern individualism is thus something new in history. This is so because the structures of mutual recognition and the subsequent selfhood of the individuals involved change at different stages in history. Although types of partial freedom existed in previous historical periods, only with modernity is the process of freedom as withdrawal and self-determination institutionalized in a more complete way.[136] For instance, in earlier society, according to Hegel, there was no separation between a person's identity as a person and his or her definite social role. Modern social freedom achieves this union:

> First, socially free individuals have a subjective relation to their social order that is similar to the one Greek citizens had to theirs but also crucially different from it in that, in the case of modern social members, having identity-constituting attachments to one's institutions is compatible with conceiving of one's self as an *individual*—that is, as a person with rights and interests separate from those of the community and as a moral subject that is able and entitled to pass judgment on the goodness of existing social norms and practices. Second, the institutions within which modern individuals achieve their particular identities objectively promote personal and moral freedom in the sense that, when functioning properly, one of their effects is to bring about the various social conditions that make the realization of those freedoms possible.[137]

Even though a person could have drawn such a separation, the separation was not recognized within the structures by which people confirmed one another's selfhood in society. Thus, Hegel seeks the integration and transcendence of the respective merits of antiquity and modernity through the conceptual reformulation of the state.

Civil society, for Hegel, involves institutions that allow human beings to live defined by their pure human freedom. It does this in structures of mutual recognition that distinguish the formal process of freedom from its contents. As illustrated in the previous chapter, when a person recognizes others as free people capable of property, contract, and labor, they are recognized in a way that affirms self-determination. We do not contract with animals that are incapable of the self-control needed to keep a promise. Thus, in modern society, people are recognized as pure selves that are not identified with any particular role or content of choice. Free individuality can become a focal aspect of existence in a way that it could not in earlier culture. Hence, Hegel sees civil society as something radically new, which creates a kind of individuality that did not previously exist, even in a hidden fashion.

The tension between liberalism's individual freedom and communitarianism's social-political bond is one of the most widely contested issues of political theory. Champions of individual freedom consider the essence of politics to be the defense of personal rights and liberties against encroachments emanating from government and tradition. From this perspective, all community standards appear questionable and possibly repressive. Countering liberalism, communitarians are quick to mention the corrosive effects that egotism and possessive individualism have on moral and political life. An appealing aspect of Hegel's thought resides precisely in its attempt to reconcile and transcend this conflict by integrating and preserving facets of both liberalism and communitarianism.[138] For instance, the *Philosophy of Right* constitutes a multifaceted edifice that makes room for both free individual initiative and shared moral bonds.

> Rather, one of Hegel's most important and explicit aims in his social theory is to integrate liberalism's concern for the fundamental rights and interests of individuals with certain aspects of romantic political thought, including its tendency to view the social order as an organism . . . and to emphasize the importance of substantive, identity-constituting attachments to social groups.[139]

Besides unequivocally endorsing universal individual rights, Hegel stresses the need that individuals have to belong to a greater social reality, a reality that transcends their own particular projects.

Hegel not only celebrates the achievement of modern freedom, he also worries about its excesses. Civil society is based on separation, but full freedom demands unity as well. Although the institutions of civil society embody self-determination, they do not do so fully.[140] Civil society requires that people respect others and choose goals that fit into the circulation of needs and commodities. It tells one a great deal about means but nothing about ends. Consequently, it leaves people free to choose their own goals. Hegel sees this as less than ideal. He argues against this type of individualism. In fact, civil society left to itself has harmful effects. Modern modes of mutual recognition imply no natural limits on society's activity. As the system of production and exchange expands, Hegel says that the means of production grows more refined, which means more specialized. Workers come to lead a more machinelike existence, while the rich live a more opulent life.[141] Since nothing is sacred, more and more aspects of human life come to be treated as commodities to be exchanged. Hegel seems to have accepted most of the negative economic effects of civil society as inevitable. The state can exercise ameliorative action, but it cannot eradicate the harms rooted in the very structure of civil society. He sees no solution to the growing inequalities in the distribution of wealth and creation of a rabble, or economic underclass.[142]

Hegel designs his political institutions as a bulwark against the fragmenting tendencies of economic self-interest and the overbearing influence of economic factors on politics. Substantively, he maintains that liberalism collapses the state into civil society. "From the very outset, liberal theory puts itself in jeopardy of undermining the common validity of freedom and justice by depriving both of their requisite self-determined character."[143]

Historically, under pressure by economic interests and developments, few of Hegel's institutions were ever developed at all, much less in the specific form he described. By grounding legitimate law and institutions in social practices, including those that are part of the economy, he comes much closer to historical materialism than Marx recognized.[144] His rational community is one that is designed to ensure the freedom of its members. He does not mean freedom in the political sense alone. Hegel is interested in freedom in a deeper, more metaphysical sense. His concern is with freedom in the sense in which one is free when able to choose without being coerced either by other human beings, natural desires, or social circumstances. Hegel believes such freedom can exist only when one chooses rationally, which is choice in accordance with universal principles. If these choices are to bring individual satisfaction, the universal principles must be embodied in an organic community organized along rational lines.

Hegel's dialectical criticism preserves what he found of value in classical liberalism while reformulating it in ways that are more sensitive to the historical context of rights. The central feature of his theory of state is its respect for rights, including the crucial right to recognition.[145] While liberalism in one sense has liberated modern individuals from the tyranny of social custom and tradition, however, in another sense, it has left them enslaved to their passions. Moreover, Hegel objects to empirical theories of natural rights, such as Hobbes' and Locke's, insofar as they cannot establish what they want to prove. If empiricism wants to be more than just a description of what rights people happen to enjoy, it must have some way of showing that these rights are necessary and universal. In other words, it must have some way of demonstrating that these rights are rooted in certain permanent features of human nature, but empiricism is not capable of providing this.[146] Since categories of necessity and universality are not given in experience, they must be discovered by other means. For Hegel, empiricism lacks all criteria for drawing the boundary between the accidental and the necessary. "Therefore, the interactions of right can have no necessary relation to the given particularities of species being or to any other prior ground. Rights rather have their legitimacy by being self-determined structures of interaction and for that very reason, *they do not have foundations*."[147] Put differently, one can reject the notion of natural rights and still speak of property rights, civil rights, and political rights. For Hegel, rights derive their content from the different normative modes of freedom specific to each of their interactions, not from natural differences.

If Hobbes and Locke rely too much on experience for their approach, Kant is too abstract. Hegel's response to the abstract character of Kantian morality is to stress that moral duty has a history and that to conceive it as something apart from social and political circumstances is to misconceive it.[148] In identifying moral conduct as a part of ethical life, Hegel is returning to an Aristotelian conception of the community as a structure of relations within which moral powers can develop. His goal is to combine the ancient emphasis on the dignity and architectonic character of political life with the modern concern for freedom, rights, and mutual recognition. "Rights are constituted through specific enacted structures of reciprocal recognition in which members of a plurality of individuals can choose a certain mode of action towards one another and have its legitimacy mutually respected."[149] The modern state, for Hegel, is a place where individual interests and the interests of the whole are in harmony. Thus, in choosing to do one's duty one chooses freely because it is a rational choice; and individual fulfillment is achieved in serving the objective form of the universal, the state. Hegel, remedying one of the defects of Kant's ethics, maintains that because the universal law is embodied in the concrete institutions of the state, it ceases to be abstract and empty, but prescribes individual duties of one's role in the community. In short, individual liberty and community are reconciled.

The state is supposed to be a successful unification of universality with particularity. For Hegel, freedom does not imply a world ungoverned by any regulative principles, but rather a world inhabited by subjects capable of supplying such principles. The Hegelian state is an organization of laws, that is, a *Rechtsstaat*, since law is what purges the state of caprice and makes modern freedom possible. Given the nexus of ethics and freedom, Hegel sees the state as the actuality of free will achieved through a universalized self-consciousness.[150] Civil society provides the public social space in which individuals, as free persons and subjects, pursue their welfare in their own way, choose their own way of life, and enter into voluntary relations with others. Hegel recognizes, however, that civil society cannot permit economic relations to have free sway. The economy is subordinate to the state; political economy is a necessity.[151] As long as the economy is left to its own logic of independent self-determinations, there is nothing to prevent economic relations from resulting in crises, overproduction, unemployment, and growing economic inequality.

Civil society is constituted in such a way that it necessarily produces this condition, and it will persist as long as the state does not create a rational organization whose overriding aim is the realization of freedom and recognition of all by all. Among these are rules regulating the conduct of business and commerce, requirements of mandatory education, and provisions for sanitation, health care, and social welfare. Between the extremes of complete individual freedom and extensive government intervention, Hegel steers a middle course that seeks to give both sides their due and that mediates individual self-interest with the general social matrix enabling the pursuit of such interest.[152] In his view, individuals have the right to demand subsistence from civil society and the latter has the responsibility for feeding its members. Nevertheless, while recognizing public responsibility in this domain, Hegel is skeptical about the ability of society to eradicate misery, especially under conditions of progressive industrialization.

As discussed in Chapter 9, postmodern critics charge Hegel with being caught up in the philosophy of consciousness. While this criticism is valid to some extent, it fails to recognize an important intersubjective dimension to Hegel's thought. In the *Phenomenology of Spirit*, self-consciousness, and thus human freedom, only advance through intersubjective recognition. Moreover, the highest categories of Hegel's logic, those that provide the entry into *Geist*, are linked with human agency and activity.[153] With this emphasis on human agency, Hegel is within the realm of intersubjectivity. Consciousness is consciousness by dialogue, and it is only the dialogue-character of consciousness that allows mental representation to be brought forth.[154] Hegel's concept of *Geist* transcends the subjective forms of self-consciousness.[155] For Hegel, consciousness becomes universal only by entering into a world of culture, mores, institutions, and history.[156] Furthermore, historical comprehension requires a common understanding and thus a unique *logos* of communication. As noted above, debates in the legislature, with their quality of give and take, are a form of communicative action, a device through which truth, and the public interest, can emerge.

For Hegel, there is no self prior to mutual recognition, and one can only be an individual within a particular community.[157] Intersubjectivity does not do away with subjectivity or with individual subjects as bearers of rights and personal interests. Norms and law are developed through the interaction of subjects in their quest for truth and are therefore an intersubjective process. Put differently, Hegel's *Sittlichkeit* reaches its completion in community. Hegel is reacting against the excessive individualism of modern liberalism. The parts of the community are related as parts of an organism. For Hegel, freedom is the historical achievement of beings who are mindful of their social dependence. Human beings attain a universal existence by gaining a collective identity that rationally reflects upon the common interest. On one hand, the social whole's universal will is dependent on the particular will of individuals, since it is only through them that its universal ends can be realized.[158] On the other hand, as discussed above, the particular wills of individuals are dependent on the universal, since particular ends can only be achieved through participation in community life. For Hegel, political freedom is best exemplified by a dialectic of individual wills and the universal will.

The Hegelian *Geist* progresses through the advancement and development of human civilizations, which is clearly in the realm of intersubjectivity because it comes from social interaction.[159] In fact, Hegel's dialectic comes from a dialogue of sorts, where truth advances through argumentation and reconciliation. The role of communication is important to Hegel, and he sees thinking and being as practical.[160] Hegel recognizes separate spheres of civil society and a constitutional state for homes of private and public freedom. He falls between the extremes of liberalism and communitarianism in order to find the proper relationship between the individual and community. He further separates representative lawmaking from administration, and his political theory respects and attempts to protect the rights and interests of individual modern subjects. Hegel rejects societies that reduce politics to the contingencies of economic relations. "In [today's] liberal democracies, the spectacle certainly seems to suggest the economic domination of society and the social subordination of politics that Hegel feared."[161]

If intersubjectivity means reconciling the needs of individuals with those of the community, Hegel's thought is certainly intersubjective. Nothing can claim to be a real social decision unless it is arrived at in a full discussion in which all participants are fully conscious of what is at stake.[162] And philosophically, he attempts to reconcile the particular with the universal in the socio-political world. Hegel recognizes that human freedom can only reside in a just society, which is one that balances the needs of the one with those of the many. Citizens exercise their personal autonomy in civil society and their public autonomy in the public sphere, and more importantly they can only achieve their personal goals through cooperative efforts. Even while trying to accomplish what appears to be purely selfish behavior, Hegel stresses the universal social connection and interdependence of all people within a particular political culture, even one that is highly individualistic:

> Individuals in their capacity as burghers in this state are private persons whose end is their own interest. This end is mediated through the universal which thus appears as a means to its realization. Consequently, individuals can attain their ends only so far as they themselves determine their knowing, willing, and acting in a universal way and make themselves links in this chain of social connexions.[163]
>
> In the course of the actual attainment of selfish ends—an attainment conditioned in this way by universality—there is formed a system of complete interdependence, wherein the livelihood, happiness, and legal status of one man is interwoven with the liveliness, happiness, and rights of all.[164]

The next chapter assesses the immediate impact of Hegel's philosophy and examines some of the important paths and variations that emerge historically under his influence. No sooner does Hegel's tenure at the University of Berlin end than his followers split into various camps and factions, each claiming to be true to Hegel's thought and representing the next phase of philosophy, while others react critically against Hegel's systematic attempt at absolute truth.

## NOTES

1. Thomas Carlyle, "Past and Present," in *The Norton Anthology of English Literature, Volume 2* (New York: W. W. Norton & Company, 1993), 966.

2. Ronald Beiner, *What's the Matter with Liberalism?* (Berkeley: University of California Press, 1992), 119.

3. Paul Franco, *Hegel's Philosophy of Freedom* (New Haven: Yale University Press, 1999), 278. Although the state is the actuality of freedom, it is not freedom understood in terms of the arbitrary or particular will of the individual, but rather in terms of the individual's substantial or rational will.

4. Georg W. F. Hegel, *Philosophy of Right*, trans. T. M. Knox (Oxford: Oxford University Press, 1975), 105.

5. Georg W. F. Hegel, *Phenomenology of Spirit*, trans. A. V. Miller (Oxford: Oxford University Press, 1977), 113–114.

6. Hegel, *Philosophy of Right*, 160. The true giving of content to morality cannot occur at the level of conscious inwardness; it demands a surrender to *Sittlichkeit*, the concrete ways of a well-organized society.

7. Eric Weil, *Hegel and the State*, trans. Mark Cohen (Baltimore: Johns Hopkins University Press, 1998), 21. See Hegel, *Philosophy of Right*, 14–16.

8. Hegel, *Philosophy of Right*, 164–165.

9. Hegel, *Philosophy of Right*, 23.

10. Fred R. Dallmayr, *G. W. F. Hegel: Modernity and Politics* (Newbury Park: Sage, 1993), 103.

11. Robert R. Williams, *Hegel's Ethics of Recognition* (Berkeley: University of California Press, 1997), 293.

12. Allen Wood, "Hegel's Ethics," in *The Cambridge Companion to Hegel*, ed. Frederick Beiser (New York: Cambridge University Press, 1993), 230.

13. Hegel, *Philosophy of Right*, 154–155.

14. Hegel, *Philosophy of Right*, 278.

15. Hegel, *Philosophy of Right*, 156.

16. Hegel, *Philosophy of Right*, 189.

17. Wood, "Hegel's Ethics," in *The Cambridge Companion to Hegel*, 231.

18. Quentin Lauer, *A Reading of Hegel's* Phenomenology of Spirit (New York: Fordham University Press, 1993), 123–124.

19. Paul Redding, *Hegel's Hermeneutics* (Ithaca, N.Y.: Cornell University Press, 1996), 16.

20. Alan Patten, *Hegel's Idea of Freedom* (New York: Oxford University Press, 1999), 130. To this extent, a community of mutual recognition can be realized only if it has a certain objective institutional structure.

21. Patten, *Hegel's Idea of Freedom*, 109.

22. Williams, *Hegel's Ethics of Recognition*, 283. With contract theory, the whole is not prior to but derivative from its parts.

23. Georg W. F. Hegel, *The Philosophy of History*, trans. J. Sibree (Buffalo, N.Y.: Prometheus Books, 1991), 40–41. See also, Dudley Knowles, *Hegel and the* Philosophy of Right (New York: Oxford University Press, 2002), 234, where he notes that Hegel's social organicism is designed to block conceptions of the state as aggregations or mechanical constructions of powers of individual persons. Hobbes' contract theory is typically seen as a form of methodological individualism that claims that the properties of social entities can be fully understood in terms of the intentional behavior of the individuals who compose them.

24. Hegel, *The Philosophy of History*, 41. See also Patten, *Hegel's Idea of Freedom*, 116–117. People in a Hobbes' state of nature are like animals and not free, since they lack the mental complexity necessary to evaluate and regulate their impulses. They are not self-determining in anything but the weakest sense. In the state of nature, human beings would be like children, who have the potential for freedom and reason. Realizing this potential requires *Bildung*. As noted in the previous chapter, *Bildung* is the process of education and acculturation that individuals must go through to achieve freedom and rationality.

25. Georg W. F. Hegel, *Lectures on the History of Philosophy: Medieval and Modern Philosophy, Volume 3*, trans. E. S. Haldane and Frances Stimson (Lincoln: University of Nebraska Press, 1995), 402.

26. Hegel, *Philosophy of Right*, 59.

27. Hegel, *The Philosophy of History*, 42.

28. Hegel, *Philosophy of Right*, 165.

29. Patten, *Hegel's Idea of Freedom*, 111. Although freedom in the state is not something utterly divorced from the subjective awareness of individuals, the emphasis remains on the objective character of the freedom realized in the state, on its substantiality and rationality, not the individual's subjective willing it.

30. Hegel, *Lectures on the History of Philosophy, Volume 3*, 402.

31. Hegel, *Philosophy of Right*, 59.

32. Patten, *Hegel's Idea of Freedom*, 110.

33. Hegel, *Philosophy of Right*, 242. See also Knowles, *Hegel and the* Philosophy of Right, 310, where he writes that Hegel argues directly against social contract philosophers that "those who are by nature citizens can no more detachedly consider whether allegiance to the state is in their best interests than can members of families query their familial duties on the basis of a personal cost-benefit appraisal of continuing affiliation. Citizenship is no more a matter of voluntary subscription than the child's finding of her family membership."

34. Hegel, *Philosophy of Right*, 242. See Franco, *Hegel's Philosophy of Freedom*, 284, where he writes that it is not just the social contract that Hegel is rejecting, but

the whole classical liberal understanding of the state for which the social contract serves as the chief theoretical construct. According to classical liberal doctrine, such as Locke's, the end of the state is to secure the life, liberty, and property of the individual.

35. Patten, *Hegel's Idea of Freedom*, 113.

36. Hegel, *Philosophy of Right*, 157.

37. Hegel, *Philosophy of Right*, 33. Although Rousseau and Fichte share Hegel's conviction that a form of rational freedom is realized in the state, they still attach too much importance to the idea of freedom as *Willkür*. By contrast, Hegel asserts that the kind of freedom that is relevant to the authority of the state is concrete freedom, which includes social obligations.

38. Patten, *Hegel's Idea of Freedom*, 120.

39. Williams, *Hegel's Ethics of Recognition*, 265. This is reflected in Hegel's criticism of Rousseau and Fichte. He believes that they both start from the fundamental Cartesian standpoint of the *cogito*, with the self-sufficient individual and then proceed to the intersubjective level of the state. In contrast, Hegel decenters subjectivity and transforms it into ethical subjectivity.

40. Hegel, *Philosophy of Right*, 21–35.

41. Hegel, *Philosophy of Right*, 28. This type of freedom is nothing else but empty self-activity.

42. Hegel, *Phenomenology of Spirit*, 111.

43. Kenneth Westphal, "The Basic Context and Structure of Hegel's *Philosophy of Right*," in *The Cambridge Companion to Hegel*, 236. In this respect, Hegel is acknowledging the force of Romantic criticisms of the Enlightenment's a-historical, a-social, individualist account of reason.

44. Hegel, *Philosophy of Right*, 107. Hegel notes that the bond of duty can appear as a restriction only on indeterminate subjectivity or abstract freedom. The truth is that in duty individuals find their liberation: First, liberation from dependence on mere natural impulse, and second, liberation from indeterminate subjectivity. Thus, substantive freedom is acquired in duty.

45. Hegel, *The Philosophy of History*, 252.

46. Michael O. Hardimon, *Hegel's Social Philosophy: The Project of Reconciliation* (Cambridge: Cambridge University Press, 1994), 34.

47. Hegel, *Philosophy of Right*, 162.

48. See Hardimon, *Hegel's Social Philosophy*, 32.

49. Hegel, *Philosophy of Right*, 124

50. Hegel, *Philosophy of Right*, 126–134.

51. Hegel, *Philosophy of Right*, 122–123.

52. Hegel, *Philosophy of Right*, 123.

53. Hegel, *Philosophy of Right*, 127–128.

54. Hegel, *Philosophy of Right*, 129–130.

55. See Hardimon, *Hegel's Social Philosophy*, 146–153.

56. Hegel, *Philosophy of Right*, 133.

57. Hegel, *Philosophy of Right*, 108.

58. Hegel, *Philosophy of Right*, 105–106, 109, and 163–164.

59. Hegel, *Philosophy of Right*, 110.

60. Hegel, *Philosophy of Right*, 124–145.

61. Hegel, *Philosophy of Right*, 126–130 and 134–145.

62. Hegel, *Philosophy of Right*, 127–129.

63. Hegel, *Philosophy of Right*, 155.

64. Weil, *Hegel and the State*, 23.

65. Hegel, *Philosophy of Right*, 176.

66. Franco, *Hegel's Philosophy of Freedom*, 307. See also, Knowles, *Hegel and the* Philosophy of Right, 328, where he writes: The sovereign is a constitutional monarch that is the culmination of the development of ethical life in universal world history. Hegel rejects the traditional trichotomy of monarchy, aristocracy, and democracy on grounds that it is outdated. The rational state contains elements of each.

67. Frederick Neuhouser, *Foundations of Hegel's Social Theory: Actualizing Freedom* (New Haven, CT: Yale University Press, 2000), 13.

68. Neuhouser, *Foundations of Hegel's Social Theory*, 128. The social world functions only in and through the conscious wills, attitudes, and beliefs of its constituent parts, all of which exist within the world as individual bearers of consciousness.

69. Shlomo Avineri, *Hegel's Theory of the Modern State* (Cambridge: Cambridge University Press, 1972), 99.

70. Hegel, *Philosophy of Right*, 196.

71. Weil, *Hegel and the State*, 46.

72. Hegel, *Philosophy of Right*, 177. See Franco, *Hegel's Philosophy of Freedom*, 309, where he notes that in Hegel's lectures of 1817–18 the principle of particularity is not contained in democracy. Therefore, democracy is not compatible with the modern principle of subjective freedom. In contrast with democracy, constitutional monarchy does not presuppose a virtuous disposition on the part of its citizens. It operates largely through law rather than disposition.

73. Hegel, *Philosophy of Right*, 176.

74. Hegel, *Philosophy of Right*, 176.

75. Hegel, *Philosophy of Right*, 181.

76. Herbert Marcuse, *Reason and Revolution: Hegel and the Rise of Social Theory* (Atlantic Highlands, N.J.: Humanities Press, 1941), 172 and 182.

77. Hegel, *Philosophy of Right*, 176.

78. Hegel, *Philosophy of Right*, 181.

79. Hegel, *Philosophy of Right*, 181–184.

80. Hegel, *Philosophy of Right*, 187.

81. Hegel, *Philosophy of Right*, 181.

82. Hegel, *Philosophy of Right*, 185.

83. Hegel, *Philosophy of Right*, 179.

84. Hegel, *Philosophy of Right*, 187.

85. Hegel, *Philosophy of Right*, 190.

86. Hegel, *Philosophy of Right*, 189–190.

87. Hegel, *Philosophy of Right*, 191. See also, Max Weber, "Bureaucracy," in *From Max Weber: Essays in Sociology*, ed. Gerth and C. Wright Mills (New York: Oxford University Press, 1946), 198–204.

88. Hegel, *Philosophy of Right*, 193.

89. Hegel, *Philosophy of Right*, 191.

90. Hegel, *Philosophy of Right*, 193–194. See Knowles, *Hegel and the* Philosophy of Right, 331, where he notes that Hegel's proposals for the Estates derive from various reform proposals charted by Stein, von Humholdt, and Hardenberg (see Chapter 2).

91. Hegel, *Philosophy of Right*, 195–197.

92. Weil, *Hegel and the State*, 67. See Richard Dien Winfield, *The Just State: Rethinking Self-Government* (Amherst, MA: Humanity Books, 2005), 209, where he says: "So long as corporate legislators promote the shared interests of their social constituents, the legislative will they wield remains intimately connected to the type of economic activity their electorate has selected and expressed in their election. In this respect, the corporate electorate does not cease to be free after electing their corporate representatives."

93. Hegel, *Philosophy of Right*, 198.

94. Avineri, *Hegel's Theory of the Modern State*, 162. He also notes that Hegel is among the first political theorists to recognize that direct suffrage in a modern society would create a system very different from that envisaged by the advocates of such a system. Hegel maintains that in very large states universal suffrage inevitably leads to electoral indifference, since the casting of a single vote is of no significance where there is a multitude of electors. See also Hegel, *Philosophy of Right*, 198, where he also notes that the legislative assembly is neither a mere indiscriminate multitude nor an aggregate dispersed into atoms. With direct suffrage people are identified as a formless mass whose commotion and activity could only be irrational.

95. Hegel, *Philosophy of Right*, 198. Political life must be grounded into the circles and associations of civil life so that its universality will not lack concreteness.

96. Hegel, *Philosophy of Right*, 197.

97. Hegel, *Philosophy of Right*, 202.

98. Hegel, *Philosophy of Right*, 203–204.

99. Hegel, *Philosophy of Right*, 203.

100. Hegel, *Philosophy of Right*, 175.

101. Franco, *Hegel's Philosophy of Freedom*, 311.

102. Hegel, *Philosophy of Right*, 286.

103. Hegel, *Philosophy of Right*, 176–179.

104. Georg W. F. Hegel, "The Positivity of the Christian Religion," in *Early Theological Writings*, trans. T. M. Knox (Philadelphia: University of Pennsylvania Press, 1948), 86–87.

105. Georg W. F. Hegel, "The Spirit of Christianity," in *Early Theological Writings*, 301.

106. Franco, *Hegel's Philosophy of Freedom*, 298.

107. Hegel, *Philosophy of Right*, 165.

108. Hegel, *Philosophy of Right*, 283.

109. Hegel, *Philosophy of Right*, 165–166.

110. Hegel, *Philosophy of Right*, 171.

111. Hegel, *Philosophy of Right*, 166.

112. Hegel, *Philosophy of Right*, 170–171.

113. Hegel, *Philosophy of Right*, 279.

114. Hegel, *Philosophy of Right*, 167. See also, Hegel, *The Philosophy of History*, 449, where he writes: "It is, indeed, regarded as a maxim of the profoundest wisdom entirely to separate the laws and constitution of the State from Religion, since bigotry and hypocrisy are to be feared as the results of a State Religion." Religious fanaticism can lead to political fanaticism.

115. Williams, *Hegel's Ethics of Recognition*, 329.

116. Hegel, *Philosophy of Right*, 285.

117. Hegel, *Philosophy of Right*, 168. See Knowles, *Hegel and the* Philosophy of Right, 321, where he says that "genuine religion may be necessary within the state, particularly for the uneducated who cannot achieve rational insight and who must rely on religion and faith for their ethical disposition."

118. Hegel, *Philosophy of Right*, 168.

119. Williams, *Hegel's Ethics of Recognition*, 328–329. This means that the state should be open to religious difference and pluralistic, rather than exclusive. Toleration is a function of the ethical strength and complexity of the social organism, that is, its ability to sustain reciprocal recognition, not in spite of, but because of its diversity. The more articulated and developed a state is, the more likely it is to be tolerant of diversity.

120. Hegel, *Philosophy of Right*, 169.

121. Hegel, *Philosophy of Right*, 173. See also, Williams, *Hegel's Ethics of Recognition*, 329, where he notes that ethical life requires the state between neutral: "In the midst of sectarian conflict, the state has emerged as an independent mediator of sectarian and religious differences. Hegel observes that the state first emerged historically as an independent rationality in its mediation of sectarian religious disputes and differences. Hegel's state is thus religiously pluralistic in principle; it is supposed to be the medium of interfaith recognition and mediation. Rather than take sides in sectarian disputes, the state is supposed to be the institution that brings out and defends the universal aspects of interhuman relationships and thereby maintains the fluidity and openness of the social organism."

122. Hegel, *The Philosophy of History*, 50.

123. Franco, *Hegel's Philosophy of Freedom*, 302.

124. Hegel, *The Philosophy of History*, 449.

125. Hegel, *The Philosophy of History*, 445–446.

126. Hegel, *The Philosophy of History*, 453.

127. Georg W. F. Hegel, *Philosophy of Mind*, trans. A. V. Miller (New York: Oxford University Press, 1971), 284–285.

128. Georg W. F. Hegel, *Lectures on the Philosophy of Religion, Volume 1*, trans. R. Brown, P. Hodgson, and J. Stewart (Berkeley: University of California Press, 1984), 457–458.

129. Hegel, *Lectures on the Philosophy of Religion, Volume 1*, 459–460.

130. Franco, *Hegel's Philosophy of Freedom*, 305.

131. David Kolb, *The Critique of Pure Modernity: Hegel, Heidegger, and After* (Chicago: The University of Chicago Press, 1986), 22.

132. Richard Dien Winfield, *Freedom and Modernity* (Albany, N.Y.: State University of New York Press, 1991), 129.

133. Hegel, *Phenomenology of Spirit*, 298. An individual could only exist in culture.

134. Hegel, *Phenomenology of Spirit*, 111.

135. Hegel, *Philosophy of Right*, 133.

136. Kolb, *The Critique of Pure Modernity*, 29.

137. Neuhouser, *Foundations of Hegel's Social Theory*, 35.

138. Dallmayr, *G. W. F. Hegel*, 5.

139. Neuhouser, *Foundations of Hegel's Social Theory*, 15.

140. Hegel, *Philosophy of Right*, 23.

141. Hegel, *Philosophy of Right*, 150.

142. Hegel, *Philosophy of Right*, 150.

143. Richard Dien Winfield, *Reason and Justice* (Albany, N.Y.: State University of New York Press, 1988), 78. The moment it conceives the institutions of justice as structures derived from a principle of freedom, they are no longer self-determined, but determined by a freedom that figures logically prior to and separately from them.

144. Westphal, "The Basic Context and Structure of Hegel's *Philosophy of Right*," 263.

145. Smith, *Hegel's Critique of Liberalism*, x. Smith argues that Hegel offers a way out of the impasse between modern liberalism and communitarianism. "Like the modern communitarians, he is critical of the individualistic and ahistorical conceptions of rights underlying the liberal polity, but like many liberals in both his day and ours, he is skeptical of any attempt to return to some form of democratic participatory *gemeinschaft* based upon immediate face-to-face relations" (6).

146. Smith, *Hegel's Critique of Liberalism*, 67.

147. Winfield, *Freedom and Modernity*, 79.

148. Smith, *Hegel's Critique of Liberalism*, 71.

149. Winfield, *Freedom and Modernity*, 83.

150. Dallmayr, *G. W. F. Hegel*, 135.

151. Weil, *Hegel and the State*, 102.

152. Dallmayr, *G. W. F. Hegel*, 129.

153. Charles Taylor, "Hegel's Philosophy of Mind," in Charles Taylor, *Human Agency and Language: Philosophical Papers 1* (New York: Cambridge University Press, 1985), 83.

154. Martin Heidegger, *Hegel's Concept of Experience*, trans. Kenley Dove (San Francisco: Harper & Row, 1970), 118.

155. Hans-Georg Gadamer, *Hegel's Dialectic: Five Hermeneutical Studies*, trans. P. Christopher Smith (New Haven, CT: Yale University Press, 1971), 78.

156. Paul Ricoeur, *From Text to Action: Essays in Hermeneutics, II*, trans. K. Blamey and J. Thompson (Evanston, IL: Northwestern University Press, 1991), 229.

157. Hegel, *Phenomenology of Spirit*, 298. See also, Neuhouser, *Foundations of Hegel's Social Theory*, 21, where he notes that practical freedom, for Hegel, involves certain cognitive relations to oneself, to others, and to the world. Subjects who are practically free enjoy a species of being-with-themselves-in-an-other.

158. Neuhouser, *Foundations of Hegel's Social Theory*, 42.

159. Hegel, *The Philosophy of History*, 48.

160. See Gadamer, *Hegel's Dialectic*, 92, where he says: "For Hegel, language thus reaches its perfection in the idea of logic since the latter thinking goes through all of the determinations of thought occurring within itself and operating in the natural logic of language. . . ."

161. Winfield, *Freedom and Modernity*, 133. Most contemporary criticism of public welfare appeal to their constituencies not as participants in self-government but as private members of society, taxpayers rather than citizens.

162. Charles Taylor, *Hegel* (Cambridge: Cambridge University Press, 1975), 384.

163. Hegel, *Philosophy of Right*, 124.

164. Hegel, *Philosophy of Right*, 123.

## Chapter Seven

# The Emergence of Hegelianism: Right and Left Movements

> But men can consciously resolve to develop themselves toward a new culture; which formerly they only developed unconsciously and by chance, they can now create better conditions for the rise of human beings for their nourishment, education, and instruction; they administer the earth economically as a whole, and can generally weigh and restrain the powers of man. This new, conscious culture kills the old, which, regarded as a whole, has led an unconscious animal and plant life; it also kills distrust in progress—process is possible.[1]
>
> —Alfred Schmidt, *History and Structure*

Hegel uses *Geist* to refer to human culture and society. As discussed in Chapter 2, *Geist* must have its seat in embodied, living subjects, and must be expressed in an external medium, such as language, custom, and social practice. To a significant extent, Hegel's philosophy is empirical. Since *Geist* becomes embodied only through its own activity, *Geist* is self-actualizing.[2] *Geist* first expresses, embodies, and objectifies its self-understandings through its action and then attains self-consciousness by appropriating these self-understandings. Furthermore, as illustrated in Chapter 3, *Geist* expresses, embodies, and objectifies itself through human history in the world. Thus, Hegel's approach to philosophy is fundamentally historical. He understands human history in terms of the drive of human beings to attain a fully adequate understanding of themselves and to form a world that corresponds to this understanding. He further contends that *Geist* attains self-knowledge by developing successively more adequate interpretations of itself. Although we can know *a priori* that the social world is rational, Hegel maintains that we can only ascertain the details of its rationality by examining the actual social world.

Hegel argues that human beings are essentially spiritual beings, which means that they are essentially self-interpreting. As spiritual beings, they are defined by their self-understanding. Their "spiritual reality" [*geistige Wirklichkeit*] consists of the self-understandings that are expressed in their social forms of life.[3] For Hegel, being spiritual means that human beings are also essentially social and cultural in the sense that they can only actualize themselves as spiritual beings as the result of being raised and socialized within human communities. In addition, human beings are essentially social and cultural in that their needs and desires are socially and culturally formed. Since each person is a product of his or her time, Hegel sees human beings as radically cultural and historical. Therefore, human beings are essentially vehicles of their particular national state.

Philosophy, according to Hegel, is supposed to comprehend in thought the rational structure of the central social institutions of its own historical period. He thinks that the *Rechtsstaat* was realized, to an extent at least, by the European states of the early nineteenth century. Since the institutions and practices of *Sittlichkeit* reflect the development of *Geist*, Hegel's goal is to help people rationally endorse and affirm the social world. In the *Philosophy of Right*, he stresses this as the goal of his political philosophy:

> This book, then, containing as it does the science of the state, is to be nothing other than the endeavour to apprehend and portray the state as something inherently rational. As a work of philosophy, it must be poles apart from an attempt to construct a state as it ought to be. The instruction which it may contain cannot consist in teaching the state what it ought to be; it can only show how the state, the ethical universe, is to be understood. . . . To comprehend what is, this is the task of philosophy, because what is, is reason. Whatever happens, every individual is a child of his time; so philosophy too is its own time apprehended in thoughts.[4]

Since freedom dialectically advances through human history, existing social institutions are rational, and since reality is rational, philosophy's task is to comprehend and justify the modern state. With his famous *Doppelsatz* [*Double Dictum*], Hegel boldly asserts: "What is rational is actual and what is actual is rational."[5] As Hegel uses the term, rational has both an epistemic and a normative aspect; it means both rationally intelligible and reasonable or good.[6]

The *Doppelsatz* has led to conservative interpretations of Hegel's political philosophy. The conservative reading of this passage suggests that everything that exists is rational and that it is rational simply because it exists. Thus, philosophy's purpose is to reconcile humans with the existing social order and its political institutions. On this view, Hegel's claim that philosophy can only comprehend things in its own time means that people are reconciled to the actual social world in which they live here and now, not to some future, ideal state. Nevertheless, Hegel does not merely endorse the status quo as such, and, contrary to appearances, the *Doppelsatz* does not mean that everything that exists is rational. Nor does it mean that things are rational simply because they exist. In fact, Hegel explicitly denies that everything that exists is rational:

> But even Experience, as it surveys the wide range of inward and outward existence, has sense enough to distinguish the mere appearance, which is transient and meaningless, from what in itself really deserves the name of actuality. As it is only in form that philosophy is distinguished from other modes of attaining an acquaintance with this same sum of being, it must necessarily be in harmony with actuality and experience.[7]

In Hegel's usage, actuality [*Wirklichkeit*] is contrasted with mere existence [*Existenz*]. Actuality is the unity of essence [*Wesen*] and existence.[8] Consequently, for Hegel, things are actual only to the extent that they realize their essence. In Hegel's terminology, not everything that exists is rational. There is a dialectical tension within Hegel's conception of reality: One side looks toward the ideal, the other side looks toward existence. "It is true enough to say that reality is truly real only when it is thought-reality; but it is equally true that thought is truly thought only as a process of coming to terms with the real."[9]

When Hegel says "what is is reason," he does not mean everything that exists, but instead refers to what "genuinely" is actual. Thus, while Hegel does endorse the family, civil society, and the state, he does not endorse them merely because they exist and are in place. He affirms them because he believes that they have an underlying rational structure that is realized to a significant extent in the modern world, and he maintains that particular families, civil societies, and states are worthy of affirmation only to the degree that they realize the underlying rational structure of the family, civil society, and the state as depicted in the *Philosophy of Right*.[10] Consequently, individuals do not endorse just any existing political order. The *Doppelsatz* does not mean that existing political states are rational just because they exist. Hegel's assertion of the rationality of the actual is not the rejection of change, but its anchor to the objective dialectic of the actual.[11] For Hegel, it is perfectly acceptable to hold that the social world is both worthy of reconciliation and in need of reform. "Everything which is not reasonable must on that very ground cease to be held actual."[12] The point of Hegel's conception of actuality is to bridge the gap between what is ideal and what exists. In other words, the existing features of modern society are sufficiently rational to warrant acceptance yet not too rational for reform. As we saw in Chapter 3, Hegel was a strong advocate of political reform in Prussia in his day. Furthermore, Hegelian philosophy provides a basis for constructive criticism globalization and today's existing order.

Hegel's position regarding reconciliation and reform in the social world is complex and leads to a tendency to place him into one of two extreme directions. Either Hegel is classified as an arch-conservative defender of the status quo who is dead set against any reform, or since he is an advocate of reform, he is thought to be against reconciliation of the existing social world. As discussed in a later section of this chapter, the first position is one of the basic sources of right Hegelianism, and the second is a source of left Hegelianism. However, Hegel's political philosophy does not fit neatly into either left or right Hegelianism. Instead, his aim is to maintain the synthesis according to which the social world, although imperfect, is worthy of reconciliation—a synthesis that would make it possible to unite basic acceptance of the social world with liberalizing reform.[13] Hegel's social philosophy furnishes the necessary tools to engage in philosophically informed criticism of the existing social world. Thus, it is possible to be reconciled to one's social world and still try to overcome its shortcomings. Nonetheless, the failings of the modern social world do not undermine its basic rationality and goodness. For Hegel, the *Doppelsatz* is the result of the historical process through which the rational becomes actual and the actual becomes rational.

There is a difference between the claim that philosophy reaches a high point in Hegel's theory and the claim that it reaches its end in his theory. Since Hegel consciously builds on prior philosophical positions, he is justified in believing that his philosophy represents a high point in the Western tradition. However, Hegel never said that philosophy ends with his system; nonetheless, the conviction that it was no longer possible to carry on philosophy as before was widespread at that time.[14] To a significant extent, subsequent philosophy happens in the wake of Hegel. Philosophers as diverse as Marx, Kierkegaard, and Nietzsche are situated in the Hegelian aftermath, and their respective thought can be understood as reactions to Hegel. Each reacts differently to Hegel's philosophy. While Kierkegaard and Nietzsche claim to reject Hegel's theory, Marx attempts to transform Hegel's theory by correcting its fatal flaws. This chapter draws some conclusions regarding Hegel's philosophy and assesses the state of philosophy in its aftermath. To this end, it is organized into three parts. The first section discusses Hegel's concept of reconciliation and its place in philosophy. The second section examines post-Hegel Hegelianism, especially Ludwig Feuerbach and Karl Marx. The third section argues that existentialism developed as a critical reaction to Hegel's philosophical system, and it focuses on the thought of Kierkegaard and Nietzsche. The final section of the chapter explores Hegel's materialism, and defends him against many of the charges brought by Feuerbach and Marx.

## HEGEL'S PHILOSOPHY OF *VERSÖHNUNG*

Although Hegel suggests that the modern social world—especially the more advanced states of Europe—could be said to realize its essence, he does not claim that every existing institution conforms to its essence on the whole. In fact, it is part of Hegel's normative conception that existing institutions will inevitably fail to realize their essence in certain respects. Hegel maintains that such failure is inevitable because existing institutions exist in the finite sphere of arbitrariness, contingency, and error constituted by human action, and anything existing in this sphere will necessarily exhibit defects and imperfections.[15] Thus, imperfections are a necessary condition of actuality. Since everything that exists in the world is finite and contingent, everything will be defective in some respect or another. Consequently, since social and political institutions exist in the finite world, they are also defective is some respects. One of the problems that Hegel's political philosophy is intended to address is that of convincing citizens to understand this fact and continue to accept the basic rationality of modern social institutions.

Alienation [*Entfremdung*], a growing concerning for human beings in Hegel's time, is still a major problem in our world. Many people feel disconnected from social and political institutions and divided by the conflicting aims of realizing their individuality and being members of the community. A primary aim of Hegel's political philosophy is to reconcile his contemporaries to the modern social world. He tries to help the people of the nineteenth century overcome their alienation from the institutions of *Sittlichkeit*—the family, civil society, and the state—and be at home with them. Hegel was one of the first modern thinkers to claim explicitly that reconciliation [*Versöhnung*] is the proper aim of political philosophy. Since *Geist* represents God's will for human beings and manifests itself in historical social and political institutions, it is necessary that people embrace these institutions. As Hegel uses it, reconciliation is a technical term referring to the process of overcoming alienation.[16] More specifically, reconciliation is the process of overcoming the disconnection and conflict that divide human beings from their social world. Even though the social world that Hegel hopes to reconcile his contemporaries to is not identical to today's world, it is not that different from it either. Both contain the nuclear bourgeois family, the market economy, and the *Rechtsstaat*.

As we saw in Chapter 2, Hegel's dialectic can be described as a process of overcoming conflict, division, and alienation in an attempt to restore harmony, unity, and peace. Although *Versöhnung* is usually translated into English as reconciliation, like most translations, it is not a perfect match. In contrast to reconciliation, *Versöhnung* connotes a process of transformation. When two people split over a disagreement about something, they do not merely resume their old relationship unchanged. With *Versöhnung*, they change their behavior and attitudes in some fundamental ways. Instead, their reunion is the result of a new, transformed state. Although the word reconciliation does not deny that a transformation takes place, it does not convey that it takes place as *Versöhnung* does. Another major difference between the English and German words is that, in its ordinary English use, reconciliation can mean submission or resignation. Hegel's project does not aim at surrender and acquiescence.[17] It is not simply a matter of resigning oneself to the status quo. *Versöhnung* does not share this aspect of reconciliation.

In German, reconciliation as resignation would be *abfinden*, not *versöhnen*. *Versöhnung* sees reconciliation to the social world in a positive light. Another important difference between the English and German versions of reconciliation concerns consolation. In German, reconciliation [*Versöhnung*] should also be contrasted with consolation [*Trost*]. Although the two concepts are very close in meaning and both involve acceptance, the two are distinct. While consolation entails providing comfort or relief for some loss, with reconciliation [*Versöhnung*] a person has no need for consolation, since he or she has fully accepted the situation. In German, reconciliation is regarded as something necessary and good. It involves accepting the present in its own right and being satisfied with it. Nevertheless, reconciliation is not a matter of thinking that everything is wonderful. Suffering and wickedness are inevitable:

> Hegel maintains that it is possible *both* to be genuinely reconciled *and* to recognize (i) that the fundamental features of the modern social world include divorce, poverty, and war, and (ii) that particular families, civil societies, and states will inevitably exhibit defects and imperfections. . . . Reconciliation, as Hegel understands it, is thus compatible with recognizing that the social world exhibits features that are genuinely problematic.[18]

The state is not a work of art; it exists in the world, a sphere of contingency, arbitrariness, and error.[19] Similarities aside, this should not lead to resignation. Maintaining the synthesis of affirmation and realism is not easy. Hegel proposes that although maintaining the attitude of reconciliation will be difficult, it is not impossible.

Since reconciliation is frequently understood as a process of overcoming conflict, Hegel's project is seen by some as a totalitarian smothering of conflict and difference. However, it is important to note that Hegel does not think that reconciliation will lead to a situation of perfect harmony free of all conflict. In fact, he asserts that conflict is an integral component of reconciliation. In the modern social world, human beings will inevitably come into conflict, even if society is well ordered and they are reconciled with it.[20] As discussed in Chapter 5, people will experience conflict between separate and particular interests that they have as individuals. Furthermore, there often will be conflict between interests and obligations that individuals have as family members, members of civil society, and citizens. These types of conflict are not accidental. People will be raised to have separate and particular interests, some of which inevitably conflict with the demands of their social roles.[21] For Hegel, a well-ordered social world is in fact a world that generates conflict. Individuality and particular freedom make a certain degree of social conflict inevitable. Thus, reconciliation involves embracing social tension. Democratic political institutions and personal freedom certainly tend toward political conflict.

Human beings need separate institutional spheres in which they may find intimacy and actualize their individuality. Social conflict also is the byproduct of the social differentiation needed to support modern economic life. According to Hegel, conflict is the price of differentiation. Consequently, conflict—even antagonism—is internal to Hegel's conception of reconciliation.[22] What is intrinsic for Hegel is that there are no *fundamental* conflicts between the interests of people as individuals and the demands of their *Sittlichkeit*. In the well-ordered modern world, individuals will be raised to identify with the roles of their *Sittlichkeit*.[23] Specifically, people will be taught to embrace the norms internal to their social roles and will regard them as both a substantial component of their self-conception and their own individual good:

> Because the substance is the absolute unity of individuality and universality of freedom, it follows that the actuality and action of each individual to keep and to take care of his own being, while it is on one hand conditioned by the presupposed total in whose complex alone he exists, is on the other a transition into a universal product.—The social disposition of the individuals is their sense of the substance, and of the identity of all their interests with the total; and that the other individuals mutually know each other and are actual only in this identity, is confidence (trust)—the genuine ethical temper.[24]

Since the well-ordered social world will promote and foster the individuality of its members, it is reasonable that members embrace social institutions and practices as part of their own good.

Hegel argues that the members of the well-ordered social world will be free of the painful personal and psychological alienation that characterized the early modern world. And if people do feel this alienation, Hegel thinks that it is possible to overcome it through philosophical reflection:

Hegel's conception of reconciliation is thus one that understands itself as preserving conflict at one level and overcoming it at another. Both elements are attractive. The fact that it seeks to preserve conflict is attractive because the idea of a perfect harmony is both utopian and dangerous: utopian because unrealizable, dangerous because invidiously anti-individualistic. The fact that Hegel is willing to embrace conflict makes his thought quite appealing. He is far too often placed in the camp of the enemies of conflict. In fact, Hegel, in contrast, say, to Marx, is one of the great friends of conflict. Nonetheless, Hegel's attitude toward conflict is not Nietzschean. He does not regard the existence of conflict as something to be celebrated in its own right. It is important that Hegel argues that, at the most fundamental level, conflicts are overcome because, in so doing, he secures the status of his conception as a conception of reconciliation.[25]

In short, Hegel advocates a "conflict-embracing" form of unity.

In Hegel's technical sense, reconciliation refers both to a process and to a result.[26] The process is that of overcoming alienation from the social world, and the result is being at home in the social world. Reconciliation is the movement that makes alienation [*Entfremdung*] disappear, and Hegel characterizes the final state of *Geist*'s reconciliation as that in which it is reconciled with itself in the object.[27] Since being at home in the social world is the key to Hegel's social philosophy, reconciliation is the answer to alienation. For Hegel, reconciliation is both an objective and subjective matter. Since there is an objective condition that the social world must meet, it is not wholly subjective. As illustrated in the previous two chapters, there are specific objective conditions that must be met if the social world is to be a home to human beings. Nevertheless, being at home in the social world is not wholly objective either, since there is a set of subjective conditions that people must satisfy in order to be at home.[28] Human beings must truly believe that the social world is a home. For Hegel, feeling at home in the social world means feeling connected to its central institutions and practices. Thus, feeling at home is also a matter of subjective appropriation. Hegel's use of reconciliation allows him to assert that people are both individuals and social members. In order to be a home, the social world must be organized in such a way that people can actualize their individuality and social membership by participating in its central social institutions.[29] If the social world makes it possible for human beings to actualize themselves as both individuals and social members, it is good, since that is what reconciling individual liberty and community is all about. That is, it is as it ought to be and has achieved its essence.

## IMMEDIATE REACTIONS TO HEGELIANISM

Hegel's philosophy reigned supreme in Germany from 1818 into the 1840s. His influence on succeeding philosophers was transmitted in multiple forms, directly through the writings of his closest admirers, who were members of what is known as the Hegelian school. Hegel's influence reached its peak in Germany during the decade following his death. The Hegelian school took shape during Hegel's lifetime, in the 1820s, while he lived in Berlin. With the *Doppelsatz*, Hegel's philosophy seems to be little more than the self-aware-ness of its own age and the articulation of its highest ideals. Hegel in fact contributed to its formation through his philosophical renown and through academic maneuverings, in which he strove to counter his rivals.[30] Almost all of Hegel's early followers saw his philosophy as the rationalization of the Prussian Reform movement. Initially, most members of the Hegelian school were convinced that the Hegelian system discovered the bridge from the fi-nite to the infinite. "The Hegelian conversion did not transport the individual from the finite relationships of the empirical world [*Diesseits*] into an infinite unity in the beyond [*Jenseits*], but culminated in the reconciling recognition that the spirit [*Geist*] was actual and present in the world."[31] Hegelian think-ing was not defined as abstract ratiocination but as the systematic comprehen-sion of the real.

Accommodation, critique, and historical transcendence were three dimen-sions of Hegel's politics. As individual disciples emphasized different dimen-sions of Hegel's politics, increasing differentiations developed in Hegelian-ism. "The appropriation of Hegelianism by members of different historical generations living in different political and cultural environments naturally exacerbated existing tensions and produced new conflicts within the Hegelian school."[32] Thus, despite shared sympathies, there were deep tensions from the very beginning. Published in 1835, David Strauss's *Life of Jesus* contributes the polarization of Hegelians. Strauss argues that the biblical story of Jesus is mythical. Some regarded Strauss's argument as a betrayal of Hegel's legacy, while others saw it as its fulfillment.[33] The Hegelians split into conserva-tive and radical camps over a dispute regarding the proper relationship of Hegel's philosophy to religion. Although the tension began over theological issues, it soon expanded into political questions, such as the extent to which existing conditions in Prussia realized Hegel's ideals. The schism of the Hegelian school into right and left wings was further abetted by an ambiguity of Hegel's dialectical *Aufhebungen*, which had both conservative and revo-lutionary interpreters.[34] Both sides of the schism pointed to the *Doppelsatz*: the reason of actuality and the actuality of reason. The right wing emphasized that only the actual is real, while the left wing stressed that only the rational is real. For left Hegelians, *Zeitgeist*, as the consciousness of the age, is the criterion of what is true and what is false, because only history in the course of time reveals what is the truth of the age, through its success. In addition, left Hegelians reduced *Geist* to the human species.

During the 1830s, the divergent tendencies within the Hegelian school become more obvious and extreme. For some, Hegel's philosophy of *Geist* and its political theory is seen merely as a justification of the status quo. The members of this conservative wing of the Hegelian School are known as right Hegelians. Under this banner, reactionary political and religious groups that resisted modernizing reforms in Prussia gained influence. After Hegel's death, this position was articulated by the University of Berlin theologian, K. P. Marheineke (1780–1846), the administrative aid for higher education in the Prussian Ministry of Culture, Johannes Schulze (1786–1869), and the editor of the Hegelian *Jahrbuecher*, Leopold von Henning (1791–1866). This wing of Hegelianism boldly asserts that the legal, administrative, and political institutions of the post-reform German state, especially Prussia, constituted the perfected or complete objectification of reason in the world, which represents absolute *Geist* as fully present.[35] For them, the only political tasks that remained for the present generation are educational and philosophical, the production of public recognition of actualized reason. This simply requires a translation of the existing language of Protestant religious culture into the language of self-conscious knowledge. "The overwhelming emphasis in this self-consciously epigonal stance was on the historical completion of the progressive actualization of reason in history, a process brought to self-consciousness in Hegelian philosophy."[36] Schulze and Henning became pillars of the "accommodationist" Hegelian establishment in the late 1820s.

In the *Lectures on the Philosophy of Religion*, Hegel claims that his speculative philosophy elevates religious faith and dogma to the sphere of knowledge and truth in a way that provides a conceptual understanding religious faith. Thus, the historical reality of the Christian reconciliation of God and man can be demonstrated intellectually. Marheineke argues that the Hegelian transformation of faith into knowledge did not threaten the viability of the Christian faith or existing church, but provided the basis for their revitalization.[37] Christian images and narratives are understood as objectifications of the development of *Geist*. For instance, Christian doctrines concerning the end of time, the last judgment, and the final union of the blessed in heaven are comprehended as representations [*Vorstellung*] of spiritual truth. Unlike Enlightenment rationalism, Marheineke says that Hegelian philosophy does not challenge the truths of Christianity. Furthermore, the right Hegelians stress the essential unity of philosophical form and spiritual content, of Hegelianism as formulated by Christianity. Marheineke and other right Hegelians interpreted Hegelian philosophy as a modern form of Christian apologetics. They further hold that the historical facts of Christianity and the present conditions in Prussia are realization of Hegel's ideas. They stripped Hegel's philosophy of religion of most of its critical, dynamic, and historical qualities.

Both sides in schism could point to some aspects of Hegel's teaching to support their case. The right argued that Hegel maintains that the universal exists only in the particular, that theory must conform to practice, and that the real is rational; the left contended that Hegel holds that the universal, the rational, is the very purpose of history, to which everything eventually must conform.[38] The left held that it is a mistake to think that the rational ideal must exist in the existing particulars. The following sections examine the transformations of Hegelianism, specifically left Hegelianism, Marxism, and existentialism. The left wing revindicated Hegel's dialectical method, turning it into a revolutionary principle. For these left, or young, Hegelians, the circle of history does not end in the modern state. Hegel's claim that the owl of Minerva flies only at dusk merely announces the end of a particular historical epoch, not the end of history itself. Thus, left Hegelians argue that Hegel's effort in the *Philosophy of Right* to absolutize his own era betrayed the dialectical dynamics that are more fundamental to his system. Also the distinction between the theoretical and practical satisfaction of freedom in the world eventually begins to stir up the longing for the realization of man's humanity in world in some of Hegel's followers.

## Left Hegelianism

Left Hegelian philosophers demand that philosophy be realized in what they call "praxis." They see Hegelianism as a revolutionary gospel of the apotheosis of mankind. In brief, they sought to place philosophy at the service of social revolution, following the process of time.[39] These young followers of Hegel attempt to develop the spirit of philosophy beyond Hegel. Left Hegelians reject the idea that Hegelianism is a finished and inactive collection of thought, and instead see it as the first self-conscious movement in the history of philosophy. They "perceived of themselves not simply as midwives for the incarnation of the Hegelian Logos in the world, but as prophets of new forms of cultural integration and human freedom that would relegate Hegel's absolute spirit to a religious and metaphysical stage of human self-alienation."[40] As an identifiable philosophic movement, left Hegelianism endured for less than two decades, from 1830 to 1848. Alarmed by what he saw as an anti-Christian and revolutionary movement in Berlin, Friedrich Wilhelm IV, the new king, wanted someone with the intellectual profile and political sensibility capable of mounting a successful counter-offensive against the Hegelian school.[41] Consequently, in 1841, Friedrich Schelling was appointed as Hegel's replacement at the University of Berlin, which had been vacant for ten years after Hegel's death.

Schelling helped to promote the multi-pronged attack on Hegel by the left Hegelians with his lectures at the University of Berlin. Schelling turns against Hegel's rational philosophy to a philosophy centered on existence.[42] More precisely, Schelling charged that Hegel's philosophy was only a system of thought, not a system about reality. He held that Hegel's system was one about reason and logic, that is, a system of if-then propositions but not a system of telling us what the world is really like. Schelling argued that "Hegel simply confused the way we must logically think of things with the system of the existing world, and that confusion lay at the basis of what was wrong with all post-Kantian idealism."[43] Schelling's appointment to the distinguished chair at the University signaled an end to critical thought. Thus, the hopes of left Hegelians to engage in a free-flowing theological and cultural dialogue was tempered, and then turned to silence in the face of an adamant union between a defensive Church and a reactionary monarchy.[44] Left Hegelianism includes figures such as Ludwig Feuerbach (1804–1872), Bruno Bauer (1809–1882), David Strauss (1808–1874), August von Cieszkowski (1814–1894), Moses Hess (1812–1875), Max Stirner (1806–1856), and Arnold Ruge (1802–1880). Their intellectual efforts focus on uncovering and overcoming the obstacles to the realization of philosophy. This position expresses dissatisfaction with the abstraction from the contingencies of social life that they see as the price of Hegel's philosophic reconciliation.

Hegel's system consists of measuring the course of history according to temporal progress. Spirit [*Geist*] has finally revealed itself in Hegel's philosophy; it is now the mission of Spirit to rationalize the world, which is the task of the left Hegelians. "The critical acuity of the left-wing Hegelians has its historical measure in the completeness of Hegel's reconciliation."[45] They argue that in order to realize itself, philosophy must return to the real limits of human experience and action. Thus, they demand a return from Hegelian idealism to "common sense" reality and an unprecedented transfiguration of that reality. Instead of constructing an absolute state by means of the categories of logic, the present existence of the state must be criticized historically with reference to the immediate future.[46] Consequently, the left Hegelians attempt to transform Hegel's retrospective and reminiscent historicism into a historical futurism. In other words, they long for more than the consequence of history; they want to be epoch-making and thus historic themselves. During the decade after Hegel's death, moderate Hegelians maintained control of the academic world. Consequently, left Hegelians withdrew from academic life and "sought their historical identity as the vanguard of a post-Hegelian cultural order that was yet to be born."[47]

For left Hegelians, since freedom has yet to be realized, philosophy's task is not yet accomplished. Their starting point is the criticism of religion, particularly institutional Christianity. This means a critical attack upon the dualism of God and man that lay at the foundation of the Hebraic-Christian tradition. For instance, David Strauss's *Life of Jesus* formulates the idea of unity of the divine and human natures.[48] This idea was inspired by Hegel's dynamic monism of God and man. While Hegel thinks that the content of religion and philosophy is identical, Strauss asserts that Hegel favors the theoretical content of religion at the expense of its historical form. He further rejects Hegel's identification of religion with philosophy. With Strauss's work, Hegelianism is transformed into the rival, if not actual destroyer, of Christian orthodoxy. According to Strauss's Hegelian perspective, there could be no other practical consequence but that the individual, to be saved—to overcome his alienation—should consciously enter into the secular equivalent of the Christ, the community.[49] For Strauss, historical study is needed to lead to a proper understanding of Christian myth.

Bruno Bauer, like Strauss, was a philosophical theologian and biblical scholar who focused on the relationship between historical truth and the universal truth of biblical revelation. Like Strauss, he also defined the model of cultural integration for the future era in immanent terms. However, "Bauer criticized the *Life of Jesus* as a symptomatic expression of the historical stage of one-sided subjective negation, which would inevitably have to give way to a reaffirmation of the objective reality of the absolute in history."[50] That is, Strauss's anti-Christian humanism was ensconced in the theological perspective. Bauer's criticism is also easily derived from Hegel's picture of the advancement of knowledge as a progressive puncturing of illusions. Bauer interpreted this to mean the evolution of critical consciousness via the progressive exposure of dogmas, and saw it as the present task of critical consciousness to expose the "God-illusion" and show man to be the "reality deity."[51] For Bauer, the reconciliation of God and man does not take place in an actualized Kingdom of God on earth, but as the reconciliation of man with his universal essence in a state of humanity. Philosophy becomes the critic of the established order: "And so philosophy must be active in politics, and whenever the established order contradicts the self-consciousness of philosophy, it must be directly attacked and shaken."[52] For Bauer, Hegelian reconciliation means the ability to reconcile the self with the suffering and alienation of its finite historical existence. Nevertheless, mankind has not yet arrived at its ultimate destination. Consequently, the Hegelian philosophical idea is transformed into a will to revolt against a world not yet completed.

August von Cieszkowski argues that the universal remains dominant for Hegel, so that in spite of Hegel's protestations of arriving at the concrete "one," the individual is surrendered to universality. His goal is a philosophy of life in activity, a radical resolution of the problem regarding the relationship between theory and practice. He transforms Hegelianism from a doctrine that is considered to be merely retrospective and theoretical into a program of fundamental change. His *Prolegomena zur Historiosophie* marks the change

from impotent theory to world-revolutionary praxis, from philosophic contemplation to social action.[53] In contrast to Hegel's division of history into the
Oriental world, the Greco-Roman world, and the Christian-Germanic world,
Cieszkowski divides it into the ancient world to Christ, the Christian-Germanic world to Hegel, and the future, which is a component of all historicity
because history is a free and responsible activity. In his writings, he discusses
the concrete question of the future world as the reform of Christianity and of
political society.[54] He is also more sensitive to the class divisions and social
anarchy produced by the rise of capitalism.

## Ludwig Feuerbach

Ludwig Feuerbach (1804–1872) is of particular importance, since he plays
an intrinsic part in Karl Marx's development. He denies that Christianity is
a crucial aspect of the Hegelian system. In his eyes, Hegel's philosophy is
not the truly critical philosophy that it claims to be, for it is essentially and
unalterably a form of justification of the status quo. Rather than try to expose
the rational core of Hegel's system and adjust the entire system accordingly,
Feuerbach attempts to expose the irrationality of Hegel's entire philosophic
enterprise.[55] A truly critical philosophy would have to expose the deceptive
nature of the Hegelian synthesis by demonstrating that it is not a truly critical
philosophic theory as it claims. He sees Hegel as a philosophical theologian.
Feuerbach tries to demonstrate that the entire history of religious and philosophic thought is the history of the development of alienated forms of human
self-consciousness. In fact, he holds that modern philosophy is the product
of theology—that is, nothing other than theology broken up and transformed
into philosophy.[56] The principle of Feuerbach's own philosophy is not absolute spirit, but instead is man, the flesh-and-blood result of all previous
philosophy. Put differently, he asserts that real human life is the proper starting point for thought. The beginning of truly positive philosophy cannot be
God or the Absolute, not being in itself, but only what is real, definite, and
finite. Feuerbach, therefore, is important for the originality and fundamental
character of his critique of philosophy itself.

Hegel's philosophy, according to Feuerbach, derives the finite from the
infinite, definite from the indefinite, and will never arrive at a true placing of
the finite and definite. To be sure, Feuerbach acquires his historical method
from Hegel, but what he thinks takes him beyond Hegel is his distinctive
characterization of philosophy as human activity. In true Hegelian fashion,
he conceives philosophical progress as a dialectical development. Feuerbach,
however, proceeds from the basis of an anthropological and cultural critique
of philosophy. Instead of stressing the idea and thought, he focuses on the

contexts of human social existence.[57] The social or species nature becomes the very condition and ground of philosophy. Philosophy, for Feuerbach, is the attempt at human self-understanding, one that goes beyond Hegel's speculative idealism. His critique of philosophy is carried out by way of his critique of religion and of religious consciousness. Hence, philosophy simply continues the mystification and conceptual inversion that theology has begun. Feuerbach maintains that the philosophy of the future has the task of leading philosophy from the realm of departed souls back to the realm of embodied and living souls; that is, philosophy must be pulled down from the divine to the realm of living human misery.[58] Feuerbach attempts to overcome human alienation by applying the dialectic exclusively to mankind's relation to the supernational.

For Feuerbach, God of the theologians and being or substance of the metaphysicians are both nothing but human consciousness of its own nature. In this respect, Feuerbach wants to free mankind from the illusion of God, restore their full freedom, and make them true human beings. The task of Feuerbach's anthropology is to awaken mankind to the truth of religion and to eliminate its falsity. The human capacity for feeling, thought, and action make it possible for people to create knowledge concerning the world and universe. It is, however, a reflection of man's world and life.[59] Thus, the error of Hegel's idealism is that it reduces existence to thought. Hegel makes man's being an emanation of God conceived as a thought-process, instead of showing the divine thought-process to be an emanation of man's own being in the material world. Although Feuerbach retains Hegel's dialectic, he uses it against Hegel. He argues that Hegel used the dialectic on the thought of others before him but failed to use it on his own thought. The Feuerbachian dialectic is not intended to destroy philosophy, but to translate and interpret it dialectically, as alienated forms of an essentially human activity.[60]

The Hegelian system, according to Feuerbach, begins with a denial of physical reality. Hegel fails to recognize the independent status of nature, which is reduced to the "otherness" of thought. The Feuerbachian dialectic is thus a move toward materialism. It is the content and thrust of this materialism as a critical materialism that gives it force. Its objects of criticisms are the mystification and alienation of everyday life, including political and economic realms of existence. Hegelian philosophy is not critical and ignores the contradictions of real existence. In short, Feuerbach's radical move is seeing the dialectic as a dialectic of consciousness that is rooted in the very condition of material human existence, such as human needs, wants, and interests. By material Feuerbach means something real or existing, as opposed to consciousness alone. Human thought and ideas are a reflection of material conditions that come through the senses, and then conscious thought reacts

to the objects of the senses. Hegel's speculative philosophy is merely a projection of man as a thinking being. Feuerbach's attack on Hegel's idealism
is a move toward empirical materialism. Nevertheless, Marx, as is discussed
in the following section, criticizes Feuerbach for not going far enough with
materialism.

Feuerbach argues that the definition of man's essence as his thinking activity is inadequate and false. Therefore, he attempts to redefine human essence,
and says that classical philosophy is at an end. In the *Critique of Hegelian
Philosophy*, Feuerbach writes:

> My essential mode of thought is not "system" but rather "mode of explanation."
> My relation to my subject matter . . . is the same as that of the scientist to his
> subject matter. I seek to explain a fact; but not in the sense that it is somehow
> already "contained" in thought, not as a "fact of consciousness" to be explained
> by explication of its content. Rather, I seek to explain it as an empirical fact, by
> empirical means. . . . I therefore distinguish myself utterly from earlier specula-
> tive philosophers. I don't ask, as Kant did: "How are *a priori* judgments pos-
> sible?" or "How is religion possible?" but rather, "What is religion?" "What is
> God?" And I ask these questions on the grounds of the facts as given.[61]

Thus, Feuerbach claims to break with Hegel's idealism. Hegel represented the
most rigorous, most abstract, and most rational form of Christian or theological philosophy. Feuerbach attacks what he sees as speculative philosophy's
explicit attempt to include a personal God in a systematic philosophy. This
paradigm of fantasy, for Feuerbach, is the absolutization of self-consciousness, in which the speculative philosopher fosters the illusion that the object
of his speculation is not his own self, but an other, divine self. Hegel's absolute is not an absolute at all, but is merely a fantasy objectified.

Hegelianism, like preceding philosophical systems, exempts itself from the
very critique leveled at other philosophers. Feuerbach maintains that there is
a formal similarity between the foundations of theology and the foundations
of absolute philosophy, which he says are uncritical and irrational. Every
philosophy appears as a specific phenomenon of its time, with presuppositions. It appears to itself presuppositionless, however, when compared to
earlier systems of thought. But a later time recognizes that it has its presuppositions after all. Feuerbach is not criticizing the making of presuppositions,
but rather the tendency of philosophy to absolutize these suppositions, to
take any presupposition as ultimate, unconditional, and necessary. In brief,
a given philosophical system fails to note the assumptions of its foundations
and takes them as absolute truths. A philosopher's task is not merely to criticize the presuppositions of other philosophies, but to examine critically the
presuppositions of his or her own philosophy as well.

Feuerbach questions the place that thought plays in determining human essence. To be sure, thinking is seen as an inner process. However, with thought and the importance played in it by language, he looks toward the species. In his *Towards a Critique of Hegel's Philosophy*, Feuerbach says that "language is nothing other than the realization of species; i.e., the 'I' is mediated with the 'You' in order, by eliminating their individual separateness, to manifest the unity of the species."[62] The outward forms of shared thought are thus not the reality of thought, or thinking activity itself, but only the means or its instrument. Every presentation of a philosophical system is not itself the truth, but only a means of one's coming closer to the truth, by means of one's own thinking activity.

Feuerbach's primary attack on Hegel's concept of Being derives from his attack on the concept of an absolute or immediate beginning. Abstractions like Hegel's "Being and Nothing" are constructions of the fantasy, of imagination, and express the limits of reason, beyond which reason cannot function, rather than the heights to which reason can rise. Hence, Feuerbach sees Hegel's contradiction between Being and Nothing as an empty, merely formal contradiction. The real contraction to the abstract concept of Being is not Nothing, but rather sensory, concrete Being. Feuerbach does not, therefore, reject the notion of dialectical opposition, but attempts to reinstate it in nonformal terms: "Dialectics is not a monologue that speculation carries on with itself, but a dialogue between speculation and empirical reality."[63] The dialectic requires the real opposition of sensory, empirical consciousness with speculative rationalism.

Hegel's philosophical terms are seen as empty universals that have no reality because they lack particular relations with actual, concrete existences. Individuals exist, and universals are derived by abstraction. The Platonic view of universals is replaced by the Baconian sense that universals are only generalizations from particular instances by abstraction. So it is Feuerbach who first sees the possibility of a radical inversion of analysis and attempts to stand Hegel back on his feet. Hegelian philosophy is seen as rational mysticism. All speculation that attempts to go beyond nature and man is in vain. The ultimate foundation of critique, according to Feuerbach, is the necessities of human life. Since man is also a creature of needs, sensing, feeling, as well as thinking, Feuerbach wants to demystify theology and philosophy.

Feuerbach's later works represent a major break with the whole dominant tradition of German idealist philosophy. *The Essence of Christianity* introduces an empiricist and materialist-oriented humanism into a philosophical tradition in which this emphasis had previously been alien. It promises a complete reinterpretation of both theology and philosophy. In brief, it asserts that man created the gods, and that the gods embody man's own conception of his own humanity, his own wishes, fears, needs, and ideas. Man creates the gods in his own image: "All the attributes of the divine nature are, therefore, attributes of the human nature."[64] In other words, God is an expression of the thought-process of man. Feuerbach examines the process of concept formation in religion in order to discover the formation of man's knowledge of himself as man. He sees this process as historical in that it is cumulative, it develops, and it matures. Religious consciousness, for Feuerbach, is not a matter of theoretical reflection but of human action.

The Feuerbachian dialectic, therefore, begins with the existing individual, the concrete and particular. Religion is seen as the alienated forms of man's recognition of his own nature. Thought is merely the reflection of sensory and feeling existence. In Feuerbach's interpretation of the dialectic, the subject, as opposed to Hegel's, is not the idea but rather is man as a species being. The task of the philosophy in the future is to lead philosophy from the realm of spirits back to the world of living men. That is, its task is to demonstrate that the consciousness of God is the consciousness of the species, and that which mankind adores in itself. For this purpose, the philosophy of the future requires no more than human understanding and human language.[65] To be conscious is to be conscious of something. In short, there is no consciousness without an object. Something must exist to generate thought. Objectivity, Feuerbach claims, is given to us by our senses.

Feuerbach's discovery is that the proper subject is the growing awareness of man as subject. His human subject, however, is the human race, the species. The love of God is seen as being the love of man in its esoteric but not yet self-conscious form. The result, according to Feuerbach, is man's estrangement from himself. He holds, therefore, that man's species character is the true object of religion. Feuerbach draws a distinction between the existing individual human as finite and the human species as incomplete, and thus infinite. The expression of man's infinite, species quality has been historically expressed in religion. In other words, the real object of man's religious consciousness is seen to be the infinity of man's capacities as a species. He asserts that religion is the relation of man to his own nature, that the essence of religion is the projection of human essence as other.[66] Knowledge of God is man's knowledge about himself. In short, Feuerbach charges that religion expresses human wants, needs, fears, hopes, and desires. He argues that when all the ideas of God are analyzed, apart from human feelings and wants, there are no ideas of God left. In brief, man is the subject, and God is the predicate. The essence of man is infinite, since man creates his essence infinitely in the process of a dialectical developing a self-consciousness with respect to his existence. For Feuerbach it follows that the emancipation of mankind from religion is the only possible path of escape from alienation, the only means by which man can actualize himself as a human being.

Feuerbach maintains that he takes the Hegelian dialectic to its extreme conclusion and thus completes its task. He does this by rejecting Hegel's idealism, and substitutes the view that basic reality is not *Geist* but is material. By reviving philosophical materialism, Feuerbach rejects that the thought and behavior of a particular epoch is the work of *Geist*, but for him it is the total sum of the material circumstances of any historic period. His view attempts to invert the Hegelian assumption of the primacy of spirit and idea by substituting for it the primacy of material order. Feuerbach shifts the focal point of historic development from God to man. While the Hegelian dialectic sees *Geist* as attempting to realize itself in history, the Feuerbachian dialectic holds that it is really mankind struggling to realize itself. It is necessary for mankind to realize this in order to overcome its self-alienation. Thus, Hegel's self-alienated God becomes Feuerbach's self-alienated man, and history as the process of God's attaining to full self-consciousness through man turns into history as a process of man's attaining to full self-consciousness through God.[67] In the Feuerbachian reformulation of Hegelianism, the goal of history is simply for mankind to become fully human.

> Bauer, Ruge, Feuerbach, and other Left Hegelians believed that the humanistic inversion of Hegelian metaphysics preserved the real, immanent content of the Hegelian dialectic. Their theories of "man" and "state" were to be conceived not as mere abstractions, but as true self-comprehensions of the real structure of human activity and consciousness previously veiled by the self-alienating forms of religious faith and philosophical speculation. Because theory was the comprehension of concrete existence, practice made self-aware, their primary "political" task was defined as public enlightenment, as the destruction of illusions and critical unveiling of the real human needs and interests previously hidden and distorted by these illusions.[68]

Like other left Hegelians, Feuerbach expects a radical change in political forms. The task is to educate human consciousness and transform passive victims into active subjects who make their own history.

## Marx's Dialectic

Although Karl Marx (1818–1883) begins with a Hegelian dialectic, he radicalizes it. As a student at Berlin in 1836, Marx attended lectures by Eduard Gans, Hegel's former student, on the philosophy of right. From Gans' course, Marx was first drawn to the revolutionary aspect of Hegel's dialectic.[69] While a student at Berlin, Marx also joined a Young Hegelian club in order to discuss his problems with Hegel. Marx's epistemological achievement is the identification of human consciousness with the practical process of reality as shaped by mankind. Marx sees himself as completing Feuerbach's project.

Reality is always human reality, not in the sense that human beings exist within nature, but in the sense that people shape nature. His materialist conception of history is composed of four elements: German idealist philosophy, Hegel's dialectic, French socialism, and English classical economics. The materialist conception of history is seen as one of the most fundamental and distinct tenets of Marxism:

> My inquiry led me to the conclusion that neither legal relations nor political forms could be comprehended whether by themselves or on the basis of a so-called general development of the human mind, but that on the contrary they originate in the material conditions of life, the totality of which Hegel, following the example of English and French thinkers of the eighteenth century, embraces as with the term "civil society:" that anatomy of this civil society, however, has to be sought in political economy.[70]

Its central claim is that people's economic behavior, their mode of production in material life, is the basis of their social life generally. This economic basis determines both society's social and political institutions and its prevalent ideas. History is the activity of human beings seeking to achieve ends, but these ends are inspired and shaped by economic realities. In this respect, Marx is greatly influenced by a Moses Hess, a left Hegelian. Hess postulated that productive activity is the essential attribute of the species. The foundations of social life are not to be found in elevated spheres but in earthly facts. In the Preface to *A Critique of Political Economy*, Marx boldly asserts that:

> In the social production of their life, men enter into definite relations that are indispensable and independent of their will, relations of production which correspond to a definite stage of development of their material productive forces. The sum total of these relations of production constitutes the economic structure of society, the real foundation, on which rise a legal and political superstructure and to which correspond definite forms of social consciousness. The mode of production of material life conditions the social, political, and intellectual life process in general. It is not the consciousness of men that determine their being, but, on the contrary, their social being that determines their consciousness.[71]

Marx's thesis is that people's thoughts and actions are greatly influenced by economic facts. With this assertion, he attacks views of politics that see it as a function of ideas and doctrines without reference to production and the economic interests of society.[72] A proper inquiry into Marx's tenets requires a look at his rejection of Hegel's idealism.

Although Marx's social theory stands on its own, it is indebted to Hegel. He acknowledges that Hegel's philosophy is of great service in constructing his economic theory. Hegel's greatness, for Marx, consists in his comprehension of man's self-generation. Marx begins with Hegel's conception of history and then both preserves its structure and changes its content.[73] Consequently, although Marx dismisses Hegel's *Geist* as a metaphysical specter, in a decisive sense, he is more Hegelian than ever. Nonetheless, Marx also strongly attacks the "mysticism" of Hegel's method. For example, in *The Holy Family*, he asserts that:

> Hegel's conception of history assumes an Abstract or Absolute Spirit which develops in such a way that mankind it a mere mass bearing it with a varying degree of consciousness or unconsciousness. Within empiric, exoteric history he therefore has a speculative, esoteric history develop. The history of mankind becomes the history of the abstract spirit of mankind, a spirit beyond all man![74]

Thus, thought does not determine material reality, but material reality determines thought. For Hegel the thought-process is the demiurge of the actual, and with Marx the idea is nothing more than the material transposed and translated in the human head.

In *Towards a Critique of Hegel's Philosophy of Right: Introduction*, Marx lashes out at German idealist philosophy:

> German philosophy is the ideal prolongation of German history. So if, instead of criticizing the incomplete works of our real history, we criticize the posthumous works of our ideal history, philosophy, then our criticism will be at the center of the question of which the present age says: that is the question.[75]

Marx's break with left Hegelianism is due to his insistence that they were still idealists, as he further argues in *The Holy Family* that:

> Meanwhile, the relation between 'spirit and mass' has still a hidden sense which will be completely revealed in the course of the reasoning. . . . That relationship discovered by Herr Bruno is, in fact, nothing but a critically caricatural realization of Hegel's conception of history; this, in turn, is nothing but the speculative expression of the Christian Germanic dogma of the opposition between spirit and matter, between God and the world.[76]

In Marx's view, it is the actual engagement of men and women with their material circumstances and the ever-present necessity to recreate the material requirements of their own continuance that gives meaning, intelligibility, thrust, and essence to history. Hence, the ultimate causes of social and political changes are to be sought, not in the minds of men, but in changes in the mode of production and exchange.

Marx is strongly influenced by Feuerbach, whose materialism provides a philosophic base for challenging the Hegelian doctrine of idealism. He follows

Feuerbach's lead and redefines the goal of history in terms of "humanism." As discussed in the previous section, Feuerbach's *Essence of Christianity* substitutes materialism for Hegelian idealism. Human beings are products of nature:

> Feuerbach is the only one who has a serious, critical attitude to the Hegelian dialectic and who has made genuine discoveries in this field. He is in fact the true conqueror of the old philosophy. The extent of his achievement, and the unpretentious simplicity with which he, Feuerbach, gives to the world, stand in striking contrast to the reverse. . . . The establishment of true materialism and of real science since Feuerbach also makes the social relationship "of man to man" the basic principle of history.[77]

Thus, Marx is congenial to Feuerbach's idea that it is the material, sensuously perceptible world that is the only reality. The goal is for mankind to realize its humanity, its human nature. Human consciousness and thinking, however supra-sensuous they may seem, are the product of the material.

Ultimately, Feuerbach does not go far enough and is still seen as basically an idealist. Feuerbach takes man as his starting place but makes absolutely no reference to the world in which man lives. More precisely, Feuerbach does not fulfill the promise of his own discoveries about the nature of philosophy. Feuerbach sees in Hegelianism only a representation of the alienation of mankind in the theoretical life of religion; he does not grasp it as esoteric economics. Feuerbach's materialism is inadequate, since he is an idealist in social theory. In the *Theses on Feuerbach*, Marx notes that:

> The chief defect of all hitherto existing materialism (that of Feuerbach included) is that the thing, reality, sensuousness, is conceived only in the form of the object or of contemplation, but not as sensuous human activity, practice, not subjectivity. . . . Feuerbach wants sensuous objects, really distinct from the thought objects, but he does not conceive human activity as objective activity.[78]

Feuerbach is abstract. Feuerbach's theory is designed to suit all periods and conditions, and is therefore useless. Feuerbach's inquiries totally lack any understanding of history, which is necessary in order to escape from the realm of abstraction. Marx's main reproach is that Feuerbach accepts reality; that is, he only wants to establish a correct consciousness. Marx is also interested in exposing the state, the political sphere of life, as one of the unholy forms of human self-alienation.[79] His social theory stresses the importance of human action in moving history.

The ultimately determining element in history, according to Marx, is the production and reproduction of real life. History is shaped by material forces, not ideas. In the science of production, distribution, consumption, and exchange are the key to understanding civil society. From an understanding of those material conditions of life Marx expects to grasp legal relationships and forms of state. Human thinking is shaped by material conditions:

> The ideas of the ruling class are in every epoch the ruling ideas, i.e., the class which is the ruling *material* force of society, is at the same time its ruling *intellectual* force. The class which has the means of material production at its disposal, has control at the same time over the means of mental production. . . . The ruling ideas are nothing more than the ideal expression of the dominant material relationships, the dominant material relationships grasped in ideas.[80]

Hence, ideas of a given period reflect its material conditions. In short, social being determines consciousness. The attributes of the external world as determined by active human consciousness also make various modes of human cognition possible; the link between epistemology and history leads to a historicization of epistemology itself.[81]

Marx's material dialectic asserts that ideas are not the ultimate cause of historical change because they can only be explained in connection with the underlying mode of production. Marx's dialectic is intended to illustrate and comprehend social changes resulting from changes in economic organization. The world is a system of organically interconnected processes characterized by inherent tendencies to development, and it is subject periodically to radical changes in its organic structure. For Marx, a dialectical theory traces the hierarchical structure of society through the stages of concreteness and explains the systematic changes in this structure by the developmental tendencies inherent in it. Marx credits Hegel with being the first to present the dialectic's general forms of movement in a comprehensive and conscious way: "The outstanding thing in Hegel's *Phenomenology* and its final outcome—that is, the dialectic of negativity as the moving and generating principle—is thus first that Hegel conceives the self-genesis of man as a process. . . ."[82] Thus, Marx's thought about the natural world is inflected through and through with Hegelianism.

Thinking, viewed dialectically, becomes a historical process. Marx, however, rejects Hegel's claim that the world is no more than a manifestation of divine thought:

> My dialectical method is, in its foundation, not only different from the Hegelian, but exactly opposite to it. For Hegel, the process of thinking, which he even transforms into an independent subject, under the name of 'the idea,' is the creator of the real world, and the real world is only the external appearance of the idea. With me the reverse is true: the ideal is nothing but the material world reflected in the mind of man, and translated into forms of thought. . . . The mystification which the dialectic suffers in Hegel's hands by no means prevents him

from being the first to present its general forms of motion in a comprehensive and conscious manner.[83]

The dialectical structure of the world is a complex empirical fact about the nature of material reality. Marx rejects Hegel's idealism and replaces it with materialism. Marx retains the dialectic because he sees something very valuable in it:

> With him it is standing on its head. It must be inverted, in order to discover the rational kernel within the mystical shell.[84]

Marx's materialist point of view holds that that there is no *Geist*—or God— who creates the world. Thus, the dialectic does not need to reconcile its divine, infinite, and perfect existence with this finite and imperfect world. His inversion of Hegel consists in seeing the dialectical structure of thought not as the cause for the dialectical structure of reality, but merely as a consequence of the fact that it is thought's function to mirror a dialectically structured world.[85]

Marx does not accept Hegel's claim that the dialectic is a logic that replaces formal logic. Stripped of its theological and logical claims, Hegel's dialectic becomes an account of how thinking, now no longer the thinking of God, develops:

> But because Hegel has conceived the negation of the negation from the point of view of the positive, and from the point of view of the negative relation inherent in it as the only true act and self-realizing act of all being, he has only found the abstract, logical, speculative, expression for the movement of history; and this historical process is not yet the real history of man. . . . The outstanding thing in Hegel's *Phenomenology* . . . [is that] Hegel conceives the self-genesis of man as a process, conceives objectification as loss of the object, as alienation and as transcendence of this alienation; that he thus grasps the essence of labor and comprehends objective man . . . as the outcome of man's own labor.[86]

Thus, Marx believes that the criticism hidden and prefigured in the *Phenomenology* is a criticism of political economy. The secret that Marx unlocks in Hegelianism is the human labor process. It is not pure mental activity, but it is in the course of their practical activity that human beings solve their survival problems and make history. Marx's material dialectic describes the process in which people develop their ways of life under concrete conditions, in the course of solving concrete problems. Reality is not *Geist* unfolding in the universe; it is the total of objects and facts, existing independently of minds and ideas. Therefore, Marx relates the unfolding of the many phases of civilization to changes in the mode of production.

Marx also learned from Hegel that human activity, or labor, is always thinking activity, and that it is necessary to differentiate the thought inherent in activity from thought that reflects on what is done and tries to describe and understand it: "The production of ideas, of conceptions, of consciousness, is at first directly interwoven with the material activity and the material intercourse of men, the language of real life."[87] Activity is always conscious activity but not necessarily self-conscious. Self-awareness is not automatic but is an achievement. The thinking that accompanies human behavior is not always self-conscious. Self-consciousness is only achieved through strenuous efforts. This is another insight that Marx attributes to Hegel. The materialist dialectic provides a very general view of the outlines of past human history, but inasmuch as this human history is the development of thinking practice and its consequences, the pattern of history is also a pattern of thought. Marx holds that although Hegel understood that human beings are the outcome of their labor, he misunderstood the nature of labor and thinking. "The only labor which Hegel knows and recognizes is abstractly mental labor."[88] Thus, Marx substitutes the process in which human beings solve the problems of meeting their material needs for Hegel's grand panorama of divine thinking.

The existing order becomes a barrier to progress and must be negated by new productive forces. In Hegelian terms, the thesis must be negated by the antithesis in order for the contradiction to be resolved. A transcendence of alienation through thinking is no real transcendence. It leaves the alien real world just as alien as before. In Marx's materialist dialectic, however, a revolution resolves the contradiction by disrupting the old order and instituting a new productive system that embodies alike the new productive forces and some phases of the old form of production. In the Preface to *A Critique of Political Economy* he asserts that:

> At a certain stage of their development, the material productive forces of society come into conflict with the existing relations of production . . . with the property relations within which they have been at work hitherto. From forms of development of the productive forces these relations turn into their fetters. Then begins an epoch of social revolution. With the change of the economic foundation the entire immense superstructure is more or less rapidly transformed.[89]

After the social revolution, a new synthesis is achieved, and corresponding institutions begin to emerge. Class struggle plays a prominent part in the dialectics of social revolution.

Human history displays a portrait of all types of wars and conflicts over a variety of reasons. It appears that the history of human society is the history of religious, political, economic, and social struggles. Marx makes a much more restricted claim, however: "The history of all hitherto existing society is the history of class struggles."[90] To be sure, class struggle is a struggle between classes, but it is much more. There is class struggle in which some of the participants are not yet classes in a full sense but instead are groups that are on the way toward developing into a class. In saying that all history is the history of class struggle, Marx is identifying class struggle as the source of revolutionary change in societies. In brief, the flourishing and decay of different cultures is due to class struggle.

Marx classifies historical periods according to their mode of production and specifically by the way in which product of the many has been taken and used by the few. For example, the glory of Rome flowed from the strenuous work and sweat of slaves who did not share in that glory. In feudal society, the hard work of the serfs supported a class of largely idle landowners. In Marx's time, the productive wealth of the capitalists is produced by workers who do not own or control the wealth that they produce. Marx summarizes the history of class struggle as follows:

> Freeman and slave, patrician and plebeian, lord and serf, guildmaster and journeyman, in word, oppressor and oppressed, stood in constant opposition to one another, carried on an uninterrupted, now hidden, now open fight that each time ended, either in a revolutionary reconstitution of society at large, or in a common ruin of the struggling classes. . . . The modern bourgeois society that has sprouted from the ruins of feudal society has not done away with class antagonisms. It has only established new classes, new conditions of oppression, new forms of struggle in place of the old ones.[91]

The great transitions in human history occur when one mode of production replaces another. These transitions, as well as the processes that lead up to them, are the effects of class struggle, because the very essence of these transitions is the replacement of one class, with its characteristic mode of production, by another class with its different mode of production. Thus, the motor of his materialist dialectic is class struggle: "Revolutions are the locomotives of history."[92] The dialectical contradictions of each economic epoch are finally overcome through class struggle that eventually results in a revolution and a new relationship of production.

Marx criticizes Hegel for reducing reality to a logical, not-real Idea. Marx identifies consciousness with Ideal and assumes that they are both opposed to real. However, Marx mistakenly criticizes his own interpretation of Hegel rather than Hegel himself.[93] When Hegel says that reality is Idea he means more than consciousness. While pure ideality is conscious, for Hegel, it is much more. As noted in previous chapters, the basic assumption of Hegel's philosophy is the identity of the real and the idea. Surreptitiously, Marx introduces a separation of the ideal and the real that Hegel would never accept.

For Hegel, reality is not a product of the Idea, it is the Idea itself. Reality is not a product of the Idea, since Idea is both substance and subject for Hegel.[94] Marx misunderstands Hegel's thought; instead of being the "science of the ideal in the real," it becomes an abstraction from the real. Furthermore, Hegel's philosophical categories are not abstract but are concrete and dynamic. Marx asserts that while Hegel proceeds from the state and turns man into a subjectified state, democracy proceeds from man and turns the state into an objectified man. While the separation of the state from both religion and economic life liberates the state from religion and economics, it does not liberate mankind from their impact. Like Hegel, Marx's goal is the freedom of mankind. However, in pursuing this goal he places much more stress on economic equality than does Hegel. Thus, Marx gives much more attentions to continuous conflict between civil society and the state.

## HEGEL AND THE REAL WORLD

Contrary to Feuerbach's and Marx's criticisms, Hegel does not ignore the real world of existing human beings. In fact, he argues that philosophy's task is to understand and explain existing reality. As discussed in Chapter 2, Hegel not only sees *Geist* as the essential reality behind empirical phenomena, but also as the rational self consciousness of man. To be sure, Hegel believes the world to have a rational structure, and his dialectical conception of categories does justice to the dynamism of life. In their complex dialectical conception, Hegel's categories are capable acquiring philosophical knowledge of the world. With the *Phenomenology of Spirit*, Hegel clearly illustrates that man is a self-conscious being that is informed by the dynamic structure of self-consciousness. He criticizes metaphysics for operating with fixed categories and oppositions that serve as the foundation for thought. Hegel agrees with some of the empiricist criticisms of metaphysics. Since the foundations of metaphysical knowledge are the products of a priori thought, empiricists object that they are not firm enough and ultimately lack concrete determinations; consequently, empiricists try to place knowledge on a firmer base by replacing the presupposed objects and axioms of philosophy with the immediacy of sense-experience.[95] In this way, empiricism claims to found knowledge on presuppositions that are concrete in themselves. Since Feuerbach and Marx charge Hegel with ignoring existing reality, it is necessary to examine Hegel's position on empiricism more carefully in order to determine the validity of this charge.

According to Hegel, Francis Bacon as one of the first thinkers to react against the metaphysical manner of deducing the nature of reality from rational principles. Against the Scholastic a priori anticipation of nature, Bacon emphasizes the importance of empirical explanations and thus directs attention to empirically given experience.[96] For Hegel, empiricism is a remedy for a deficiency of metaphysics:

> In Empiricism lies the great principle that whatever is true must be in the actual world and present to sensation. This principle contradicts what 'ought to be' on the strength of which 'reflection' is vain enough to treat the actual present with scorn and to the point to a scene beyond—a scene which is assumed to have place and being only in the understanding of those who talk of it. . . . For the main lesson of Empiricism is that man must see for himself and feel that he is present in every fact of knowledge which he has to accept. [97]

The empirical principle is necessary for the development of true philosophical knowledge. This principle allows Hegel's speculative philosophy to progress beyond metaphysics. Even though speculative philosophy does not derive all its ideas from sense-perception, it shares empiricism's concern for the immediacy and dynamic life of thought and concern for the manner in which reason is manifested in the empirical world.[98] In contrast with metaphysics and no less than empiricism, Hegel's philosophy recognizes only "what is."[99] Hegel's speculative philosophy argues that although fundamental conceptual determinations about the natural and human world can be derived from reason, the development of reason must be based on the rational reconstruction of empirical experience. Contrary to the charges of Feuerbach and Marx, Hegel does pay close attention to the real world.

Hegelian political philosophy is effective as a critical perspective on other views, such as modern liberalism. As indicated in Chapter 6, Hegel makes sound criticisms of excessively economistic and individualistic theories, such as liberalism. In our own time, civil society has had difficulties in fulfilling its own principles of universal human freedom and dignity, since it systematically consigns whole classes to conditions of life that are subhuman by its own standards.[100] Nevertheless, Hegel can help us better understand a basic problem of modern political world, the wish to have a form of political participation that is both genuinely meaningful and compatible with the pursuit of one's private life. As illustrated above, Hegel's discussion of labor and poverty within civil society foreshadows aspects of Marxism. Concentration of economic power and the unlimited pursuit of profit on the part of those who control wealth create a contradiction within civil society. Overproduction, underconsumption, and alienation are chronic problems of modern society. Furthermore, Hegel's discussion of the dialectic between the slave and the master in the *Phenomenology of Spirit* illustrates the importance of work. Only in and by work does man finally become aware of the significance and necessity of his experience. More precisely, through work consciousness comes to itself:

> Therefore, it is by work, and only by work, that man realizes himself objectively as man. Only after producing an artificial object is man himself really and objectively more than and different from a natural being; and only in this real and objective product does he become truly conscious of his subjective human reality. Therefore, it is only by work that man is a supernatural being that is conscious of its reality; by working, he is "incarnated" Spirit, he is historical "World," he is "objectivized" History.[101]

In the beginning, it is work that frees man from natural contingencies.

Alexandre Kojève argues that Hegel's dialectic is much closer to Marx than is usually recognized. According to Hegel, religion and philosophy are only an ideological superstructure that is born and exists solely in relation to a real substructure; and this substructure is nothing but the totality of human actions realized in the course of universal history—that history in and by which man has created a series of specifically human worlds.[102] Human beings are not only the planks that are used in the construction of history, they are also the carpenters who build it and architects who conceive the plan for it. Even more importantly, human beings are not only the material, the builder, and the architect of the historical edifice; they are also the ones for whom this edifice is constructed. Consequently, they live in it, they see and understand it, and they describe and criticize it.[103] While Hegel appears to think that edifice is reconciled in the modern state Marx strongly rejects that contention. As indicated above, Marx builds explicitly upon Hegel's historical dialectic. Later liberal ideas are influenced as well by Hegelian streams, thus illustrating the never-ending dialectic characteristic of the history of political ideas in general. As examined in the next two chapters, since the perfection of *Geist* in the modern state, as depicted by Hegel, has yet to be realized, his thought does provide a basis for either building an alternative to or modifying the liberal state.

Marx claims that Hegel's dialectic was upside down; he further asserts that his material dialectic corrects the intrinsic flaws in Hegel's dialectic. Up to this point in time, Marx's followers seem to have failed miserable in achieve a just state. Hegel recognizes that justice demands that civil society must act to ensure that everyone have a sufficient means to earn a livelihood when necessary. This implies that at times the state must redistribute wealth through taxation. Since fair commodity relations mandates regulation, the economy must be subordinate to justice. However, unlike with Marx, democratic government must not be relegated to the management of the economy. As discussed in Chapter 6, Hegel places civil society under the rule of constitutional self-government. Although Hegel does not explicitly comment on the limits of redistribution, he seems to suggest that whatever is necessary to eliminate social disadvantage is justified to the extent that the freedoms of commodity relations are upheld.[104] As argued in Chapter 10, Hegel would not be pleased with the direction taken by the United States over the last couple of decades. Democratic government is being stripped of its ability to regulate the economy responsibly and to protect the public. This tendency harms responsive citizenship in ways that Hegel would find unacceptable. The following chapter examines the criticisms lodged against by existentialism in general, and Kierkegaard and Nietzsche in particular.

# NOTES

1. Alfred Schmidt, *History and Structure: An Essay on Hegelian-Marxist and Structuralist Theories of History*, trans. J. Herf (Cambridge: MIT Press, 1981), 1.

2. Georg W. F. Hegel, *Philosophy of Mind*, trans. William Wallace (New York: Oxford University Press, 1971), 26.

3. Michael O. Hardimon, *Hegel's Social Philosophy: The Project of Reconciliation* (New York: Cambridge University Press, 1994), 47.

4. Georg W. F. Hegel, *Philosophy of Right*, trans. T. M. Knox (New York: Oxford University Press, 1967), 11.

5. Hegel, *Philosophy of Right*, 10.

6. Michael J. Inwood, *Hegel* (London: Routledge, 2002), 497. Referring specifically to Hegel's *Doppelsatz*, Inwood writes that for Hegel the problem about the goodness of the world and the problem about its intelligibility are one and the same problem with one and the same solution. Rational [*Vernunftig*] means both rationally intelligible in the sense of exemplifying thought-determinations and reasonable in the sense of being more or less as it ought to be.

7. Georg W. F. Hegel, *Logic*, trans. William Wallace (New York: Oxford University Press, 1975), 8.

8. Hegel, *Logic*, p. 200. See also Michael Inwood, *A Hegel Dictionary* (Oxford: Blackwell, 1992), 33–34.

9. Quentin Lauer, *Hegel's Idea of Philosophy* (New York: Fordham University Press, 1983), 2

10. Hardimon, *Hegel's Social Philosophy*, 26. Reconciled individuals do endorse their social world, but they do not endorse it qua existing social world. They endorse it qua actual and qua rational. "Actual" preserves the contrast with potential and undeveloped that is central to Hegel's conception of *Wirklichkeit*.

11. Domenico Losurdo, *Hegel and the Freedom of the Moderns*, trans. Marella and Jon Morris (Durham: N.C.: Duke University Press, 2004), 36.

12. Hegel, *Logic*, 201. See also Hardimon, *Hegel's Social Philosophy*, 57, where he writes: "The phenomenal world is not identical with reality of this world, for it contains much that is not real. A large portion of this consists of mere appearance:

appearances that fail to live up to their essence and appearances that have no essence. But the real is not a Platonic, ontological 'beyond' [*Jenseits*] either. It is not a realm of ideas that are not realized in this world. Nor is the real a Kantian, epistemic "beyond": a thing in itself that lies beyond the bounds of human cognition. The real has external existence in the phenomenal world and is accessible to human cognition. One grasps the reality of things by seeing how their existing features express and embody their essence and how their essence is expressed and embodied in their existing features."

13. Hardimon, *Hegel's Social Philosophy*, 27. Although Hegel did not advocate the uncritical endorsement of the status quo, Hardimon says that Hegel did think that it was far more important to grasp the positive and valuable qualities of the modern social world than to detect its shortcomings.

14. Tom Rockmore, *Before and After Hegel: A Historical Introduction to Hegel's Thought* (Berkeley: University of California Press, 1993), 144.

15. Georg W. F. Hegel, *Aesthetics: Lectures on the Fine Arts, Volume 1*, trans. T. M. Knox (Oxford: Oxford University Press, 1988), 99.

16. Hardimon, *Hegel's Social Philosophy*, 2.

17. Hardimon, *Hegel's Social Philosophy*, 86. The English word reconciliation carries baggage that the German word does not.

18. Hardimon, *Hegel's Social Theory*, 90.

19. Hegel, *Philosophy of Right*, 279.

20. Hegel, *Philosophy of Right*, 108.

21. Hegel, *Philosophy of Right*, 130–131.

22. Hardimon, *Hegel's Social Philosophy*, 93.

23. Hegel, *Philosophy of Right*, 124–125.

24. Hegel, *Philosophy of Mind*, 254.

25. Hardimon, *Hegel's Social Philosophy*, 94.

26. Hegel, *Aesthetics: Lectures on Fine Arts, Volume 1*, 55.

27. Georg W. F. Hegel, *Lectures on the Philosophy of Religion, Volume 1*, trans. R. Brown, P. Hodgson, and J. Stewart (Berkeley: University of California Press, 1984), 177.

28. Hardimon, *Hegel's Social Philosophy*, 96.

29. Hardimon, *Hegel's Social Philosophy*, 105. Hegel maintains that the social world is a home only if its structures unify individuality and social membership in a fundamental way. It must be possible for people to regard their social membership as an essential aspect of their individuality and to regard their individuality as an essential aspect of their social membership.

30. Rockmore, *Before and After Hegel*, 139.

31. John Edwards Toews, *Hegelianism: The Path Toward Dialectical Humanism, 1805–1841* (Cambridge: Cambridge University Press, 1980), 93.

32. Toews, *Hegelianism*, 88.

33. Frederick Beiser, *Hegel* (New York: Routledge, 2005), 308.

34. Karl Löwith, *From Hegel to Nietzsche: The Revolution in Nineteenth-Century Thought*, trans. David Green (Garden City, N.J.: Anchor Books, 1964), 67. See Toews, *Hegelianism*, for a more detailed discussion of Hegelianism. Toews divides the Hegelian school into three different factions, right, center, and left.

35. John Toews, "Transformations of Hegelianism, 1805–1846," in *The Cambridge Companion to Hegel*, ed. Frederick Beiser (New York: Cambridge University Press, 1993), 388.

36. Toews, "Transformations of Hegelianism, 1805–1846," 388.

37. Toews, *Hegelianism*, 148.

38. Beiser, *Hegel*, 310.

39. Löwith, *From Hegel to Nietzsche*, 82. They protest against the arrogance of absolute philosophy that justifies the status quo.

40. Toews, *Hegelianism*, 206–207.

41. Terry Pinkard, *German Philosophy 1760–1860: The Legacy of German Idealism* (Cambridge: Cambridge University Press, 2002), 317.

42. Löwith, *From Hegel to Nietzsche*, 113. Schelling claims that Hegel's ontology lacks an immediate reference to existence. In the final section of this chapter, I respond to criticisms that Hegelianism disregards and disrespects the empirical world.

43. Pinkard, *German Philosophy 1760–1860*, 327. Contrary to Hegel, Schelling held to the notion that there has to be a "final dichotomy" to our thinking, namely, the opposition between a system of thought for which logic and reason are authoritative and that which is beyond thought.

44. Lawrence Stepelevich, "Introduction," in *The Young Hegelians: An Anthology*, ed. L. Stepelevich (Atlantic Highlands: N.J.: Humanities Press, 1983), 2.

45. Löwith, *From Hegel to Nietzsche*, 43. The reconciliation found its most intelligible expression in his political and religious philosophy. Its destruction was the goal of the left Hegelians, because they were concerned with the "real" state and with "real" Christianity.

46. Löwith, *From Hegel to Nietzsche*, 84.

47. Toews, *Hegelianism*, 235.

48. David Strauss, "The Life of Jesus," in *The Young Hegelians*. For Strauss, Hegel's accomplishment was the reconciliation of God and man, of the transcendent and the immanent.

49. Stepelevich, "Introduction," 7.

50. Toews, *Hegelianism*, 288.

51. Robert Tucker, *Philosophy & Myth in Karl Marx* (New Brunswick: NJ.: Transaction Publishers, 2001), 74.

52. Bruno Bauer, "The Trumpet of the Last Judgement," in *The Young Hegelians*, 184.

53. August von Cieszkowski, "Prolegomena to Historiosophie," in *The Young Hegelians*, 70.

54. Löwith, *From Hegel to Nietzsche*, 143.

55. For an excellent discussion and analysis of Feuerbach's thought and its development, see Marx Wartofsky, *Feuerbach* (Cambridge: Cambridge University Press, 1977).

56. Löwith, *From Hegel to Nietzsche*, 74. Feuerbach asserts that Hegelian philosophy is the last ambitious attempt to re-establish lost, defeated Christianity by means of philosophy.

57. Ludwig Feuerbach, *The Essence of Christianity*, trans. George Eliot (Buffalo, N.Y.: Prometheus, 1989), xiv–xvi.

58. Ludwig Feuerbach, *Principles of the Philosophy of the Future*, trans. M. Vogel (Indianapolis, IN: Hackett, 1986), 3.

59. Feuerbach, *The Essence of Christianity*, xv.

60. Feuerbach, *Principles of the Philosophy of the Future*, 64–72.

61. This quote is found in Wartofsky, *Feuerbach*, 139–140.

62. Ludwig Feuerbach, "Towards a Critique of Hegel's Philosophy," in *The Young Hegelians*, 103.

63. Feuerbach, "Towards a Critique of Hegel's Philosophy," 110.

64. Feuerbach, *The Essence of Christianity*, 14.

65. Feuerbach, *Principles of the Philosophy of the Future*, 3.

66. Feuerbach, *The Essence of Christianity*, 13–14.

67. Tucker, *Philosophy & Myth in Karl Marx*, 87. For Hegel, it is the self-realization of God in man, for Feuerbach, the self-realization of man qua man after he has ceased to project himself as God.

68. Toews, *Hegelianism*, 361.

69. Louis Dupré, *The Philosophical Foundations of Marxism* (New York: Harcourt, Brace & World, 1966), 67.

70. Karl Marx, *A Contribution to the Critique of Political Economy*, trans. S. Ryazanskaya (New York: International Publishers, 1970), 20.

71. Karl Marx, *Selected Writings*, ed. David McLellan (Oxford: Oxford University Press, 1977), 389.

72. See Terrell Carver, *Marx's Social Theory* (Oxford: Oxford University Press, 1982).

73. See G. A. Cohen, *Karl's Marx's Theory of History: A Defence* (Princeton: Princeton University Press, 2000).

74. Marx, *Selected Writings*, 143.

75. Marx, *Selected Writings*, 67.

76. Marx, *Selected Writings*, 144. See also Karl Marx, *Economic and Philosophic Manuscripts* (Buffalo, N.Y.: Prometheus, 1988), 142, where Marx says that Bruno Bauer still remains wholly within the confines of the Hegelian Logic.

77. Marx, *Economic and Philosophic Manuscripts*, 143–144.

78. Marx, *Selected Writings*, p. 156. See also Friedrich Engels, *Ludwig Feuerbach and the Outcome of Classical German Philosophy* (New York: International Publishers, 1941), for a discussion the influence of Feuerbach on the development of Marx and Engels materialism. However, Engels also says that Feuerbach reduces all human relations into the realm of religion; such etymological tricks are the last resource of idealist philosophy (p. 34). Engels also suggests that "as a philosopher . . . he [Feuerbach] stopped halfway; the low half of him was materialist, the upper half idealist (42)."

79. Tucker, *Philosophy & Myth in Karl Marx*, 103.

80. Karl Marx and Friedrich Engels, *The German Ideology* (New York: International Publishers, 1970), 64.

81. Shlomo Avineri, *The Social and Political Thought of Karl Marx* (Cambridge: Cambridge University Press, 1972), 75. The attributes of objects derive from the object's standing in the human social context, and their meaning derives from the modes of concrete human consciousness that relates to them. Reality is a human reality, not only because it is shaped by men, but also because it reacts on man himself.

82. Marx, *Economic and Philosophic Manuscripts*, 149.

83. Karl Marx, *Capital: A Critique of Political Economy, Volume One* (New York: Vintage Books, 1976), 102–103.

84. Marx, *Capital, Volume One*, 103.

85. Allen Wood, *Karl Marx* (London: Routledge, 1981), 209.

86. Marx, *Economic and Philosophic Manuscripts*, 145 and 149.

87. Marx and Engels, *The German Ideology*, 47.

88. Marx, *Economic and Philosophic Manuscripts*, 150.

89. Marx, *Selected Writings*, p. 390.

90. Karl Marx and Friedrich Engels, *The Communist Manifesto* (New York: Washington Square Press, 1964), 57.

91. Marx and Engels, *The Communist Manifesto*, 58.

92. Karl Marx, *Class Struggles in France: 1848–1850* (New York: International Publishers, 1964), 120.

93. Dupré, *The Philosophical Foundations of Marxism*, 94.

94. Dupré, *The Philosophical Foundations of Marxism*, 96. Marx says that for Hegel the Idea is subject and the concrete reality of the state is the predicate. Marx claims that this separates the ideal and the real. From Hegel's point of view, it is Marx who separates subject and predicate into the distinct spheres of thought and reality. By confining the predicate entirely to the order of thought, Marx destroys the original identity of thought and being.

95. Hegel, *Logic*, 60.

96. Georg W. F. Hegel, *Lectures on the History of Philosophy: Medieval and Modern Philosophy, Volume 3*, trans. E. S. Haldane and Frances Simson (Lincoln: University of Nebraska Press, 1995), 180.

97. Hegel, *Logic*, 61.

98. Stephen Houlgate, *Hegel, Nietzsche and the Critique of Metaphysics* (Cambridge: Cambridge University Press, 1986), 106.

99. Hegel, *Logic*, 62.

100. Allen Wood, *Hegel's Ethical Thought* (Cambridge: Cambridge University Press, 1990), 260.

101. Alexandre Kojève, *Introduction to the Reading of Hegel*, trans. James Nichols (Ithaca, N.Y.: Cornell University Press, 1969), 25. The master, who does not work, produces nothing stable outside of himself. Thus his enjoyment and his satisfaction remain purely subjective: They are of interest only to him and therefore can be recognized only by him; they have no "truth," no objective reality revealed to all. The slave can work for the master only by repressing his own desires. Hence, he transcends himself by working. The master is the catalyst of the historical process, since this process would not be possible without him.

102. Kojève, *Introduction to the Reading of Hegel*, 32.

103. Kojève, *Introduction to the Reading of Hegel*, 33.

104. Richard Dien Winfield, *Freedom and Modernity* (Albany, N.Y.: State University of New York, 1991), 253. Due to the contingency of the market, the measures taken by public administration must be continually revised in reaction to the changing situation of the economy.

## Chapter Eight

# Nineteenth-Century Rejections of Hegelianism: Kierkegaard, Nietzsche, and Criticisms of Metaphysics

> [I]n every truth the opposite is equally true. For example, a truth can only be expressed and enveloped in words if it is one-sided. Everything that is thought and expressed in words is one-sided, only half the truth; it all lacks totality, completeness, and unity.[1]
>
> —Hermann Hesse, *Siddhartha*

As noted in the last chapter, it is necessary to recognize that Hegel's claim that with his dialectic method represents a culmination of all historical philosophy is not the same as saying that philosophy reaches its end in his theory. To be sure, since he consciously builds on prior philosophical positions, his assertion that his philosophy represents a high point in the Western tradition is justified. However, Hegel never said that philosophy ends with his system; nonetheless, the conviction that it was no longer possible to carry on philosophy as before was widespread at that time.[2] To a significant extent, subsequent philosophy happens in the wake of Hegel. Kierkegaard and Nietzsche are sharp critics of modernity and are situated in the Hegelian aftermath; consequently, their respective philosophy can be understood as reactions to Hegel. Each reacts differently to Hegel's philosophy. While Kierkegaard and Nietzsche claim to reject Hegel's theory, Marx attempts to transform Hegel's theory by correcting its fatal flaws.

Marxism completely rejects the idea that an invisible hand can guarantee the welfare of all and criticizes Hegel as failing to see this. In fact, Marxists hold that any free enterprise system entails social injustice and must be rejected. However, social justice cannot be reached by replacing the market with a totally planned economy. As indicated in Chapter 5 and discussed more fully in Chapter 10, even though Hegel recognizes the imperfections of a market system, he also finds that social justice cannot be achieved by eliminating it. In short, Hegel notes that socialism would eliminate the freedom of particularity that is required by commodity relations in order to allow individuals to choose independently what they need and how they will earn a living. For Hegel, it is the inability of some to exercise this freedom that is the wrong that should be corrected. To put it differently, social justice does not consist in eliminating commodity relations, as Marx argues, but rather in providing everyone the opportunity to participate in the reciprocal satisfaction of freely chosen needs; "Hegel understands this far better than those who stand him on his head: and, therefore, he recognizes that the remedy to social inequality lies not in the overthrow of commodity relations, but outside the economic order altogether in two separate civil institutions that he calls corporations and the police."[3]

Hegel recognizes that civil society gives its members the right to form economic interest groups to advance their own needs. Since they are voluntary and can only pursue their common cause by participating in, and not supplanting, civil society, Hegel asserts that they are legitimate. Nevertheless, by themselves, corporations cannot remove social injustice and the extreme inequality of wealth. If social justice is to be achieved, the civil society must be subject to an additional enforcement of welfare, which Hegel sees as the job of the "police," or public administration:

> The very rights founded in commodity relations require that the economic interest group activity be supplemented by a *public* administration of welfare, addressing all members of society and issuing from a universally respected civil authority empowered to guarantee them the chance to satisfy their freely selected commodity needs through economic activity of their own choice. Hegel introduces his "police" to carry out just this task, duly aware of its decisive role in setting the economy in its proper subordinate position within the just society.[4]

Not only does Marx's communism fall short of the requirements that a just economy ordains, today's neoliberal imperative of free trade and globalization desperately fail in this regard. While the market brings employment opportunities and skilled labor together, Hegel sees that his interconnectedness has a downside. Well-trained workers often find their skills redundant in the modern economy, and they become unemployed when their skills are no longer needed, through no fault of their own. Increasing economic efficiency and globalization creates surplus production and replaces workers with technology. When a surplus of goods is produced, workers are laid off, creating unemployment. The modern economy frequently renders workers superfluous, wreaking havoc on their personal lives, especially with the outsourcing of so many jobs to take advantage of cheap foreign labor. Moreover, by failing to earn a livelihood, Hegel says that the victims of poverty are deprived not just of goods but also the opportunity to exercise their autonomy as a rightful member of the community.

This chapter draws some conclusions regarding Hegel's philosophy and assesses the state of philosophy in its aftermath. To this end, it is organized into four sections. The first section briefly argues that existentialism developed as a critical reaction to Hegel's philosophical system. The second section examines Kierkegaard's criticisms of Hegel's approach. Kierkegaard opposes the very idea of a Hegelian system, and holds that the very idea of system and existence are incompatible. The third section discusses Nietzsche's rejection of Hegel. Nietzsche also scorns the idea of a philosophical system, and opposes the concept of truth that has run through the Western philosophical tradition. Nietzsche further rejects the idea of a neutral philosophical perspective. The final section of the chapter explores Hegel's critique of modern metaphysics, and defends him against many of the charges brought by his nineteenth-century critics.

## EXISTENTIALISM AS A RESPONSE TO HEGELIANISM

Although a clearly delineated existentialist platform does not exist due to the wide variety of existentialists, there are some common themes that existential writers tend to share. Many existentialists profess hostility to closed systems, secular or religious, that pretend to be exact mirrors of essential reality.[5] Holding that rational and comprehensive explanations of the universe and world do not work, existentialism rejects systematic attempts that claim to capture the world of human existence with tidy systems. For many existentialists, Hegel's philosophy represented the grandest system of all. Also, themes such as freedom, decision, and responsibility are prominent in existential philosophy. Man is never merely part of the cosmos, but stands apart from it, and there is a tension that opens possibilities for tragic conflict. Hegel's speculative philosophy is blamed for ruining the nineteenth century for the seriousness of existence. The existentialist responds to the contemporary malaise as a diagnostician who recommends the fervent revolt of the individual man. The particulars of this revolt, however, vary with each existentialist.

Life is gripped totally by the drama of human existence, and existentialists frequently speak of authentic existence, showing through philosophical analysis the impossibility of man's building a universally valid system of thought that enables him to view truth from the outside like another object. There are always loose ends; human experience and knowledge are always incomplete and fragmentary. Existentialism emerges as a philosophy that demands a radical, personal, and never-ceasing questioning of the purpose of human life. Thinkers, such as Nietzsche, Kierkegaard, and Ortega y Gasset, have expressed their misgivings about the so-called mass society and what it does to the individual.[6] Also, they tend to think passionately, as one who is involved in the actualities of existence. The concept of freedom central to existentialism posits that people are free but cannot be sure what, if anything, they can count on. As such human beings make the choices on how they live their lives and are essentially thrown into life with no anchors or pre-established values. The freedom to create meaning allows us to create ourselves. And we bear the full responsibility for that creation. For some, like Jean-Paul Sartre (1900–1980), we make ourselves through our actions.[7] Nothing has meaning independent of those human beings who endow the world with meaning. If existence precedes essence, human reality must constantly create and recreate itself.

## SØREN KIERKEGAARD:
## PHILOSOPHY WITHOUT FOUNDATIONS

Like those commonly associated with existentialism, Søren Kierkegaard (1813–1855) emphasizes the significance of individual choice. Like Marx and Nietzsche, Kierkegaard emerges as one of the rebels of the nineteenth century whose works were composed in conscious opposition to the prevailing assumptions and conventions of the age. He also sees himself historically, as a corrective against the age. Hegel saw *Weltgeist* as unfolding in history, and at the core of this grandiose system is his view of history as a single process with one beginning, one development, and one end. Nothing is left to chance and chaos has no place in the world. Unlike Marx, who disliked specific features of Hegel's system and attempts to put it on its feet, Kierkegaard answers with a more radical "no," which was not provoked by any particular feature of the Hegelian system, but by its very image of man and the world. He opposes the very idea of a systematic theory as a methodological error. In fact, system and existence are incompatible for Kierkegaard, who objects that the full-blooded reality of life has been swallowed up by Hegel's *Geist*, which alone has actual reality. All Kierkegaard's writings bear witness to the necessity of affirming the integrity of the individual in the face of such grand systems. His notion of subjective truth against the claim of objective truth shifts the locus of the argument from logic to life: "The real subject is not the cognitive subject . . . the real subject is the ethically existing subject."[8] Although critical of Hegel, Kierkegaard often employs a Hegelian vocabulary. Kierkegaard took courses from Schelling in Berlin and was strongly influenced by Schelling's reading of Hegel.[9] Even though he was disappointed by Schelling's performance, Kierkegaard took some of Schelling's ideas and fashioned them into a highly original philosophy.

Like most existentialists, Kierkegaard opposes the very ideal of a philosophical system, such as Hegel's. Existence cannot be reduced to a mere part in a system. While philosophical systems seek a unity between thought and being, Kierkegaard asserts that existence calls for their separation. Speculative philosophers, such as Hegel, forget their own existence and confuse themselves with humanity in general.[10] His emphasis on existence leads Kierkegaard to adopt an antisystematic form of discussion. Kierkegaard denies the viability of Hegel's effort to capture truth within a system. A logical system, such as Hegel's, offers only an objective truth to which Kierkegaard prefers the subjective truth, or, more precisely, a concept of truth as subjective.[11] He further objects to Hegel's concept of mediation between two incompatible possibilities. Hegel avoids the need to choose between opposing possibilities through his strategy of mediating difference. Since he links opposing concepts through a middle term, Hegel never has to choose between what are often incompatible perspectives. In the *Science of Logic*, for instance, "Becoming" mediates between "Being" and "Nothing." Since Kierkegaard rejects the idea of a system, he also rejects the constant mediation that makes such a system possible. Furthermore, since Hegel mediates all distinctions, he avoids the need to choose. Kierkegaard insists on the need to choose among different possibilities. For him, the need to choose is not intellectual; the deeper problem concerns existence to the extent that is necessary to choose, that is, to choose one's own form of life.[12]

Kierkegaard believes there is a problem with the way that the majority of his contemporaries think of themselves and lead their lives. He argues that they succumb to an impersonal and anonymous mode of consciousness that precludes spontaneous feeling and is devoid of a secure sense of self-identity:

> My principal thought was that in our age, because of the great increase in knowledge, we had forgotten what it means to exist, and what inwardness signifies, and that the misunderstanding between speculative philosophy and Christianity was explicable on that ground. . . . If men had forgotten what it means to exist religiously, they had doubtless also forgotten what it means to exist as human beings.[13]

Hence, everything tends to be seen in abstract terms, as theoretical possibilities that could be contemplated and compared but not to the concrete realization of which people are unwilling to commit themselves. Life seems to be purged of passion and feeling, and action is replaced by thought and becomes a matter of thinking instead of doing. For Kierkegaard, "to exist" is precisely to act, and "to know," separated from action, is precisely to avoid "existing."[14]

Social decisions are reached by accumulating information as opposed to making decisions that bear the stamp of individual passion or conviction. Public discourse, for Kierkegaard, becomes a pure abstraction, and as a form of abstract thought reasoning is not profoundly dialectical enough. As an opinion and conviction, it lacks full-blooded individuality:

> In fact there are handbooks for everything, and very soon education, all the world over, will consist in learning a greater or lesser number of comments by heart, and people will excel according to their capacity for singling out the various facts like a printer singling out the letters, but completely ignorant of the meaning of anything. Thus our own age is essentially one of understanding, and on the average, perhaps, more knowledgeable than any former generation, but it is without passion.[15]

These trends are also accompanied by a propensity to identify with amorphous abstract entities like "the public" or "humanity." In this way, Kierkegaard maintains that people absolve themselves from individual responsibility. Thus, society bands together in the safety of numbers and in this sense one could do anything on principle and avoid all personal responsibility.[16] Thus, Kierkegaard argues that we have lost sight of ourselves as unique individuals under the domain of bland generalities and the bloodless universals of collective thought. This has allowed people to avoid all personal responsibility. "Indeed, the private world of the emotions and personal judgments that constitute them are so important for Kierkegaard that the objective world in which truth is determined impersonally and apart from the passions fades from view and becomes only a backdrop for the quite dramatic personal performances that give us the truth, the only real truth for 'an existing human being'—subjective truth."[17] While an objective truth is a descriptive truth, a subjective truth is a performative truth.

According to Kierkegaard, what is needed is to bring home to people what it means for each individual to be a human being. This involves leading people to recognize for themselves, through an appeal to their own inner experience, the limitations of their particular mode of living. This enlargement of an individual's self-understanding and critical self-awareness could not be achieved by abstract instruction. Outward answers always fall short. In part, Kierkegaard's *Either/Or* is a protest against the Hegelian notion that distinct forms of consciousness follow one another in a dialectically necessary sequence in the progressively unfolding of universal mind or spirit.[18] In *Fear and Trembling*, faith is presented as possessing a wholly independent status, lying beyond the province of ethical thinking and resisting elucidation in universal or rational terms.[19] Kierkegaard concludes that faith constitutes the highest passion of a person. For him, it is a simple fact of existence that people suffer from anxiety. The primary cause of this anxiety is that people are separated from God. With his emphasis that religion is higher than ethics, Kierkegaard inverts a fundamental Hegelian theme. In stressing the paramount importance of the religious element against the ethical element, he rehabilitates a subjective form of theory that Hegel subordinates to objective forms of thought.[20] Faith is beyond the aegis of human reason, and is not susceptible to justification in rational terms. On the contrary, one must make a radical leap to a commitment to something that is objectively uncertain in order to pass from ethical to religious existence.

It was therefore necessary to counter the contention that Christianity represented a doctrine that could be objectively justified. Kierkegaard suggests that Christianity rests upon presuppositions totally at variance with those he has ascribed to thinkers of the Platonic tradition. Truth is not merely found by looking within as Plato suggested. Truth is not possessed by the individual, but can only be brought to him from the outside, but he must be inwardly changed if he is to be in a position to accept it: "One who gives the learner not only the Truth, but also the condition for understanding, is more than teacher . . . if it is to be done, it must be done by God himself." [21] Faith and reason cannot be reconciled, and either the one or the other must give way. Faith reveals itself when reason is set aside and the individual makes the leap, which God demands. In fact, Kierkegaard says that "faith is itself a miracle."[22] In every case faith demands not only a leap, but a leap into the rationally unthinkable that presupposes divine assistance. His references to the miraculous character of religious faith render it totally incommensurable with all accepted forms of human cognition. Reason has limits and is thus unable to access the infinite.

In *Concluding Unscientific Postscript*, he undertakes a sustained and comprehensive critique specifically addressed to the implications of Hegelian theory. He rejects Hegel's idealism that reality could be rendered wholly transparent to human reason and holds that Hegel's position that thought was logically prior to existence reverses the true order. For Kierkegaard, Hegel's procedure involves inverting the relation of thought to reality, including human beings as part of that reality. Existence has been absorbed within thought, the contingent reduced to the necessary, the individual subordinated to the universal. It is subjectivity that Christianity is concerned with, and it is only in subjectivity that its truth exists, if it exists at all; objectively, Christianity has absolutely no existence.[23] Like left Hegelianism and Marxism, Kierkegaard's existential philosophy has been characterized as a reaction of the philosophy of man against the excesses of the philosophy of ideas and the philosophy of things.

Kierkegaard is concerned with people themselves, as opposed to the rest of nature, as responsible and self-determining participants in the existential process. It is central to his vision of the human condition that human beings should lead their lives in a way that requires them to be continuously attentive to their ultimate worth and destiny as individual persons. Christian belief demands acceptance of what is from a rational standpoint uncertain and even absurd. In Christian faith, inwardness is intensified to the utmost degree, and, as such, it can be said to constitute the highest passion in the sphere of human subjectivity.[24] Subjectivity, according to Kierkegaard, is the truth. He is thus unfailingly insistent upon the unique character of the subjective acceptance of Christianity. He assumes that human nature is so structured that an individual can only free himself from despair and fulfill his fundamental aspirations as a person by embracing the Christian message.[25]

Besides offering a criticism of rationalism, Kierkegaard also speaks out against contemporary life in Europe, arguing that his age is essentially one of understanding and reflection, but is also one without passion. The modern age also has too much thought and deliberation, but not enough action. People are not strong or passionate enough to pull themselves away from reflection:

> A revolutionary age is an age of action; ours is the age of advertisement and publicity. Nothing ever happens but there is immediate publicity everywhere. In the present age a rebellion is, of all things, the most unthinkable.[26]

Such an expression of strength would, in Kierkegaard's eyes, seem ridiculous to the calculating thought of his time, according to which one is not satisfied with doing something or action, but each wants to reflect and flatter themselves with the illusion that they discovered some new truth.[27]

Existence requires more than reflection; we must lead and take decisive action. Kierkegaard says that in the past men stood or fell by their actions, but in modernity, everyone idles about and reflects. For, being without passion, the present world has lost all feeling for the values of Eros, for enthusiasm and sincerity in politics and religion, or for piety, administration, and domesticity in everyday life.[28] An age without passion is an age without values; everything is transformed into representational ideas. As long as people merely search for money and profit, there is little originality. In the end, therefore, money will be the one thing people will desire, which is moreover only representation, an abstraction.[29] People hardly ever envy the natural gifts of others, but only envy money. In a way, Kierkegaard is expanding on some of the problems with modern life in civil society.

Apparently, for Kierkegaard, too much thinking can be dangerous: ". . . one thing, however, is certain, an increased power of reflection like an increased knowledge only adds to man's affliction."[30] In modern Europe, he thinks that this pitfall is nearly impossible to escape. Reflection curbs the passion to act, and empties everything of significance. No one is any longer carried away by the desire for the good to perform great things. This reflective tension ultimately constitutes itself into a principle, and just as in a passionate age enthusiasm is the unifying principle, so in an age that is very reflective and passionless any envy is the negative unifying principle.[31] This envy in reflection prevents the individual from making a decision passionately, and the envy imprisons man's will and strength. In the age of reflection, people are imprisoned by it and not by tyrants, priests, or secret police. It is a fundamental truth of human nature that man is incapable of remaining permanently on the heights, of continuing to admire anything.[32] Human nature needs variety.

Kierkegaard's attitude toward his own age also affects his relationship to Hegel's philosophy. He sees it as representative of the leveling of individual existence in the universality of the historical world, of the "dispersion" of man in the world process.[33] Kierkegaard then moves to some criticisms of the mass of people that has significant implications for democracy. People resent those with power or those who are perceived to be their betters. When this resentment permeates politics it establishes itself as a process of leveling, which stifles and hinders all actions. This leveling process leads to an abstract power that establishes the victory of abstraction over the individual. In the present age, this tends toward equality. Kierkegaard is responding to the way in which the individual is threatened by equality: It must be obvious to every one that the profound significance of the leveling process lies in the fact that it means the predominance of the category "generation" over the category "individuality."[34] Leveling is the destruction of the individual.

The problem is exacerbated by the fact that no single individual, even one of outstanding leadership potential, will be able to arrest the abstract process of leveling. Kierkegaard sees this leveling process as likely to continue. Individuals can resist it by drawing from internal religious courage, which springs from his individual religious isolation. Leveling can also be accomplished by one particular caste, e.g., the clergy, the bourgeois, the peasants, by the people themselves.[35] He says that in order for everything to be reduced to the same level, it is first necessary to procure a phantom, which is a monstrous abstraction that embraces all. This phantom, according to Kierkegaard, is the public: "The public is, in fact, the real 'Leveling Master' rather than the actual leveler, for whatever leveling is only approximately accomplished it is done by something, but the public is a monstrous nothing."[36] The public is an abstraction consisting of unreal individuals who are never united in an actual situation, yet they are held together in a whole. In cannot be represented because it is an abstraction. People are absorbed into the mass of public opinion, and individuality is lost. It is easy and nonthreatening, since the public is only an abstraction and possess no threat. Made up of individuals at the moments when they are nothing, the public is a kind of gigantic something, an abstract and deserted void that is everything and nothing.[37] The illusion is that the public is greater than a king above his people. Another illusion is that the public stands for, or consists of, the individual will. Rather, it is against individualism. Mass society, according to Kierkegaard, levels every one to the lowest common denominator.

Kierkegaard claims that individual responsibility can be lost when succumbing to the public will. Following the public will enables us to avoid all personal responsibility. It is only after the individual has acquired an ethical outlook, in face of the whole world, that there can be any suggestion of really joining together.[38] Life's existential tasks have lost their connection with reality. From now on the great individuals or great leader will be without authority because he or she will not be recognized or understood. The leveling process renders these potential great leaders unrecognizable. Numerical equality among people has rid modern life of the individual and everything organic and concrete. For this reason, Kierkegaard's existentialism is quite hostile to both equality and modern democracy. Although there are some very important differences, Nietzsche's political thought shares this criticism of democratic politics in the mass society. The two agree that modern life has essentially killed the individual.

## FRIEDRICH NIETZSCHE AND THE CRITICISM OF METAPHYSICS

Like Kierkegaard, Friedrich Nietzsche (1844–1900) scorns the idea of a philosophical system. In fact, Nietzsche opposes the concept of truth that has run through the Western philosophical tradition since its beginning. Philosophy up to and through Hegel presupposes that there is a single truth that can be known through a neutral perspective. Nietzsche rejects the idea of a neutral philosophical perspective. Hegel, for Nietzsche, represents the model of what we should not do if we wish to philosophize.[39] Human beings are motivated by power as subjectivity. That is, they strive to experience themselves as agents, beings who determine their future. Although there are many dimensions to politics, it is partly about the abilities of people to choose and make a difference—in other words, it is about people as political agents.[40] Human beings see themselves as agents of historical change and therefore as experiencing the self as contributing to the transformation of the past. Nietzsche sees the nihilism of nineteenth-century Europe as the result of a loss of identity of mankind as political agents. The contemporary human condition, as Nietzsche describes it, is one of estrangement.

Like Kierkegaard, Nietzsche holds that human beings have the responsibility to create meaning for their world. Thus, genuine philosophers have a creative function. A philosopher is not someone who analyzes values, but rather is someone who creates them.[41] The true philosopher is the legislator who determines the tasks and the essential goals of human reason. Therefore, the philosopher is not someone like Hegel who scrutinizes the past. Rather, Nietzsche asserts that all the sciences have from now on to prepare the way for the future task of the philosophers, which is the solution to the problem of values and the order of rank among values.[42] Values exist only because human beings posit them: Whatever has value in our world now does not have value in itself, according to its nature, but has been given value at some time by human beings.[43]

Nietzsche is definitely not an advocate of equality, however. Human beings are not equal by nature nor should they possess equal political rights. In fact, he repeatedly maintains that he is not writing for the many but for the few:

> It is important that as few people as possible should think about morality; hence it is very important that morality should not one day become interesting. . . . None of these ponderous herd animals with their unquiet consciences . . . wants to know or even sense that "the general welfare" is no ideal, no goal, no remotely intelligible concept . . . ; in short, that there is an order of rank between man and man, hence also between morality and morality.[44]

The act of self-creation is devoid of egalitarian implications. Furthermore, there are times when the course of action is at the expense of the many: "What serves the higher type of men as nourishment or delectation must almost be poison for a very different and inferior type."[45]

Due to the inherent inequality of human beings, Nietzsche's social theory lends itself to charges of elitism. Since the vast bulk of humanity is incapable of decisive action, it is up to the few who are strong and bold enough to take control and reshape the human condition. In fact, it seems that the important variable of human nature is strength for Nietzsche. Only the few are capable of leading in any meaningful fashion, the rest can only follow. His philosophy is a call to challenge the depreciation of all striving in contemporary mass society. To a significant extent, he sees the contemporary crisis as one of leadership: Modern culture is drifting aimlessly along without any real direction. Old values no longer work in today's world. His project consists in instilling a passion for greatness in a world without gods.[46] Nietzsche presents a new kind of strength, one that would be capable of establishing a golden age of order and growth. The *Übermensch* is Nietzsche's term for this heroic elite, and has been translated into English as superman, overman, and higher man. These actors are the only ones with the strength to break the stranglehold of nihilism.

Like Kierkegaard, Nietzsche rejects the notion that human society should place its faith and hope in increased rationalization. The solution to mankind's problems cannot be found in systems of thought that are seen as carriers of objective truth. Nietzsche also dismisses the claim that any system of thought can rest upon proven propositions. He was convinced that the subtleties of rationalism and the discoveries of scientific research never really touch upon truth. Men take particular world views, which essentially rest upon unproven assumptions, and turn them into convictions that are then seen as valid:

> Against positivism, which halts at phenomena—"There are only facts"—I would say: No, facts is precisely what there is not, only interpretations. We cannot establish any fact "in itself. . . ." In so far as the word "knowledge" has any meaning, the world is knowable; but it is interpretable otherwise, it has no meaning behind it, but countless meanings.—"Perspectivism."[47]

Truth, for Nietzsche, is the creative commitment that actively determines the world. In brief, truth is personal and highly subjective. Nietzsche asserts that since Socrates, Western philosophy has excluded every aspect of man except reason from the truth-finding process, which is a fatal mistake.

From its very beginning, Western philosophy has been driven by a "will to truth."[48] Nietzsche believes that the question of the value of truth necessarily originates in this will to truth. Human beings pursue truth because they find it useful to their purposes. The traditional ideal of knowledge, according to Nietzsche, assumes that at least in principle everything that is can be known. However, knowledge involves, for Nietzsche, an inherently conditional relation to its object, a relation that presupposes or manifests specific values, interests, and goals.[49] Mankind cannot contemplate knowledge without interests. Rejecting ideas such as "absolute knowledge," "pure reason," and "absolute intelligence," Nietzsche asserts that:

> All these concepts presuppose an eye such as no living being can imagine, an eye required to have no direction, to abrogate its active and interpretative powers—precisely those powers that alone make of seeing, seeing something. All seeing is essentially perspective, and so is all knowing. The more emotions we allow to speak in a given matter, the more different eyes we can put on it order to view a given spectacle, the more complete will be our conception of it, the greater our "objectivity." But to eliminate the will, to suspend the emotions altogether, provided it could be done—surely this would be to castrate the intellect, would it not?[50]

These different eyes could never produce a single unified picture. Perspectivism implies that there can be no total or final theory or understanding of the world. Objectivity is merely nothing but an extension of subjectivity. Because they are used to construct societies, Nietzsche recognizes the importance of these attempts at truth and knowledge. In short, an interpretation is nothing short of a table of values, by which one's very life is guided and even constituted.[51] Nietzsche calls social views and practices interpretations because he believes that every view of the world makes possible and promotes a particular kind of life, and thus presupposes and manifests specific interests and values. By calling them interpretations, he is asserting that they are neither detached nor disinterested, nor are they objective in the usual sense.

In modern society, consciousness takes an anti-individualistic turn. Like Kierkegaard, Nietzsche believes that social consciousness leads to a herd existence, and tries to shape individual experience into common knowledge. Western society has attempted to turn the individual's monopoly of experience into communicable knowledge:

> My idea is, as you see, that consciousness does not really belong to man's individual existence but rather to his social or herd nature; that, as follows from this, it has developed subtlety only insofar as this is required by social or herd utility. Consequently, given the best will in the world to understand ourselves as individually as possible, "to know ourselves," each of us will always succeed in becoming conscious only of what is not individual but "average.". . . Fundamentally, all our actions are altogether incomparably personal, unique, and infinitely individual; there is no doubt of that. But as soon as we translate them into consciousness they no longer seem to be.[52]

Communication, or making common what is individually experienced, for Nietzsche, inevitably involves a falsification. Experiences are communicated, but at the cost of robbing them of their essential uniqueness. Society is not composed of individuals but members.

The individual, as Nietzsche sees it, is his or her own law and therefore unpredictable and unmanageable. Society, on the other hand, requires rules, conventions, and morality so that human beings can be made uniform and calculable. Law and morality are employed as social straitjackets in order to prevent people from becoming individuals. Thus, the price of social membership is forfeiture of self-rule thorough the establishment of social norms:

> . . . and so we continue on with custom and morality: which latter is nothing other than simply a feeling for the whole content of those customs under which we live and have been raised—and raised, indeed, not as an individual, but as a member of the whole, as a cipher in a majority.—So it comes about that through his morality the individual outvotes himself.[53]

Hence, the individual plays an active part in his own socialization and the end of self-rule. Man is a herd animal and has an internal drive toward conformity: "Morality is the herd instinct in the individual."[54] Morality, according to Nietzsche, trains the individual to be a function of the herd and to ascribe value to himself only as that function.

Contrary to liberal thinkers who see the development of the autonomous individual, Nietzsche finds modern man to be not a personality, but merely an isolate. The modern individual represents all atoms against the communality, and instinctively sets himself up with other atoms.[55] What the individual fights, he fights not as a personality but as the representative of atoms against the whole. In *Schopenhauer as Educator*, Nietzsche writes: "we live in the age of atoms, of atomistic chaos."[56] The modern state represents the demands and the rule of the herd:

> There are still peoples and herds somewhere, but not with us my brother: here there are states. The State? What is that? Well then! Now open your ears, for now I shall speak to you of the death of peoples. The state is the coldest of all cold monsters. . . . Where a people still exists, there the people do not understand the state and hate it as the evil eye and sin against custom and law.[57]

The Nietzsche's conception of the modern state is far from that of Hegel and seems to represent the herd-nature of mankind, and the same time it is a manifestation of human weakness. Nietzsche says that only true individuals are responsible: Multiplicities are invented in order to do things for which most individuals lack the courage.[58] Most of mankind follows the herd and is too weak to break out on its own. Society's law and norms reinforce this. In such a society, truly being an individual is an existential plight.

The nihilism confronting European culture is supported and maintained by the herd, according to Nietzsche. In this situation anything that the individual of strength does is immoral by herd standards. Individualistic valuations and actions are thus the antitheses of those coming from any moral system. Like Hegel, Nietzsche strongly rejects any conception of Kantian morality with universalizable maxims. The merit of any deed must be determined on a strictly individualistic basis: "That your Self be in the action, as the mother is in the child: let that be your maxim of virtue!"[59] Actions performed out of a sense of duty or respect for the law are merely pseudonyms for herd instinct. For Nietzsche, virtue must be an individual invention: "And so should each in his own manner do his best for himself—that is my moral:—the only one that still remains for me."[60] In the Nietzschean sense, an individual is one with the strength and mind to go against the herd. Only the heroic individual is capable of resisting this enslavement to his own habits, and for Nietzsche the truly heroic individual is extremely rare.

Nietzsche places all life in one of two camps: ascending or declining. The ascending camp is one of a growing affirmation of life, while the descending is decadent and resentful. Ascending, growing, and affirmative life is known as "Dionysian."[61] Of course since all life entails suffering and strife, the Dionysian individual affirms life in spite of suffering:

> Every art, every philosophy may be viewed as remedy and an aid in the service of growing struggling life; they always presuppose suffering and sufferers. But there are two kinds of sufferers: first, those who suffer from the over-fullness of life—they want a Dionysian art and likewise a tragic view of life, a tragic insight—and then those who suffer from the impoverishment of life and seek rest, stillness, calm seas. . . . He that is richest in the fullness of life, the Dionysian god and man, cannot only afford the sight of the terrible and questionable but even the terrible deed and any luxury of destruction, decomposition, and negation.[62]

Hence, the Dionysian individual lives in the same world as the decadent herd, but this individual is strong enough to transform the meaningless of life whereas the herd is not. Since the chief threats to individuality are timidity and laziness, the strength and boldness allows the Dionysian individual to escape the mediocrity of the herd.

Life and action, according to Nietzsche, require illusion in order to give meaning to chaos. By rejecting the rationalism of Western metaphysics, he is asserting that there can be no justification in the nature of things. If contemporary society is to pass through the chaos, like the ancient Greeks did, Dionysian individuals are needed to create new meaning. For Nietzsche, Socrates and Euripides remove values from the immediacy of experience, absolutize them, and tend to endow conclusions with validity independently of the social and historical situations that give rise to them. In his attempt to bring order to the political and moral chaos of Greece, Socrates finds it necessary to establish a science of ethics:

> Against this practical pessimism, Socrates represents the archtype of the theoretical optimist, who, strong in the belief that nature can be fathomed, considers knowledge to be the true panacea and error to be radical evil. . . . So it happened that ever since Socrates the mechanism of concepts, judgments, and syllogisms has come to be regarded as the highest exercise of man's powers, nature's most admirable gift. Socrates and his successors, down to our own day, have considered all moral and sentimental accomplishments . . . to be ultimately derived from the dialectic of knowledge, and therefore teachable.[63]

Socrates' success has been at the expense of the heroic individual. Since then Western metaphysics contends that the intellectual and moral skills needed to counter chaos can be taught.

Socrates' choice of the rational dialectic method, as Nietzsche sees it, set in motion the processes that eventually led to contemporary nihilism. Socratic logic is the constant pursuit of a goal that can never be reached. Prior to Socrates, the old foundation of Greek culture and state had been mythological rather than rational. Nietzsche maintains that the Greeks were involuntarily impelled to relate all their experiences immediately to myths that necessarily informed all their actions:

> Yet every culture that has lost myth has lost, by the same token, its natural, healthy creativity. Only a horizon ringed about with myths can unify a culture. . . . Here we have our present age, the result of a Socratism bent on the extermination of myth. Man today, stripped of myth, stands famished among all his pasts and must dig frantically for roots, be it among the most remote antiquities.[64]

Human beings need to break the hold of the past, and they do so by creating myths and holding on to an illusion, which allows the foundations of the time and culture to escape from the past. Contemporary European culture is caught in a past that has long since failed to work. The Nietzschean individual must break the hold and crush the existing morality.

In one of his most famous, and infamous, statements, Nietzsche proclaims that: "God is dead."[65] His philosophical enterprise, to a significant extent, is devoted to coming to terms with and transcending this important event. The death of God establishes the challenge of creating new meaning for the modern world. When Nietzsche declares that God is dead, he means that the belief in the Christian God has become unbelievable and it is already casting its shadow over Europe.[66] In other words, the entire European morality must now fall because it was built upon this belief in God. Nihilism, for Nietzsche, is loss of values. It means that not only are all theological faiths dead but that the various metaphysical faiths that have served as surrogates since antiquity as well. This includes the faith in science since he sees a metaphysical faith underlying the faith in science:

> Strictly speaking, there is no such thing as a science without assumptions; the very notion of such a science is unthinkable, absurd. A philosophy, a "faith" is always needed to give science a direction, a meaning, a limit. . . . The faith on which our belief in science rests is still a metaphysical faith.[67]

Thus, science alone leads into the abyss; it can destroy values, but it can neither create them nor tell human beings how they are to live. Put differently, science cannot assume the mantle of the religion that it has destroyed. In the broadest sense, the death of God means more than the demise of all absolutes and all ultimate sources of authority; it means the demise of faith in the possibility of absolutes.[68] The death of God is thus intrinsically connected with the advent of Western nihilism.

Since the highest values of society devaluate themselves, they no longer function. The decline of these values is the collapse of all prior truth concerning human existence. This, for Nietzsche, is the fundamental event of Western history. With the death of God and the absence of transcendent values, the creation of values assumes an unmatched urgency:

> What I relate is the history of the next two centuries. I describe what is coming, what can no longer come differently: the advent of nihilism. . . . For some time now, our whole European culture has been moving as toward a catastrophe, with a tortured tension that is growing from decade to decade. . . . Because the values we have had hitherto thus draw their final consequence; because nihilism represents the ultimate logical conclusion of our great values and ideals—because we must experience nihilism before we can find out what value these "values' really had.[69]

Without deities, nihilistic human beings lack any ideal for which they may strive. This is a stern warning: If nihilism is not to destroy life, human beings must be capable of setting new goals and determining new values and meaning for life.

Nietzsche considers the Christian Church the mortal foe of everything noble on earth. For him, it stands for a slave or herd morality, and it fights all human greatness by representing the weak and sick through fraud. The commandments of Christian morality, for example, are categorical, universal, non-reflexive, and external to willing. Although Christianity holds individuals responsible for their acts, it subverts the possibility of responsible agency by holding individuals to universal and categorical maxims of behavior that proscribe their conduct. Christian morality externally regulates behavior through promises of salvation and threats of damnation. While Christian doctrine asserts that individuals are endowed with free will and moral responsibility, it simultaneously denies them an understanding of the worldly conditions of agency, and thus undermines the worldly possibility of moral agency.[70] Instead, it uses the doctrine of free will to constrain the individual's sense of agency to a system of spiritual rewards and punishments. Christianity, for Nietzsche, instills a reflexive examination of one's motives, but it does so in such a way that the self is externalized from and defined against worldly experiences. Hence, Nietzsche sees Christian morality as slave morality that trains the individual to be a function of the herd and ascribe value to oneself only as a function.[71] Christianity denies the possibility of a worldly self by constructing a transcendental self tied to correct behavior. With the fate of mankind hanging in the balance, it is necessary for Nietzschean individuals to go boldly beyond conventional standards of good and evil and create new values.

Since Western thought has destroyed the faith in God and the values based upon this belief, a void remains. Nietzsche sees the agony, the suffering, and the misery of a godless world so intensely where others were yet blind to its tremendous consequences:

> Nietzsche was more deeply impressed than almost any other man before him by the manner in which the belief in God and a divine teleology may diminish the values and significance of man: how this world and life may be completely devaluated *ad maiorem dei gloriam*. . . . To escape nihilism—which seems involved both in asserting the existence, and also in denying God and thus robbing everything of meaning and value—that is Nietzsche's greatest and most persistent problem.[72]

Instead of rationalizing current valuations and accepted truths, he offers a critique and prepares the ground for the creation of new values in order to fill the void. If Nietzsche is the prophet of nihilism, it is not in the sense of proclaiming its arrival as something to be celebrated, but in the sense of warning mankind of the accelerating decline of Western society. Nihilism, however, must first be experienced in order to comprehend the need for new values. His political message is that the time is now at hand to go boldly beyond good and evil.

## HEGEL'S CRITIQUE OF MODERN METAPHYSICS

Nietzsche's philosophy represents a revolution in Western thought. In fact, he is typically seen as one of Hegel's most radical critics. Gilles Deleuze asserts that Nietzsche saw Hegel as the primary target of his philosophical assault on nihilism.[73] However, it is necessary to remember that Feuerbach, Marx, and Kierkegaard also each argued that Hegel's philosophy ignored the real, empirical world. This section is intended to redeem Hegel against charges that his philosophy lacks a concrete basis. To this end, it considers Hegel's criticisms of modern metaphysics in order to illustrate that many of the charges brought forth by Feuerbach, Marx, Kierkegaard, and Nietzsche are not based on an accurate understanding of Hegel's philosophy. Nietzsche's philosophical, postmodern descendents and their criticisms of Hegel are addressed in the next chapter. Hegel is a systematic philosopher who places his faith in the rigorous and methodical unfolding of dialectical reason, while Nietzsche is an unsystematic, highly literary writer who uses isolated perceptions and colorful metaphors to make his point. However, the two philosophers share an important common aim: Bringing an end to a previous metaphysics and initiating a radically new way of thinking.[74] Both thinkers criticize traditional modes of thought. In his later writings, Nietzsche comes to appreciate Hegel's concern with historical change and development as a possible antidote to static essentialism; this is especially true of Hegel's emphasis on historical and social contradictions as a possible gateway to insight into the contradictory character of all things.[75]

Deleuze thinks that Nietzsche is a powerful critic of the Hegelian dialectic. His view is shaped by the belief that Nietzsche knew Hegel's texts well and exposes the "life-denying" mentality of Hegel's philosophy.[76] However, as Stephen Houlgate argues, Nietzsche did not study Hegel's texts in any depth and relied mainly on secondary sources for his interpretation and evaluation of Hegel's thought:

> Although of course it is difficult to prove that Nietzsche did not study Hegel in depth, nothing in his work suggests that he accorded more than cursory attention to Hegel's texts. Nor, *pace* Deleuze, can we assume that Nietzsche was well acquainted with the works of Hegel's immediate successors either, expect perhaps Feuerbach and D. F. Strauss. . . . It seems, therefore, that Nietzsche's understanding of Hegel was not founded on a close study of either Hegel or of the works of those who might most obviously be expected to have known Hegel's philosophy well, but it was derived rather from other secondary sources.[77]

Houlgate concludes that the major sources of Nietzsche's ideas about Hegel are likely to have been Arthur Schopenhauer's writings, lectures by Jakob Burckhardt, and Friedrich Lange's *The History of Materialism*. Schopenhauer's influence seems to be most pronounced, especially during Nietzsche's early years. For Schopenhauer, Hegel is guilty of naïve optimism because he constructs an overall plan of a purposeful development for history. In fact, history reveals the never-changing self-will of man and the actions and sufferings of man that follow from that will.[78] Schopenhauer therefore charges Hegel with serving the ignoble ends of the state rather than the interests of philosophical truth.

Agreeing with Schopenhauer, Nietzsche also charges Hegel with false historical optimism and the deification of the state. The problem, for Nietzsche, is that Hegel's philosophy encourages an attitude of uncritical acceptance of historical necessity by arguing that whatever occurs in history is determined by an all-powerful, rational Idea. In other words, Nietzsche thinks that Hegel's *Doppelsatz* transforms "what is" into "what must be." He charges Hegel's philosophy with being hostile to independent, critical thought. As we see in this chapter's introduction, Hegel does not merely endorse the status quo as such, and, contrary to appearances, the *Doppelsatz* does not mean that everything that exists is rational. Nor does it mean that things are rational simply because they exist. In fact, Hegel explicitly denies that everything that exists is rational. Things are rational only to the extent that they fulfill their essence in reality. As Hans-Georg Gadamer observes: "I think Hegel's statement, 'What is rational is real, and what is real is rational,' articulates a task for each individual rather than a legitimation for the inactivity of us all."[79]

Contrary to Feuerbach's, Marx's, Kierkegaard's, and Nietzsche's criticisms, Hegel does not ignore the real world of existing human beings. In fact, he urges that philosophy's task is to understand and explain existing reality. As illustrated in Chapter 2, he does not see *Geist* only as the essential reality behind empirical phenomena, but rather as the rational self consciousness of man. However, it is true that Hegel believes the world to have a rational structure, and Nietzsche's opposition to this belief distinguishes Hegel's "this-worldly" ontology from Nietzsche's.[80] Hegel's dialectical conception of categories does justice to the dynamism of life. In their complex dialectical conception, Hegel's categories are capable acquiring philosophical knowledge of the world. With the *Phenomenology of Spirit*, Hegel clearly illustrates that man is a self-conscious being that is informed by the dynamic structure of self-consciousness. Like Nietzsche, Hegel criticizes metaphysics for operating with fixed categories and oppositions that serve as the foundation for thought. Hegel agrees with some of the empiricist criticisms of metaphysics. Since the foundations of metaphysical knowledge are the products of a priori thought, empiricists object that they are not firm enough and ultimately lack concrete determinations; consequently, empiricists try to place knowledge on a firmer base by replacing the presupposed objects and axioms of philosophy with the immediacy of sense-experience.[81] In this way, empiricism claims to found knowledge on presuppositions that are concrete in themselves. Feuerbach, Marx, Kierkegaard, and Nietzsche each charge Hegel with ignoring existing reality. Consequently, it is necessary to examine Hegel's position on empiricism more carefully in order to determine the validity of this charge.

Hegel sees Francis Bacon as one of the first thinkers to react against the metaphysical manner of deducing the nature of reality from rational principles. Against the Scholastic a priori anticipation of nature, Bacon emphasizes the importance of empirical explanations and thus directs attention to empirically given experience.[82] For Hegel, empiricism is a remedy for a deficiency of metaphysics:

> In Empiricism lies the great principle that whatever is true must be in the actual world and present to sensation. This principle contradicts what 'ought to be' on the strength of which 'reflection' is vain enough to treat the actual present with scorn and to the point to a scene beyond—a scene which is assumed to have place and being only in the understanding of those who talk of it. . . . For the

main lesson of Empiricism is that man must see for himself and feel that he is present in every fact of knowledge which he has to accept.[83]

The empirical principle is necessary for the development of true philosophical knowledge. Indeed, this principle has enabled Hegel's speculative philosophy to progress beyond metaphysics. Although speculative philosophy does not derive all its ideas from sense-perception, it shares empiricism's concern for the immediacy and dynamic life of thought and concern for the manner in which reason is manifested in the empirical world.[84] In contrast with metaphysics and no less than empiricism, Hegel's philosophy recognizes only "what is."[85] Hegel's speculative philosophy argues that although fundamental conceptual determinations about the natural and human world can be derived from reason, the development of reason must be based on the rational reconstruction of empirical experience. Contrary to the charges of his critics, Hegel does pay close attention to the real world. Herbert Marcuse notes that Hegel's most abstract and metaphysical concepts are saturated with experience. Marcuse further says: "The negation which applies to them is not only a critique of a conformistic logic, which denies the reality of contradictions, it is also a critique of the given state of affairs on its own grounds—of the established system of life."[86]

For Hegel, empiricism is an essential condition of the Idea reaching its full development. However, empiricism is not yet speculative philosophy, since what is present to empirical consciousness is still a relatively simple sensuous immediacy that does not reflect reality's dialectic character.[87] While empiricism claims to base knowledge on sensuous perceptions, it also tries to transform its sensuous perceptions into thoughts through a process that Hegel refers to as analysis. It attempts to abstract different empirical qualities from perceived objects and translate them into pure conceptual determination. "Yet analysis is the process from the immediacy of sensation to thought; those attributes, which the object analyzed contains in union, acquire the form of universality by being separated."[88] Since analysis leads to thought-determinations, Hegel thinks that empiricism shares the conviction that the truth of things lies in thought. Like metaphysics, empiricism differentiates between objects and consciousness and holds that objects are known in terms of determinations of consciousness. Nevertheless, empiricism is an important advance over metaphysics because its analysis proceeds from what is concretely given.

For Hegel, John Locke most clearly exemplifies this type of metaphysical empiricism.[89] Locke starts from sense-experience and observation and then derives thought-determinations from it. Hegel credits Locke with solving the problem of the origin and legitimization of philosophical concepts and ideas. In Locke's view, all concepts are empirical in origin. Even though Hegel sees the value of Locke's attempt to derive concepts from concrete experience, he is critical of the residual of positivism in Locke's method. Empiricism considers ideas to be positive determinations abstracted or separated out from external things by an external process of comparing, distinguishing, and contrasting.[90] Sense-objects are therefore conceived as the standard of concreteness that legitimize all thought-determinations. For Hegel, the important difference between a priori metaphysics and a posteriori empiricism resides in the nature of the foundation on which knowledge is held to rest. While a priori metaphysics presupposes that the content is infinite and *noumenal*, empiricism's presuppositions are finite and sensuous. "To this extent, both modes of philosophizing have the same method; both proceed from data or assumptions, which they accept as ultimate."[91] Since it still operated with the same categories as metaphysics, empiricism did not change the philosophical method enough.

Empiricism cannot provide the warrant for scientific laws as hoped for by the empiricists. Sense-experience lacks the universals needed to ground thought-determinations. Hegel says that David Hume is the first to draw attention to the impossibility of legitimizing determinations empirically. Although Hume begins from the position of Bacon and Locke, his achievement lay in drawing what Hegel sees as the logical conclusion from the empiricist position:

> Here Hume really completed the system of Locke, since he consistently drew attention to the fact that if this point of view be adhered to, experience is indeed the principle of whatever one knows, or perception itself contains everything that happens, but nevertheless the determination of universality and necessity are not contained in, nor were they given use by experience. Hume has thus destroyed the objectivity or absolute nature of thought-determination.[92]

Given that empiricism holds that sensuous perception lacks the determinations of rational necessity and universality, by definition those determinations cannot be justified by being derived from perception. Thus, Hume concludes that the most we can do is to habitually treat the connections observed in experience as necessary and universal, even though they cannot be established as intrinsically necessary or universal. Hegel agrees with Hume that no explicit universal and necessary determinations are found in particular, immediate perceptions. In contrast to Hume, Hegel does not treat sensuous perception as the ultimate foundation of all thought about the world, but only as the source of contingent, empirical conceptions.[93] Hegel does claim that reason can determine intrinsic, necessary relations between phenomena in experience. Just because empirical perception cannot itself provide insight into intrinsic rational connections in experience, unlike Hume, Hegel does not conclude that reason cannot establish such connections in experience.

According to Hegel, Kant's critical philosophy arises out of Hume's skepticism. Kant begins with Hume's contention that necessary, universal thought-determination cannot be legitimized by sense-perception. Unlike Hume, Kant cannot accept the position that the concept of necessity is merely the product of habit. Kant's answer to the problem regarding the legitimacy of judgments on causal connection is that they are not derived from the empirical sphere but belong to the spontaneity of thought; in other words, it is a priori.[94] Since necessity is the a priori product of thought and is not abstracted from sense-perception, it should be seen as a subjective necessity. For Kant, conceptual categories have legitimate application only within the sphere of objects as they appear to the mind. There is no transcendent ontological application to the things themselves. In contrast to empiricism, Kant locates authority within thought itself. We do not simply accept what is given to us by perception. Rather we are active, rational beings who understand what we perceive in terms of concepts and categories that our own thought supplies. However, he does simply return to metaphysics, since the rational critique of metaphysical categories is the primary task of philosophy. For Hegel, Kant's great achievement is to recognize that the problem with metaphysics is not just its lack of empirical foundations, but is in the inadequacy of the limited categories that it employs to understand reality:

> A very important step was undoubtedly made, when the terms of the old metaphysics were subjected to scrutiny. The plain thinker pursued his unsuspecting way in those categories which had offered themselves naturally. It never occurred to him to ask to what extent these categories had a value and authority of their own. . . . They accepted their categories as they were, without further trouble, as an *a priori* datum, not yet tested by reflection. The Critical Philosophy reversed this, Kant undertook to examine how far the forms of thought were capable of leading to the knowledge of truth.[95]

Because forms of thought themselves must be made the object of knowledge, Hegel holds that this is the correct thing to do.

Nevertheless, Hegel also thinks that Kant's categorical critique of metaphysics is imperfect. Kant argues that the categories of understanding are inadequate to the knowledge of realty because they are generated by the mind and thus subjective. Categories give the multiplicity of sense-perceptions a consistency and objectivity that they otherwise lack. In Kant's account, this objectivity is still subjective, since it only pertains to reality as senses perceive it and not as reality is in itself. In contrast to Kant, Hegel believes that thought can articulate the structure of reality itself. While he agrees with Kant that necessary, categorical connections are not explicitly present in perception but are generated by reason, Hegel does not agree that these categorical connections are merely for us and not also the logical forms inherent in the real world.[96] Hegel holds that the world that our senses perceive is in itself structured according to the logical principles with which we operate. Sense-perception, in Hegel's view, is an imperfect knowledge of reality and thus lacks explicitly universal, rational determinations and cannot provide a reliable foundation for rational thought. The logical character of reality is only revealed in thoughts made explicit and produced by the mind. Thus, the categories do not confine human beings within the alleged limits of human experience. Instead, they equip people to see and understand "what is." Like Kant, Hegel believes that human beings bring categories to bear on the world of perception. Unlike Kant, he maintains that those categories make genuine knowledge of the world possible and do not merely bring order to limited human experience. Because their minds are conceptually prepared for the truth of things, human beings can gain access to that truth.

Hegel also thinks that Kant only drew the negative conclusion from the antinomies that the categories of formal logic are not applicable to reality in itself.[97] Kant fails to draw the positive conclusion that reality is contradictory in itself:

> The true and positive meaning of the antinomies is thus: that every actual thing involves a coexistence of opposed elements. Consequently, to know, or, in other words, to comprehend an object is equivalent to being conscious of it as a concrete unity of opposed determinations.[98]

With the exclusion of contradiction and negation from his concept of reality, Kant employs the metaphysician's concept of identity in order to conceive reality. Kant's critique ultimately fails to satisfy Hegel because it removes forms of thought from reality, increasing the separation between thought and reality. Hegel avoids this by undertaking an immanent critique of the categories of metaphysics, a critique in which the categories must examine themselves, determine their intrinsic limits and show up the defects in their very nature.[99] It is only through such an immanent critique that the true character of the categories can be revealed, since it is only through an immanent critique that thought displays the dialectic which it possesses within itself.[100] As discussed in Chapter 2, Hegel criticizes the one-sided conception of the categories by revealing the dialectical complexity inherent in each category. The categories unite opposing determinations in themselves and are thus developing logical forms. By conceiving of categories in this dialectical way, Hegel reveals the concreteness, "the life-pulse," within reason itself.[101] While categories in their finite, static conception are too abstract and subjective to be adequate to philosophical knowledge, categories in their dialectical conception will be capable of yielding definitive philosophical knowledge of reality. In this way, Hegel conceives of speculative logic as offering the true critique of the abstract categories of metaphysics and as recovering the important conviction, which both Kant and Nietzsche contested in varying ways, that reality can be known determinately in conceptual thought.[102]

Against Kant's transcendental idealism, Hegel rejects the idea that there is a dimension of reality that cannot be comprehended by the categories of thought. Hegel argues that such knowledge can be achieved only by employing the correct categories, which requires understanding the inherent logical structure of thought. Hegel's speculative philosophy is intended to fulfill the task that metaphysics set out to accomplish and failed, to achieve conceptual knowledge of reality. The specific difference between speculative philosophy and metaphysics is that speculative philosophy challenges certain of the basic assumptions on which metaphysics is founded; it challenges the absolute distinctions between categories and the very notion of a foundation to philosophy itself.[103] As illustrated in Chapter 2, Hegel's dialectical method begins by developing concepts of particular areas of the experienced world by deriving pure a priori conceptual determinations immanently from the logical structure of reason. Next, it looks at experience in order to find the particular empirical phenomena that manifest those determinations and provide the contingent details that extend and fill out an understanding of those determinations. Hegel's method combines a straightforward empirical investigation with an a priori dialectical derivation of the fundamental logical determinations that are recognized in the empirical phenomena.[104] Thus, philosophical truth depends on the proper logical derivation of conceptual determinations and the correct identification of the empirical phenomena that correspond to them. Experience can alert the philosopher to possible logical errors, but, for Hegel, only reason itself can demonstrate that the speculative derivation of logical determinations is false.[105]

Hegel's dialectic is a process of conceptual redefinition. A conceptual category is held to have a greater complexity than it initially appeared to and contradictions are revealed within the concept. Consequently, a category's determination is revised in order to articulate better the form of the category. With redefinition, thought advances to new determinations and categories. The sequence of categories in Hegel's dialectic therefore forms a continuous and increasingly complex determination of what thought is:

> It must be admitted that it is an important consideration—one which will be found in more detail in the logic itself—that the advance is a *retreat into the ground*, to what is *primary* and *true*, on which depends and, in fact, from which originates, that with which the beginning is made. . . . The essential requirement for the science of logic is not so much that the beginning be a pure immediacy, but rather that the whole of the science be within itself a circle in which the first is also the last and the last is also the first.[106]

By revealing a contradiction in an initial conception, Hegel's logic demonstrates that thought in its very immediacy is inherently dynamic. As the initial characterization of thought responds to contradiction, it develops a new conceptual determination. For Hegel, the process of logical development is not a series of external reflections, but consists in the deepening and intensification of an initial determination by the dialectic immanent in that determination.[107] Dialectical self-determination continuously redefines the conceptual categories. Thus, for Hegel, thought is self-determining and dialectic, not merely reflective. Furthermore, categories of thought are not fixed, eternal forms that remain unchanged throughout history. Instead, they are concepts that alter their meaning in history. Therefore, while Kant's categories constitute a permanent transcendental framework of knowledge, Hegel's constitute the changing historical precondition of knowledge.

As discussed in the *Phenomenology of Spirit*, the logic of self-consciousness determines that consciousness passes through different levels of development before it reaches full self-awareness and self-determination. Along the way, dialectical rationality gives rise to forms of consciousness that fail to conform to dialectic reason completely. It is essential to recognize that Hegel does not assert that the absolute determinations of reason will guarantee that all aspects of reality will be fully rational. Instead, the determinations of reason will ground multiple forms of existence and determination, and it is up to science and other forms of inquiry to discover, and these forms only manifest a fully dialectical rational character late in the day.[108] Hegel claims that the determinations of dialectical reason are absolute categories of all human thought. However, this does not mean that thought for Hegel is always explicitly and uniformly rational. The logical determinations that Hegel establishes with his dialectical method make possible a wide variety of human responses to experience and do not stifle the openness, freedom, and exploratory tentativeness of consciousness.[109] Although Hegel's dialectical philosophy claims to be the definitive articulation of the general categories in which we operate, it does not preclude caution and self-criticism. It grounds the possibility of caution in experience and establishes its proper character.[110] Since it reveals the intrinsic limits within all modes of consciousness, Hegel's dialectic retains a critical moment.

One of the most important differences between Hegel and Nietzsche is that Nietzsche bases his critique of metaphysics on the distinction between life and thought, while Hegel subjects all distinctions to an immanent, dialectical critique in which the speculative, dialectical character of reason is seen to inhere in the categories and forms of thought themselves. Hegel's philosophy is not metaphysical in the tradition usage of the term:

> Hegel's is a non-metaphysical philosophy because it does not conceive the subject as a foundational entity or as a simple substance in the manner of a Leibnizian monad. The subject for Hegel is constituted in the activity of thinking and

speaking; it is not merely a spiritual 'thing' which underlies that activity. Hegel is not denying that each human subject is a unique individual, conscious of himself as distinct from all other selves, but he is insisting that such unique individuality, and the freedom of self-determination which individuals can enjoy, is itself made possible by social relations and by the public medium of language that constitutes the element of consciousness.[111]

The inherently public, contextual character of consciousness is brought out in the *Phenomenology of Spirit*, where he says that consciousness is "the 'I' that is 'We' and the 'We' that is 'I.'"[112] Like Nietzsche, Hegel rejects the view that there is a subjectivity that transcends the historical specificity of human existence. Hegel's *Phenomenology* studies historical modes of consciousness. As discussed above, it examines and describes these modes of consciousness in their own terms and not against some external standard. The subject does not have other-worldly connotations. It does not reside beyond the historical human activity, but is immanent in human history. Hegel redefines subjectivity as the conscious identity that human beings develop in historical linguistic communities.[113] Thus, subjectivity has an intrinsically dialectical structure, which makes it intersubjective.

Unlike Nietzsche, Hegel does not think that human life need always be dominated by selfish instinctual drives, as he holds that the will can be brought to exhibit an intersubjective character that reconciles conflicting interests and that is not reducible to one will's dominance over another.[114] In several of his works, Nietzsche writes that there are no moral facts, only moral interpretations. In one sense, however, there are moral facts: the facts of the acceptance of certain principles as moral principles within a given social context (Hegel's *Sittlichkeit*).[115] For Hegel, as for Nietzsche, morality does not consist of principles but of practices. As illustrated in Chapter 4, it is doing, not willing, that is of moral significance. Hegel's notion of modern *Sittlichkeit* entails an individuality that is nurtured with regard to shared norms and ethical values, and his conception of *Rechtsstaat* includes an ethical life in which individual and community undergo a reconciliation that preserves the interest and realizes the potential of each only by incorporating the aspirations of the other. For Hegel, a properly conceived conception of community does not pose the threat to individuality that it is thought to by Nietzsche and many other existentialists. Moral autonomy is conceived within the objective relations and institutions of society. Therefore, properly conceived, modernity does provide necessary ethical values and practices. Although Hegel is critical of traditional metaphysics, he does not succumb to moral relativism.

Experience reveals that liberal society cannot hold together simply by the satisfaction of its members' needs and interests, but also requires a common set of beliefs to link its structure and practices with what members see as of ultimate significance.[116] Hegel had insight into some of the perennial, recurring problems of liberalism. For example, the increasing alienation in a society that has eroded its traditional foci of allegiance makes it harder and harder to achieve the basic consensus that is required for a democracy.[117] Hegel notes that participation of all in a decision is only possible if there is a ground of agreement, or of underlying common purpose, but this becomes extremely difficult since the tight unity, say of the Greek *polis*, cannot be recaptured in the modern world that knows the principle of individual freedom. Nevertheless, Hegel resurrects the standpoint of ethical life [*Sittlichkeit*] that was destroyed with modernity. In this way, Hegel opposes the self-enclosed subjectivity of modernity. While Kierkegaard and Nietzsche lament the loss of individuality, Hegel, like Marx, recognizes that modernity's excessive individuality threatens community and can actually increase alienation.

Concerning many of the issues that we confront in the age of globalization, Hegel recognizes that at times economic justice demands that contemporary society must act to ensure that everyone have a sufficient means to earn a livelihood. This implies that at times the state must redistribute wealth through taxation. As illustrated in the previous chapter, fair commodity relations mandate regulation, the economy must be subordinate to justice. However, unlike with Marx, democratic government must not be relegated to the management of the economy. As discussed in Chapter 6, Hegel places civil society under the rule of constitutional self-government. Although Hegel does not explicitly comment on the limits of redistribution, he seems to suggest that whatever is necessary to eliminate social disadvantage is justified to the extent that the freedom of commodity relations are upheld.[118] As argued in Chapter 10, Hegel would not be pleased with the direction taken by the United States over the last couple of decades. Democratic government is being stripped of its ability to regulate the economy responsibly and to protect the public. This tendency harms responsive citizenship in ways that Hegel would find unacceptable. The next chapter examines some of Hegel's more recent critics.

# NOTES

1. Hermann Hesse, *Siddhartha* (New York: Bantam Books, 1951), 143.

2. Tom Rockmore, *Before and After Hegel: A Historical Introduction to Hegel's Thought* (Berkeley: University of California Press, 1993), 144.

3. Richard Dien Winfield, *Freedom and Modernity* (Albany, N.Y.: State University of New York, 1991), 251.

4. Winfield, *Freedom and Modernity*, 252. "Although Hegel's account of the 'police' is brief at best, his conception of commodity relations already prescribes the twofold way in which public authority must secure the welfare of all as an exercise of

civil freedom: At one and the same time, public authority must insure that the commodities needed by individuals be in adequate and affordable supply in the market and that they all have the commodities they require to obtain through exchange what they need."

5. See Ernst Breisach, *Introduction to Modern Existentialism* (New York: Grove Press, 1962), Diane Raymond, *Existentialism and the Philosophic Tradition* (Englewood Cliffs, N.J.: Prentice-Hall, 1991), and John Macquarrie, *Existentialism* (London: Penguin Books, 1972), for superb introductions to existentialism and its major contributors. Existentialists illustrate through philosophical analysis the impossibility of man's building a universally valid system of knowledge that will enable him to view truth from outside like any other object.

6. For example, see José Ortega y Gasset, *The Revolt of the Masses* (New York: W. W. Norton & Company, 1932), where he discusses the encroachments of the mass-man which threaten Western culture.

7. See Jean-Paul Sartre, *Being and Nothingness* (New York: Washington Square Books, 1956) and Jean-Paul Sartre, *Existentialism and Human Emotions* (Secaucus, N. J.: Citadel Press, 1985).

8. Søren Kierkegaard, *Concluding Unscientific Postscript*, trans. D. Swanson and W. Lowrie (Princeton, N.J.: Princeton University Press, 1969), 183.

9. Rockmore, *Before and After Hegel*, 146. Kierkegaard follows but radicalizes Schelling's objection to Hegel's abstract approach to existence that, for Kierkegaard, resists rational comprehension. In fact, Kierkegaard's critique of Hegel consists in bringing against Hegel an objection concerning abstractness that Hegel consistently brought against the theories of his predecessors. While a logical system might be possible, an existential system is not.

10. Kierkegaard, *Concluding Unscientific Postscript*, 99–103.

11. Rockmore, *Before and After Hegel*, 147.

12. Rockmore, *Before and After Hegel*, 148.

13. Kierkegaard, *Concluding Unscientific Postscript*, 223.

14. Robert Solomon, *From Hegel to Existentialism* (New York: Oxford University Press, 1987), 77. One does not simply choose an action or course of action; one chooses a way of life.

15. Søren Kierkegaard, *The Present Age*, trans. A. Dru (New York: Harper Torchbooks, 1962), 77.

16. Kierkegaard, *The Present Age*, 79.

17. Solomon, *From Hegel to Existentialism*, 83.

18. Søren Kierkegaard, *Either/Or, Parts I and II* (Princeton, N.J.: Princeton University Press, 1987).

19. Søren Kierkegaard, *Fear and Trembling*, trans. H. Hong and E. Hong (Princeton, N.J.: Princeton University Press, 1983).

20. Rockmore, *Before and After Hegel*, 145.

21. Søren Kierkegaard, *Philosophical Fragments*, trans. D. Swenson (Princeton, N.J.: Princeton University Press, 1962), 18.

22. Kierkegaard, *Philosophical Fragments*, 81.

23. Kierkegaard, *Concluding Unscientific Postscript*, 116.

24. Kierkegaard, *Concluding Unscientific Postscript*, 118.

25. Søren Kierkegaard, *The Concept of Anxiety*, trans. R. Thomte (Princeton, N.J.: Princeton University Press, 1980) and Søren Kierkegaard, *Sickness unto Death*, trans. A. Hannay (Princeton, N.J.: Princeton University Press, 1980).

26. Kierkegaard, *The Present Age*, 35.

27. Kierkegaard, *The Present Age*, 36.

28. Kierkegaard, *The Present Age*, 39.

29. Kierkegaard, *The Present Age*, 40.

30. Kierkegaard, *The Present Age*, 42.

31. Kierkegaard, *The Present Age*, 47.

32. Kierkegaard, *The Present Age*, 49.

33. Löwith, *From Hegel to Nietzsche*, 109. Similarly, his attack on Hegel's system is directed not only against systematic philosophy, but also against the system of the entire existing world, as the ultimate wisdom of which he saw Hegel's philosophy of history.

34. Kierkegaard, *The Present Age*, 52.

35. Kierkegaard, *The Present Age*, 59.

36. Kierkegaard, *The Present Age*, 60.

37. Kierkegaard, *The Present Age*, 63.

38. Kierkegaard, *The Present Age*, 79.

39. Rockmore, *Before and After Hegel*, 163.

40. Gary Warren, *Nietzsche and Political Thought* (Cambridge: MIT Press, 1988), 6.

41. Friedrich Nietzsche, *Beyond Good and Evil: Prelude to a Philosophy of the Future*, trans. Walter Kaufmann (New York: Vintage, 1966), 137–138.

42. Friedrich Nietzsche, *The Genealogy of Morals*, trans. F. Golffing (New York: Doubleday, 1956), 188.

43. Friedrich Nietzsche, *The Gay Science*, trans. Walter Kaufmann (New York: Vintage, 1974), 242 and see also Nietzsche, *Beyond Good and Evil*, 136, where he says that genuine philosophers are commanders and legislators who create new values.

44. Nietzsche, *Beyond Good and Evil*, 156–157.

45. Nietzsche, *Beyond Good and Evil*, 42.

46. Leslie Thiele, *Friedrich Nietzsche and the Politics of the Soul: A Study of Heroic Individualism* (Chicago: The University of Chicago Press, 1990), 11.

47. Friedrich Nietzsche, *The Will to Power*, trans. Walter Kaufmann (New York: Vintage, 1967), 267.

48. Friedrich Nietzsche, *Beyond Good and Evil*, 9.

49. Alexander Nehamas, *Nietzsche: Life as Literature* (Cambridge: Harvard University Press, 1985), 50. See also Thiele, *Friedrich Nietzsche and the Politics of the Soul*, 38, where he says that knowledge, for Nietzsche, is not a product of depersonalized observation and thought, but of the stimulation of the senses and passions, of their multiplication and agglomeration.

50. Nietzsche, *The Genealogy of Morals*, 255–256.

51. Nietzsche, *The Gay Science*, 336.

52. Nietzsche, *The Gay Science*, 299.

53. Friedrich Nietzsche, *Human, All Too Human: A Book for Free Spirits*, trans. R. Hollingdale (Cambridge: Cambridge University Press, 1986), 232.

54. Nietzsche, *The Gay Science*, 175.

55. Tracy Strong, *Friedrich Nietzsche and the Politics of Transfiguration* (Berkeley: University of California Press, 1988), 201.

56. Friedrich Nietzsche, *Untimely Meditations*, trans. R. Hollingdale (Cambridge: Cambridge University Press, 1983), 150.

57. Friedrich Nietzsche, *Thus Spoke Zarathustra*, trans. R. Hollingdale (London: Penguin, 1969), 75–76.

58. Nietzsche, *The Will to Power*, 382.

59. Nietzsche, *Thus Spoke Zarathustra*, 120.

60. This is from a letter of April, 18, 1874, as taken from *Nietzsche Briefwechsel*, found in Thiele, *Friedrich Nietzsche and the Politics of the Soul*, 39.

61. Friedrich Nietzsche, *Ecco Homo*, trans. R. Hollingdale (London: Penguin, 1979), 80.

62. Nietzsche, *The Gay Science*, p. 328.

63. Friedrich Nietzsche, *The Birth of Tragedy*, trans. F. Golffing (New York: Doubleday, 1956), 94.

64. Nietzsche, *The Birth of Tragedy*, pp. 136–137.

65. Nietzsche, *The Gay Science*, 167. See Martin Heidegger, *Nietzsche: Volume Three*, trans. David Krell (New York: Harper-Collins, 1987), 203, says Nietzsche's statement that God is dead applies to the suprasensuous realm in general.

66. Nietzsche, *The Gay Science*, 279.

67. Nietzsche, *The Genealogy of Morals*, 288.

68. Bruce Detwiler, *Nietzsche and the Politics of Aristocratic Radicalism* (Chicago: The University of Chicago Press, 1990), 69.

69. Nietzsche, *The Will to Power*, 3–4.

70. Friedrich Nietzsche, *The Antichrist*, trans. H. L. Mencken (Costa Mesa, CA: Noontide, 1988), 64–68.

71. Nietzsche, *Beyond Good and Evil*, p. 76.

72. Walter Kaufmann, *Nietzsche: Philosopher, Psychologist, Antichrist* (Princeton, N.J.: Princeton University Press, 1978), 103.

73. Gilles Deleuze, *Nietzsche and Philosophy*, trans. H. Tomlinson (Minneapolis: University of Minnesota Press, 1983), 8. Deleuze says that Nietzsche's philosophy is an "absolute anti-dialectics." He also asserts that Hegel's dialectics fosters an attitude of uncritical acquiescence of the fictional necessity of what "is" and what is objectively "rational." Deleuze sees the Hegelian dialectic as the product of a tired, nihilistic will that is weary of willing.

74. Stephen Houlgate, *Hegel, Nietzsche and the Criticism of Metaphysics* (Cambridge: Cambridge University Press, 1986), 2. Hegel and Nietzsche are both critics of dualism and thinkers who hope to surpass metaphysical thinking. Houlgate credits David Breazeale, "The Hegel-Nietzsche Problem," *Nietzsche-Studien*, 4 (1975), 146–164, with first developing this justification for a comparative study of Hegel and Nietzsche.

75. Fred R. Dallymer, *G. W. F. Hegel: Modernity and Politics* (Newbury Park, N.J.: Sage, 1993), 202.

76. Deleuze, *Nietzsche and Philosophy*, 8 and 162–163.

77. Houlgate, *Hegel, Nietzsche and the Criticism of Metaphysics*, 25. Houlgate writes that Hegel, in general, seems to have relished criticizing great philosophers rather than actually reading them.

78. Arthur Schopenhauer, *The World as Will and Representation, Volume 1*, trans. E. Payne (New York: Dover, 1966), 147.

79. Hans-Georg Gadamer, *Reason in the Age of Science*, trans. F. Lawrence (Cambridge: MIT Press, 1981), 36.

80. Houlgate, *Hegel, Nietzsche and the Criticism of Metaphysics*, 5. From Hegel's point of view, Nietzsche is justified in criticizing the abstract conception of being which negates becoming, development, and history; but he is not justified in believing uncritically that life is becoming without logical form or identity, without being.

81. Hegel, *Logic*, 60.

82. Georg W. F. Hegel, *Lectures on the History of Philosophy: Medieval and Modern Philosophy, Volume 3*, trans. E. S. Haldane and Frances Simson (Lincoln: University of Nebraska Press, 1995), 180.

83. Hegel, *Logic*, 61.

84. Houlgate, *Hegel, Nietzsche and the Critique of Metaphysics*, 106.

85. Hegel, *Logic*, 62.

86. Herbert Marcuse, "A Note on Dialectic," in Herbert Marcuse, *The Essential Marcuse: Selected Writings of Philosopher and Social Critic Herbert Marcuse*, ed. Andrew Feenberg and William Leiss (Boston: Beacon Press, 2007), p. 64.

87. Hegel, *Logic*, 63.

88. Hegel, *Logic*, 62–63.

89. Hegel, *Lectures on the History of Philosophy, Volume 3*, 298.

90. Hegel, *Lectures on the History of Philosophy, Volume 3*, 305.

91. Hegel, *Logic*, 63.

92. Hegel, *Lectures on the History of Philosophy, Volume 3*, 371.

93. Houlgate, *Hegel, Nietzsche and the Critique of Metaphysics*, 110. Nietzsche's criticism of empiricism resembles Hume's in that it casts doubt on the legitimacy of our necessary judgments about the world by asserting that life does no manifest the determinations and principles that such judgments express. Consequently, Houlgate concludes that Hegel's critique of Hume also extends to Nietzsche.

94. Hegel, *Logic*, 65.

95. Hegel, *Logic*, 66.

96. Hegel, *Logic*, 67. These categories are not removed from the structure of things, but are the very preconditions that give access to the structure of things.

97. Hegel, *Logic*, 78.

98. Hegel, *Logic*, 78.

99. Hegel, *Logic*, 66.

100. Georg W. F. Hegel, *Science of Logic*, trans. A. V. Miller (Amherst, MA: Humanity Books, 1969), 54.

101. Hegel, *Science of Logic*, 37.

102. Houlgate, *Hegel, Nietzsche and the Critique of Metaphysics*, 121. See Hegel, *Science of Logic*, 64.

103. Houlgate, *Hegel, Nietzsche and the Critique of Metaphysics*, 123.

104. Georg W. F. Hegel, *Philosophy of Nature*, trans. A. V. Miller (New York: Oxford University Press, 2004), 91.

105. Hegel, *Philosophy of Nature*, 10–11.

106. Hegel, *Science of Logic*, 71.

107. Houlgate, *Hegel, Nietzsche and the Critique of Metaphysics*, 137.

108. Georg W. F. Hegel, *The Philosophy of History*, trans. J. Sibree (Buffalo, N.Y.: Prometheus, 1991), 57.

109. Houlgate, *Hegel, Nietzsche and the Critique of Metaphysics*, 141.

110. Hegel, *Science of Logic*, 19.

111. Houlgate, *Hegel, Nietzsche and the Criticism of Metaphysics*, 167.

112. Hegel, *Phenomenology of Spirit*, 110.

113. Hegel, *The Philosophy of History*, 40–41.

114. Houlgate, *Hegel, Nietzsche and the Criticism of Metaphysics*, 94.

115. Solomon, *From Hegel to Existentialism*, 99. Morality is an expression of character rather than a display of practical reason.

116. Charles Taylor, *Hegel* (Cambridge: Cambridge University Press, 1975), 459.

117. Charles Taylor, *Hegel and Modern Society* (Cambridge: Cambridge University Press, 1979), 115.

118. Winfield, *Freedom and Modernity*, 253. Due to the contingency of the market, the measures taken by public administration must be continually revised in reaction to the changing situation of the economy.

## Chapter Nine

# Hegel and Postmodernism

Of one thing we are sure. Every thing is elusive. God is elusive. Revolutionary morality is elusive. Justice is elusive. Human character.[1]

—E. L. Doctorow, *The Book of Daniel*

Today, Hegel is more criticized than carefully read. Opinions on Hegel are mixed, and he is widely seen as either the embodiment of all that is good in philosophy or as the best example of what can go wrong in philosophical thought. He is also alternatively seen as a theologian, a historian, a social critic, a conservative, a historicist, or an overzealous rationalist. An actual reading of Hegel's body of work should demonstrate that Hegel did not subscribe to most of the outrageous beliefs typically ascribed to him. A closer reading reveals his "argumentative strength and depth of vision rather than the pompous although insightful obscurantist he has so often been portrayed to be."[2] Despite the difficulty of Hegel's thought, he has had an unparalleled impact on the modern world. As discussed in Chapter 7, Marx's analysis of capitalism is greatly indebted to Hegel's dialectic, and as covered in Chapter 8, Kierkegaard's existentialism develops in response to Hegelian philosophy. Modern theologians, such as Karl Barth and Dietrich Bonhoeffer, would be inconceivable without the background of Hegel's ideas. Furthermore, John Dewey's pragmatism, Hans-Georg Gadamer's hermeneutics, Jürgen Habermas' social theory, and Jacques Derrida's deconstruction have all been profoundly influenced by Hegel. Given the extraordinary way in which Hegel's thinking invades contemporary intellectual life, no one today who seriously seeks to understand the shape of the modern world can avoid coming to terms with Hegel.[3] The landscape of modern political life is dominated by the institutions of *Sittlichkeit*; the family, civil society, and the state. Most contemporary theorists recognize that these institutions are necessary to a full enjoyment of subjectivity and freedom.

The historical importance of Hegel's thought alone justifies the continuing study of his work. A more important reason for engaging with Hegel's ideas, however, is that they are actually of great value and relevance to current so-cial, political, aesthetic, theological, and philosophical discussions. Hegel's is still a viable philosophical endeavor with important things to contribute to contemporary debates, particularly the debates about historical relativism, poverty and social alienation, the nature of freedom and political legitimacy, the future of art, and the character of Christian faith.[4] While Hegel's philoso-phy marks the culmination of a phase of modern Western history, it does not represent the end of history itself. Today, economic imperatives of scale demand a steady expansion of production, which has triggered a scramble for international markets and lower production costs. Simultaneously, the same imperatives place a premium on scientific and technological innovation as a means to increase production efficiency and to reduce dependence on hu-man labor. Hegel's philosophy is not simply a finished artifact, a congealed monument of a past era, but rather is a steady companion of ongoing discus-sions open to new insights and arguments.[5] His work still responds to today's inquiries and provides a critical foil for assessing contemporary experiences and theoretical predilections. As Derrida notes, Hegel's discourse "still holds together the language of our era by so many threads."[6]

Hegel's philosophy arises out of the epistemological and practical ques-tions of modernity. Subsequently, although he is critical of specific aspects of modernity, he is certainly not antimodern. As discussed in the previous two chapters, antimodernism begins with Kierkegaard, Marx, and Nietzsche, who each see the modern bourgeois as hollow and corrupt. Since Nietzsche, the very possibility of philosophy has become increasingly challenged. In the late twentieth century, what has emerged from the work of Heidegger, Gadamer, Foucault, Lyotard, Derrida, Wittgenstein, and other postmodern thinkers, is a mode of philosophizing that is rooted in what they see as a need to direct the critical capacities of philosophy upon the traditional conception of philosophy itself. Although these theorists are very diverse, they are connected by their attacks on foundationalism. Tying together hermeneutics, deconstruction, post-structuralism, post-humanism, postmodernism, neopragmatism, post-analytic philosophy, and post-philosophical philosophy is an agreement that foundationalism with its goal of a philosophical science needs to be rejected.[7] Despite differences, these postmoderns assert that the philosophical pretension to an aperspective, presuppositionless standpoint is unwarranted.

History has shown that the whole approach to theoretical and practical justification is plagued by the skeptical objection that every candidate for first principle—reason or reality—is equally unjustifiable due to its own privileged status.[8] Each of modernity's critics argue in various ways that the self-grounding standpoint of absolute knowing to which foundationalism must lay claim is unattainable, since every standpoint necessarily must be one from amongst several possible perspectives. They link the widely proclaimed collapse of modernity with this demise of foundationalism. Antifoundationalism consists of the rejection of Cartesianism, understood as the modern attempt to legitimate philosophy through a project of self-reflection that would result in the discovery of indubitable principles of truth. Cartesian modernity establishes its privileged access to the conditions of cognition through critical self-reflection and demonstrates its capacity to arrive at foundational knowledge. Furthermore, through this self-ground, Cartesian thought justifies its claim to authority and to judge all other claims to knowledge. Postmodern theories reject modernity's claim of a foundational standpoint of cognitive self-transparency "view from nowhere."[9] Each perspective of cognition is a limited standpoint that is unavoidably conditioned by determinative factors that can neither be made fully transparent nor transcended. Without access to an Archimedean point of view, postmodern thinkers assert that we cannot claim to have revealed the foundation of knowledge. However, as the following sections illustrate, Hegel offers a strategy for conceiving reality without metaphysical or transcendental arguments. His philosophy demonstrates in full detail how indeterminacy does in fact give rise to a development leading to categorical totality.[10]

As antifoundationalists, postmodern philosophers argue that all knowledge—and thus all philosophical reasoning—is finite, perspective, or conditional, and is tied to conceptual schemes, embedded in horizons, governed by language games, ruled by paradigms, or inextricable from forms of life and sets of social practices. Much of the philosophical controversy surrounding modernism and postmodernism can be profitably formulated within the framework first proposed in German Idealism, especially in Hegelian discussions of agency, self-determination, and rationality.[11] Critical theory, poststructuralism, and philosophical hermeneutics—three of the major strands of contemporary continental thought—criticize the modern Cartesian legacy. The development of the Frankfurt School of Critical Theory has been linked with the appropriation and reinterpretation of German Idealism, particularly Hegel. The Frankfurt theorists—Theodor Adorno, Max Horkheimer, Herbert Marcuse, and Jürgen Habermas—believe that truth is attained by unfolding both the truth content and the contradictions of thought by connecting them to social context. Like Hegel's dialectic, this leads to a historically relativized truth that is universal precisely through awareness of its historical and social situation and limitations. Furthermore, they hold that Hegel's focus on

the negative and the power of negation and contradiction inherent in thought
and reality is the key to rescuing the negative form from the overwhelming
affirmative power of modern industrial society.

Herbert Marcuse (1898–1979) and Theodor Adorno (1903–1969) see
Hegel, despite his conservative tendencies, as a true revolutionary thinker,
especially if rescued from his embeddedness in a doctrine of undialectical
affirmation.[12] In their interpretation, Hegel provides a philosophical basis for
a "negative thinking," or "determinate negation," that can serve as a basis
for liberation from the domination of existing reality. Since we presently live
in a contradictory, antagonistic society, negative experience is the authentic
form of experience.

> In other words, Hegel's philosophy is eminently critical philosophy, and the ex-
> amination to which it subjects its concepts, beginning with that of being, always
> accumulates within itself, like an electrical charge, the specific objections that
> can be made to it. Of all the distortions perpetuated on Hegel by a dim-witted
> intelligentsia, the most pitiful is the notion that the dialectic has to admit as valid
> either everything whatsoever or nothing whatsoever. In Kant, critique remains
> a critique of reason: in Hegel, who criticizes the Kantian separation of reason
> from reality, the critique of reason is simultaneously a critique of the real.[13]

Since Hegelian philosophy is the first articulation of the saturation of experience with negativity, Adorno asserts that "these days it is hardly possible for a
theoretical idea of any scope to do justice to the experience of consciousness,
and in fact not only the experience of consciousness but the bodily experience of the human being, without having incorporated something of Hegel's
philosophy."[14] Adorno holds that for individuals living in a contradictory,
perverted society, dialectical experience is an essential vehicle for the preservation of truth. Thus, negative experience is not only a negation but also
an affirmation. As discussed in Chapter 2, real truth about reality includes
an awareness of the potentiality, the desire for transcending the perverted
world.

In the 1920s, Martin Heidegger began to pursue the "question of being,"
which he feels was long-neglected by Western metaphysics. Like Hegel, Heidegger attempts to demonstrate that modernity is located within a context, but
while Hegel wants to correct the problems of modernity, Heidegger laments
the direction of modern times. Subjectivity stands over objects and manipulates
them for its own goals. Heidegger, like Hegel, sees the rise of modern subjectivity as a trajectory from the ancient Greeks onward. They agree that the most
obvious phenomenon distinguishing modernity is empty subjectivity, and both
stress the need to go beyond the modern contentless self.[15] The self-sufficiency
of the modern subject is illusory, and human beings exist only by inhabiting

something deeper than the subject-object relations, such as *Sittlichkeit*. The following subsections discuss contemporary critiques of modern subjectivity, and I argue that, despite important differences, they all bear a resemblance to Hegel's critique of modernity. In others words, Hegel was already dealing with many of the important postmodern criticisms of modernity.

However incomplete and misunderstood his efforts may be, Hegel provides a strategy for remedying the dilemmas of postmodern thought. This chapter examines the continuing importance of Hegel's philosophy and defends him against the chargers that postmodern philosophers tend to levy against him. Hegel foresees many of the problems that make up the postmodern criticisms of modern philosophy without succumbing to its shortcomings. To this end, the chapter is organized into four sections. The first section examines the relationship between Theodor Adorno's negative dialectics and Hegel's. The second part refutes Jürgen Habermas' charge that Hegel fails to break away from the philosophy of consciousness and recognize the importance of intersubjectivity. Poststructuralism and deconstruction, particularly the philosophy of Jacques Derrida, is explored in the next section. The final section discusses the contemporary continental philosophy of hermeneutics and poststructuralism, focusing on Martin Heidegger and Hans-Georg Gadamer, noting their relation and dependence on Hegel.

## CRITICAL THEORY AND NEGATIVE DIALECTICS

Theodor Adorno (1903–1969) asserts that Hegel's philosophy leads to "essential insights through critical self-reflection of critical-Enlightenment philosophy and the scientific method."[16] Although Adorno appreciates many important aspects of Hegel's dialectic, he rejects Hegel's Idealism, which he sees as based on the illusion that the power of thought is sufficient to grasp the totality of the real.

> As though the dialectic had become frightened of itself, in the *Philosophy of Right* Hegel broke off such thoughts by abruptly absolutizing one category—the state. This is due to the fact that while his experience did indeed ascertain the limits of bourgeois society, limits contained in its own tendencies, as a bourgeois idealist he stopped at that boundary because he saw no real historical force on the other side of it. He could not resolve the contradiction between his dialectic and his experience: it was this alone that forced Hegel the critic to maintain the affirmative.[17]

Idealism's rationale is the redemption of the metaphysical concept of truth as the self-presentation of actuality, the whole, from the context of idealist ontology. Even though the course of history has shattered the basis on which speculative metaphysical thought could be reconciled with experience, Adorno argues that the problem of truth is not abolished.[18] His conception of truth is derived from the immanent critique of the inherently identificatory character of all conceptual thought, which he labels "identity thinking." It is out of this critique of identity-thinking that "negative dialectics," or non-identity thinking occurs.[19] In brief, truth is only approached negatively. Adorno's arguments are dialectical in the sense that they focus on the unavoidable tensions between polar opposites whose oppositions constitute their unity and generate historical change. His dialectic is negative in that it refuses to affirm any underlying identity or final synthesis of polar opposites. Furthermore, Adorno formulates his thinking as critical thinking without transcendental method.

The primary task, for Adorno, is an immanent critique of philosophy because only a systematic critique of philosophy can adequately dispense with old problems and set limits for new projects. Most previous philosophies fail to provide an adequate account of the relation between subject and object. In his view, this relationship is "neither an ultimate duality nor a screen hiding ultimate unity."[20] Although subject and object are constituted by one another, they are not reducible to each other and neither can be wholly subsumed by the other. They are internally related, interdependent structures within which the cognitive process unfolds. The reduction of subject to object or vice versa, according to Adorno, proclaims false identities. It is Adorno's aim to transcend the separation of pure philosophy and the substantive subject matter. He is particularly anxious to expose the fallacies of subjectivism, such as the bourgeois idealism in Hegel.[21] Bourgeois idealism—the idea that the subject's concepts produce the world—embraces identity thinking, which aims at the subsumption of all particular objects under general definitions and a unity system of concepts. This type of thinking falsely affirms dominant ideologies.[22]

In order to grasp the distinctive characteristics of Adorno's thought, it is necessary to understand some of the determining influences on this thinking. Among them, three are crucial: First, he accepts aspects of Marx's critique of Hegel's notion of history. Second, Adorno is concerned with Walter Benjamin's criticism of conceptual thinking, and finally, he adheres to Nietzsche's views on the absence of ultimate foundations in epistemology and the falsity of identity thinking. He draws a distinction between those aspects of Hegel's work that could be legitimately employed for the development of a materialistic and dialectical method and those that had to be discarded. *Negative Dialectics* sets out to free dialectics from affirmative traits that are entailed in Hegel's notion of the negation of the negation, which frees the understanding of history from the fallacies that follow from too great an emphasis on subjectivity.[23] The central task of philosophy is to reflect upon socio-life processes and describe their structure and development. Cognition is to be understood in light of its development in actual social processes, not by describing in advance the cognitive achievement in accordance with a logical or scientific model. Philosophy is practical.

Although Hegel's writings suggest the logic of this kind of perspective, Adorno thinks that he fails to pursue it: Not only did he falsify "the object ideologically, calling it a free act of the absolute subject; he also recognized in the subject a self-representing objectivity," thus failing to appreciate the degree to which ideology impinges upon the individual.[24] In opposition to Hegel, Adorno argues that reality cannot be grasped from a single view. Like Nietzsche, Adorno rejects the position that the mind has privileged access to such an Archimedean point and can achieve self-sufficiency. Like Marx, he holds that thinking is a form of praxis, always historically conditioned; and just as physical labor transforms and negates the material world under changing historical circumstances, so mental labor, also under changing historical conditions, alters its object world through criticism.

The capacity of dialectics to transcend opposition is limited, however. Against Hegel's notion of a cognitive process that unfolds into a unity in *Geist*, Adorno's understanding suggests only negativity, that the difference between subject and object cannot be abolished. Hence, the power of reflection is inadequate to grasp the totality of the real. Since reason is bound by historical circumstances that constrain thinking, the only way in which the historical process might be conceived as a whole is negatively:

> Universal history must be construed and denied. After the catastrophes that have happened, and in view of the catastrophes to come, it would be cynical to say that a plan for a better world is manifested in history and unites it. Not to be denied for that reason, however, is unity that cements the discontinuous, chaotically splintered moments and phases of history—the unity of the control of nature, progressing to rule over men, and finally to that over men's inner nature. No universal history leads from savagery to humanitarianism, but there is one leading from the slingshot to the megaton bomb.[25]

For Adorno, it seems that if history has any unity at all, it is created by suffering. The desire to control the world lies behind all philosophical attempts, especially those that lead to the construction of systems representing totality. History defies systems. Disorder in reality fuels the desire to find order in thought. Adorno chastises those philosophies, including Hegelian and Marxist, which seek a perfect oneness of man and world.

Adorno agrees with Marx that as the principle of exchange extends to the living labors of human beings it changes into objective inequality, namely

social classes. However, he differs from Marx in his explanation of the ultimate source of the exchange process. Rather than emphasizing the role of
alienated and abstracted labor in creating the world of commodities, Adorno
insists that abstract thought is a function of the market place, which he sees
as the "original sin" in the division of mental from manual labor:

> Abstraction—without which the subject would not be the *constituens* at large
> at all, not even according to such an extreme idealist as Fichte—reflects the
> separation from physical labor, perceptible by confrontation with that labor.
> When Marx, in his critique of the *Gotha Programme*, told the Lassalleans that
> in contrast to the customary litany of popular socialist literature labor was not
> the sole source of social wealth, he was philosophically . . . saying no less than
> that labor could not be hypostatized in any form, neither in the form of diligent
> hands nor in that of mental production. Such hypostasis merely extends the illu-
> sion of the predominance of the productive principle.[26]

Thus, he asserts that orthodox Marxism's privileging of production merely
repeats the subject's domination of the object. Although he appears at times
to reflect Georg Lukács' usage of reification, for Adorno reification is not
equivalent to the alienated objectification of subjectivity, that is, the reduction
of a fluid process into a dead thing.[27] Instead, reflecting a use of Nietzsche,
reification, when used in a pejorative sense, means the suppression of heterogeneity in the name of identity.

Reification, for Adorno, is a forgetting. However, the reversal of forgetting
that Adorno wants is not the same as remembering something forgotten—the
recovery of a perfect wholeness or original plentitude—but means rather the
restoration of difference and non-identity to their proper place in the nonhi-
erarchical constellation of subjective and objective forces he called peace.[28]
Adorno's use of reification is not merely a relationship among human beings,
but also entails the domination of the otherness of the natural world. Both
positivism and idealism utilize a sort of conceptual imperialism that reifies
the natural world into quantitatively fungible fields for human control and
manipulation. Hence, both Lukács and Antonio Gramsci are wrong in simply
privileging history or society over nature as the locus of freedom. Rather than
giving priority to one or the other, a negative dialectic plays off nature against
history or society and vice versa chiasmically.[29] To put it differently, ending
reification in the Hegelian sense used by Lukács merely fosters its perpetua-
tion in the Nietzschean sense employed by Adorno.

Adorno is, however, clearly aware of this paradox, and he is suspicious of
the claim that all reification might ultimately be overcome. It is not a matter
of repeating the Hegelian verdict against reification, but rather of a critique

of reification that discloses the contradictory moments that are contained in forgetting. In short, there is a difference between good and bad reification:

> Humanity includes reification as well as its opposite, not merely as the condition from which liberation is possible but also positively, as the form in which, however brittle and inadequate it may be, subjective impulses are realized, but only by being objectified.[30]

His defense of some measure of good reification makes sense only if his assumption that the tyranny of identity, the exchange principle, and the domination of the constitutive subject over both the contingent subject and the object are all accepted as synonymous. Conversely, his much more frequent attacks on bad reification means that he is no less hostile to the denigration of any subjective agency, which characterized philosophies ranging from positivism to structuralist Marxism.[31] His insistence on the permanence of some subjectivity, collective and individual, sets him apart from structural Marxists, such as Louis Althusser.

Although Adorno's dialectic compares with Hegel and Marx in some respects, he differs significantly from both since he sees no linearity in this movement, while they project history toward a goal and an end. This change of dialectical perspective can be linked to Adorno's understanding of the negative. Hegel and Marx see the negative as a necessary component of history and of any movement and development, and since they believe in an end to history they also see the suspension of negativity—the negation of the negation—at some point. In contrast, Adorno believes in the existence of the negative as long as something exists at all. Dialectical thinking is merely an attempt to purge thinking of all misidentification, and is a recognition of the insufficiency of any given identification. Consequently, it is not a new and non-identificatory kind of thinking, but a demonstration of the insufficiency of identification. In other words, Adorno cannot imagine that there could be a real totality one day, that everything could ever be as it is supposed to be and that it will ever reach a quiet end: All that is thought can never become social reality, and reality can never be identical with thought.[32]

Adorno's materialism does not comply with Marx in making organized work the starting-point of social development. He sees social life reproducing itself in the back-and-forth struggle of man—who is also nature—with nature, as a biological-natural struggle to produce a human, rational, and social nature. The fluctuation between the historic-socially separated moments makes it clear, for Adorno, that the classic terminological separation of idealism and materialism is outdated. His view of science and philosophy is not idealistic, and his understanding of the materialistic basis of society is purely economic. He intends to demonstrate that the traditional separations of theory and reality have lost their purpose. For example, idealism has become a materialistic force, since it perpetuates the existing balance of power; and materialism has become the leitmotif that controls everything.[33] Adorno's philosophy is propelled by establishing that the existing circumstances are perceived by man differently from what they really are. His proof is the fact that human beings experience and think about themselves, others, and their social relations in terms of abstractions that are carried to extremes in exchanging goods. In this respect, his philosophy has a material basis.

Concepts are historically imprinted, even those that are attempting to express that something is unchangeable. Like Hegel, Adorno argues that concepts, like everything experienced, are of a historical nature.[34] He asserts that the perception of immutability is connected with abstract thinking in the way it effects society and establishes control. The abstraction of exchange values, according to Adorno, is analogous to abstract thinking in science and philosophy. The concept of eternally valid truths uses standards that are defined by the human mind; however, this conceals that these eternal values are merely expressions of certain interests, the interest of exercising control. Immutable concepts isolate the scientific, philosophical, and practico-political moment from the grand picture of existence, but Adorno asserts that this isolation is a mere artifice, since it contradicts the characteristics of all existing meaning. These historical characteristics reveal themselves in everything existing that is given to human consciousness, and if consciousness itself is of a historical nature then everything else is likewise of a historical nature.[35]

The dialectical moment of Adorno's philosophy reveals that he does not perceive the existing reality as a closed, completely identical unity but as conflict between opposing forces. In short, his dialectic is negative because it cannot be regarded as either a method or a world-picture. This conflict separates conceptually what is held in reality as one: subject and object, nature and history, content and form, individual and society, and thought and reality. These moments are defined by Adorno as forms of appearance and fact that complement each other. One cannot exist without the other, and their conceptual separation is artificial. Unlike Marx who considers one of the two opposing moments superior to the other, Adorno does not in principle grant any superiority to one or the other moment of a dialectical relation. He rejects attempts to dichotomize reality into a contrast of change and immutability that creates the prerequisites for everything to conform to the ideal of immutableness. To put it simply, Adorno opposes any theory that holds that everything is both changeable and unchangeable.

The struggle for emancipation depends on particular material and historical conditions, which Adorno believes are less and less favorable to success. However, within the pessimism, there is a glimmer of hope:

> To this end, dialectics is obliged to make a final move: being at once the impression and the critique of the universal delusive context, it must now turn even against itself. The critique of every self-absolutizing particular is a critique of the shadow which absoluteness casts upon critique; it is a critique of the fact that critique itself, contrary to its own tendency, must remain within the medium of the concept. It destroys the claim of identity by testing and honoring it; therefore, the claim can reach no farther than that claim. . . . It is up to the self-reflection of critique to extinguish that claim, to extinguish it in the very negation of negation that will not become a positing. . . . It lies in the definition of negative dialectics that it will not come to rest in itself, as if it were total. This is the form of hope.[36]

To be sure, Adorno does not leave much room for optimism; but historical circumstances, within which all metaphysical and belief systems are anchored, might change. Although negative dialectics cannot lead to change alone, it can help to break the grip of all conceptual systems that freeze the object and ignore its genesis.

Negative dialectics is the position of the particular—changing configurations of objects, whether natural or social things, or human practices—that Adorno seeks to explicate. To put it another way, he wants to demonstrate the priority of the object and, at the same time, confirm the mediation of subject and object:

> Due to the inequality inherent in the concept of mediation, the subject enters into the object altogether differently from the way the objects enters into the subject. An object can be conceived only by a subject but always remains something other than the subject, whereas a subject by its very nature is from the outset an object as well. Not even as an idea can we conceive a subject that is not an object, but we can conceive an object that is not a subject. To be an object also is part of the meaning of subjectivity; but it is not equally part of the meaning of objectivity to be a subject.[37]

His goal is to show how the history of the mind, which he sees as the subject's attempt to gain distance from the object, continually reveals the superiority of objectivity. Although objects cannot be grasped without conceptuality, they do not dissolve into concepts. By means of negative dialectics, Adorno aims to transcend the concept and reach the non-conceptual.[38]

In salvaging the particular through remembrance, Adorno suggests that the hold of all-embracing rationalities might be broken revealing a space for freedom—creative, spontaneous thought and action. In order to comprehend something, its immanent connections with other things must first be perceived and then the conditions under which it exists must be examined.[39] Adorno insists upon the necessity of tracing out the inner history of the object, which is the way it is mediated in history. His philosophical goal is to help critical theory, which is embroiled in tradition, to be able to transcend it. Negative dialectics seeks to make the real antagonisms visible, as contradictions, which are masked by philosophy's striving for logical identity. The key is nonidentity thinking, which depends upon, and yet alters, existent convention. This entails examining the contradiction between the object's idea of itself and its actual existence. Since the object's self-image is surpassed, it is brought into flux. Thus, the immanent method, through its capacity to produce a heightened perception of the thing itself, cannot escape a certain transcendent quality.[40] However, the transcendent element of Adorno's approach does not lead to a once and for all grasp of the totality.

The idea of rational identity, contained within the ideal, preserves a place for utopia—a notion of the possible, which is in danger of being overlooked or suppressed. Nonidentity thinking can uncover this moment:

> To define identity as the correspondence of the thing-in-itself to its concept is *hubris:* but the ideal of identity must not simply be discarded. Living in the rebuke that the thing is not identical with the concept is the concept's longing to become identical with the thing. This is how the sense of nonidentity contains identity. The supposition of identity is indeed the ideological element of pure thought, all the way down to formal logic; but hidden in it is also the truth moment of ideology, the pledge that there should be no contradiction, no antagonism. In the simple identifying judgment, the pragmatist, nature-controlling element already joins with a utopian element. . . . The untruth of any identity that has been attained is the obverse of truth. The ideas live in the cavities between what things claim to be and what they are. Utopia would be above identity and above contradiction; it would be a togetherness of diversity.[41]

A certain range of concepts, such as justice, beauty, or freedom, are not simply abstractions from the characteristic unit of individual objects but contain within themselves definitions that the object might fail to fulfill. Thus, they can become a means to reveal the difference between the actuality and potentiality of a given thing.

Cognition of nonidentity, for Adorno, allows identification of an object in more ways and to a greater extent than identity thinking. An object's concept provides access to an understanding and evaluation of the object. For example, Adorno says that:

the judgement that man is free refers to the concept of freedom; but this concept in turn is more than is predicated of the man, and by other definitions the man is more than the concept of his freedom. The concept says not only that it can be applied to all men defined as free; it feeds on the idea of a condition in which individual qualities would not to be ascribed to anyone here and now.[42]

This condition would be one in which human beings meet and fulfill all the properties and conditions contained in the notion of freedom. The concept of freedom lags behind when it is applied empirically.[43] In contemporary society, the inequality of social power ensures that the alleged identity between the concept of freedom and the objective state of affairs is false. Hence, this negation of the concept of freedom in practice points to aspects of society that aid, restrict, and restrain freedom's actuality.

The analysis of a particular entity begins with its concept and reveals nonidentity where identity is frequently assumed. Through this immanent method, Adorno suggests that the individuality of the particular can be uncovered through categories that are intrinsic to it rather than through notions that are imposed from without. Negative dialectics depends on the internally related employment of the categories of concept and object, appearance and essence, particular and universal, and part and whole. Through the examination of the formation of concepts and the disjuncture between them and the objects that they seek to cover, Adorno's negative dialectic attempts to disclose the processes of mutual constitution and alteration between object and totality. The examination of the object is also assessed in terms of what it appears to be and its essence, which reveals the universal within the particular. Critical theory aims to understand, analyze, and enact in the subjective ground of society. Simply put, to comprehend society it is necessary to know it from the inside, or know its formative processes.

Adorno's final position seems to draw closer to aspects of Kantian philosophy. The antinomies of Kant's metaphysics are said to represent accurately the position of metaphysics in a contradictory historical situation.[44] Although Adorno does not accept Kant's transcendental method, he does believe that Kant's stress on the import of what lies beyond the mind must be saved. For Adorno, the preservation of this moment is the preservation of the moment of possibility, of possible transcendence:

To want substance in cognition is to want utopia. It is this consciousness of possibility that sticks to the concrete, the undisfigured. Utopia is blocked off by possibility, never by immediate reality; this is why it seems abstract in the midst of exact things. The inextinguishable color comes from nonbeing. Thought is its servant, a piece of existence extending—however negatively—to that which is not. The utmost distance alone would be proximity; philosophy is the prism in which its color is caught.[45]

Although negative dialectics continually evokes the possibility of the transcendence of existing belief systems and material conditions, it does not give an absolute status to this idea. Dialectics allows one to think the absolute, but the absolute as transmitted by dialectics always remains in bondage to conditioned thinking; and dialectics cannot escape this bondage.[46] No absolute can be expressed other than in topics and categories of immanence.[47] Since the concept of immanence is historical, negative dialectics seeks to be the self-consciousness of the context of delusion. Adorno, however, does not claim that it has entirely escaped this context, though he hopes to break out of the context from within.[48]

## POSTMETAPHYSICAL INTERSUBJECTIVITY

Jürgen Habermas (1929–present) says that Hegel is caught up in the philosophy of consciousness, since Hegel locates the core of modernity in the principle of subjectivity.[49] Hegel's principle of subjectivity contains an emancipatory potential that both represents a world of progress and of alienated spirit. Habermas sees the notion of civil society as Hegel's main contribution. By separating and simultaneously linking society and the state, Hegel promotes a self-transcendence of modernity under modern auspices.[50] While praising Hegel's intention, Habermas finds his effort flawed and ultimately unsuccessful, because of its subjectivist moorings and its excessively theoretical-contemplative character:

> Thus, Hegel's philosophy satisfies the need of modernity for self-grounding only at the cost of devaluing present-day reality and blunting critique. . . . Philosophy cannot instruct the world about how it ought to be; only reality as it is reflected in its concepts. It is no longer aimed critically against reality, but against obscure abstractions shoved between subjective consciousness and an objective reason.[51]

Like Adorno, Habermas thinks that Hegel absolves philosophy from the task of confronting its concept with the decadent existence of social and political life.[52] This muffling of critique, according to Habermas, is a close corollary of the devaluation of actuality by Hegel's philosophy.

In attempting a philosophical reconciliation, Hegel slides into the illusory solution offered by his concept of absolute knowledge—that is, the overcoming of subjectivity within the limits of the philosophy of the subject.[53] Habermas' remedy for Hegel's philosophical shortcomings is a different model of reconciliation, or the mediation of the universal and the particular. Instead of subordinating the freedom of individuals to a higher subjectivity, Habermas claims that communicative action relies on the higher intersubjectivity of an uncoerced will formation within a communication community obeying the need for cooperation.[54] As opposed to appealing to the power of *Vernunft*, synthesis is derived from the universality of an uncoerced consensus achieved between free and equal individuals.

While some of Habermas' criticism is valid, he fails to recognize important intersubjective dimensions to Hegel's thought. In the *Phenomenology of Spirit*, self-consciousness and thus human freedom only advance through intersubjective recognition. Moreover, as discussed in Chapter 2, the highest categories of Hegel's logic, those that provide the entry into *Geist*, are linked with human agency and activity.[55] With this emphasis on human agency, Hegel is within the realm of intersubjectivity. Consciousness is consciousness by dialogue, and it is only the dialogue-character of consciousness that allows mental representation to be brought forth.[56] This is close to Habermas' communicative action. Hegel's concept of *Geist* transcends the subjective forms of self-consciousness.[57] For Hegel, consciousness becomes universal only by entering into a world of culture, mores, institutions, and history.[58] Furthermore, historical comprehension requires a common understanding, and thus a unique *logos* of communication. For Hegel, debates in the legislature, with their quality of give and take, are a device through which truth, and the public interest, can emerge, i.e., a form of communicative action.

Compare this to where Habermas says that the interrelation between individuality and community define the unimpaired intersubjectivity of a relation of reciprocal recognition.[59] This is very Hegelian. For Hegel, there is no self prior to mutual recognition, and one can only become an individual within a particular community, or culture.[60] Intersubjectivity does not do away with subjectivity, or individual subjects as bearers of rights and personal interests. Norms and law are developed through the interaction of subjects in their quest for truth and is therefore an intersubjective process. Put differently, Hegel's *Sittlichkeit* reaches its completion in community. Habermas makes essentially the same point, and both he and Hegel are reacting against the excessive individualism of modern liberalism. Moreover, both try to reconcile individual liberty with community. For Hegel, the parts of the community are related as parts of an organism. Furthermore, both theorists argue that freedom is the historical achievement of beings who are mindful of their social dependence.[61]

The Hegelian *Geist* progresses through the advancement and development of human civilizations, which is clearly in the realm of intersubjectivity since it comes from social interaction.[62] In fact, Hegel's dialectic comes from a dialogue of sorts, where truth advances through argumentation and reconciliation. The role of communication is important to Hegel too, and, like Habermas, he sees thinking and being as practical.[63] Moreover, although there are philosophical differences in their arguments, Habermas' deliberative democracy closely resembles Hegel's *Rechtsstaat*. Both develop separate spears of civil society and a constitutional state for homes of private and public freedom. Both fall between the extremes of liberalism and communitarianism in order to find the proper relationship between the individual and community.[64] Both separate representative lawmaking from administration. While Habermas talks about intersubjectivity, his political theory respects and attempts to protect the rights and interests of individual modern subjects. Both Habermas and Hegel reject an atomistic ontology that sees individuals as existing prior to society, and they both insist that political rights must be grounded in the intersubjective relations of recognition.

Even though they take different philosophical paths, Habermas and Hegel essentially reach the same political conclusion. If intersubjectivity means reconciling the needs of individuals with those of the community, Hegel's thought is certainly intersubjective. Nothing can claim to be a real social decision unless it is arrived at in a full discussion in which all the participants are fully conscious of what is at stake.[65] And philosophically, he attempts to reconcile the particular with the universal in the socio-political world. Like Habermas, Hegel recognizes that human freedom can only reside in a just society, which is one that balances the needs of the one with those of the many. Citizens exercise their personal autonomy in civil society and their public autonomy in the public sphere, and more importantly they can only achieve their personal goals through a cooperative endeavor. As illustrated in Chapter 5, even while trying to accomplish what appears to be purely selfish behavior, Hegel stresses the universal social connection and interdependence of all people within a particular political culture, even one that is highly individualistic:

> Individuals in their capacity as burghers in this state are private persons whose end is their own interest. This end is mediated through the universal which thus appears as a means to its realization. Consequently, individuals can attain their ends only so far as they themselves determine their knowing, willing, and acting in a universal way and make themselves links in this chain of social connexions.[66]
>
> In the course of the actual attainment of selfish ends—an attainment conditioned in this way by universality—there is formed a system of complete interdependence, wherein the livelihood, happiness, and legal status of one man is interwoven with the liveliness, happiness, and rights of all.[67]

## PHENOMENOLOGICAL AND
## PHILOSOPHICAL HERMENEUTICS

Martin Heidegger (1889–1976) attempts to discover a method that will disclose life in terms of itself, not the abstract subject of Hobbes and Locke. He seeks a method of going behind and to the root of Western conceptions of Being—that is, a phenomenological hermeneutics that will enable him to render visible the presuppositions on which they have been based. In doing so, Heidegger calls the entire Western metaphysical tradition into question. The phenomenology of Edmund Husserl (1859–1938) helped provide Heidegger with the conceptual tools that might lay open the processes of "Being" in human beings. Phenomenology opens up the realm of the pre-conceptual apprehending of phenomena. However, whereas Husserl approaches it with an idea of bringing into view the functioning of consciousness as transcendental subjectivity, Heidegger sees in it the vital medium of man's historical being-in-the-world [*In-der-Welt-Sein*].[68] The importance of Heidegger's philosophy begins with his insistence on historicity and "situatedness" in the world that cannot be overcome through scientific method or further reduced to a transcendental basis. What is at stake is the difference between epistemological and practical orientation for philosophy. In its historicity and temporality, he sees clues to the nature of Being—as it discloses itself in lived experience and escapes the conceptualizing and atemporal categories of idea-centered thinking. Heidegger shifts phenomenology from the transcendent, subject-centered phenomenology of Husserl to the question of Being.

Heidegger claims that the Western philosophical tradition has misinterpreted human being [*Dasein*]. Hence, he attempts to work out a new analysis of what it is to be human. The traditional misunderstanding of human beings goes back to Plato's fascination with theory. Plato tries to understand and explain the universe in a detached way, by discovering the principles that underlie the profusion of phenomena. Philosophy, therefore, gets on the wrong track by thinking that one could have a theory of everything. In criticizing the conceptual treatment of Being, Heidegger challenges Hegel's quasi-Platonic metaphysics, particularly the notion of timeless permanence of the idea as distinguished from the temporal flux of the phenomenal world.[69] Heidegger argues that Hegel's aim was to overcome finite knowledge through the attainment of infinite knowledge.[70] Hegel's criticisms of modernity fail because he remains caught within the destiny of metaphysics. With the renewal of the question of Being, Heidegger wants to reassess Hegel's finitude-infinity nexus:

> Whether the finitude which was prevalent in philosophy up to Hegel, was the original and effective finitude operative in philosophy, or whether it was only

an incidental finitude that was carried along nilly-willy. What needs to be asked is whether Hegel's conception of infinity did not itself arise from the incidental finitude, in order to reach back and absorb it.[71]

For Heidegger, the status of finitude in its relation to absoluteness is key to understanding Hegel's *Phenomenology*. Hegel's dialectics tries to sublate everything finite into the Absolute.[72] According to Heidegger, Hegel follows the tradition of metaphysics in equating infinite Being with idea or logos, terms that in the aftermath of Descartes and Kant are identified with reason, spirit, and subjectivity.

Heidegger sees Hegel as the culmination of the Cartesian phase of metaphysics. Heidegger shifts the focus of philosophy from idea or *logos* to time and temporality. However, as illustrated in Chapter 2, Hegel is not the Cartesian that Heidegger claims, since he sees knowledge as dialectical. Heidegger develops his hermeneutic phenomenology in opposition to Husserl's transcendental phenomenology. Husserl develops an account of mankind as essentially a consciousness with self-contained meaning that gives intelligibility to everything people encounter. Heidegger rejects Husserl's notion of intentionality as a self-sufficient individual subject directed at the world by means of its mental content. Instead, Heidegger's ontological approach is an attempt to break free of Descartes' distinction between subject and object that has traditionally dominated modern philosophy. His new approach is a phenomenology of mindless, everyday coping skills as the basis of intelligibility—that is, a hermeneutical phenomenology.

Hermeneutics is applied to those situations where human beings encounter meanings that are not immediately understandable but require interpretative effort. Hans-Georg Gadamer (1900–2002) borrows and modifies Heidegger's hermeneutic legacy. His philosophical hermeneutics is a reaction against both relativistic historicism and the insistence on a methodology that was inspired by the natural sciences. Using Heidegger as his starting point, Gadamer develops a critique of German Idealism that tries to overcome the primacy of self-consciousness. Like Hegel, Gadamer's hermeneutics has its origins in intersubjectivity. In *Truth and Method*, Gadamer sees the philosophical encounter with historical texts as broadly patterned on Hegel's dialectics. Furthermore, he notes: "Even the language of the Hegelian dialectic, which strives to sublate the language rigidly conceptualized in statement and counterstatement, dictum and contradiction, and to raise it beyond itself, succeeds in promoting language through thinking and in being itself converted into language, inasmuch as that is the means by which and in which the concept is brought to conceptualization."[73] Gadamer's notion of effective history [*Wirkungsgeschichte*] closely resembles the concept of experience of Hegel's *Phenomenology*. The past has a truly pervasive power in the phenomenon of understanding. Human understanding must take into account the interpreter's present participation in history. Hegel tries to demonstrate that every new achievement of knowledge is a mediation or refocusing the past within a new and expanded context. Despite criticizing Hegel, Gadamer nevertheless takes him very seriously and defends him against Kantian critics. It is of central importance for hermeneutics that it should come to grips with Hegel.[74] While Plato, Aristotle, and Heidegger are the major influences on Gadamer's development, Hegel is not far behind. Gadamer defends Hegel against charges that his philosophy is abstract and neglects concrete immediacy.[75] Gadamer is also extremely sympathetic to Hegel's denial of transcendental subjectivity and his attempt to situate human subjects in time. Gadamer sees that Hegel recognizes the need to find a way to reject formalism and to establish a socio-historical basis for thought without ending up with a non-philosophical enterprise.[76] He further appreciates Hegel's rehabilitation of Greek philosophy and attempt to break with modern metaphysics.

Like Hegel, Gadamer's thought illuminates the human context within which understanding occurs. Unlike most other postmodern critics, Gadamer recognizes that Hegel's completion of transcendental idealism is effected in and through a critique of egological subjectivity and the epistemology founded on it:

> For it is Hegel who explicitly carried the dialectic mind or spirit beyond the forms of subjective spirit, beyond consciousness and self-consciousness.[77]
>
> In particular, Hegel's powerful speculative leap beyond the subjectivity of the subjective Spirit established this possibility and offered a way of shattering the predominance of subjectivism. . . . Was it not Hegel's intention, also—i.e., together with Heidegger after the latter's "turn"—to surpass the orientation to self-consciousness and the subject-object schema of a philosophy of consciousness?[78]

Unlike Habermas, Gadamer recognizes that Hegel's thought goes beyond subjectivity.[79] Hegel's dialectic shares some important characteristics with Gadamer's hermeneutical attack on transcendentalism and relativism. However, Gadamer thinks that Hegel's rejection of subjectivity is still incomplete, since it is only a rejection of its egological form. Despite the fact that Hegel's concept of Geist transcends the subjective form of consciousness, Gadamer contends that the ultimate structure of consciousness remains dominant for Hegel's thought.[80] More precisely, Gadamer holds that although Hegel does overcome a variety of modes of subjective consciousness, the basic form of consciousness prevails and is absolutized. Both Hegel and Gadamer recognize the dynamic and self-transcending quality of knowledge in a higher universality, but Gadamer argues that this universality remains finite and is not to be equated with Hegel's absolute knowledge. Gadamer's hermeneutics

is an attempt to overcome Hegel. The key to Gadamer's critique of Hegel lies
in its affirmation of the primacy of finitude, as the notion that the thinking
subject cannot attain the full self-transparency of an absolute knowing. This
is fundamental, and Gadamer's critique of Hegel hinges on it: "In its uniqueness, finitude and historicity, however, human *Dasein* would preferably be
recognized not as an instance of an eidos, but rather as itself the most real
factor of all."[81] It is not absolute knowledge but the moving, dialectical life
of reason that finds expression in Gadamer's hermeneutics.

Despite his rejection of Hegel's transcendence of *Dasein* in its uniqueness
and finitude, Gadamer nevertheless sees Hegel's dialectic as useful. Insofar
as it articulates finitude philosophically, rather than as a dogmatic article of
faith, it must make use of and is a version of the philosophy of reflection.[82]
Consequently reflection cannot be renounced fully, because human beings
reach an awareness of their finitude through reflection. Reflective self-understanding is an activity through which human beings become aware of their
situatedness. Therefore, Gadamer's hermeneutics seems to require that the
truth claims of the philosophy of reflection be properly realized:

> Hermeneutics requires its actual productivity only when it musters sufficient
> self-reflection to reflect simultaneously about its own critical endeavors, that is,
> about its own limitations and the relativity of its own position. Hermeneutical
> reflection that does that seems to me to come closer to the real ideal of knowl-
> edge, because it also makes us aware of the illusion of reflection.[83]

Gadamer seems to rely on reflection and yet wants to breaks the spell of
Hegelian reflection. Although he recognizes this difficulty, Gadamer thinks
that hermeneutics is superior to Hegel. Because of his realization of the inadequacy of Kant's and Heidegger's critiques of reflective idealism, Gadamer
turns to the experience and phenomenon of language in order to affect his
own conception of a reality that is beyond the omnipotence of reflection.[84]
Hegel's emphasis on history and the necessity of historical consciousness for
philosophy is a central point at which Hegel's and Gadamer's projects meet.
"Hegel states a definite truth, inasmuch as the essential nature of the historical
spirit consists not in the restoration of the past but in thoughtful mediation
with contemporary life."[85] For Gadamer, understanding is essentially dialectical because a new concretization of meaning comes from the interplay that
goes on continually between the past and present.

Despite its dialectical transcendence, Gadamer notes that Hegel's conception of *Geist* is still the basis for the critique of subjectivity. Nevertheless, although the concept of *Geist* that transcends the subjectivity of the ego has its
counterpart in the phenomenon of language, Gadamer thinks that, in contrast
to *Geist*, "the phenomenon of language has the merit of being appropriate to

our finitude."[86] Language is the medium in which past and present actually interpenetrate. For Gadamer, since word and subject matter, language and reality, are inseparable, the limits of human understanding coincide with the limits of common language:

> Language is not one of the means by which consciousness is mediated with the world. . . . Language is by no means simply an instrument or a tool. For it belongs to the nature of the tool that we master its use, which is to say we take it in hand and lay it aside when it has done its service. . . . Rather, in all our knowledge of ourselves and in all knowledge of the world, we are always already encompassed by the language which is our own.[87]

In this respect, Gadamer agrees with Heidegger's assertion that language and understanding are inseparable aspects of human being-in-the-world [*In-der-Welt-Sein*]. The experience and manipulation of objects is not self-founding, but always presupposes that human beings are already oriented to a particular world by means of language. In its life as conversation, language constantly presses against the limits of established conventions and moves between the sedimented meanings and usages that are at its basis and the new that it strives to express.[88] In this sense, language allows ever new concretizations of its subject matter. Gadamer also values Hegel's recognition of the importance of the historical development of freedom. "No higher principle is thinkable than that of the freedom of all, and we understanding actual history from the perspective of this principle: as the ever-to-be-renewed and the never-ending struggle for this freedom."[89]

## POSTSTRUCTURALISM AND DECONSTRUCTION

Poststructuralism problematizes the foundations of philosophy and political thought by rejecting the precision of language. Under the influence of a radicalized Nietzscheanism, poststructuralism tends to downplay philosophical connections in favor of separateness and particularity. Instead of complex efforts to overcome traditional metaphysics, poststructuralist movements tend to question metaphysics entirely. In a large part, the roots of poststructuralism lie in a general opposition to the philosophical tradition, particularly Hegel. Shunning Hegel's notion of sublation, poststructuralists tend to privilege rupture over continuity in a manner that reverses traditional metaphysical priorities from universality to particularism, holism to diversity, and reason to decision. As a corollary emphasis is placed on an agonistic struggle that does not necessarily lead to mutual recognition. In the political arena, the Nietzschean upsurge is opposed to all "totalizing" institutions, especially structures of the modern state and comprehensive modes of integration and mediation.[90] In this context, Hegel is frequently charged with a totalitarianism that is detrimental to individual freedom and diversity. Even though poststructuralists and deconstructionists often differ over the details, they typically reflect a Nietzschean perspective that is combined with anti-Hegelianism. For instance, Gilles Deleuze (1925–1995) sees Nietzsche as a thinker who shattered traditional philosophy. For Deleuze, Hegel's dialectic absorbs and dissolves human distinctions into a uniform rationality.[91] Against this, Nietzsche's philosophy emerges as the life-affirming antipode of Hegel's dialectics.

With deconstruction, Jacques Derrida (1930–2004) is charged with licensing an arbitrary free play in flagrant disregard of all established requirements of thought. His deconstructive work is seen as merely a private and anarchic project, closer to literature than to philosophy. However, Derrida himself refers to a "Hegelian law" where one cannot speak out against reason except by being for it; this means that the revolution against reason can be made only from within it and so is limited to an internal disturbance.[92] In brief, it is argued that within Derrida's thought, anything is possible. But for others, deconstruction designates the content and style of Derrida's thinking and reveals a well-ordered procedure, a step-by-step type of argumentation based on the acute awareness of level-distinctions, and a marked thoroughness and regularity. For example, Rodolphe Gasché asserts that "all adequate comprehension of the nature and implications of the order characteristic of deconstruction is, indeed, possible only on the condition that one also develops a sense of what deconstruction is to achieve."[93] As long as its goal is believed to promote licentious free play, and the nihilistic canceling out of opposites, Gasché holds that deconstruction's definite and logical procedure cannot be grasped. For him, Derrida is not part of the move to debunk truth.

It is a mistake to judge Derrida's work as literary and to exclude it from philosophical discussion.[94] Derrida is a philosopher whose work is committed to an ongoing critical dialogue with previous thinkers, and centrally concerned with issues in the realm of truth, knowledge, and representation.

> First, what Derrida has to say is mediated by the cannon of the traditional problems and methods of philosophical problem solving, as well as by the history of these problems and methods. . . . Second, . . . the specific displacements of traditional philosophical issues by deconstruction amount not to an abandonment of philosophical thought as such, but rather to an attempt at positively recasting philosophy's necessity and possibility in view of its inevitable inconsistencies. Indeed, Derrida's inquiry into the limits of philosophy is an investigation into the conditions of possibility and impossibility of a type of discourse and questioning that he recognizes as absolutely indispensable.[95]

Thus, deconstruction attempts to account for a heterogeneous variety of non-logical contradictions and discursive inequalities of all sorts that continue to haunt philosophical arguments. In fact, Derrida devotes a significant number of texts to the study of traditional philosophers. Nevertheless, he does not simply repeat or conserve their heritage, but instead attempts to find out how their thinking works, to find the tensions or contractions with their corpus.[96] In this respect, Derrida's deconstruction is not far from Hegel's dialectic. Both philosophers respond critically to the philosophical tradition. For Derrida, deconstruction is not merely a method or tool that you apply to a text from the outside; it is something which happens and which happens inside.[97] Likewise, Hegel's dialectic is not applied to thought, but rather is the movement found within thought itself. Christina Howells notes that:

> In all his books and essays Derrida is a scrupulous, meticulous, patient reader, determined to disentangle what has been conflated, to bring to light what has been concealed, and to pay scrupulous attention to marginalia and footnotes, in the expectation that what has been relegated to the margins may prove paradoxically central to a less parochial understanding of the text. . . . Deconstruction may set out to 'read between the lines,' or even 'read against the grain,' but it always attempts to read, and understand.[98]

The essence of the deconstructive project is the demonstration of textual self-contradiction. For instance, Derrida asserts that there is a deconstruction at work within Plato's work.

Derrida's deconstruction contains Nietzschean suspicions about the tradition of Western philosophy's epistemological picture of truth as a glassy correspondence or clear and distinct representation between the mind and external reality. It is necessary to interrogate those various pre-critical ideas of reference that envisage a straightforward matching-up between language and the outside world. Thus, deconstruction, building on Heidegger, must work to problematize such habits of thought by showing how strictly impossible it is to draw a firm line between reality and representation. As Christopher Norris puts it, Derrida's deconstruction must fasten on those blindspots in the discourse of commonsense empiricism that betray its naïve ontological commitments and traditional philosophy's failure to think through the issues raised by a rigorous epistemological critique.[99] Philosophical confusion can only be avoided by a scrupulous attention to the problems involved in arriving at "the real" through representations of it. This clearly places Derrida within the same tradition as Hegel.

From Plato's forms to Cartesian certainty, philosophy has struggled to discover, or determine, something known as "truth." In short, Derrida's texts

stand squarely within the tradition of Western philosophy, and nonetheless so
for his attempt to contest, or deconstruct, that tradition:

> Then perhaps it will be understood that the value of truth (and all those values
> associated with it) is never contested or destroyed in my writings, but only rein-
> scribed in more powerful, larger, more stratified contexts. And within interpre-
> tative contexts (that is, within relations of force that are always differential—for
> example, socio-political-institutional—but even beyond these determinations)
> that are relatively stable, sometimes apparently almost unshakeable, it should be
> possible to invoke rules of competence, criteria of discussion and of consensus,
> good faith, lucidity, rigor, criticism, and pedagogy.[100]

Without these indispensable protocols, regardless of how complex their articulation in the reading of specific texts, deconstruction would lack all critical
force and become a sophisticated bag of tricks as its critics charge. Such criticisms mistake its target by assuming that deconstruction is synonymous with
a handful of overworked catchwords, such as freeplay or textuality.[101] Derrida
has always insisted that deconstruction be held accountable to the standards
of logical rigor and argumentative consistency. Deconstructionist criticism
obeys laws and intentions of its own.[102] Deconstruction is not a nihilistic
undermining of truth, but rather an exploration of the prejudices and precon-
ceptions that underlie much of what is generally accepted without question.[103]
Thus, like Hegel's dialectics, deconstruction is always on the side of truth.
Nevertheless, what Derrida is trying to articulate is an order of insight into the
workings of language that necessarily eludes the sort of "clear-cut" conceptualization that "mainstream" philosophers sought in their work.

Similar to philosophical hermeneutics and Nietzschean perspectivism, deconstruction rejects the certainty of both an Archimedean point and holistic
philosophical systems. Nonetheless, Derrida holds that it is a meaningful operation as long as critique is construed as a search for minimal syntheses that
regulate the non-philosophical problems that haunt philosophical discourse.
Although they do not destroy the possibility of philosophizing, they do significantly limit it. Derrida is attempting to shake and reinscribe philosophy's
endeavor to account by itself for itself by knowledge's systematic and system-
forming self-exposition. Like Hegel, Derrida is concerned with determining
the limits of the possibility of systematicity and system-formation.

Derrida's deconstruction, like Hegel's dialectics, is also acutely sensitive
to the contingency of human constructs and to the deeply historical, social,
and linguistic "constructedness" of human beliefs and practices. Derrida's
work, like Hegel's, is not exclusively anti-Enlightenment, but a new enlightenment questioning the "axioms and certainties of Enlightenment," doing so
precisely in order to affect what should be the enlightenment of contemporary

times.[104] While Enlightenment makes everything turn on "Reason," his new enlightenment wants to know "the reason for Reason." Thus, although he is critical of the Enlightenment, critique is an intrinsic aspect of enlightenment. For Derrida, philosophy is the right to ask any question about all that is held intellectually sacred, including about reason and philosophy itself. In brief, the effect of his new enlightenment would not be to jettison reason but to redefine and redescribe it; deconstruction means to continue the struggle for emancipation but by another means.[105]

## HEGEL'S ANTIFOUNDATIONAL DEFENSE OF MODERNITY

Theoretical and practical justifications of knowledge are plagued by the skeptical objection that every candidate for first principle, such as reason or reality, are unjustifiable because they favor some foundation. Most postmodern critics argue in different ways that the self-grounding standpoint of absolute knowing to which foundationalism lays claim is unattainable, since each standpoint is only a possible perspective. Postmodern theorists typically connect the widely proclaimed collapse of modernity with this demise of foundationalism.[106] This usually entails the rejection of Cartesianism, understood as the modern attempt to legitimate philosophy through a project of self-reflection that would result in the discovery of indubitable principles of truth. Cartesian modernity establishes its privileged access to the conditions of cognition through critical self-reflection and demonstrates its capacity to arrive at foundational knowledge. Through this self-ground, Cartesian thought justifies its claim to authority and therefore judges all claims to knowledge. Postmodern theories reject modernity's claim of a foundational standpoint of a neutral, detached vantage point. Each perspective of cognition is a limited standpoint that is unavoidably conditioned by determinative factors that can neither be made fully transparent nor transcended. Without access to an Archimedean point of view, postmodern thinkers assert that we cannot claim to have revealed the foundation of knowledge.

Modern foundationalism is rooted in the belief that subjectivity could somehow liberate itself from contingency and attain a transparent framework of "giveness." As argued above, Hegel offers a strategy for conceiving reality without metaphysical or transcendental arguments. Put differently, his defense of modernity rejects Cartesianism. His philosophy demonstrates in full detail how indeterminacy does in fact give rise to a development leading to categorical totality.[107] As antifoundationalists, postmodern philosophers argue that all knowledge—and thus all philosophical reasoning—is finite, perspective, or conditional, and is tied to conceptual schemes, embedded in horizons, governed by language games, ruled by paradigms, or inextricable from forms of life and sets of social practices.[108] Because many postmodern philosophers have Nietzschean roots, they tend to blur the distinction between knowledge and power. Consequently, there are good reasons to be suspicious of antifoundational theories, since they often lack a sound basis for differentiating between the authority of reason and that of power. Much of the philosophical controversy surrounding modernism and postmodernism can be profitably formulated within the framework proposed in Hegelian discussions of agency, self-determination, and rationality.

Hegel clearly recognizes problems with many features of foundationalism. Nevertheless, he also unquestionably believes that both a standpoint of autonomous rational objectivity and philosophy as a rigorous science are possible. That is, Hegel accepts the idea of an autonomous reason. William Maker notes that "Hegel proposed to introduce the standpoint of autonomous reason and philosophical science through a radical and consummately deconstructive *critique* of foundational epistemology and transcendental philosophy."[109] He further observes that Hegel completes the philosophical tradition in a way that already incorporates the legitimate features of postmodernism, and does so in a way that does not succumb to the problematic features of postmodernism. Hegel's dialectic provides the self-constitution of an autonomous reason that makes critique possible. Nevertheless, Hegel's philosophy is still modern in that it provides a framework for analyzing claims about the primacy of autonomy and reason. His project is distinctly modern in that is concerned with two characteristics of modernity: Hegel is interested in both epistemological issues that arise out of the emergence of modern scientific thought and in practical issues that arise out of the French Revolution and their break from prevailing intellectual traditions.[110]

As illustrated in Chapter 2, Hegel assesses the inadequacies of his philosophical predecessors and their various attempts at foundationalism. However, his rejection of modern foundationalism does not lead him to skepticism, relativism, or nihilism. Even though it is nonfoundational, his philosophy is still critical philosophy. Hegel's approach tries to conceive reality from the standpoint of autonomous reason. Nonetheless, his system does not absolutize reason in the sense of denying that there is any limit to it.[111] Since autonomous reason rejects the exclusive primacy that "givenness," Hegel's social and political institutions are derived from the notion that individuality and freedom are not givens. As demonstrated in Chapter 6, individual freedom and consciousness originate from and are dependent upon a network of specific institutions, whose character is more properly understood as intersubjectively constituted. While Hegel does not reject individual freedom, he does not approve of it when conceived in atomistic, egological terms of modern contract theory.

Hegel's philosophy of the dialectic provides a firm basis for the critique of contemporary political and social institutions and practices, such as the global economy. Hegel is well aware that the ethical imperative of a market economy makes justice more problematic that merely protecting individual property. He reminds us that it is necessary to view economic self-interest within the broader context of human nature, that is, a concrete ethical life [*Sittlichkeit*]. Today, the deregulation of markets and the move toward global economic integration has provided rich financial rewards to those at the top and has widened the gap between the rich and poor. Furthermore, governments are becoming less democratic to the extent that public policy becomes dictated by the need to compete in the global economy. Decisions that were once made in legislative chambers are now being made in corporate boardrooms. Globalization contributes to the spread of aggressive individualism to the detriment of community values. Hegel's ethical theory warns of the dangers that follow when economic relations are disconnected from *Sittlichkeit*. The next chapter examines contemporary globalization and looks to Hegel for help and guidance.

## NOTES

1. E. L. Doctorow, *The Book of Daniel* (New York: Plume, 1971), 42.

2. Terry Pinkard, *Hegel's Dialectic: The Explanation of Possibility* (Philadelphia: Temple University Press, 1988), 4.

3. Steven B. Smith, *Hegel's Critique of Liberalism: Rights in Context* (Chicago: The University of Chicago Press, 1989), 14.

4. Stephen Houlgate, *An Introduction to Hegel: Freedom, Truth and History* (Oxford: Blackwell, 2005), 2.

5. Fred R. Dallmayr, *G. W. F. Hegel: Modernity and Politics* (Newbury Park, N.J.: Sage, 1993), 184.

6. Jacques Derrida, *Margins of Philosophy*, trans. Alan Bass (Chicago: The University of Chicago Press, 1982), 119.

7. William Maker, *Philosophy Without Foundations: Rethinking Hegel* (Albany, N.Y.: State University of New York Press, 1994), 2.

8. Richard Dien Winfield, *Reason and Justice* (Albany, N.Y.: State University of New York Press, 1988), 5. Winfield illustrates how classical appeals to privileged givens and modern appeals to a privileged determiner ultimately fall prey to skepticism.

9. Thomas Nagel, *The View from Nowhere* (Oxford: Oxford University Press, 1986).

10. Richard Dien Winfield, *Freedom and Modernity* (Albany, N.Y.: State University of New York Press, 1991), 49.

11. Robert B. Pippin, *Idealism as Modernism: Hegelian Variations* (Cambridge: Cambridge University Press, 1997), 5. Pippin argues that many possible Idealist interpretations and justifications for foundational norms in modern thought have not been sufficiently appreciated by recent critics of modernity.

12. Herbert Marcuse, *Reason and Revolution: Hegel and the Rise of Social Theory* (Atlantic Highlands, N.J.: Humanities Press, 1941), 11.

13. Theodor Adorno, *Hegel: Three Studies*, trans. Shierry Nicholsen (Cambridge: MIT Press, 1993), 77.

14. Adorno, *Hegel*, p. 2.

15. David Kolb, *The Critique of Pure Modernity: Hegel, Heidegger, and After* (Chicago: The University of Chicago Press, 1986), 206.

16. Adorno, *Hegel*, 65. Hegel goes beyond the limits of a science that merely ascertains and arranges data, and he attacks mere epistemology by showing that the forms that epistemology considers to constitute knowledge depend as much on the content of knowledge as vice-versa. Adorno therefore considers Hegel to be anti-positivist.

17. Adorno, *Hegel*, 80.

18. Adorno, *Hegel*, 37.

19. Adorno, *Hegel*, 24.

20. Theodor Adorno, *Negative Dialectics* (New York: Continuum, 1973), 174.

21. Adorno, *Hegel*, 31.

22. Adorno, *Hegel*, 32.

23. Adorno, *Negative Dialectics*, 334–340. See also Theodor Adorno, "Subject and Object," in *The Essential Frankfurt School Reader*, ed. A. Arato and E. Gebhardt (New York: Continuum, 1982).

24. Adorno, *Negative Dialectics*, 198 and 350. See also Simon Jarvis, *Adorno: A Critical Introduction* (London: Routledge, 1998), 151, where he says: "Adorno attempts to think anew not by producing a supposedly self-sufficient new method or new system, but through the criticism of the tradition from which it emerges. This is why Adorno described his own philosophical work as undertaking a 'transition to interpretation.' Such a transition aims to rescue thinking from an endless repetition of its dialectic of enlightenment."

25. Adorno, *Negative Dialectics*, 320.

26. Adorno, *Negative Dialectics*, 177–178.

27. Adorno, *Negative Dialectics*, 190.

28. Martin Jay, *Adorno* (Cambridge: Harvard University Press, 1984), 68.

29. Chiasmus entails the inversion of the word order on one clause in another that follows. See Maurice Merleau-Ponty, *The Visible and the Invisible* (Evanston, Ill.: Northwestern University Press, 1968), where he also emphasizes chiasmus as an appropriate way to convey dialectical reversal without premature reconciliation.

30. Theodor Adorno, *Prisms* (Cambridge: MIT Press, 1967), 106.

31. Jay, *Adorno*, 70–71. The mistake of idealism is to give absolute primacy to the collective over the individual subject, just as existentialists like Kierkegaard erred by doing precisely the opposite. In both cases, an identity theory replaces that force-field of irreconcilable moments acknowledged by negative dialectics. Truth cannot be reduced to a reflection of what exists in the social totality of the moment.

32. Willem van Reijen, *Adorno: An Introduction* (Philadelphia: Pennbridge Books, 1992), 53.

33. Adorno, *Negative Dialectics*, 204–207.

34. Adorno, *Negative Dialectics*, 153–155.

35. Adorno, *Negative Dialectics*, 189–193.

36. Adorno, *Negative Dialectics*, 406.

37. Adorno, *Negative Dialectics*, 183.

38. Adorno, *Negative Dialectics*, 9.

39. Adorno, *Negative Dialectics*, 25 and 52.

40. Adorno, *Prisms*, 32.

41. Adorno, *Negative Dialectics*, 149–150.

42. Adorno, *Negative Dialectics*, 150.

43. Adorno, *Negative Dialectics*, 151. It is not what it says. The contradiction between the concept of freedom and its realization remains the insufficiency of the concept. The potential of freedom calls for criticizing what an inevitable formalization has made of the potential.

44. Adorno, *Negative Dialectics*, 484–493.

45. Adorno, *Negative Dialectics*, 56–57.

46. Adorno, *Negative Dialectics*, 405.

47. Adorno, *Negative Dialectics*, 407.

48. Adorno, *Negative Dialectics*, 406.

49. Jürgen Habermas, *Philosophical Discourses on Modernity*, trans. F. Lawrence (Cambridge: MIT Press, 1987), 27.

50. Habermas, *Philosophical Discourses on Modernity*, 38–40.

51. Habermas, *Philosophical Discourses on Modernity*, 42-43.

52. Habermas, *Philosophical Discourses on Modernity*, 42.

53. Habermas, *Philosophical Discourses on Modernity*, 22.

54. Habermas, *Philosophical Discourses on Modernity*, 40.

55. See Charles Taylor, "Hegel's Philosophy of Mind," in Charles Taylor, *Human Agency and Language: Philosophical Papers 1* (New York: Cambridge University Press, 1985), 83.

56. Martin Heidegger, *Hegel's Concept of Experience*, trans. Kenley Dove (San Francisco: Harper & Row, 1970), 118.

57. Hans-Georg Gadamer, *Hegel's Dialectic: Five Hermeneutical Studies*, trans. P. Christopher Smith (New Haven: Yale University Press, 1971), 78.

58. Paul Ricoeur, *From Text to Action: Essays in Hermeneutics, II*, trans. K. Blamey and J. Thompson (Evanston: Northwestern University Press, 1991), 229.

59. Jürgen Habermas, *The Future of Human Nature* (London: Polity, 2003), 34.

60. Georg W. F. Hegel, *Phenomenology of Spirit*, trans. A. V. Miller (Oxford: Oxford University Press, 1952), 298.

61. Habermas, *The Future of Human Nature*, 34; Georg W. F. Hegel, *Philosophy of Right*, trans. T.M. Knox (London: Oxford University Press, 1952), 172.

62. Georg W. F. Hegel, *The Philosophy of History*, trans. J. Sibree (Buffalo, N.Y.: Prometheus Books, 1991), 48.

63. See Gadamer, *Hegel's Dialectic*, 92, where he says: "For Hegel, language thus reaches its perfection in the idea of logic since the latter thinking goes through all of the determinations of thought occurring within itself and operating in the natural logic of language. . . ."

64. Jürgen Habermas, *Between Facts and Norms: Contributions to a Discourse Theory of Law and Democracy*, trans. W. Rehg (Cambridge: MIT Press, 1996), 296.

65. Charles Taylor, *Hegel* (Cambridge: Cambridge University Press, 1975), 384.

66. Hegel, *Philosophy of Right*, 124.

67. Hegel, *Philosophy of Right*, 123.

68. Martin Heidegger, *Being and Time*, trans. J. Macquarrie and E. Robinson (New York: Harper & Row, 1962), 78–80.

69. Dallmayr, *G. W. F. Hegel*, 225.

70. Martin Heidegger, *Hegel's Phenomenology of Spirit*, trans. Parvis Emad and Kenneth Maly (Bloomington: Indiana University Press, 1988), 38.

71. Heidegger, *Hegel's Phenomenology of Spirit*, 38.

72. Heidegger, *Hegel's Phenomenology of Spirit*, 65.

73. Hans-Georg Gadamer, *Reason in the Age of Science*, trans. F. Lawrence (Cambridge: MIT Press, 1981), 4.

74. Hans-Georg Gadamer, *Truth and Method*, trans. J. Weinsheimer and D. Marshall (New York: Continuum, 1989), 353–355.

75. Gadamer, *Truth and Method*, 342–243.

76. Robert Pippin, "Gadamer's Hegel," in *The Cambridge Companion to Gadamer*, ed. R. Dostal (New York: Cambridge University Press, 2002), 226.

77. Gadamer, *Hegel's Dialectic*, 104.

78. Hans-Georg Gadamer, "Reflections on my Philosophical Inquiry," in *The Philosophy of Hans-Georg Gadamer*, ed. L. Hahn (Chicago: Open Court, 1997), 34.

79. Gadamer, *Reason in the Age of Science*, 32. One of Hegel's greatest merits is the recognition that the emergence of the family, society, and state arise from the overcoming and surpassing of the subject spirit, of the individual consciousness, in the direction of a common consciousness.

80. Gadamer, *Hegel's Dialectic*, 78.

81. Hans-Georg Gadamer, *Philosophical Hermeneutics*, trans. D. Lingis (Berkeley: University of California Press, 1976), 135.

82. Maker, *Philosophy Without Foundations*, 151.

83. Gadamer, *Philosophical Hermeneutics*, 152.

84. Gadamer, *Philosophical Hermeneutics*, 61–62.

85. Gadamer, *Truth and Method*, 168–169.

86. Gadamer, *Philosophical Hermeneutics*, 128.

87. Gadamer, *Philosophical Hermeneutics*, 62.

88. Gadamer, *Philosophical Hermeneutics*, 127.

89. Gadamer, *Reason in the Age of Science*, 9.

90. Dallmayr, *G. W. F. Hegel*, 234.

91. Giles Deleuze, *Nietzsche and Philosophy*, trans. H. Tomilson (Minneapolis: University of Minnesota Press, 1988), 40.

92. Jacques Derrida, *Writing and Difference*, trans. Alan Bass (Chicago: The University of Chicago Press, 1978), 111–112.

93. Rodolphe Gasché, "Infrastructures and Systematicity," in *Deconstruction and Philosophy: The Texts of Jacques Derrida*, ed. J. Sallis (Chicago: The University of Chicago Press, 1987), 3.

94. Rodolphe Gasché, *The Tain of the Mirror: Derrida and the Philosophy of Reflection* (Cambridge: Harvard University Press, 1986), 1.

95. Gasché, *The Tain of the Mirror*, 1–2.

96. Jacques Derrida, *On the Name*, trans. T. Dutoit (Stanford: Stanford University Press, 1995), 119–121. See also Gasché, "Infrastructures and Systematicity," 5–6, where he says that deconstruction is a meaningful operation only if it is construed as a search for minimal syntheses that regulate the noncanonical and nonphilosophical problems that haunt philosophical discourse and limit it. As a result, all philosophy in the aftermath of deconstruction will have to live with this new type of finitude that is brought to light by deconstruction.

97. Jacques Derrida, *Memories for Paul de Man*, trans. C. Lindsay et al. (New York: Columbia University Press, 1989), 123. "This is another way of saying: there is always already deconstruction, at work in works. . . . Deconstruction cannot be applied, after the fact and from the outside, as a technical instrument of modernity. Texts deconstruct themselves by themselves, it is enough to recall it or recall them to oneself."

98. Christina Howells, *Derrida: Deconstruction from Phenomenology to Ethics* (Cambridge: Polity Press, 1999), 2–3.

99. Christopher Norris, *Derrida* (Cambridge: Harvard University Press, 1987), 142.

100. Jacques Derrida, *Limited Inc*, trans. S. Weber (Evanston, IL: Northwestern University Press, 1988), 146. For arguments against deconstruction as philosophy, see John Ellis, *Against Deconstruction* (Princeton, N.J.: Princeton University Press, 1989); and for counter-arguments, see "Limited Think: How not to read Derrida," in Christopher Norris, *What's Wrong with Postmodernism: Critical Theory and the Ends of Philosophy* (Baltimore: The Johns Hopkins University Press, 1990).

101. Norris, *What's Wrong with Postmodernism*, 139.

102. Gasché, *The Tain of the Mirror*, 3.

103. Howells, *Derrida*, 154.

104. Derrida, *Points*, 428.

105. John Caputo, "The Right to Philosophy," in *Deconstruction in a Nutshell: A Conversation with Jacques Derrida*, ed. John Caputo (New York: Fordham University Press, 1997), 55.

106. Maker, *Philosophy Without Foundations*, 2. Heidegger, Wittgenstein, Gadamer, Derrida, and Rorty all direct the critical capacities of philosophy upon the traditional conceptions of the philosophical enterprise itself, in order to liberate it from itself. Thus, it is fashionable to be against philosophical foundations. Maker asserts that hermeneutics, deconstruction, poststructuralism, postmodernism, neopragmatism, and postanalytic philosophy all agree that foundationalism needs to be rejected.

107. Winfield, *Freedom and Modernity*, 49.

108. Maker, *Philosophy Without Foundations*, 4.

109. Maker, *Philosophy Without Foundations*, 13-14. Maker argues that, properly construed, the failure of foundationalism leads not to the rejection, but to the vindication of modernist notions of objectivity and rationality.

110. Maker, *Philosophy Without Foundations*, 21.

111. Maker, *Philosophy Without Foundations*, 39.

## Chapter Ten

# Conclusion: Hegel Today

McBride moved past a newsstand . . . with newspapers and colorful like Time, The Weekly Newsmagazine headlining the collapse of Russian socialism, the grandeur of American capitalism, and the latest business bankruptcy, unemployment figures, and sale of another national mercantile landmark to foreigners, and they came to the entrance of on of the emergency stairwells. . . . But the odors in the this civilization were strong, the air reeking of smoke and unwashed bodies and their waste, a stench of rot and degradation that was violently disgusting and vilely intolerable to all but the mass producing it daily.[1]

—Joseph Heller, *Closing Time*

Although the political and economic world has undergone profound changes since the time of Hegel, his thought can still shed some light on contemporary issues. In fact, in light of many of the problems and concerns that are brought forth by globalization, we could argue that we need him now, more than ever. Today, globally dispersed corporations have rendered local political societies more vulnerable. For example, Jürgen Habermas notes that "globalization raises questions about fundamental presuppositions of classical international law—the sovereignty of states and the sharp division between domestic and foreign policy."[2] He further asserts that:

Nongovernmental actors such as multinational corporations and internationally influential private banks undermine the formal sovereignty of nation-states. Today each of the thirty largest corporations operating on a global scale has an annual turnover greater than the gross domestic product of ninety countries represented in the UN. But even the governments of the economically most powerful countries are keenly aware of the gulf that is opening up between the

345

limits of the range of action of nation states and imperatives, not of world trade,
but of global networks of productive relations.[3]

Thus, globalization has created new challenges for democracy. Habermas,
like Hegel, says that sovereign nations profit from their economies only so
long as they functioned as "national economies" over which they could exercise influence by political means. As discussed in Chapter 5, Hegel stresses
the necessity of submitting the economy under control by the political system and ethical life at large. However, "with the denationalization of the
economy, in particular with the increasing global interconnection of financial
markets and industrial production itself, national politics loses its control over
the general conditions of production."[4] This is clearly the case in the United
States and most of the world today.

In the past three decades, democratic capitalism, which accepts a certain
amount of regulation and oversight by democratic authority, has been replaced by a strong distain for regulatory government. With globalization and
neoliberalism, democratic politics is trumped by economics. Benjamin Barber
argues that while today's global economy tends to nurture individual liberty
and prizes productivity, it neglects equality and places profits before people
and products before jobs.[5] He further observes that this has destroyed the
delicate balance of democratic capitalism. As illustrated below, Hegel's conceptions of ethical life [*Sittlichkeit*] and modern state [*Rechtsstaat*] provide
powerful intellectual tools for restoring the balance. In short, the essence of
democracy is the right of the people to oversee their common goods, and this
right has been under siege by neoliberalism and globalization. Democracy
today not only suffers from neoliberalism, but also from a version of modern
liberalism that often leads to excessive individualism. Hegel reminds us that
democracy is the condition of democracy and not the other way around.

Hegel can help us better understand the problems of modern political
life. This chapter addresses the various ways that Hegel's philosophy can
still serve us today. The first section of the chapter assesses the relationship
between Hegel's philosophy and economic justice, including subsections
on political economy and alienation and issues in contemporary globalization, and discusses ways that his philosophy can help us with many of the
economic problems that we face. The final section of the chapter looks to
Hegel for remedies for modern dilemmas. In particular, his philosophy is very
useful as an antidote for excessive individualism, and his conception of *Sittlichkeit* provides firm basis for the reconciliation of individual rights within
the social framework of a community and the reestablishment of economics
as a subsection of the socio-politico system at large.

## HEGEL AND ECONOMIC JUSTICE

It is important to remember that Hegel sees poverty as a major flaw in the modern world, caused by a variety of factors, such as extravagance, idleness, and dereliction of duty. As illustrated in Chapter 5, Hegel portrays civil society as a well-oiled machine that functions smoothly according to the laws of economics. Nevertheless, it is far from perfect. Although individual instances of poverty may the consequences of particular choices, poverty overall is more likely to result from external conditions. As covered in the following section, poverty is still a serious problem even in advanced industrial nations, such as the United States. While Hegel does not suggest that poverty originates in modern society, he thinks that modern society does exacerbate the problem. Unlike traditional methods of production, the modern economy pulls individuals away from the family. Self-sufficient individualism and unmitigated pursuit of private interests spawns and legitimates an atomistic principle that abandons all individuals to contingency. Each individual is supposed to fend for him- or herself. While the market brings employment opportunities and skilled labor together, this interconnectedness has a downside. Well-trained workers often find their skills redundant in the modern economy, and they become unemployed when their skills are no longer needed, through no fault of their own. Increasing economic efficiency and production creates surplus production and replaces workers with machines. When a surplus of goods is produced, workers are laid off, creating unemployment. The modern economy frequently renders workers superfluous, wreaking havoc on their personal lives, especially with the outsourcing of so many joins to take advantage of cheap foreign labor. Moreover, by failing to earn a livelihood, the victims of poverty are deprived not just of goods but also the opportunity to exercise their autonomy as a rightful member of the community.

In the *Philosophy of Right*, Hegel recognizes that poverty is not only absolute, but can be relative as well. The poor are poor not only in that they have been deprived of property and the possibility of acquiring property, this deprivation also leads to others, such as nonrecognition and marginalization. The denial of recognition and the exclusion from civil society while living in its midst can constitute a spiritual death. The poor are pushed to the margins of society and become invisible. Deprived of resources and recognition, they are without determinate being or status in civil society. The recognition of universal freedom disappears, or turns out to be freedom for a few, and the general recognition [*Anerkanntsein*] is thereby undermined.[6] This greatly resembles the situation for most of the homeless in contemporary United States. Most Americans move through their daily lives with little to no contact with the homeless and the desperately poor. In fact, we barely see them. For Hegel, this deprivation threatens the possibility of membership and inclusion in civil society. In addition, it can threaten one's right to life. Life itself has needs, and property resources are among the most basic way of meeting life's needs; to be deprived of the resources to meet these needs is to be deprived of one's ultimate right to life itself.[7] Since recognition, for Hegel, is a condition of having rights, the poor do not really have any rights in civil society in a meaningful fashion.

Hegel's conception of modern *Sittlichkeit* requires that civil society and the state be balanced. At times, government intervention is required to address some of the harsh side-effects of life in civil society. As discussed in Chapter 5, Hegel does not advocate complete laissez-faire.

> Hegel points out these problems and suggests the method for redistributing wealth that avoids them, while insuring the greatest fairness and respect for the exercise of economic freedom: redistribution not through transfers of goods and services, but through monetary taxation and reimbursement. . . . [R]eliance on taxation allows the equitably determined transfer to be mediated through the choice of all parties concerned. By virtue of taxation, the economically privileged, be they individual or private or public enterprises, are allowed to fulfill their economic duty to the disadvantaged without relinquishing their freedom to decide what commodities to exchange and what services to render in obtaining the money they must pay. Similarly, monetary reimbursements leave the disadvantaged with the full prerogative to decide how to translate the abstract form of wealth they have received into particular goods and earning opportunities.[8]

Thus, while the separation between government and economy is an important part of Hegel's modern state, the state has specific powers and responsibilities in the economic realm. In fact, Hegel would not likely be pleased with the political direction taken by the United States over the last couple of decades. Democratic government is being stripped of its ability to regulate the economy responsibly and to protect the public. This tendency not only harms responsive citizenship; Hegel would find the number of people living below the poverty line unacceptable.[9] Furthermore, the recent wave of globalization is exacerbating the gulf between individualism and community, and excessive privatization is threatening the public realms and commons. Globalization denotes the expanding scale, growing magnitude, speeding up, and deepening impact of transcontinental flows and patterns of social interaction.

## Political Economy and Alienation

Perhaps the most serious problem posed by civil society is the problem of poverty. While unemployment and poverty may not be violations of abstract right, they are social wrongs caused by private economic interaction. It is a terrible evil, according to Hegel, generated by the basic structure of civil society itself, and it is a problem for which there is no easy solution. Although Hegel definitely praises the important contributions of the market, he also realizes that the mechanisms of the market can and often do create social polarization, poverty, and alienation. In fact, he supports the necessity of state intervention in order to mitigate some of the harsher aspects of poverty. Ultimately he is unable to provide a solution, however. Thus, poverty clearly poses a significant obstacle for Hegel's project. The most obvious aspect of poverty is material deprivation for human beings, since it is a condition of destitution, want, and need. Nevertheless, it is still imperative that government actively wrestles with the problems of poverty and does not merely turn its back on it. The criticisms of this section focus primarily on poverty, since its existence points to an acute objective inequality.

Hegel's acceptance of Adam Smith's "invisible hand" does not include following the overly optimistic and harmonistic implications of the model. He accepts Smith's view that behind the senseless and conflicting clash of egoistic interests in civil society a higher purpose can be discerned; but he does not agree with the assumption that everyone in society is therefore being taken care of. Poverty, which is marginal in Smith's model, assumes another dimension for Hegel, who holds that pauperization and the subsequent alienation from society are not incidental to the system but endemic to it. Moreover, poverty, according to Hegel, grows in proportion to the growth of wealth. Far from being a relic of the old, undeveloped society, poverty in modern society is a phenomenon as modern as the structure of commodity-producing society itself:

> When social conditions tend to multiply and subdivide needs, means, and enjoyments indefinitely—a process which, like the distinction between natural and refined needs, has no qualitative limits—this is luxury. In the same process, however, dependence and want increase *ad infinitum*, and the material to meet these is permanently barred to the needy man because it consists of external objects with the special character of being property, the embodiment of the free will of others, and hence from his point of view its recalcitrance is absolute.[10]

Thus, it is the economic expansion of civil society that brings, creates, and intensifies social polarization.

Modern poverty is accompanied by industrial overproduction that cannot find enough consumers who have sufficient purchasing power to buy the products offered on the market. Therefore, it is not the malfunction of civil society that causes poverty, but precisely its opposite, the smooth functioning of the powers of the market:

When civil society is in a state of unimpeded activity, it is engaged in expanding internally in population and industry. The amassing of wealth is intensified by generalizing (a) the linkage of men by their needs, and (b) the methods of preparing and distributing the means to satisfy these needs, because it is from this double process of generalization that the largest profits are derived. That is one side of the picture. The other side is the subdivision and restriction of particular jobs. This results in the dependence and distress of the class tied to work of that sort, and these again entail inability to feel and enjoy the broader freedoms and especially the intellectual benefits of civil society.[11]

He also points out that there is no minimum standard of living that can be fixed and determined beforehand. The historicity of needs and the development of civil society turn the minimum standard of living into a measure always relative to prevailing conditions.[12] The problem is that while the poor cannot attain a decent level of consumption in their particular society, they nevertheless feel the need to achieve this level. Civil society internalizes its norms about consumption into the consciousness of its members even though it is unable to satisfy these norms for everyone.

Poverty becomes a dialectical concept; it is the expression of the tension between the needs created by civil society and its inability to satisfy them:

Not only caprice, however, but also contingencies, physical conditions, and factors grounded in external circumstances may reduce men to poverty. The poor still have the needs common to civil society, and yet since society has withdrawn from them the natural means of acquisition and broken the bond of the family . . . their poverty leaves them more or less deprived of all the advantages of society, of the opportunity of acquiring skill or education of any kind, as well as the administration of justice, the public health services, and often even of the consolations of religion, and so forth.[13]

This is a strikingly modern and sophisticated description of the culture of poverty, and it parallels many much more recent attempts to drive home the point that poverty cannot be described merely in quantitative terms.[14] The culture of poverty, for Hegel, also entails the deprivation of educational and vocational skills, exclusion from the system of justice, and the exclusion from many of society's important institutions.

When poverty reaches this qualitative dimension of exclusion Hegel maintains that a rabble [*Pöbel*] is created. He describes the rabble as a heap of human beings utterly atomized and alienated from society, feeling no allegiance to it and no longer even wishing to be integrated into it. They are hopeless. This group sees itself as being completely outside of civil society:

When the standard of living of a large mass of people falls below a certain subsistence level—a level regulated automatically as the one necessary for a member of the society—and when there is a consequent loss of the sense of right and wrong, of honesty and the self-respect which makes a man insist on maintaining himself by his own work and effort, the result is the creation of a rabble of paupers.[15]

Hence, poverty is not an accident, a misfortune, or the result of human error or vice; rather it is produced by the complications of civil society. The modern problem of poverty poses a serious obstacle for Hegel, since it and the creation of the rabble are structural features of civil society. This suggests that civil society has the character of a zero-sum game, so that the rich become rich only at the expense of the poor.[16] Hegel also recognizes that the development of the modern economy leads to increased specialization, which, in turn, leads to a growing class of workers being thrown into stifling, low-paying, unrewarding jobs. Moreover, he characterized the modern economy as having recurrent crises of overproduction that also throw people out of work into poverty.

Some possible solutions are considered by Hegel and then rejected. For example, private charity is private and as such violates the condition of public agency. Private charity is also not effective. Being dependent upon the private decisions of particular individuals, charity is contingent, and thus unreliable. It also tends to humiliate its recipients and undermines their self-respect. Hegel does not disapprove of private charity, but argues that although it is valuable and important, it cannot provide a solution to the problem of poverty. Hegel then weighs the possibility of providing direct financial aid to the poor that would be funded by taxes imposed upon the wealthy or other public sources.[17] However, he ultimately rejects this since it would contradict the basic principle of civil society, which is that people are to support themselves through their own labor. Hegel also rejects the proposal that the state provide the poor with productive work through public institutions.

It appears that Hegel can see no way of solving the problem of poverty. Besides material deprivation, a significant evil of poverty is that being poor means being alienated. Poverty is a circumstance of alienation; the poor cannot be at home in the social world.[18] Nonetheless, it is not clear that Hegel fully grasps this point. He never specifically states that poverty is a circumstance of alienation. Had he clearly seen the problem of poverty as a problem of alienation, then it is likely that it would have held a more central place in his work than it does. The poor, for Hegel, are objectively cut off from participation in the modern world. His primary concern is with the subjective alienation of the members of the bourgeoisie and not the objective alienation of the poor.[19] To be sure, Hegel does take the problem of poverty to be very serious, but he does not think that it is so serious as to undermine his conception of the modern state as *Geist* perfected. Since it is a problem that must be overcome and a tension that needs to be reconciled, political economy and philosophy must devote considerable time and effect to the problem of poverty.

Hegel's philosophy can demonstrate that all temporal existence is subject to defects and accidents, and thus the wise do not expect perfection of anything in this world. All human things are marred by contingency. As discussed in previous chapter, the actual state is rational, but the existing state is never wholly actual.[20] Actual states are always marred by the error and misconduct of those in charge of public affairs. Hegel's political philosophy also provides no solution to the problem of poverty, because in civil society it is not an accident:

> As the dialectic had become frightened of itself, in the *Philosophy of Right* Hegel broke off such thoughts by abruptly absolutizing one category—the state. This is due to the fact that while his experience did indeed ascertain the limits of bourgeois society, limits contained in its own tendencies, as a bourgeois idealist he stopped at that boundary because he saw no real historical force on the other side of it. He could not resolve the contradiction between his dialectic and his experience: it was this alone that forced Hegel the critic to maintain the affirmative.[21]

Hence, poverty is not the result of contingent imperfections that befall a rational system. Its emergence is a necessary consequence of civil society. Ultimately Hegel offers no solution.[22] Dialectical reason must be applied to Hegel's conception of the state. Consequently, it is imperative that contemporary thinkers wrestle with the problem of poverty and continue to look for solutions. "'Trickle-down' theories of prosperity are implausible enough in advanced countries such as the United States and Britain. They are Borgesian fictions in Mexico."[23] Put another way: "First, Second, and Third Worlds, North and South, developed and developing countries have all suffered the results of downward leveling. . . ."[24]

## Contemporary Globalization

Globalization refers to a transformation in the scale of human organization that links distant communities and expands the reach of economic power relations across the world's regions and continents. As Soviet-style communism was being dismantled, free market capitalism declared a global victory. With Marxist ideology wholly discredited, the state in decline as a significant institution, and economic globalization and neoliberalism erasing national borders, many concluded that the full force of the market could now be unleashed to focus human attention exclusively on the production and consumption of endless material wealth:

A process of global command, brought about in large part through the imposition of the economic norm (principally through the World Bank and the International Monetary Fund), . . . extended on a truly global scale. The acceptance of Russia . . . in the World Bank and IMF is one of the final pieces in the puzzle. Economic command over the First, Second, and Third Worlds can now be presented as global political command. The right of capital to intervene at a world level . . . can now be posed as a juridical power.[25]

The long path of human history is held by many to be reaching its ultimate conclusion—a universal, consumer society. Of course, much of the world remains a long way from universal peace and prosperity, even within free market capitalism's own borders. However, this does little to moderate its claim to victory. The deregulation of markets and the move toward global economic integration has provided rich financial rewards to those at the pinnacles of financial power and has widened the gap between the market's winners and losers, rich and poor.[26] Furthermore, nations with capitalist economies are becoming less democratic to the extent that public policy becomes dictated by the need to compete and flourish in the transnational political economy.[27] Decisions that were once made in legislative chambers are now being made in corporate boardrooms. As economic activities increasingly transcend regions and national frontiers, a direct challenge is mounted to the territorial principle that underpins the modern state.[28] The globalization emanating from the West has lead to the spread of aggressive individualism to the detriment of community values. Hegel's ethical theory warns of the dangers that follow when economic relations are disembedded from other cultural and institutional structures.[29]

Although every recent generation seems to be living through great changes that transform human lives and practices, what gives contemporary change its power is globalization. The interaction of extraordinary technological innovation is combined with a worldwide reach driven by global capitalism. The substitution of machines and computers for workers is going to force every nation to rethink the role of human beings in the social process.[30] Moreover, it has a speed, inevitability, and force that it has not had before. There is a quantum leap in scale and nature of both risk and opportunity. Although capitalism has existed for more than two centuries, today society is encountering a new form of capitalism:

They simply call it the free market, but by that bit of short-hand they mean very much more than the freedom to buy and sell. What they celebrate, preach and demand is private enterprise liberated from governmental regulation, unchecked by effective trade unions, unfettered by sentimental customs barriers or investment restrictions, and molested as little as possible by taxation. What they insistently demand is the privatization of state-owned businesses of all kinds. . . . What they promise is a more dynamic economy that will generate new wealth, while saying nothing about the distribution of any wealth, old or new. They call it free market, but I call it turbo-charged capitalism, or turbo-capitalism for short, because it is so profoundly different from the strictly controlled capitalism that flourished from 1945 until the 1980s.[31]

Globalization is such a powerful idea because there seems to be no escaping it. For instance, the remote Asian farmer is as likely to be affected by farming of genetically modified wheat in the United States' Midwest as is the European consumer. Furthermore, giant multinational corporations dwarf the GNPs of all but the few very largest countries in the world and are globally deploying the latest technology. In many important respects, political and economic borders are coming down, and there is a new conception of time, risk, and opportunity. To put it differently, the economy transforms the world, but it transforms it into a world of the economy.[32]

Globalization arguably involves the most profound redesign of the planet's political economic arrangements since the Industrial Revolution. Although it sounds rather simple, commoditization does capture the process by which almost every relationship is turned into a commercial exchange. It seems that more and more human relationships and decisions are determined by markets and economic efficiency. As Hegel notes, this can, and often does, have a dehumanizing effect upon people. Furthermore, a global market system is an application of a strictly economic calculus to the satisfaction of human needs and wants. In this respect, market systems promote amorality.[33] An ethical society is not one where markets flood into everything and all values are commercialized; nevertheless, without some spaces for the market, Hegel warns that freedom and prosperity can be threatened. As discussed in Chapter 5, when a government is too strong it might become oppressive, but when it is too weak, the society will lack the necessary steering mechanisms. Contrary to the Hegelian view that anticipates a global civil society—featuring diversity, and roughly equalitarian roles for participants—the evidence overwhelmingly points to a world order organized by, and in the interests of, large-scale private economic enterprises.[34] In order words, the destruction of national *Sittlichkeit* is not being replaced by a global *Sittlichkeit*. Moreover, as Hegel notes, an ethical life is not possible without a properly established *Sittlichkeit*. And without an ethical life, it is not possible to reconcile the individual and the community.

Through the new global free trade rules and deregulation, policies that are questionable—or even undesirable—at the national level are now being applied globally. Critics charge that these ideas have brought the disintegration of the social order, an increase in poverty and homelessness, alienation, ecological destruction, and an anxiety about the future. The passage of the Uruguay Round of GATT (General Agreement on Tariffs and Trade) with its associated WTO (World Trade Organization) is celebrated by the world's political leadership and transnational corporations as a global economic rebirth. It is claimed that these new arrangements will bring an expansion of economic activity in a short time, with benefits trickling down to everyone. However, the promises of global enthusiasts have fallen short in many respects:

> Yet, to their great and continuing embarrassment, growth . . . was much more rapid in the 1950s, 1960s, and 1970s than it is today. Evidently there was not all that much inefficiency, or perhaps there was, but it was outweighed by the hidden advantage of stability: secure incomes sustain families that save more, providing more capital for others to invest, and they also invest more themselves in the human capital of their children.[35]

> We have a wealth of data about how widespread and severe global poverty is today: out of a total of 6 billion human beings, 790 million are malnourished, 880 million lack access to health services, 1 billion are without adequate shelter, 1 billion without access to safe drinking water, 2 billion without electricity, and 2.4 billion without access to basic sanitation; 850 million adults are illiterate. One-quarter of all children between age five and fourteen, 250 million in all, do wage work outside their household, often under harsh or cruel conditions. Some 50,000 human deaths per day, fully one-third of all human deaths, are due to poverty-related causes.[36]

> In the United States free markets have contributed to social breakdown on a scale unknown in any other developed country. Families are weaker in America than in any other country. . . . They have generated a long economic boom from which the majority of Americans has hardly benefited. Levels of inequality in the United States resemble those of Latin America countries more than those of any European society.[37]

By expanding the boundaries of the market beyond the boundaries of nation-states, market power inevitably moves beyond the reach of national governments. "The NAFTA has benefited multinational companies, but has led to reduced real wages in the United States and Canada and a marked decline in Mexico's labor standards. It has had severe environmental consequences in the border regions especially."[38] As a result, governance decisions are transferred from governments, to multinational corporations. This violates Hegel's conception of *Rechtsstaat* by upsetting the proper balance within *Sittlichkeit*, particularly between civil society and the state. As indicated in Chapter 5, a properly constituted ethical life requires a certain amount of political regulation of economic activity, or community intervention to curb excessive individualism. By treating market relations as products of natural necessity, political economy excludes fundamental elements of freedom and responsibility that could bring markets within the field of justice.[39]

Consequently, corporations now have enormous political power that they are actively using to reshape the rules of the market. The GATT has now become one of the corporation's most powerful tools for reshaping the market. "Under the new GATT agreement, a World Trade Organization, the WTO, has been created with far-reaching powers to provide corporations the legal protection they feel they need to continue expanding their far-flung operations without the responsibility to serve any interest other than their own bottom line."[40] For instance, the WTO hears disputes brought against national or local laws that are held to be barriers against free trade. Secret panels of unelected trade experts hear the disputes and render rulings, which are rarely overturned. In general, any health, safety, or environmental standard that exceeds international standards set by industry representatives is likely to be considered a trade barrier. Nevertheless, there are important opportunities and benefits that can be gained from this new world. Capitalism is good at risk, change, and modernization. In fact, in can introduce new technologies that profoundly overturn many vested interests. In Asia and parts of Latin American, the pace of economic development has reached levels that would have been unlikely in earlier times. For example, the transfer of technology via foreign investment and the free dissemination of information have allowed rapid industrialization and a sharp rise in standards of living in many places.

Whatever one might think about the results, it is safe to say that contemporary human beings are living in a business civilization that is increasingly global. This trend has significant consequences for political economy. First, governments everywhere are less confident about the merits of the public domain and the effectiveness of public action. More frequently, governments are abdicating initiative to the private sector. Consequently, the decline of national sovereignty reflects globalization. Second, the diminishing role of the welfare state and competitive pressures at the bottom of the labor market make life for the poor as relatively harsh as in the more unregulated periods of capitalism. Third, there is also an accompanying intensification and insecurity of work as businesses strive to maximize shareholder value. Average wage-earners in the United States have seen their pay stagnate or fall in real terms over the last two decades, and they feel exposed to job insecurity. Global unemployment has reached its highest level since the great depression, with more than 800 million people unemployed or underemployed in the world.[41] Businesses today are under a severe threat from technological competition to reduce jobs in order keep profits up. Capitalism seems to have two faces:

> It's a very febrile capitalism, but for all that and its short-termism it has been a very effective transmission agent for the new technologies and for creating the new global industries and markets. It is a tool both of job generation and of great

inequality. One can't imagine a planned economy managing to be as creative or as destructive.[42]

In brief, new capitalism is clearly a driving force of globalization.

Colonial rule changed the social and economic structures of the third world. New structures, consumption styles, and technological systems have become so ingrained in third world economies that even after the attainment of political independence, the importation of Western values, products, technologies, and capital have continued and expanded.[43] Third world nations have grown more dependent upon global trading and financial systems, as well as on multinational corporations. Formal colonialism came to an end not because the colonial powers decided to forgo its economic advantages, but because these conditions can be obtained by more politically acceptable and more effective methods.[44] In other words, the influence of Western commerce, trade, and political organization outlived direct rule: "Powerful national economic interests have often been able to sustain hegemonic positions over former colonial territories through the replacement of a 'visible presence of rule' with the 'invisible government' of corporations, banks, and international organization."[45] In order to finance the import of modern technology, third world countries are forced to export even more goods and crops. Economically, financially, and technologically, third world nations are sucked deeper into the whirlpool of the world economic system and consequently losing their indigenous skills, their capacity for self-reliance, and in many cases the very resource base on which their survival depends.[46]

For more than a century, the conventional economic wisdom has been that new technologies boost productivity, lower the costs of production, and increase the supply of cheap goods, which, in turn, stimulates purchasing power, expands markets, and generates more jobs. This proposition provides the operating rationale for the economic policy of nearly every industrial nation in the world. Furthermore, it is believed that the dramatic benefits brought on by advances in productivity eventually filter down to the mass of human beings in cheaper goods, greater purchasing power, and more jobs. As foretold by Hegel, it seldom seems to happen that perfectly. Although stockholders have greatly profited from new technologies and advances in productivity, benefits have not trickled down to the average worker. So far, the promises have not been realized. As trade and financial markets have been widely opened, incomes have not risen faster, but slower. Moreover, equality among nations has not improved, with many of the poorest countries suffering an absolute decline in incomes. Between 1980 and 1995, income growth was actually negative among the least developed countries, dropping 0.4 percent per year.[47] Thus, over the past two decades, forced economic integration has led to a greater inequality of global incomes. For example, in what can be referred to as a "trickle-up" process, in Mexico there has been a massive transfer of resources from the salaried population to owners of capital and from public control to a few private hands.[48] Moreover, the world seems to reflect a polarized class structure. About twenty percent of the world's population can be labeled over-consumers, about sixty percent of the population are presently meeting most of their basic needs, and about twenty percent are essentially excluded—that is, eating a nutritionally inadequate diet, drinking contaminated water, and living in rudimentary shelters or in the open.[49] This bottom twenty percent of the world's population is essentially Hegel's "rabble."

Although it was not recognized as a concern in Hegel's time, it is becoming clear that the environment is not capable of sustaining the growing impact of economic activity. "Rapid transport from here-to-there is the condition of the global economy and of the proliferation of global pollutants."[50] The bottom line is that because of population growth and the more than fivefold economic expansion since the 1950s, the environmental demands on the economic system now fill the available environmental space of the planet.[51] Everywhere forests are overlogged, agriculture overcropped, grasslands overgrazed, wetlands overdrained, groundwater overtapped, seas overfished, and nearly all terrestrial and marine environment is overpolluted with chemical and radioactive poisons. Worse still, the atmospheric environment is becoming less capable of absorbing either the ozone-depleting gases or the greenhouse gases generated by these activities without creating new climactic conditions to which human beings cannot indefinitely adapt.[52] Although increased trade is seen as being the most effective way to increase economic development, it has dire environmental consequences. In Taiwan, for instance:

> Following "free trade" principles, efforts to maximize agricultural production for export-oriented plantations have led to the tripling of fertilizer use between 1952 and 1980, which has led to soil acidification, zinc losses, and decline in soil fertility, with water pollution and fertilizer runoff contaminating groundwater—the main source of drinking water for many Taiwanese. The use of pesticides has also increased massively, and it's a major source of contamination of Taiwan's surface waters and groundwaters. Because of deregulation, pesticide sale is subject to no effective government controls.[53]

With the advent of the global economy, economic competitiveness is the order of the day. Subsequently, this leads to the elimination of environmental regulations. The biosphere is incapable of sustaining six billion people at the consumption level of the developed nations.[54]

Caught in the throes of increasing global competition, multinational corporations seem determined to hasten the transition from human workers to machine surrogates.[55] Moreover, their ardor has been fanned by compelling bottom-line considerations. A firm can save money by lowering standards for pollution control, wages, and health care—all choices that externalize some of its costs.[56] A relatively small number of these multinationals are becoming the true power wielders of the contemporary era. "Multinational corporations now account . . . for at least 25 per cent of world production and 70 percent of world trade, while their sales are equivalent to almost 50 percent of world GDP."[57] This new world order has been a major force in greatly reducing the influence of nation-states. Corporate enterprise is a locus of irreducibly unaccountable power.[58] Unaccountability of the multinational corporation is now the prevailing condition in most countries. With fewer and fewer exceptions, the world-active company makes decisions that affect huge numbers of people and reports to no one, except its own executives and its major shareholders.[59] At the same time, the strength of these multinational corporations continues to grow as they expand.

For Hegel, a modern *Sittlichkeit* that is appropriate for human beings requires the proper balance between economics and politics. At times, government power is necessary to check excessive economic power. Tony Clarke notes that, in effect, what has taken place is a massive shift in power, out of the hands of nation-states and democratic governments and into the hands of multinational corporations. It is now the multinational companies that effectively govern the lives of the vast majority of the people on Earth, even though these new world realities are seldom reflected in the strategies of citizen movements for democratic social change.[60] The *Rechtsstaat* has lost its role protecting the lives and rights of its citizens through public regulation. Ironically, this is taking place under the name of democracy, where the advance of free markets is seen as the advance of democracy. The difficulty is that the most basic rule of corporate operation is that it must show a profit, regardless of everything else. For Hegel, "the just economy is only worthy of its title if it is subject to a continual political supervision that intervenes upon the market to prevent commodity relations from interfering with the equal political opportunity of citizens and the affairs of the state."[61]

National boundaries are becoming extremely porous. The international mobility of capital simply reinforces the capitalist market's constraints on the state and its policies.

> When the economies are merged, capital flows to whatever locality offers the maximum opportunity to externalize costs through case subsidies, tax breaks, substandard pay and working conditions, and lax environmental standards. Income is thus shifted from workers to investors, and costs are shifted from investors to the community.[62]

Furthermore, one type of disinvestment in a society is the transfer of investment to another society where the multinational corporation has a presence. If a state is pursuing policies that a business does not like—be it corporate taxation, social spending, labor market regulation, or pollution abatement— that business can simply move elsewhere.[63] This aspect of globalization has greatly altered the balance between government and the economy in the modern state and is not a properly instituted *Sittlichkeit*. Although this has been possible for some time, it has proliferated with today's global economy. In recent decades, the international economy has changed rather dramatically in terms of the increasingly free movement of goods, services, capital, and labor across national boundaries. The new developments in the transnational order are leading to a withering away of the autonomy of national governments. Thus, modern states are no longer able to balance the particular with the universal.

The drive to privatize and bring under corporate management as many elements of economic and social activity as possible in the last half-century has tipped the balance of democratic existence to an uncomfortable precariousness.[64] As Hegel noted, the real challenge lies not so much with economic problems, but rather in the political and moral values that always enter into economic determinations. While private property makes individuals responsible for their actions relating to that property, it only encourages them to be responsible in relation to their own self-interests, and it does not rule out any antisocial or environmentally unsound action.[65] Moreover, when rights are a function of property rather than personhood, only those with property have rights.[66] Economics is a language that discusses the workings and options of society in a specific sphere, but it is not the language of all social values. As Hegel depicts with his conception of *Sittlichkeit*, politics and morality—collective wills and private value systems—must remain the bedrock of society. Economic freedom, however, is a euphemism for private enterprise unfettered by social accountability.[67] In other words, it accepts an unchallenged sovereignty of the market and the absolute primacy of economic efficiency over almost any societal purpose. Finally, in the market, one dollar is one vote, and people get as many votes as they have dollars. No dollar, no votes; markets are inherently biased in favor of people of wealth.[68]

The world's top corporations are now engaged in unprecedented global mergers, acquisition, and concentration. Robert Kuttner argues that corporations have become not only centers of concentrated economic and financial power, but are bearers of the prevailing laissez-faire global ideology. Furthermore, as their economic power grows, so does their political and intellectual reach, at the expense of nations-states that once balanced private economic power with public interest.[69] Global deregulation greatly reduces the role of the citizen. The World Trade Organization addresses the concerns of investors, but not workers or citizens. In fact, it lacks rules of evidence, due process, public hearings, or conflict of interest. Moreover, Kuttner suggests that while the regulatory role of the nation-state was based on understanding the instability of laissez-faire and the necessity of countervailing intervention, the WTO is the opposite, since its mission allows laissez-faire to operate at its pleasure. Governments are supposed to stay clear, since entrepreneurs need to be free to move capital and production and seek markets anywhere in the world, without political intrusion. Global laissez-faire pulls capital into corners of the globe where there is less regulation, which in turn makes it harder for all nations to police their banks, stock exchanges, capital markets, and social standards. Kuttner concludes that the very existence of laissez-faire unravels the safety net by further limiting the realm of the public sphere. In essence, the WTO is the world's highest judicial and legislative body.[70] As illustrated in Chapters 5 and 6, Hegel rejects a pure laissez-faire approach to political economy. Since markets are shaped by human expectations, their behavior cannot be rationally predicted.

Many workers are no longer able to find full-time employment and long-term job security. In 1993, BankAmerica Corporation—then the nation's second largest bank—announced that it was turning 1,200 full-time positions into part-time ones.[71] Across the United States, other corporations are creating a new structure of employment, composed of a small core of permanent full-time employees and a growing pool of part-time, contingent employees. The lack of employment opportunities is not a temporary, short-run aspect of the United States' economy, but is permanent and endemic.[72] Faced with a highly competitive economy, many companies are paring down their core labor pool and hiring temporary workers to be able to add and drop workers quickly in response to changing trends in the market. Temporary employment agencies are providing American companies with over a million employees every day. For instance, Manpower, the nation's largest temp agency, is now the country's single largest employer with over a half of a million workers.[73] In the last couple of decades, there has been significant growth in contingent work. In fact, between 1982 and 1992, temporary employment grew ten times faster than overall employment. Today, temporary workers are being used in virtually every industry and sector. More people now labor at short-term tasks and change employers frequently. Lifetime employment in one place is a thing of the past. As a result, people cannot identify themselves with a particular labor or single employer. Thus, it has disturbed identities based on place—that sense of "home," of belonging somewhere particular in the world.[74] That is, today's economy increased alienation and works against a firmly established *Sittlichkeit* that is necessary for a reconciled human life.

The growing gap in income between top management and the rest of the American workforce is creating a deeply polarized nation. One cannot help thinking of Hegel's discussion of the great wealth and abject poverty of the modern economy. The gross domestic product of the United States has grown more than 40 percent in past quarter century, while the real median income of more than 60 percent of American workers has fallen.[75] The middle class, once the signature of American prosperity, is statistically shrinking. Since the 1980s, the income gap in the United States began to dramatically widen. By the end of the decade, the richest 0.5 percent of families owned 30.3 percent of the household net worth, an increase of over 4 percent from 1983.[76] During the same time period, the poorest fifth of the population experienced a decline in income. In other words, the American rich became richer while the rest of the workforce saw their wages and benefits cut. During the last two decades of the twentieth century, average wages dropped even while productivity increased. Moreover, less than one percent of the people had more wealth than the bottom 90 percent combined. To those that argue that this extreme inequality of income is required to provide the necessary incentive, the evidence is strong that both worker participation in management and profit sharing tend to enhance productivity and the worker-run enterprises often are more profitable than their counterparts.[77]

Two very different Americas are emerging in the twenty-first century. The new high-technology revolution seems to be exacerbating the growing tensions between rich and poor. Kevin Phillips is concerned about the emergence of "dual economies" and points to Pennsylvania, where high-tech cities like Philadelphia are prospering in the new global economy, while other areas of the state are losing steel mills and textile plants.[78] Census Bureau statistics provide statistical evidence of the growing gap between rich and poor. In 1992, 36.9 million people were living in poverty, an increase of 5.4 million from 1989.[79] Most of the nation's poor work, they just do not make enough to make ends meet. In the last two decades, although productivity grew by 22 percent, the median hourly wage actually fell 13 percent.[80] Furthermore, the gap between top executive officers and average workers is increasing as well. In the mid-1960s, with growth rising at about 6 percent per year, the ratio between the income of CEOs and average workers was 39 to 1; in 1997, however, it was 254 to 1.[81] As if that is not enough, tax reform during the same period actually exacerbated economic inequality. "America is no longer a bourgeois society. It has become a divided society, in which an anxious majority is wedged between an underclass that has no hope and an overclass that denies any civil obligations."[82]

Despite tremendous economic growth over the years, Hegel's rabble still exists in great numbers. Hegel was well aware that the ethical imperative of the market makes social justice a problem much more formidable than the liberal task of protecting the person and property of each individual.[83] Thus, the economy cannot be divorced from other dimensions of society. "What contemporary economists might learn from Hegel is that the economy is moral, legal, and political. . . ."[84] His basic account of the modern state provides resources for the reconciliation of the state and civil society, the universal and the particular. "It can be shown employing the categories of Hegel's philosophy of right, that civil society and the state can be reconciled, provided that social inequalities are counteracted through a pervasive public regulation of market activity and that social factors are prevented from becoming bases of political privilege."[85] Moreover, Hegel's thought furnishes a framework for criticizing social and political institutions that fail to meet these requirements. He recognized that a just economics requires a vigilant political system. Hegel's discussion of political economy warns us of the consequences that follow when economic forces get out of control. With globalization, individual nations no longer possess the ability to safeguard the public interests, and international institutions have not yet been developed to do the job. In short, a global economic requires a global *Sittlichkeit* and *Rechtsstaat*.

## HEGEL AND CONTEMPORARY DILEMMAS

Hegel certainly disagrees with specific postmodern views on the limited possibility of philosophy, and he clearly believes that a standpoint of autonomous rational objectivity is attainable. Philosophy is possible as a rigorous science, and many features of modernity can be demonstrated as distinctively rational. Consequently, Hegel's task is to defend a conception of autonomous reason: "Henceforth the principle of the independence of Reason, or of its absolute self-substance, is made in a general principle of philosophy, as well as a forgone conclusion of the time."[86] However, it is a grave mistake to think that Hegel was not aware of the difficulties and paradoxes consequent upon the foundational project. As illustrated in Chapter 2 and Chapter 7, Hegel is clearly aware of the inherent difficulties involved in grounding philosophy. The *Phenomenology of Spirit* is nothing other than an immanent and thoroughgoing critique of the traditionally conceived manner of establishing philosophy as a science. In fact, William Maker argues that Hegel introduces the standpoint of autonomous reason and philosophical science through a radical and consummately destructive critique of foundational epistemology and transcendental philosophy.[87] He further asserts that Hegel completes the philosophical tradition in a way that already incorporates the legitimate features of postmodern criticism of it, and Hegel does so without undermining the force of critique or succumbing to the problematic features of postmodernism, such as excessive relativism. If this is so, then contemporary oppositions between modernity and postmodernity are false dichotomies; that is, the philosophical revelation of the failure of foundationalism is part of the modernist tradition of the self-critique of reason.[88]

Hegel is not a foundationalist in the sense attacked by Nietzsche, Heidegger, or Derrida. "He rejects the whole idea that philosophy must begin with premises or 'first principles' which are accepted from the outset and then derive or deduce a number of consequences which are its 'results.'"[89] Strange as it may sound, if there is anything that can lead to a determinacy of reality, it has to be nothing; that is, nothing that is stipulated, nothing that is real in itself, nothing that can be claimed about knowing.[90] Hegel's *Science of Logic* and *Encyclopedia* can be seen as taking this anti-foundational course. Although the investigation of the conditions of knowledge is intended as a necessary preliminary to any knowledge, Hegel castigates it as "knowing before knowing."[91] His philosophical project is modern to the extent that it is concerned with epistemological issues that arise out the emergence of modern scientific thought and practical issues that arise out of the French Revolution. Both the advent the modern scientific method and French Revolution result in the break from specific aspects of philosophical and political traditions. Like modern thinkers, Hegel believes that the decisive breaks heralded by the scientific and French revolutions stand in need of legitimation. His own philosophical project is more specifically shaped by his perception of the inadequacies of predecessors in successfully legitimating the breaks from past authority announced by these two revolutions.[92]

For Hegel, previous modern thinkers substitute new allegedly rational privileged givens for old privileged and authoritarian givens as principles for cognition and conduct. With Descartes, philosophy, whether rationalist or empiricist, becomes defined by its investigation into the foundations of knowledge that is conducted by the reflecting subject. Prior to Hegel, modern philosophy tries to demonstrate that the ultimate foundations for determining truth is not found in privileged traditions, but rather is found within the thinking-rational subject. Hegel sees rationalists, empiricists, and transcendental idealists alike as engaged in the task of seeking to discover some given, universally shared bases for knowledge and action within the individual, either as rational or natural sensing being.[93] Like contemporary postmodern thinkers, Hegel agues that this approach is fruitless. "By repudiating the foundationalism underlying praxis and liberal philosophies of justice, and following out the logic of the philosophy of right, Hegel paves the way for a systematic investigation of what the economy ought to be."[94] His *Science of Logic* illustrates how reason attains normative validity by achieving a foundation-free autonomy. "In regard to the quest for knowledge, this involves developing an autonomous reason, that instead of resting on foundations, generates its own method and content in the course of its self-determination."[95] Hegel attempts to free the quests for truth and justice of all privileged foundations by seeking justification in self-determined determinacy or freedom.

Even though Hegel recognizes the inadequacies of his predecessors and agrees with some of the postmodern arguments against foundationalist epistemology, his rejection of the adequacy of consciousness as a paradigm in philosophy does not lead him to skeptical, relativistic, or nihilistic conclusions. Nevertheless, Hegel refuses to subordinate reason to some other authority. His philosophical system conceives of reality from the standpoint of autonomous reason, not given assumptions of tradition. As we saw in Chapters 3 through 6, Hegel's conception of the *Sittlichkeit* and *Rechtsstaat* are derived from notions of individuality and freedom that are not given. His system denies that the determinate primacy for reason of any such given can be demonstrated. However, the price of the claim to reason's autonomous self-constitution, as based on the rejection of the given as foundational, is an appreciation of the self-closure of the system.[96] In other words, Hegel's system does not "absolutize" reason in the sense of denying that there are any limits to it. Therefore, while Hegel is a nonfoundationalist, his philosophy is still a critical one that does not fall into relativism. Hegel's development of self-determined determinacy has a noncollapsing structure: Its structure is not immediately given, but entirely produced through the mediation of its own self-determination.[97]

Only by being determined through itself can justice avoid being relative to the given conditions of particular circumstances and attain the unconditioned universality constitutive of normative validity; therefore, Hegel concludes that justice can have no foundations, but must be its own ground and standard.[98] If the demands of normativity are met by self-determination, then the institutions of justice must be the reality of freedom. Freedom is not inherent in the given structure of the individual agent, but rather must involve an institutionally determined activity:

> The foundation-free systematic philosophy inaugurated by Hegel has attempted to conceive truth and justice in terms of self-determination in order to escape the dilemmas of foundationalism and the attendant opposition of natural right and conventionalism. Despite the debatability Hegel's success in working out this option, it does provide a strategy that meets the challenge of nihilism and allows for a prescriptive conception of right comprising of a theory of justice.[99]

Individual freedom and individuality originate from and depend upon a network of various institutions whose definitive character is more properly thought of as intersubjectively constituted. Unlike subjectivist theories, Hegel does not conceive of freedom in atomistic, egological terms; unlike most postmodernists, his conception of freedom is compatible with the idea of autonomous reason that postmoderns disparage.[100]

Thus, contrary to Habermas' charge discussed in the previous chapter, Hegel's philosophy is not a philosophy of the subject, but is instead a post-Cartesian, post-Kantian account of ethical intersubjectivity. In the *Phenomenology of Spirit*, self-consciousness develops out of an intersubjective account of recognition. For Hegel, recognition constitutes the ethical sphere. For Hegel, freedom is neither a natural given, nor an attribute of the self, but rather an intersubjective process of reciprocal recognition.[101] He maintains that ethics is the support and foundation of rights-based, moral sanctions:

> Hegel is indeed claiming that the human good consists in being actively related to others within certain institutions. But he is also claiming, even more controversially, that it is only in being so linked that nature, implications, and bindingness of other sorts of normative claims can be fully made out. He is especially claiming that it is only in being so linked that I can actually *be* an individual, rights-bearing, morally responsible, and therewith free individual.[102]

Social institutions and practices are the objective sphere of ethics. For Hegel, being free means to act under social norms that are self-imposed, that is, norms must count as reasons that actually motivate one's behavior. Ethical life consists in a theory of practical rationality that develops dialectically. Human freedom and political rights do not depend on fictitious givens or assumptions, such as contract theory. Rather, the legitimation of freedom and constitution of principles of action can be undertaken solely through an exercise of autonomous reason. As illustrated above, real freedom depends upon various circumstances and conditions that can only be guaranteed by human acts and by humanly created institutions. The Hegelian approach holds that abstract ideals, such as the dignity of the individual, acquire usable content only in the context of concrete institutions.[103] For Hegel, reason functions critically only when one acknowledges that claims to authority require some rational justification, not merely the appeal to coercion. Self-determination requires social institutions and practices.

### Excessive Individualism and Fragmentation

As Hegel notes in the *Philosophy of Right*, excessively individualistic conceptions of liberalism tend to empty the concept of citizenship of any meaningful content. On the contrary, Hegel demonstrates that a civic relationship to the state presupposes an underlying attachment to a concrete political community. Unless the relationship to the state is mediated by a sense of commitment to an enduring political community, then citizenship is something hollow and the whole of modern existence, of which liberalism tends to function as a theoretical encapsulation, eats away at the sources of solidaristic attachments.[104] Moreover, the globalization of contemporary economics has enormous implications for the theory of democratic citizenship. When traditional services are stripped of their social character, privatized, and put on an individual ability-to-pay basis, the common good is grievously wounded.[105] The more contractual arrangements enfold the lives of people, the less cohesiveness there is in the community. Market relationships are not the same as community and citizenship. While Hegel recognizes that free enterprise is a necessary aspect of human freedom, he clearly warns us that it can be pushed too far. Contemporary institutions and practices are failing to reconcile individuals with an ethical community.

Serious reflection of citizenship further requires an examination of the cultural dimension. In order to participate in civic life, people must be fitted for it, which presupposes a certain level of *Sittlichkeit*. This raises serious concerns regarding political and cultural education, as well as economic practices that shape the dominant culture. Either people inhabit a culture that stimulates political energies and enlivens political imagination, or they inhabit one that stifles and dulls the cultural resources that nourish citizenship. "The contemporary 'citizen' is unfitted for citizenship, not merely because of deficiencies in the political system, but because the nature of modern modes of consumption thoroughly privatizes individuals and renders them incapable of experiencing anything genuinely public."[106] Like communitarianism, Hegel notes that political citizenship requires a shared culture. The problem with contemporary mass culture is not that it merely renders people uncultured, but that it privatizes and deracinates them—that is, undermines the cultural conditions of citizenship. Hegel sees this and thinks that it could be contained within the modern state. "Only within the enacted contexts of a system of rights, such as comprise property relations, a moral community, a free family, a civil society, and a constitutional democracy, can individuals achieve genuinely self-determination."[107]

Political liberalism and unregulated capitalism overly stress private, individualistic aims. In fact, the classical ideal of the 'good life' is replaced by ever-increasing private wants and consumption. The economic practices of contemporary societies seem to rule out the very possibility of restraint of wants and desires in the interest of liberty. As public space is privatized, more and more dimensions of life are held to be outside the realm of politics in the name of property rights and economic efficiency, and therefore are unable to be touched by the public will. Hegel would likely view the contemporary situation as being one where civil society has infringed on the boundaries of the state and upset the balance of ethical life. Consequently, political action appears as necessarily futile, and, as the sense of efficacy shrinks, so too do the bounds of civic allegiance to the political community.[108] It is no wonder that voting turnout has declined sharply. Hegel correctly foresaw the danger of public apathy inherent within liberal models of representation, as well as the dangers of an unregulated—or even under-regulated—civil society. In brief, liberalism provides a state that has lost its power, both internally in its capacity to form a coherent community and externally in its ability to pursue its objectives in the face of other nations.[109] Liberal society has become fragmented and atomistic, since its institutional structure is too weak to support a common sense of meaning and to generate a morally satisfying form of community. If government becomes impotent, democracy becomes a hollow façade. Hegel recognizes that the realization of each person's liberty requires a state that creates and maintains the conditions that assure the dignity of each individual.

In *The Human Condition*, Hannah Arendt charges that modern society is quintessentially a society of laborers or jobholders. By a jobholder's society Arendt means a society in which it is dictated that "whatever we do, we are supposed to do for the sake of 'making a living:'" a society governed by the "trend to level down all serious activities to the status of making a living."[110] In this respect, it is certainly wrong to conceive of liberalism as merely offering a neutral grid within which individuals can pursue their self-defined activities. As Hegel saw it, every society is shaped by its implicit ranking of activities, or by the definition of a certain range of activities as paradigmatically worthy of pursuit. According to Arendt, what defines modern society is that it tends increasingly to conceive of itself as a society of laborers in order to maximize the possibilities of consumption: "The modern age was as intent on excluding political man, that is, man who acts and speaks, from its public realm as antiquity was on excluding *homo faber*."[111] Thus, the liberal regime is a regime of producers and consumers, not of citizens. In short, society is not merely subsumed by economic command; it is absorbed entirely by the integrated mode of production. Democracy—even liberal democracy—requires public-spirited *homo civicus* as well as narrowly selfish *homo economicus*, and to the extent that the former is displaced by the latter, politics becomes increasingly problematic.[112] Hegel's *Rechtsstaat* is based on the recognition of the needs of both *homo economicus* and *homo civicus*. Following Hegel's *Sittlichkeit* should lead to a reconciliation of public and private aspects of modern life.

Depressed wages, a frenetic pace at the workplace, and the possibility of unemployment, are all taking their psychological toll on more and more Americans. Employees are feeling trapped by the new lean-production practices and sophisticated new automation technologies. Americans, perhaps more than any other people, define themselves in relationship to their work. From childhood, children are constantly asked what they want to be when they grow up. The notion of being "productive" is so deeply imprinted on the nation's character that when one is suddenly denied access to a job, his or her self-esteem is likely to plummet.[113] Employment is more than income; for many, it is the essential measure of self-worth. Thus, to be underemployed or unemployed is to feel unproductive and worthless. Living in a society that so greatly respects and admires high-earning winners, losers find it hard to preserve their self-esteem.[114] Social problems can be directly turned into psychological dispositions, such as guilt, anxiety, conflict, and neuroses. Homicide is up in the workplace. The murdering of employers has nearly tripled since 1989 and is the fastest-growing category of workplace violence.[115] After a period of outward rage, most unemployed workers turn their rage inward. Fearing that they will never work again, they begin to blame themselves for their predicament. They experience an overwhelming sense of shame and worthlessness.[116]

The price paid by working people for economic growth has been in terms of the breakdown of human associations, the loss of solidarity, indifference between people, violence, loneliness, and a sense of loss of function and purpose.[117] The present age is one in which the social order of national, state, ethnicity, and the traditional family is on the decline. The ethic of individual self-fulfillment and achievement is the most powerful current in modern society. Modern society does not integrate human beings as whole persons into its functional system; it relies on the fact that individuals are not integrated but only partly and temporarily involved as they wander between different functional worlds. "To the extent that society breaks down into separate functional spheres that are neither interchangeable nor graftable onto one another, people are integrated into society only in their partial aspects as taxpayers, car drivers, students, consumers, voters, patients, producers, fathers, mothers, sisters, pedestrians, and so on."[118] Hegel's system offers a response, or at least, a serious starting point for reconciliation and integration. He recognizes the fragmenting and alienating tendencies of modernity, and his critical philosophy responds to its shortcomings. Dialectical reason compels us to critically engage and address these problems and shortcomings, and not ignore them.

With the *Phenomenology*, Hegel breaks the circle of consciousness and leads the self to its intersubjective self-awareness as *Geist*. The radical individualist conception of society fits Hegel's dialectic of master and slave, where each seeks to be independent. Society is seen as a constant struggle to push one's own interests to maintain his or her independence vis-à-vis others.[119] Self-knowledge is only possible through mutual recognition. In other words, the self knows itself as rational being only if it grants the same status to the other. This means that the self must recognize the free and equal reality of others. It is the single act of self-consciousness between two selves where each recognizes itself in the other as the other recognizes itself in it: the I that is We, and the We that is I [*Ich, das Wir, und Wir, das Ich ist*].[120] Contrary to the claims of his postmodern critics, Hegel rejects the claim that there is a privileged realm of subjectivity where the self knows itself independent of others and the historical world. With the life and death struggle for recognition, Hegel is taking issue with Hobbes' analysis of human nature. Against Hobbes, Hegel is claiming that freedom is a more basic drive than self-preservation, since people are willing to risk their lives for it. Independence and freedom require community. Through the dialectic, the self breaks its solipsistic shell. This allows Hegel to criticize the excesses of liberalism while keeping necessary dimensions of individualism. As discussed in Chapter 2, Hegel's argument also forges a connection between realism and intersubjectivity by combining realism with an emphasis on the social dimension of knowledge. Hegel reminds us that we cannot understand political and moral principles outside the social and historical context from which they are established. "Accordingly, freedom is not a natural endowment or a monological capacity, but an actual structure of interaction consisting in the interconnected and mutually concordant actions of a plurality of agents."[121]

## Restoring Community and Ethical Life

Although the whole of Hegel's theory of politics has been subjected to severe criticism, it is difficult to exaggerate its enormous historical significance for modern political philosophy. In retrospect Hegel is seen by different contemporary thinkers as being both progressive and reactionary depending on who is evaluating him. For example, Karl Popper argues that the Marxist extreme left wing, as well as the conservative center, and the fascist extreme right, all base their political philosophies on Hegel.[122] As illustrated in Chapters 6 and 7, this is a gross misunderstanding of Hegel's political thought. Popper seems to forget the decisive influence of Kant on the development of Hegel's concept of freedom. In fact, Popper thinks that Hegel's insistence on the absolute moral authority of the state, which overrules all personal morality and all conscience, gives Hegel an important role in the development of modern totalitarianism. From his early Berne writings to the *Philosophy of Right*, Hegel makes Kant's principle of autonomy his chief moral idea. Popper further asserts that Hegel's political philosophy is essentially an apology for Prussianism. For Popper, that is why Hegel rigorously attacks liberalism. Liberal elements of political theory are replaced by a Platonic-Prussian worship of the state. The Hegelian idea that the history of the world is the world's court of justice is merely a defense of the status quo resulting from power struggles.

Popper's interpretations of Hegel are wrong. How could Hegel, who stresses freedom to the point of making it the goal of history, be accused of totalitarianism? How could he suggest that freedom had been achieved in the autocratic German society of his time? The first step toward clearing up this puzzle is questioning whether Hegel's ideally rational state is merely a description of the Prussian state at the time he was writing. It is clearly not. Although there are some similarities, there are also significant differences. First, his constitutional monarchy is not at all like the more absolute monarchy of Frederick William III. Second, while Prussia did not have a functioning parliament, Hegel's legislature makes law and provides an outlet for the expression of public opinion. Third, Hegel was a supporter of free expression and political rights in his day. Finally, Hegel advocated trial by jury as a way of involving citizens in the legal process, and there was no right to trial by jury in Prussia at that time. Hegel's language describing the state is often extravagant and has lent itself to misuse and distortion in the service of totalitarianism, but this is a misuse. Given the pluralistic structure of Hegel's *Rechtsstaat*, especially its inclusion of intermediate groups and the whole realm of civil society, the common criticism of Hegel as a defender of absolutism is wrong. As we saw in Chapter 3, Hegel regards freedom as the foundation of *Recht*, the essence of *Geist*, and the end of history. Moreover, in the *Philosophy of Right*, Hegel advocates formal and subjective freedom in many passages, and he stresses that such freedom requires non-interference by government. No less than Locke, Rousseau, or Kant, Hegel maintains that some rights are inalienable. In addition, he repeatedly argues that the ancient Greeks failed to recognize subjective freedom and the main strength of *Rechtsstaat* is that it secures individual rights.

These differences, especially when combined with an analysis of *Sittlichkeit*, should be sufficient to acquit Hegel of the charge of having drawn up his philosophy entirely in order to please the Prussian monarchy. They do not, however, make Hegel a liberal in the modern sense. Clearly, he is not a liberal. As indicated in Chapter 6, Hegel criticized popular suffrage because it would amount to whimsical likes and dislikes and would be based on an impulse. Since arbitrary choice is not a free act, freedom consists in acting according to the laws of reason. Law must be worthy of assent by any rational being. He critically reacts to the excessive individualism of modern liberalism that leads to atomized citizens. Hegel's defense of the state is contingent upon his belief that it is only a means to the basic law and order necessary for the foundation of liberty and the enjoyment of basic human rights and property. Charles Taylor notes that for Hegel, a state so atomized must lose the allegiance of its citizens and be paralyzed in inaction for lack of consensus, or else becomes the plaything of the arbitrary will of factions.[123] Taylor also notes that the Hegelian state of the *Philosophy of Right* exists nowhere in totality, and contemporary Prussia did not fill the bill at all. Nevertheless, Hegel is not a communitarian either, since he continues to hold fundamental liberal values, such as freedom of conscience, equality of opportunity, and various other individual rights. His dialectic clearly attempts to reconcile the tension of each into a harmony that respects both individual rights and community.

Experience reveals that liberal society cannot hold together simply by the satisfaction of its members' needs and interests, but also requires a common set of beliefs that link its structure and practices with what members see as of ultimate importance.[124] Hegel, according to Taylor, has insight into some of the perennial, recurring problems of liberalism. For example, the increasing alienation in a society that has eroded its traditional foci of allegiance makes it harder and harder to achieve the basic consensus which is required for a democracy.[125] Hegel notes that participation of all in a decision is only possible if there is a ground of agreement, an underlying common purpose. However, this becomes extremely difficult because the tight unity of the Greek *polis* cannot be recaptured in the modern world that knows the principle of individual freedom. Ultimately Taylor does not accept Hegel's conception of the state, but he does believe that Hegel's posing of the problem is still one of the most acute and penetrating available. There is little question that Hegel's *Rechtsstaat* fails as a precise blueprint for modern society, especially since a hereditary monarch is not likely to be capable of rising above the private factions of society in the way that Hegel asserts. We would be well-served to read democracy in a Hegelian spirit and see it as an evolving concept. Nevertheless, Hegel avoids enclosing his thought within a Cartesian philosophy of consciousness and is thus able to develop the first truly universal concept of the state. In addition, Hegel's state is not based upon an individual or a subjective decision; it is a moment in the necessary development of individual freedom into something higher. This organic conception makes Hegel's state different from other modern philosophers, for whom the state is static.

Hegelian political philosophy is particularly effective as a critical perspective on other views, such as liberalism or communitarianism. Understood in its historical context, Hegel's philosophy is neither radical nor reactionary, but is dialectical. It is not radical because it demands that statesmen build on the historical past; and it is not reactionary because it compels them to recognize the progressive forces of history and support rational change. He makes sound criticisms of the economistic and individualistic perspectives common in liberalism. Although he tolerates inequalities and affirms the ideal of equality of opportunity, Hegel sees the danger that extremes of wealth and poverty pose to the communal values of *Sittlichkeit*. Modern civil society also cannot fulfill its own principles of universal human freedom and dignity, because it systematically consigns whole classes to conditions of life that are subhuman by its own standards.[126] Nevertheless, Hegel can help us better understand a basic problem of the modern political world—the wish to have a form of political participation that is both genuinely meaningful and compatible with the pursuit of one's private life. Hegel's *Rechtsstaat* conceives of the universality of the state against the particularity of society, and this can only be achieved if the liberal state is transformed into a democratic state. For Hegel, the process of actualizing rights is embedded in a context that requires a public discussion about a shared conception of the common good.

Hegel's *Sittlichkeit* includes moral actions, though he makes a technical distinction between ethical life and morality [*Moralität*]. While morality concerns the individual's inner sphere, moral intentions and religious conscience, Hegel's ethics considers the individual as an integral part of the social and political body. As illustrated in Chapter 4, morality views individuals as if prior to the whole, while ethical life is a concrete universal that makes the whole prior to the part. Thus, Hegel argues that morality is one-sided and abstract, since it separates individuals from their place in the social whole. Even though *Sittlichkeit* is essential holistic, it includes the interests and rights of individuals. "While the whole is prior to its parts, it also cannot function apart from them; indeed, it realizes itself only through each of them individually, only if each of them retains its own separate identity as a necessary part of the whole."[127] Hegel does not think that individuals are merely a means for some collective end. Like Kant, he stresses that each individual is an end in him- or herself. In fact, the end of the social organism is the thriving of individuals. For Hegel, the reconciliation of individuals and community requires that individuals utilize critical reflection. Like Aristotle and Plato, Hegel holds that the highest good can be achieved only within the state. Human beings find meaning by becoming good citizens and fulfilling their social duties. Hegel's concept of reciprocity ensures that social responsibility is a vital component of citizenship.

Later liberal ideas are influenced as well by Hegelian streams, thus illustrating the neverending dialectic so characteristic of the history of political ideas in general. In Hegelian fashion, we must continue to synthesize philosophical concepts, preserving their truth and canceling their errors in a single coherent account. However, we must not assume that we have reached an ultimate, final truth, but must continue to search for dialectical tensions and gaps between existing reality and rational concepts. The notion of the "end of history" originates with Alexandre Kojève's idiosyncratic reading of Hegel.[128] More recently, Francis Fukuyama applies this notion to the end of the cold war and the fall of Soviet communism.[129] Hegel certainly believes that history has an end or goal, and he identifies this end with freedom in the modern state. However, this does not mean that Hegel holds a pragmatic understanding of the dialectic of world history. In fact, the entire argument of the *Philosophy of Right* serves as a refutation of the view that history alone is the final arbitrator of the rationality of any historical political regime. The ultimate justification of the modern, rational state is not that it is the political order that emerges at the end of the historical process, but that it is the one that most fully actualizes human freedom.[130] Hegel's historicism does not assert that the future is predetermined. "The necessity Hegel is after is nothing other than this sense of progression, of order in the midst of chaos, of *Bildung* in spite of the apparent absurdity of it all."[131]

As discussed in Chapter 7, Hegel never completely conflates the normative with the empirical by identifying the rational with any set of social or historical circumstances. His *Doppelsatz* [double dictum] only makes sense if we remember that Hegel steers a middle path between rationalism and empiricism. The rational is actual only to the extent that it realizes and develops the idea. To be sure, Hegel's political philosophy is based on optimism and faith in the progress of *Geist*, but it is not a naïve optimism that uncritically accepts the status quo. Moreover, Hegel's identification of the modern state with the goal of history does not preclude the possibility of a decline in the future. To be Hegelian, we must apply the dialectic to Hegel and all subsequent philosophies and existing political states. In conclusion, although the perfection of *Geist* in the modern state, as depicted by Hegel, has yet to be realized, his thought does provide a basis for either building an alternative to or modifying the contemporary liberal state. Democracy should be read as an evolving conception of the principle of respecting the dignity of individuals.[132] Like Hegel, today's social theorists should start with a concern for human freedom and intersubjectivity, and should search for the conditions of their full expression and flourishing. Hegel's goal of realizing human freedom is still valid for the twenty-first century; however, we should not too readily translate the contingent features of his social world into the edicts of eternal reason.

There is no essential historical Hegel whose personal intentions we can retrieve, or whose historical world we can objectively reconstruct as the central necessary condition in understanding what his texts meant or mean, and there is no essential or core meaning-in-itself in Hegel's texts, eternally waiting to be unearthed. Gadamer is right: we can only look at Hegel from where we are now, from within our own "horizon."[133]

The vast majority of people in modern democracies today tend to see freedom in a way that Hegel thought was inadequate, a vehicle for pursuing their self-chosen ends. Hegel emphasizes the self-realizing and self-determining dimension of freedom, one that is not simply doing as we please, but entails self-mastery, cultivation of capacities, and achievement of important goals. But he also stresses the need to balance it with community interest. Since individual liberty and community have not yet been reconciled, Hegel still speaks to us today:

> Besides, it is not difficult to see that ours is a birth-time and a period of transition to a new era. Spirit [*Geist*] has broken with the world it has hitherto inhabited and imagined, and is of a mind to submerge it in the past, and in the labour of its own transformation. Spirit is indeed never at rest but always engaged in moving forward.[134]

# NOTES

1. Joseph Heller, *Closing Time* (New York: Simon & Schuster, 1994), 94.

2. Jürgen Habermas, *The Inclusion of the Other: Studies in Political Theory*, ed. Ciaran Cronin and Pablo De Greiff (Cambridge: MIT Press, 1998), 174.

3. Habermas, *The Inclusion of the Other*, 174.

4. Habermas, *The Inclusion of the Other*, 174.

5. Benjamin Barber, *Strong Democracy: Participatory Politics for a New Age* (Berkeley: University of California Press, 2003), xii. Barber notes that democratic capitalism has been replaced by an incautious and predatory market capitalism.

6. Robert R. Williams, *Hegel's Ethics of Recognition* (Berkeley: University of California Press, 1997), 247. To be sure, the external state is supposed to provide opportunities to all in principle, but the disappearance of the possibility of property and the opportunity to work from the situation of the poor means that their freedom no long can have any determinate existence in the world.

7. Williams, *Hegel's Ethics of Recognition*, 244.

8. Richard Dien Winfield, *The Just Economy* (New York: Routledge, 1988), 221.

9. Mark R. Rank, *One Nation, Underprivileged: Why American Poverty Affects Us All* (New York: Oxford University Press, 2005), 25. "Currently, there are 34.6 million Americans, or 12.1 percent of the population, who fall below the poverty line. . . . [I]n addition to the 34.6 million Americans in poverty, a further 12.5 to 26.3 million Americans live precariously close to the poverty line."

10. Hegel, *Philosophy of Right*, 128. See Richard Dien Winfield, *Freedom and Modernity* (Albany, N.Y.: State University of New York, 1991), 133, where he says that today's democracies reflect the economic domination of society and social subordination of politics that Hegel feared.

11. Hegel, *Philosophy of Right*, 149–150.

12. Hegel, *Philosophy of Right*, 150.

13. Hegel, *Philosophy of Right*, 148–149.

14. Shlomo Avineri, *Hegel's Theory of the Modern State* (Cambridge: Cambridge University Press, 1972), 150.

15. Hegel, *Philosophy of Right*, 150.

16. Hegel, *Philosophy of Right*, 128.

17. Hegel, *Philosophy of Right*, 150.

18. See Michael O. Hardimon, *Hegel's Social Philosophy: The Project of Reconciliation* (Cambridge: Cambridge University Press, 1994), 245–246.

19. Hardimon, *Hegel's Social Philosophy*, 246.

20. Hegel, *Philosophy of Right*, p. 22.

21. Theodor Adorno, *Hegel: Three Studies*, trans. Shierry W. Weber (Cambridge: MIT Press, 1993), 80. Adorno goes on to assert that the central nerve of the dialectic as a method is determinate negation. Only the critical idea that unleashes the force stored up in its own object is fruitful; fruitful both for the object, by helping it to come into its own, and against it, reminding it that it is not yet itself. Adorno and others at the Frankfurt School argue that Hegel's focus on the negative and the power of negation and contradiction inherent in thought and reality seemed a key to rescuing the negative from the overwhelming affirmative power of advanced industrial society. A true, negative dialectic must strive to attain precisely that otherness that is denied by a subject-oriented dialectic.

22. See Avineri, *Hegel's Theory of the Modern State*, 153–154, where he concludes that after discarding the various possible alternatives for the elimination of poverty, Hegel gloomily remarks that it remains inherent and endemic to modern society. The *Philosophy of Right* attests to the depth of this pessimism: Against nature man can claim no right, but once society is established, poverty immediately takes the form of a wrong done to one class by another. He concludes that Hegel's civil society entails a theory of pauperization and social polarization. See also, Winfield, *The Just Economy*, for a discussion of a just economy based on Hegelian modifications to today's economy.

23. John Gray, *False Dawn: The Delusions of Global Capitalism* (New York: The New Press, 1998), 50.

24. Jeremy Brecher and Tim Costello, *Global Village or Global Pillage: Economic Reconstruction from the Bottom Up* (Cambridge: South End Press, 1998), 83.

25. Michael Hardt and Antonio Negri, *Labor of Dionysus: A Critique of the State-Form* (Minneapolis: University of Minnesota Press, 1994), 297.

26. David Korten, "The Mythic Victory of Market Capitalism," in *The Case Against the Global Economy: And for a Turn toward the Local*, ed. Jerry Mander and Edward Goldsmith (New York: Sierra Club Books, 1996), 188.

27. John Dryzek, *Democracy in Capitalist Times: Ideals, Limits, and Struggles* (Oxford: Oxford University Press, 1996), 3.

28. David Held and Anthony McGrew, *Globalization/Anti-Globalization* (Cambridge: Polity, 2002), 7.

29. Winfield, *The Just Economy*, 28.

30. Jeremy Rifkin, *The End of Work: The Decline of the Global Labor Force and the Dawn of the Post-Market Era* (New York: Tarcher/Putnam, 1995), xv.

31. Edward Luttwak, *Turbo Capitalism: Winners and Losers in the Global Economy* (New York: HarperPerennial, 1999), 27.

32. Guy Debord, *The Society of the Spectacle*, trans. D. Nicholson-Smith (New York: Zone Books, 1995), 28.

33. Robert Heilbroner and Lester Thurow, *Economics Explained* (New York: Touchstone, 1994), 256.

34. Herbert Schiller, *Information Inequality: The Deepening Social Crisis in America* (London: Routledge, 1996), 112.

35. Luttwak, *Turbo Capitalism*, 30.

36. Thomas Pogge, "Human Rights and Human Responsibilities," in *Global Justice and Transnational Politics: Essays on the Moral and Political Challenges of Globalization*, eds. P. De Grief and C. Cronin (Cambridge: MIT Press, 2002), 151–152.

37. Gray, *False Dawn*, 2.

38. Teresa Brennan, *Globalization and Its Terrors* (London: Routledge, 2003), 44. Corporations have successfully attacked environment regulations as a restraint of free trade under NAFTA.

39. Winfield, *The Just Economy*, 30–31. Thus, political economy would give an incipiently asocial, normatively neutral characterization to its otherwise eminently civilizing subject matter.

40. David Korten, "The Failures of Bretton Woods," in *The Case Against the Global Economy*, 28.

41. Rifkin, *The End of Work*, xv.

42. Will Hutton, "Anthony Giddens and Will Hutton in Conversation," in *Global Capitalism*, eds. Anthony Giddens and Will Hutton (New York: The New Press, 2000), 10.

43. Martin Khor, "Global Economy and the Third World," in *The Case Against the Global Economy*, 48.

44. Edward Goldsmith, "Development as Colonialism," in *The Case Against the Global Economy*, 255.

45. Held and McGrew, *Globalization/Anti-Globalization*, 13.

46. Khor, "Global Economy and the Third World," 48.

47. Faux and Mishel, "Inequality and the Global Economy," 97.

48. Carlos Heredia and Mary Purcell, "Structural Adjustment and the Polarization of Mexican Society," in *The Case Against the Global Economy*, 282–283.

49. David Korten, *When Corporations Rule the World*, (San Francisco: Kumarian Press, 2001), 252.

50. Brennan, *Globalization and Its Terrors*, xix. The consumption of fossil fuels is the condition of rapid transport over global distances. Brennan argues that under the present system, profit can continue to be made at the present rate only at the expense of the environment.

51. Joshua Karliner, *The Corporate Planet: Ecology and Politics in the Age of Globalization* (San Francisco: Sierra Books, 1997), 16–20.

52. Edward Goldsmith, "Global Trade and the Environment," in *The Case Against the Global Economy*, 78, and Brennan, *Globalization and Its Terrors*, 52.

53. Goldsmith, "Global Trade and the Environment," 79.

54. Goldsmith, "Global Trade and the Environment," 81.

55. Rifkin, *The End of Work*, 6.

56. Herman Daly, "Free Trade: The Perils of Deregulation," in *The Case Against the Global Economy*, 232. When firms produce under the most permissive standards and sell their products elsewhere without penalty, they press on countries with higher standards to lower them. In effect, unrestricted free trade imposes lower standards. Daly suggests that this is reverse environmental imperialism.

57. Held and McGrew, *Globalization/Anti-Globalization*, 53.

58. Samuel Bowles and Herbert Gintis, *Democracy and Capitalism: Property, Community, and the Contradictions of Modern Social Thought* (New York: Basic Books, 1987), 172.

59. Schiller, *Information Inequality*, 95.

60. Tony Clarke, "Mechanisms of Corporate Rule," in *The Case Against the Global Economy*, 298.

61. Winfield, *The Just Economy*, 231.

62. Korten, *When Corporations Rule the World*, 85.

63. Dryzek, *Democracy in Capitalist Times*, 77.

64. Robert Schiller, *Culture Inc: The Corporate Takeover of Public Expression* (Oxford: Oxford University Press, 1989), 3.

65. Andrew Sayer, *Radical Political Economy: A Critique* (Oxford: Blackwell, 1995), 151.

66. Korten, *When Corporations Rule the World*, 89.

67. Schiller, *Culture Inc*, 12.

68. Korten, *When Corporations Rule the World*, 73.

69. Robert Kuttner, "The Role of Governments in the Global Economy," in *Global Capitalism*, 147.

70. Brecher and Costello, *Global Village or Global Pillage*, 59. The trade panels will in effect have dictatorial power over governments.

71. Rifkin, *The End of Work*, 190.

72. Lester Thurow, *The Zero-Sum Society: Distribution and the Possibilities for Economic Change* (London: Penguin, 1980), 205.

73. Rifkin, *The End of Work*, 190.

74. Richard Sennett, "Street and Office: Two Sources of Identity," in *Global Capitalism*, 176.

75. Brecher and Costello, *Global Village or Global Pillage*, xix.

76. Rifkin, *The End of Work*, 173.

77. David Schweikart, *Against Capitalism* (Boulder, CO: Westview, 1996), 100.

78. Kevin Phillips, *The Politics of Rich and Poor: Wealth in the American Electorate in the Reagan Aftermath* (New York: Harper Perennial, 1991), 201.

79. Rifkin, *The End of Work*, 177.

80. Faux and Mishel, "Inequality and the Global Economy," 102.

81. Faux and Mishel, "Inequality and the Global Economy," 95.

82. Gray, *False Dawn*, 111.

83. Winfield, *The Just Economy*, 107.

84. Shaun Gallagher, "Interdependence and Freedom in Hegel's Economics," in *Hegel on Economics and Freedom*, ed. William Maker (Macon, Ga.: Mercer University Press, 1987), 180. To the extent that it is made abstract, to the extent that it is seen

as separable from other dimensions of ethical life, to the extent that it is theoretically disembedded, contemporary economists fail to deal with the living economy.

85. Winfield, *Freedom and Modernity*, 278.

86. Georg W. F. Hegel, *Logic*, trans. William Wallace (New York: Oxford University Press, 1975), 93.

87. Maker, *Philosophy Without Foundations*, 13.

88. Maker, *Philosophy Without Foundations*, 14. "Modernity, with its distinctive claims to the rightful primacy of autonomy, can only be legitimated on the basis of a demonstration that the autonomies of thought and action are neither in need of nor can have any foundations."

89. Robert C. Solomon, *In the Spirit of Hegel: A Study of G. W. F. Hegel's* Phenomenology of Spirit (New York: Oxford University Press, 1983), 229.

90. Winfield, *Freedom and Modernity*, 41.

91. Richard Dien Winfield, *Law in Civil Society* (Lawrence, KS: University of Kansas Press, 1995), 20.

92. Maker, *Philosophy Without Foundations*, 26.

93. Maker, *Philosophy Without Foundations*, 28. See Winfield, *Law in Civil Society*, 29, where he notes that completely contrary to foundationalism, the subject matter and method of philosophy will not be given at the outset but will be arrived at as the outcome of philosophical investigation.

94. Winfield, *The Just Economy*, 98.

95. Winfield, *Reason and Justice*, 14. See also Winfield, *Freedom and Modernity*, 43.

96. Maker, *Philosophy Without Foundations*, 39.

97. Winfield, *Reason and Justice*, 129.

98. Winfield, *The Just Economy*, 89.

99. Winfield, *Reason and Justice*, 16.

100. Maker, *Philosophy Without Foundations*, 41.

101. Winfield, *Freedom and Modernity*, 100.

102. Pippin, *Idealism as Modernism*, 420.

103. Terry Pinkard, *Democratic Liberalism and Social Union* (Philadelphia: Temple University Press, 1987), 173. The abstract ideals are themselves extrapolated from concrete social unions.

104. Ronald Beiner, *What's the Matter with Liberalism?* (Berkeley: University of California Press, 1992), 109.

105. Schiller, *Information Inequality*, xv.

106. Beiner, *What's the Matter with Liberalism?*, 126.

107. Winfield, *Law in Civil Society*, 31. The free will cannot be a monological structure, that is, a structure of the self, determined independently of the plurality of agents.

108. Beiner, *What's the Matter with Liberalism?*, 119.

109. Hardt and Negri, *Labor of Dionysus*, 253.

110. Hannah Arendt, *The Human Condition* (Chicago: The University of Chicago Press, 1958), 126–127.

111. Arendt, *The Human Condition*, 159.

112. Dryzek, *Democracy in Capitalist Times*, 13. Because there is no reason for *homo economicus* to be committed to liberal democratic norms, the result is that the institutional status quo may run out of defenders while its politics becomes more confused and incoherent as self-interest runs wild.

113. Rifkin, *The End of Work*, 195.

114. Luttwak, *Turbo Capitalism*, 21.

115. The National Institute for Occupational Safety and Health, "Violence in the Workplace," *Training and Development*, (January 1994): 27.

116. Rifkin, *The End of Work*, 196.

117. Schiller, *Culture Inc.*, 31.

118. Ulrich Beck, "Living Your Own Life in a Runaway World: Individualisation, Globalisation and Politics," *Global Capitalism*, 165.

119. Terry Pinkard, *Democratic Liberalism and Social Union* (Philadelphia: Temple University Press, 1987), 143.

120. Hegel, *Phenomenology of Spirit*, 110.

121. Winfield, *Reason and Justice*, 164.

122. Karl Popper, *The Open Society and Its Enemies: The High Tide of Prophecy: Hegel, Marx, and the Aftermath* (Princeton, N.J.: Princeton University Press, 1966), 30.

123. Charles Taylor, *Hegel* (Cambridge: Cambridge University Press, 1975), 451.

124. Taylor, *Hegel*, p. 459.

125. Charles Taylor, *Hegel and Modern Society* (Cambridge: Cambridge University Press, 1979), 115.

126. Allen Wood, *Hegel's Ethical Thought* (Cambridge: Cambridge University Press, 1990), 260.

127. Beiser, *Hegel*, 235. In ethical life, Hegel tries to synthesize the rights both of objectivity and subjectivity.

128. Alexandre Kojève, *Introduction to the Reading of Hegel: Lectures on the Phenomenology of Spirit*, trans. James Nichols (Ithaca, N.Y.: Cornell University Press, 1969).

129. Francis Fukuyama, *The End of History and the Last Man* (New York: Free Press, 1992).

130. Paul Franco, *Hegel's Philosophy of Freedom* (New Haven, CT: Yale University Press, 1999), 338. While it is true that Hegel sees the empirical course of history as confirming his philosophical justification, it does not have independent verifying power.

131. Solomon, *In the Spirit of Hegel*, 207. "What Hegel has in mind is a kind of context-bound, *teleological* necessity, necessity within a context *for some purpose*. It is not precise; it cannot be formalized or reduced to a formula. . . . Hegel does not mean by 'necessity' what Kant means by 'a priori.'"

132. Pinkard, *Democratic Liberalism and Social Union*, 174.

133. Pippin, "Gadamer's Hegel," 236.

134. Hegel, *Phenomenology of Spirit*, 6.

# Bibliography

Adorno, Theodor. *Hegel: Three Studies*. Cambridge: MIT Press, 1993.
———. *Negative Dialectics*. New York: Continuum, 1973.
———. *Prisms*. Cambridge: MIT Press, 1967.
Althaus, Horst. *Hegel: An Intellectual Biography*. Malden, MA: Polity Press, 2000.
Aquinas, Thomas. *On Kingship*. Toronto: The Pontifical Institute of Medieval Studies, 1949.
———. *The Political Ideas of St. Thomas Aquinas*. New York: Hafner Press, 1953.
Arato, A. and Gebhardt, E. *The Essential Frankfurt School Reader*. New York: Continuum, 1982.
Arendt, Hannah. *The Human Condition*. Chicago: The University of Chicago Press, 1958.
Aristotle. *Nicomachean Ethics*. Indianapolis: Bobbs-Merrill, 1962.
———. *Physics*. Oxford: Clarendon Press, 1970.
———. *Politics*. Chicago: The University of Chicago Press, 1984.
Augustine. *The City of God*. Garden City: Image Books, 1958.
———. *On Free Choice of Will*. Indianapolis: Hackett, 1993.
Avineri, Shlomo. *Hegel's Theory of the Modern State*. Cambridge: Cambridge University Press, 1972.
———. *The Social and Political Thought of Karl Marx*. Cambridge: Cambridge University Press, 1972.
Bacon, Francis. *The New Organon*. Indianapolis: Bobbs-Merrill, 1960.
Barber, Benjamin. *Strong Democracy: Participatory Politics for a New Age*. Berkeley: University of California Press, 2003.
Beck, Lewis. *Studies in the Philosophy of Kant*. Indianapolis: Bobbs-Merrill, 1965.
Beiner, Ronald. *What's the Matter with Liberalism?* Berkeley: University of California Press, 1992.
Beiser, Frederick. *The Cambridge Companion to Hegel*. Cambridge: Cambridge University Press, 1993.
———. *Hegel*. New York: Routledge, 2005.

Bell, Daniel. *Communitarianism and Its Critics*. Oxford: Oxford University Press, 1993.

Bowles, Samuel and Gintis, Herbert. *Democracy and Capitalism: Property, Community, and the Contradictions of Modern Social Thought*. New York: Basic Books, 1987.

Brecher, Jeremy and Costello, Tim. *Global Village or Global Pillage: Economic Reconstruction From the Bottom Up*. Cambridge: Sound End Press, 1998.

Breisach, Ernst. *Introduction to Modern Existentialism*. New York: Grove Press, 1962.

Brennan, Teresa. *Globalization and Its Terrors: Daily Life in the West*. New York: Routledge, 2003.

Brod, Harry. *Hegel's Philosophy of Politics: Idealism, Identity, and Modernity*. Boulder: Westview, 1992.

Cadava, E., Connor, J., and Nancy, J. *Who Comes After the Subject?* New York: Routledge, 1991.

Caputo, John. *Deconstruction in a Nutshell: A Conservation with Jacques Derrida*. New York: Fordham University Press, 1997.

Carver, Terrell. *Marx's Social Theory*. Oxford: Oxford University Press, 1982.

Cassirer, Ernst. *The Question of Jean-Jacques Rousseau*. Bloomington: Indiana University Press, 1963.

———. *The Philosophy of the Enlightenment*. Princeton: Princeton University Press, 1951.

Cicero. *De Legibus*. London: Harvard University Press, 1928.

———. *De Re Publica*. London: Harvard University Press, 1928.

Cohen, G. A. *Karl Marx's Theory of History: A Defence*. Princeton, N.J.: Princeton University Press, 2000.

Dallmayr, Fred. *G. W. F. Hegel: Modernity and Politics*. Newbury Park: Sage, 1993.

Davies, Robertson. *The Rebel Angels*. London: Penguin, 1981.

De Greiff, Pablo and Cronin, Ciaran. *Global Justice and Transnational Politics: Essays on the Moral and Political Challenges of Globalization*. Cambridge: MIT Press, 2002.

Debord, Guy. *The Society of the Spectacle*. New York: Zone Books, 1995.

Deleuze, Gilles. *Nietzsche and Philosophy*. Minneapolis: University of Minnesota Press, 1983.

Derrida, Jacques. *Limited, Inc*. Evanston, IL: Northwestern University Press, 1988.

———. *Margins of Philosophy*. Chicago: The University of Chicago Press, 1982.

———. *Memories of Paul de Man*. New York: Columbia University Press, 1989.

———. *On the Name*. Stanford: Stanford University Press, 1995.

———. *Writing and Difference*. Chicago: The University of Chicago Press, 1978.

Descartes, René. *Mediations*. Indianapolis: Bobbs-Merrill, 1960.

Detwiler, Bruce. *Nietzsche and the Politics of Aristocratic Radicalism*. Chicago: The University of Chicago Press, 1990.

deVries, Willem. *Hegel's Theory of Mental Activity*. Ithaca, N.Y.: Cornell University Press, 1988.

Dickens, Charles. *A Tale of Two Cities*. New York: Signet Classic, 1980.

Diderot, Denis. *Political Writings*. Cambridge: Cambridge University Press, 1992.

Doctorow, E. L. *The Book of Daniel*. New York: Plume, 1971.

Dostal, R. *The Cambridge Companion to Gadamer*. New York: Cambridge University Press, 2002.

Dryzek, John. *Democracy in Capitalist Times: Ideals, Limits, and Struggles*. Oxford: Oxford University Press, 1996.

Dupré, Louis. *The Philosophical Foundations of Marxism*. New York: Harcourt, Brace & World, 1966.

Ellis, John. *Against Deconstruction*. Princeton, N.J.: Princeton University Press, 1989.

Engels, Friedrich. *Ludwig Feuerbach and the Outcome of Classical German Philosophy*. New York: International Publishers, 1941.

Etzioni, Amitai. *The Moral Dimension: Toward a New Economics*. New York: The Free Press, 1988.

——. *The New Golden Rule: Community and Morality in a Democratic Society*. New York: Basic Books, 1996.

Falzon, Christopher. *Foucault and Social Dialogue: Beyond Fragmentation*. London: Routledge, 1998.

Ferry, Luc. *Political Philosophy, Volume 1: Rights—the New Quarrel between the Ancients and the Moderns*. Chicago: The University of Chicago Press, 1990.

Feuerbach, Ludwig. *The Essence of Christianity*. Buffalo, N.Y.: Prometheus, 1989.

——. *Principles of the Philosophy of the Future*. Indianapolis, IN: Hackett, 1986.

Fichte, Johann. *The Science of Knowledge*. Cambridge: Cambridge University Press, 1982.

——. *Foundations of Natural Right: According to the Principles of the Wissenschaftslehre*. Cambridge: Cambridge University Press, 2000.

——. *The Vocation of Man*. Indianapolis, IN: Hackett, 1987.

Findlay, John. *Hegel: A Re-Examination*. Oxford: Oxford University Press, 1958.

Fox, Michael. *The Accessible Hegel*. Amherst, MA: Humanity Books, 2005.

Franco, Paul. *Hegel's Philosophy of Freedom*. New Haven, CT: Yale University Press, 1999.

Friedrich, Carl. *The Philosophy of Hegel*. New York: Random House, 1953.

Fukuyama, Francis. *The End of History and the Last Man*. New York: Free Press, 1992.

Gadamer, Hans-Georg. *Hegel's Dialectic: Five Hermeneutical Studies*. New Haven, CT: Yale University Press, 1976.

——. *Philosophical Hermeneutics*. Berkeley: University of California Press, 1976.

——. *The Philosophy of Hans-Georg Gadamer*. Chicago: Open Court, 1997.

——. *Reason in the Age of Science*. Cambridge: MIT Press, 1981.

——. *Truth and Method*. New York: Continuum, 1989.

Galileo. *Discoveries and Opinions of Galileo*. Garden City, N.J.: Doubleday, 1957.

Gasché, Rodolphe. *The Tain of the Mirror: Derrida and the Philosophy of Reflection*. Cambridge: Harvard University Press, 1986.

Giddens, Anthony and Hutton, Will. *Global Capitalism*. New York: The New Press, 2000.

Gildin, Hilail. *Rousseau's Social Contract*. Chicago: The University of Chicago Press, 1983.

Grass, Günter. *The Tin Drum*. New York: Vintage, 1961.

Gray, John. *False Dawn: The Delusions of Global Capitalism*. New York: The New Press, 1998.

Guyer, Paul. *The Cambridge Companion to Kant*. Cambridge: Cambridge University Press, 1992.

Habermas, Jürgen. *Between Facts and Norms: Contributions to a Discourse Theory of Law and Democracy*. Cambridge: MIT Press, 1996.

——. *The Future of Human Nature*. London: Polity, 2003.

——. *The Inclusion of the Other: Studies in Political Theory*. Cambridge: MIT Press, 1998.

——. *Knowledge and Human Interests*. Boston: Beacon Press, 1971.

——. *Philosophical Discourses on Modernity*. Cambridge: MIT Press, 1987.

——. *Theory and Practice*. Boston: Beacon Press, 1973.

Hampson, Norman. *The Enlightenment*. Baltimore: Penguin, 1968.

Hardimon, Michael. *Hegel's Social Philosophy: The Project of Reconciliation*. New York: Cambridge University Press, 1994.

Hardt, Michael and Negri, Antonio. *Labor of Dionysus: A Critique of the State-Form*. Minneapolis: University of Minnesota Press, 1994.

Harris, Henry. *Hegel: Phenomenology and System*. Indianapolis: Hackett, 1995.

Haym, Rudolf. *Hegel und siene Zeit*. Berlin: Rodolf Gaertner, 1857.

Hegel, Georg W. F. *Aesthetics: Lectures on Fine Arts, Volume 1*. Oxford: Oxford University Press, 1975.

——. *Aesthetics: Lectures on Fine Arts, Volume 2*. Oxford: Oxford University Press, 1975.

——. *The Difference Between Fichte's and Schelling's System of Philosophy*. Albany: State University Press of New York Press, 1977.

——. *Early Theological Writings*. Philadelphia: University of Pennsylvania Press, 1948.

——. *Faith and Knowledge*. Albany, N.Y.: State University of New York Press, 1977.

——. *Introductory Lectures on Aesthetics*. London: Penguin Press, 1993.

——. *Lectures on the History of Philosophy, Volume 1: Greek Philosophy to Plato*. Lincoln: University of Nebraska Press, 1995.

——. *Lectures on the History of Philosophy, Volume 2: Plato and the Platonists*. Lincoln: University of Nebraska Press, 1995.

——. *Lectures on the History of Philosophy, Volume 3: Medieval and Modern Philosophy*. Lincoln: University of Nebraska Press, 1995.

——. *Lectures on the Philosophy of Religion, Volume 1*. Berkeley: University of California Press, 1984.

——. *Lectures on the Philosophy of Religion, Volume 2*. New York: Humanities Press, 1962.

——. *The Letters*. Bloomington: Indiana University Press, 1984.

——. *Logic*. Oxford: Clarendon Press, 1975.

——. *Phenomenology of Spirit*. Oxford: Oxford University Press, 1977.

———. *The Philosophy of History*. Buffalo, N.Y.: Prometheus Books, 1991.

———. *Philosophy of Mind*. New York: Oxford University Press, 1971.

———. *Philosophy of Nature*. New York: Oxford University, 2004.

———. *Philosophy of Right*. Oxford: Oxford University Press, 1967.

———. *Political Writings*. Cambridge: Cambridge University Press, 1999.

———. *Reason in History: A General Introduction to the Philosophy of History*. Indianapolis: Bobbs-Merrill, 1953.

———. *Science of Logic*. Amherst, MA: Humanity Books, 1969.

———. *System of Ethical Life 1802/03 and First Philosophy of Spirit (1803)*. Albany, N.Y.: State University of New York Press, 1979.

Heidegger, Martin. *Being and Time*. New York: Harper & Row, 1962.

———. *Hegel's Concept of Experience*. San Francisco: Harper & Row, 1970.

———. *Hegel's Phenomenology of Spirit*. Bloomington: Indiana University Press, 1988.

———. *Nietzsche: Volume Three*. New York: Harper-Collins, 1987.

Heilbroner, Robert and Thurow, Lester. *Economics Explained*. New York: Touchstone, 1994.

Held, David and McGrew, Anthony. *Globalization/Anti-Globalization*. Cambridge: Polity, 2002.

Herder, Johann. *Against Pure Reason: Writings on Religion, Language, and History*. Minneapolis: Fortress Press, 1993.

Hesse, Herman. *Siddhartha*. New York: Bantam Books, 1951.

Hobbes, Thomas. *Man and Citizen*. Indianapolis: Bobbs-Merrill, 1952.

Höffe, Otfried. *Immanuel Kant*. Albany, N.Y.: State University of New York Press, 1994.

Houlgate, Stephen. *Hegel, Nietzsche and the Criticism of Metaphysics*. Cambridge: Cambridge University Press, 1986.

———. *An Introduction to Hegel: Freedom, Truth and History*. Oxford: Blackwell, 2005.

Howells, Christina. *Derrida: Deconstruction from Phenomenology to Ethics*. Cambridge: Polity Press, 1999.

Hyppolite, Jean. *Genesis and Structure of Hegel's Phenomenology of Spirit*. Chicago: Northwestern University Press, 1974.

Inwood, Michael. *Hegel*. London: Routledge, 2002.

———. *A Hegel Dictionary*. Oxford: Blackwell, 1992.

Jarvis, Simon. *Adorno: A Critical Introduction*. London: Routledge, 1998.

Jaspers, Karl. *Kant*. New York: Harvest, 1962.

Jay, Martin. *Adorno*. Cambridge: Harvard University Press, 1984.

Kant, Immanuel. *Critique of Judgment*. New York: Hafner, 1951.

———. *The Critique of Practical Reason*. New York: Macmillan, 1993.

———. *The Critique of Pure Reason*. New York: St. Martin's Press, 1961.

———. *Fundamental Principles of the Metaphysics of Morals*. Buffalo, N.Y.: Prometheus, 1987.

———. *Groundwork for the Metaphysics of Morals*. New Haven, CT: Yale University Press, 2002.

———. *Political Writings*. Cambridge: Cambridge University Press, 1991.

————. *Prolegomena to Any Future Metaphysics*. Indianapolis: Hackett, 1977.

Karliner, Joshua. *The Corporate Planet: Ecology and Politics in the Age of Globalization*. San Francisco: Sierra Books, 1998.

Kaufmann, Walter. *Hegel: A Reinterpretation*. Notre Dame, IN: University Notre Dame Press, 1965.

————. *Nietzsche: Philosopher, Psychologist, Antichrist*. Princeton, N.J.: Princeton University Press, 1978.

————. *Hegel's Political Philosophy*. New York: Atherton, 1970.

Kierkegaard, Søren. *The Concept of Anxiety*. Princeton, N.J.: Princeton University Press, 1980.

————. *Concluding Unscientific Postscript*. Princeton, N.J.: Princeton University Press, 1969.

————. *Either/Or, Volume 1*. Princeton, N.J.: Princeton University Press, 1987.

————. *Either/Or, Volume 2*. Princeton, N.J.: Princeton University Press, 1987.

————. *Fear and Trembling*. Princeton, N.J.: Princeton University Press, 1983.

————. *Philosophical Fragments*. Princeton, N.J.: Princeton University Press, 1962.

————. *The Present Age*. New York: Harper Torchbooks, 1962.

————. *Sickness unto Death*. Princeton, N.J.: Princeton University Press, 1980.

Knowles, Dudley. *Hegel and the Philosophy of Right*. New York: Routledge, 2002.

Kojève, Alexandre. *Introduction to the Reading of Hegel: Lectures on the Phenomenology of Spirit*. Ithaca, N.Y.: Cornell University Press, 1969.

Kolb, David. *The Critique of Pure Modernity: Hegel, Heidegger, and After*. Chicago: The University of Chicago Press, 1986.

Korten, David. *When Corporations Rule the World*. San Francisco: Kumarian Press, 2001.

Kundera, Milan. *The Unbearable Lightness of Being*. New York: HarperPerennial, 1984.

Lauer, Quentin. *Hegel's Idea of Philosophy*. New York: Fordham University Press, 1971.

————. *A Reading of Hegel's Phenomenology of Spirit*. New York: Fordham University Press, 1993.

Locke, John. *An Essay Concerning Human Understanding*. Bergenfield, N.J.: Meridian, 1964.

————. *The Second Treatise of Government*. Indianapolis: Bobbs-Merrill, 1952.

Losurdo, Domenico. *Hegel and the Freedom of Moderns*. Durham, N.C.: Duke University Press, 2004.

Löwith, Karl. *From Hegel to Nietzsche: The Revolution in Nineteenth-Century Thought*. Garden City, N.J.: Anchor Books, 1964.

Luther, Timothy. *Congress, Interest Groups, and Democracy: Private Money v. Public Interest*. Boston: Houghton Mifflin, 2002.

————. *Hegel and Marx: Economics and Democracy*. Boston: Houghton Mifflin, 2002.

————. *The Political Philosophy of Democracy: Its Origins, Promises, and Perils*. Boston: Houghton Mifflin, 1998.

Luttwak, Edward. *Turbo Capitalism: Winners and Losers in the Global Economy.* New York: Harper/Perennial, 1999.

McCarney, Joseph. *Hegel: On History.* London: Routledge, 2000.

Macquarrie, John. *Existentialism.* London: Penguin, 1972.

Maker, William. *Hegel on Economics and Freedom.* Macon, Ga.: Mercer University Press, 1987.

———. *Philosophy Without Foundations: Rethinking Hegel.* Albany, N.Y.: State University of New York, 1994.

Mander, Jerry and Goldsmith. *The Case Against the Global Economy: And a Turn toward the Local.* New York: Sierra Club Books, 1996.

Manuel, Frank. *Age of Reason.* Ithaca, N.Y.: Cornell University Press, 1951.

Marcuse, Herbert. *Hegel's Ontology and the Theory of Historicity.* Cambridge: MIT Press, 1987.

———. *Reason and Revolution: Hegel and the Rise of Social Theory.* Atlantic Highlands: Humanities Press, 1941.

———. *The Essential Marcuse: Selected Writings of Philosopher and Social Critic Herbert Marcuse.* Boston: Beacon Press, 2007.

Marx. Karl. *Capital, Volume One.* New York: Vintage, 1976.

———. *Class Struggles in France: 1848-1850.* New York: International Publishers, 1964.

———. *A Contribution to the Critique of Political Economy.* New York: International Publishers, 1970.

———. *Economic and Philosophical Manuscripts.* Buffalo, N.Y.: Prometheus, 1988.

———. *Selected Writings.* Oxford: Oxford University Press, 1977.

Marx, Karl and Engels, Friedrich. *The Communist Manifesto.* New York: Washington Square Press, 1964.

———. *The German Ideology.* New York: International Publishers, 1970.

Merleau-Ponty, *The Visible and the Invisible.* Evanston, IL: Northwestern University Press, 1968.

Nagel, Thomas. *The View from Nowhere.* Oxford: Oxford University Press, 1986.

Nehamas, Alexander. *Nietzsche: Life as Literature.* Cambridge: Harvard University Press, 1985.

Neuhouser, Frederick. *Foundations of Hegel's Social Theory: Actualizing Freedom.* Cambridge: Harvard University Press, 2000.

———. *Fichte's Theory of Subjectivity.* Cambridge: Cambridge University Press, 1990.

Nietzsche, Friedrich. *The Antichrist.* Costa Mesa: Noontide, 1988.

———. *Beyond Good and Evil: Prelude to a Philosophy of the Future.* New York: Vintage, 1966.

———. *The Birth of Tragedy.* New York: Doubleday, 1956.

———. *Ecco Homo.* London: Penguin, 1979.

———. *The Gay Science.* New York: Vintage, 1974.

———. *The Genealogy of Morals.* New York: Doubleday, 1956.

———. *Human, All Too Human: A Book for Free Spirits.* Cambridge: Cambridge University Press, 1986.

——. *Thus Spoke Zarathustra*. London: Penguin, 1969.

——. *Untimely Meditations*. Cambridge: Cambridge University Press, 1983.

——. *The Will to Power*. New York: Vintage, 1967.

Norris, Christopher. *Derrida*. Cambridge: Harvard University Press, 1987.

——. *What's Wrong with Postmodernism: Critical Theory and the Ends of Philosophy*. Baltimore: The Johns Hopkins University Press, 1990.

Ortega y Gasset, José. *The Revolt of the Masses*. New York: W. W. Norton & Company, 1932.

Patten, Alan. *Hegel's Idea of Freedom*. New York: Oxford University Press, 1999.

Pelczynski, Z. A. *The State and Civil Society: Studies in Hegel's Political Philosophy*. Cambridge: Cambridge University Press, 1984.

Pinkard, Terry. *Democratic Liberalism and Social Union*. Philadelphia: Temple University Press, 1987.

——. *German Philosophy 1760–1860: The Legacy of Idealism*. Cambridge: Cambridge University Press, 2002.

——. *Hegel: A Biography*. Cambridge: Cambridge University Press, 2000.

——. *Hegel's Dialectic: The Explanation of Possibility*. Philadelphia: Temple University Press, 1988.

——. *Hegel's Phenomenology: The Sociality of Reason*. New York: Cambridge University Press, 1996.

Pippin, Robert. *Hegel's Idealism: The Satisfactions of Self-Consciousness*. Cambridge: Cambridge University Press, 1989.

——. *Idealism as Modernism: Hegelian Variations*. Cambridge: Cambridge University Press, 1997.

Pippin, Robert and Höffe, Otfried. *Hegel on Ethics and Politics*. Cambridge: Cambridge University Press, 2004.

Plato. *Phaedo*. Indianapolis: Bobbs-Merrill, 1951.

——. *The Republic*. New York: W. W. Norton & Company, 1985.

——. *Sophist*. Indianapolis: Hackett, 1993.

Polybius. *The Histories*. New York: Twayne Publishers, 1966.

Popper, Karl. *The Open Society and Its Enemies: The High Tide of Prophecy, Hegel, Marx and the Aftermath*. Princeton: Princeton University Press, 1966.

Rank, Mark. *One Nation, Underprivileged: Why American Poverty Affects Us All*. New York: Oxford University Press, 2005.

Raymond, Diane. *Existentialism and the Philosophic Tradition*. Englewood Cliffs: Prentice-Hall, 1991.

Redding, Paul. *Hegel's Hermeneutics*. Ithaca, N.Y.: Cornell University Press, 1996.

Reijen, Willem van. *Adorno: An Introduction*. Philadelphia: Pennbridge Books, 1992.

Ricoeur, Paul. *From Text to Action: Essays in Hermeneutics II*. Evanston, Ill.: Northwestern University Press, 1991.

Rifkin, Jeremy. *The End of Work: The Decline of the Global Labor Force and the Dawn of the Post-Market Era*. New York: Tarcher/Putnam, 1995.

Ritter, Joachim. *Hegel and the French Revolution: Essays on the Philosophy of Right*. Cambridge: MIT Press, 1982.

Ritzer, George. *The McDonaldization of Society: An Investigation into the Changing Character of Contemporary Social Life.* Thousand Oaks, CA: Pine Force Press, 1996.

Robinson, Jonathan. *Duty and Hypocrisy in Hegel's Phenomenology of Mind.* Toronto: University of Toronto Press, 1977.

Rockmore, Tom. *Before and After Hegel: A Historical Introduction to Hegel's Thought.* Berkeley: University of California Press, 1993.

——. *Cognition: An Introduction to Hegel's Phenomenology of Spirit.* Berkeley: University of California Press, 1997.

Rousseau, Jean-Jacques. *A Discourse on Inequality.* London: Penguin, 1984.

——. *The Social Contract.* Oxford: Oxford University Press, 1995.

Sallis, John. *Deconstruction and Philosophy: The Texts of Jacques Derrida.* Chicago: The University of Chicago Press, 1978.

Sandel, Michael. *Liberalism and the Limits of Justice.* New York: Cambridge University Press, 1982.

Sarmago, José. *All the Names.* San Diego: Harvest, 1999.

Sartre, Jean-Paul. *Being and Nothingness.* New York: Washington Square Press, 1956.

——. *Existentialism and Human Emotions.* Secaucus, N.J.: Citadel Press, 1983.

Sayer, Andrew. *Radical Political Economy: A Critique.* Oxford: Blackwell, 1995.

Schaeffer, Robert. *Understanding Globalization: The Social Consequences of Political, Economic and Environmental Change.* Lanham, Md.: Rowman & Littlefield, 2005.

Schelling, Friedrich. *Ideal for a Philosophy of Nature.* Cambridge: Cambridge University Press, 1988.

——. *System of Transcendental Idealism.* Charlottesville: University of Virginia Press, 1978.

Schiller, Friedrich. *On the Aesthetic Education of Man.* Oxford: Oxford University Press, 1967.

Schiller, Herbert. *Culture Inc: The Corporate Takeover of Public Expression.* Oxford: Oxford University Press, 1989.

——. *Information Inequality: The Deepening Social Crisis in America.* London: Routledge, 1996.

Schlegel, Friedrich. *Philosophical Fragments.* Minneapolis: University of Minnesota Press, 1991.

Schmidt, Alfred. *History and Structure: An Essay on Hegelian-Marxist and Structuralist Theories of History.* Cambridge: MIT Press, 1981.

Schopenhauer, Arthur. *The World as Will and Representation, Volume 1.* New York: Dover, 1966.

Schweikart, David. *Against Capitalism.* Boulder, CO: Westview, 1996.

Shapiro, H. *Medieval Philosophy: Selected Readings from Augustine to Buridan.* New York: Random House, 1964.

Shklar, Judith. *Freedom and Independence: A Study of Political Ideas of Hegel's Phenomenology of Mind.* New York: Cambridge University Press, 1976.

Silko, Leslie. *The Almanac of the Dead.* London: Penguin, 1991.

Singer, Peter. *Hegel.* Oxford: Oxford University Press, 1983.

Smith, Steven. *Hegel's Critique of Liberalism: Rights in Context*. Chicago: The University of Chicago Press, 1989.

Solomon, Robert. *From Hegel to Existentialism*. New York: Oxford University Press, 1987.

——. *In the Spirit of Hegel: A Study of G. W. F Hegel's Phenomenology of Spirit*. New York: Oxford University Press, 1983.

Stepelevich, Lawrence. *The Young Hegelians: An Anthology*. Atlantic Highlands: Humanities Press, 1983.

Stern, Robert. *Hegel and the Phenomenology of Spirit*. London: Routledge, 2002.

Stiglitz, Joseph. *Globalization and Its Discontents*. New York: W. W. Norton, 2003.

Strong, Tracy. *Friedrich Nietzsche and the Politics of Transfiguration*. Berkeley: University of California Press, 1988.

Taylor, Charles. *Hegel*. Cambridge: Cambridge University Press, 1975.

——. *Hegel and the Modern State*. New York: Cambridge University Press, 1979.

——. *Human Agency and Language: Philosophical Papers 1*. New York: Cambridge University Press, 1985.

Thiele, Leslie. *Friedrich Nietzsche and the Politics of the Soul: A Study of Heroic Individualism*. Chicago: The University of Chicago Press, 1990.

Thurow, Lester. *The Zero-Sum Society: Distribution and the Possibilities for Economic Change*. London: Penguin, 1980.

Toews, John. *Hegelianism: The Path Toward Dialectical Humanism, 1805–1841*. Cambridge: Cambridge University Press, 1980.

Tucker, Robert. *Philosophy & Myth in Karl Marx*. New Brunswick, N.J.: Transaction Publishers, 2001.

Tugendhat, Ernst. *Self-Consciousness and Self-Determination*. Cambridge: MIT Press, 1986.

Warren, Gary. *Nietzsche and Political Thought*. Cambridge: MIT Press, 1988.

Wartofsky, Marx. *Feuerbach*. Cambridge: Cambridge University Press, 1977.

Weber, Max. *From Max Weber: Essays in Sociology*. New York: Oxford University Press, 1946.

Weil, Eric. *Hegel and the State*. Baltimore: Johns Hopkins Press, 1998.

Westphal, Kenneth. *Hegel's Epistemology: A Philosophical Introduction to the Phenomenology of Spirit*. Indianapolis: Hackett, 2003.

White, Alan. *Absolute Knowledge: Hegel and the Problem of Metaphysics*. Athens: Ohio University Press, 1983.

Wiedmann, Franz. *Hegel: An Illustrated Biography*. New York: Pegasus, 1968.

Williams, Robert. *Hegel's Ethics of Recognition*. Berkeley: University of California Press, 1997.

Winfield, Richard D. *Freedom and Modernity*. Albany: State University Press of New York Press, 1991.

——. *The Just Economy*. New York: Routledge, 1988.

——. *The Just Family*. Albany, N.Y.: State University of New York Press, 1998.

——. *The Just State: Rethinking Self-Government*. Amherst, MA: Humanity Books, 2005.

———. *Law in Civil Society.* Lawrence, KS: University Press of Kansas, 1995.

———. *Overcoming Foundations: Studies in Systematic Philosophy.* New York: Columbia University Press, 1989.

———. *Reason and Justice.* Albany, N.Y.: State University of New York Press, 1988.

———. *Stylistics: Rethinking the Artforms After Hegel.* Albany, N.Y.: State University of New York Press, 1996.

Wokler, Robert. *Rousseau.* Oxford: Oxford University Press, 1995.

Wood, Allen. *Hegel's Ethical Thought.* New York: Cambridge University Press, 1990.

———. *Karl Marx.* London: Routledge, 1981.

# Index